Da Capo
BEST
MUSIC
WRITING
2000

Da Capo
BEST
MUSIC
WRITING
2000

Peter Guralnick
GUEST EDITOR

Douglas Wolk
SERIES EDITOR

DA CAPO PRESS

List of credits/permissions for all pieces can be found on page 437.

Copyright © 2000 by Da Capo Press, A Member of the Perseus Books Group
http: www.dacapopress.com

Library of Congress Cataloging-in-Publication Data
Da Capo best music writing 2000 / edited by Douglas Wolk and Peter Guralnick.
   p. cm
  Includes index.
  ISBN 0-306-80999-0 (pbk.)
  1. Music—20th century—History and criticism.   I. Title: Best music writing 2000.
II. Wolk, Douglas.   III. Guralnick, Peter.

ML55 .D14   2000
781.64—dc21

                                      00-055513

10   9   8   7   6   5   4   3   2   1

Contents

Introduction

My grandmother was never comfortable with competition. She thought every contest should end in a tie.

After a lifetime of exposure to the same kind of gratuitous awards shows and invidious comparisons we have all experienced, I can understand her point, and it was one of the factors that held me back initially from embracing this particular type of editorial function. I never wanted to be a critic: why would I choose to be the ultimate critic, a self-appointed arbiter of taste who with a simple thumbs-up or thumbs-down makes an absolute judgment in an all-too-unabsolute world? What qualifications did I, or anyone, possess to draw those kinds of distinctions?

Well, perhaps needless to say, I got over it. In retrospect, I could put it down to a somewhat transparent need to hold on to an illusion of youthful indecision. Or fear of accountability. Or, simply, cowardice. But in the end what got me over it was the writing, probably a couple of hundred pieces in all, that I came to read with a growing appreciation that this undoubtedly was just the tip of the iceberg. There were stories from sources as varied as *Joe* and *Mean*, *Vibe* and *Spin*, the *New Yorker* and *No Depression*, on-line publications and old-fashioned 'zines. And what I came to realize—or perhaps to rationalize—was that an anthology of this sort should not be seen as a contest at all but as a celebration, an opportunity to create, in written form, the type of mix that you send out to a friend and get back in kind, offering the comforting familiarity of shared interests, the sometimes unsettling evidence of divergent tastes, and, best of all, the challenge of new directions to explore, new avenues to pursue.

With that said, let me give you a little bit of background on the bi-
ases that went into my choice. Because it is inescapably my choice—I
have nothing to hide behind, except the fact that on a different day, under a different set of circumstances, with different inputs, that choice
might shift slightly. But in the end clearly an anthology of this sort reflects its selector no less than each selection in this book reflects its author. Art lies in nothing if not in the selection of detail; the angle of
perspective will inevitably determine what is included and what is left
out of the picture, and if someone else were to read over exactly the
same mass of material that was provided to me, they would, I'm sure,
make a very different choice.

What I was looking for first and foremost was accessibility, and by
that I don't necessarily mean familiarity of either subject matter or
style. I tried to be open to subjects I knew nothing about and to approaches altogether different from my own—but, whatever the subject,
whatever the approach, I wanted something that could sweep me up,
carry me away to the places reading (and music) has always taken me
from childhood on. I guess I should qualify that. I don't mean that one
has to be transported to some exotic, fairy-tale world; you have only to
read "Don't Drink the Brown Water," David Moodie and Maureen
Callahan's unblinking portrait of the 1999 version of Woodstock Nation, to understand that. The writer's only obligation, it seems to me, is
to provide some kind of entree to a world that (s)he uniquely understands and to give the reader some reason for being there. There is no
definition to the geography of that world—it can be internal or external or, as in the case of Lester Bangs' joyously barbaric yawp, "An Instant Fan's Inspired Notes: You Gotta Listen," a combination of the
two—but it must, in some unspecified manner, permit access. And it
must, in some equally unspecified manner, go beyond the surface, accept neither received wisdom nor party line, but instead deliver writing
that lives in its own terms, that makes the reader care.

For me one of the great pleasures of immersing myself for the first
three months of this year in so much writing with which I was previously unfamiliar was the discovery of new worlds, and new ways of
looking at old ones. The revolutionary Nigerian musician Fela, for example, was someone about whom I knew very little before reading Jay
Babcock's "Fela: King of the Invisible Art." In less sure hands I might

very well have felt overwhelmed by the sheer volume of information imparted. But Babcock's enthusiasm for his subject, his utter conviction, his selection of factual and anecdotal detail drew me in in such a way that, almost without knowing it, I was hooked.

The same was true of any number of other stories in this collection, from "The Ties that Bind," Rosanne Cash's gracefully reflective personal reminiscence, to Ben Sandmel's rollicking "Mr. K-Doe Goes to Washington," to Arthur Kempton's elegantly analytic "The Lost Tycoons," in which an implicit connection is drawn between the experiences and philosophies of Elijah Muhammad and Berry Gordy. The subjects are as various as the disintegration of a young Cape Breton fiddler (Rebecca Mead's "Sex, Drugs, and Fiddling"), the fragile hopes of hip hop (David Samuels' "Hip Hop High") and the cynicism of success (Nancy Jo Sales' "Money Boss Player"), the lost history and ecstatic musical tradition of an obscure black church (Geoffrey Himes' "A Joyful Noise"), the strange hold that the discarded past has upon us (Neil Strauss' "Unearthing the New Nashville's Wax Castoffs"), and— something with which we can all identify—the mania of record collecting (Eddie Dean's brilliant portrait of an eccentric, "Desperate Man Blues"). What each has in common is its ability to lure the reader in. And, just as important, none is the product of a cynical, commodity-driven sales pitch, none is an infomercial masquerading as news.

I'm not saying that the stories in this collection should be seen as all stemming from a single school or that they in any way suggest a greater purpose or a seamless whole. What I *am* saying is that they represent the sound of the individual human voice, they insist upon their own truth, sometimes flashy, sometimes seemingly little more than the patient accumulation of facts, but always expressed in their own quirky terms. That is what I value so much about each of these pieces, the refusal to give in to the seductive blandishments of an increasingly mass-produced age. How many times have we seen the same blizzard of stories surrounding the release of this or that major motion picture, this or that political event, the long-awaited album from the otherwise reclusive superstar, with each story carefully timed to support the product that is being sold, all offering the same revelations in virtually the same words? It's not that these words are necessarily false, but they are *rendered* false by the lack of scrutiny they are given; they become false not simply by the manner in which they are offered up but by the manner in which they are reported.

That is what makes these stories different; each has its own take on the subject at hand, whether in the form of essay, satire, profile, or reportage. Many may well be offshoots of a particular occasion (Woodstock '99, Ernie K-Doe's Washington hegira, Ry Cooder's seminal role in the *Buena Vista Social Club* phenomenon, the release of a new album by Tom Waits or Steve Earle or June Carter)—but none to my mind is *confined* to that occasion, none retails the bland bromides of the age. You can open the book at any point, and I think you will be entertained, whether by a Wallace Stevens–like reflection upon the tribulations of a rap superstar (Selwyn Seyfu Hinds' "Me, Machine: The Curious Case of a Man Called Sean"), the fractured logic of Jonny Whiteside's "Love and Hell: Merle Haggard's Twin Oracles," Susan Orlean's disturbingly elegiac "Meet the Shaggs," or Sasha Frere-Jones' affectionately personal history of Run-D.M.C. Each shows an investment in its subject, each has its own highly individuated point of view—each glories in what Sun Records founder Sam Phillips likes to call the "perfect imperfection" of reality. Even a story as determinedly prosaic as J. R. Jones' "Prove It All Night," about a bar band that never made it and never will, finds cracked beauty in the mundane.

The early years of rock writing are often cited as a kind of golden age—and I know I often meet younger writers who express envy at the opportunities available then. I don't think that's true—I don't really believe there's ever been a golden age, though there are certainly formats and skills in every field that get left behind. But winnowing through all the material considered for this book did underscore one difference between the freelancing climate in which I grew up and the one that exists now: the increasing disappearance of the long-form story, the growing editorial disinclination to invest time, or space, in anything without an explicit commercial hook. I suppose it's understandable. A shortened attention span is frequently cited, and in an age of rampant consumerism it's not surprising that so much that is now fashionable amounts to little more than a smug consumer's guide. But the continued existence of pieces like these only underscores the validity of work with its own reason for being, of writing that has been allowed space to develop, of work that seeks to share a world of passionately held values and beliefs.

It's been a real treat for me to have the opportunity to read so many different pieces on so many different subjects expressed in so many different ways. The collection could easily have been half again as long without suffering in quality—and I guess one of the most gratifying aspects of the whole experience for me has been to reacquaint myself with a field that more and more I had come to treat as a kind of archive of source material without allowing myself the luxury of simply reading for pleasure. The regrets I have center around what I'm afraid I may have missed. I wish there were more jazz writing, for example—and its relative absence may well be the result of my own parochial vision. I wish there had been greater elucidation of some of the more significant pop trends, whether in the form of profiles or analysis—but, again, the aim was illumination, not self-congratulation, and so much of what is written on the latest trend or trendsetter seems to fall into the latter category.

What has been heartening, on the other hand, is the number of times the writing has sent me back to the music that was its inspiration—which I think ultimately is what all critical writing is meant to do. I can't imagine anyone reading Dave Hoekstra's measured account of no-depression country singer Steve Earle's embattled life and failing to check out the music it has produced. I know Jay Babcock's impassioned piece on Fela sent me to the reissue program that MCA has recently embarked upon, and Dave Marsh and Daniel Wolff's inspiring "No Hiding Place" had me pulling out all my Dorothy Love Coates albums. That's the wonderful thing about art. It's always there; sometimes we just need a little nudge to appreciate it. And that, I think, is what the best writing on music can do. It's one of the reasons I look forward so much to next year's selection by someone else. It will give me a whole new place to start.

"The more life that happens," Jim Walsh writes in "Baptism by Bruce," the final piece in this book, "the less you know about the meaning of life. The mystery just deepens." I can go along with that. The trick is to enjoy the mystery, as if it were happening to someone else, as if it were a thriller that captured your attention and wouldn't let go. We're all looking for that kind of release from the prison of ourselves, and music provides it as often as anything else. "When I was younger," Walsh writes in a story that goes far beyond the dimensions of a concert review, "Springsteen's music provided me with a road map to manhood and gave me permission to be both saint and sinner. Now, songs such as 'Badlands' still make me 'want to go out tonight and find out what I got,' but they elicit less of an ache, because I know that nothing compares to the art of real life and that music can be found in the mundane."

To find out how, you'll just have to read the rest of the book.

Peter Guralnick

ROSANNE CASH

The Ties
That Bind

From the time I was six until I was 12, my family lived on a barren hill-top in Southern California in the tiny town of Casitas Springs, between Ventura on the ocean and Ojai at the mountains. Although we were isolated, we had a lot of deliveries up there on the mountain: the milk-man, the Jewel Tea truck (a traveling store of candy, powdered drinks, snacks and bulk white-trash kinds of food) and the Helm's bakery truck—my favorite. I always ran outside when the Helm's truck bumped across the cattle grate at the top of our drive. One day I bolted out through the garage to greet the driver just as he flung open the back doors like it was a gypsy wagon. I practically swooned before the hundreds of cakes, pies, tarts and breads.

"Do you take the truck home at night?" I asked.

"Yes." He smiled at me.

"How do you keep from eating all this stuff when you get home?"

"Well, if you're around it all day, you want to get away from it when you go home at night. Does your daddy sit around and sing all day when he comes home off the road?"

I pondered for a moment. "Well, no."

It was the answer he expected, and so I gave it, but what I was thinking then, and what I understand more clearly now, is that it's not just the singing you bring home with you. It's the constant measuring of ideas and words, if you are a songwriter, and the daily handling of your instrument, if you are a musician, and the humming and scratching and pushing and testing of the voice, the reveling in the melodies, if you are a singer. More than that, it is the straddling of two worlds, and the struggle to make the transition from the creative realms to daily life and back with grace. My father is, and does, all of that. I do too, although I cannot claim my father's profound originality and influence. (Indeed, I go by the maxim that genius does what it must and talent does what it can.)

I belong to an extended family of musicians whose members sprawl across three generations. Some occupy positions of great acclaim (my father and my stepmother's family, the Carter Family), others of anecdotal obscurity (my maternal uncle, "Wildman" Ray Liberto, a former raucous honky-tonk piano player). At 16, I did not intend to take my place among them. Tradition was anathema to me; I understood that real rebellion would be to take a straight, nonmusical path. My mother had had a strict Italian Catholic upbringing, which pretty much defined her views about a woman's place in the world, and my father was an enormously visible performer. I had a fierce though silent desire to live a different life. I would not be a housewife, nor would I seek fame as a singer. I would be an archeologist and move to a kibbutz (odd choice for a Catholic girl, and so much the better). Change and newness: That defined life as far as I was concerned.

Then, when I was a day out of high school, my father took me on the road. It was something of a graduation gift, and a chance to catch up on some lost time with my dad. And it was a serious education: traveling the world, watching him perform, singing on the bus. He made a list of 100 Essential Country Songs, which he instructed me to learn, a wide-ranging list that ran from the old history lesson songs like "The Battle of New Orleans" through classics like Hank Williams's "I'm So Lonesome

I Could Cry." I was ushered into a treasury of song, and it was thrilling to learn more about my father through his great love for this music. I learned to play guitar from my stepmother's sister, Helen, and from Mother Maybelle Carter, and from Carl Perkins, all of whom were on the road with Dad at the time. Each day, I spent many hours in dressing rooms, practicing chords and the old songs they taught me. I discovered a passion for songwriting that remains undiminished to this day and that led me into my life as a writer and singer—into my family's vocation.

I lasted 2½ years on that bus until, too much feeling the constraint a young girl feels in the constant presence of a parent, I moved to London and then came home and went to college. But an important part of my heart and soul was given form and expression on that bus, and I came to realize how a shared passion forges deep bonds between people, defining a family more deeply than blood connection alone can do.

At the heart of real country music lies family, lies a devotion to exploring the bonds of blood ties, both in performance and in songwriting. Of course, there have been families in pop music (the Jacksons, the Beach Boys, Heart, Hanson). Parents and children have sung all manner of music together or in succession—Judy Garland and Liza Minnelli, Nat King Cole and Natalie Cole, Tim Buckley and Jeff Buckley, Loudon Wainwright III and his son, Rufus. But the community of country music emphasizes the family connection, revels in it, and there seems to be less rivalry, less need for the children to break away on their own musical terms (although that was an impulse I struggled with for the first 15 years of my career). Country treats family as a rich and fascinating source of material for its songs.

The Carter Family is the prototypical country music family, both for its artists and in the wide-ranging subjects of its songs, but there have been many, many more examples since the Carters began singing in the 1920s. It seems that members of every possible variation of the extended family have pursued careers separately, together and successively. (This is also true in bluegrass and gospel, close cousins to country.) As a teenager, I saw the Earl Scruggs Revue perform perhaps 20 times and held my breath for those moments when laconic Earl would glance at one of his sons, who had just performed a phenomenal solo, in a fleeting moment of approbation. Doc and Merle Watson also had a special resonance for me as performers. They were so close—in their genetic gifts, in their attitudes and quiet respect for each other—that it was a privilege to be in their audience. I was certain that they treated each other the same offstage as on. When Merle died in 1985, it was painful to imagine the enormity of the loss for Doc. He lost not only his son but his musical soulmate. I was thrilled recently to discover that Doc now plays music with Merle's son.

It was riveting to watch the Judds at the height of their career work out their mother-daughter tensions on stage. Every subtle gesture—mom stroking Wynonna's hair and the almost imperceptible flinch it provoked, or the intense glances from one to the other that were ignored—spoke reams, and every adult daughter in the audience would relate. In my own performing, I've found it impossible to stay mad at someone you love when you are on stage with them. Arguments and grudges melt away under the spotlights and the audience's gaze. I feel that I should somehow be better on stage, more magnanimous, for the sake of the audience, and sometimes I *am* better. One of the sweetest moments of my life occurred several years ago, the last time my dad played Carnegie Hall. I had been a little angry with him the day before the show and had brought up some old grievances, which he listened to gracefully. He invited me to sing "I Still Miss Someone" with him the next night. I demurred. The day of the performance, I had a fierce headache and told him I could not do it. I went to his hotel that evening before the show, and he asked again. I declined, but as I watched him walk out of the room I suddenly realized what it meant to him and agreed to sing the song. That night, as we sang together, all the old pain dissolved. I felt the longing to connect completely satisfied. Under the lights, in the safety of a few thousand people who loved us like crazy just then, I got something from my dad that I'd been trying to get since I was about six years old. It was truly magic, for both of us. I don't think we've ever been so close.

Performed by families and often about family, traditional country music spares nothing and no one in its gaze. In the deeply maudlin early

country songs about dead babies, for example, lie the hard truths about
mountain life. The best in this tragic bunch—according to my dad,
anyway—is an old tune called "The Railroad Engineer." The engineer's baby is sick, but he has to go to work and drive ol' No. 9, or
whatever it is, so he bids his wife:

> *Just hang a light when I pass tonight—*
> *Hang it so it can be seen.*
> *If the baby's dead, then show the red;*
> *If it's better, then show the green.*

Happily the engineer sees green, but most babies did not fare so well
in the early Appalachian songs, which were a way to count the losses
and gather comfort.

Mother is the most revered member of the family in traditional
country music, the person whose mention holds the greatest emotional
charge. The "country classic of them all" (again, according to Dad) is
"Sweeter Than the Flowers," co-written by Ervin Rouse, who also
wrote "Orange Blossom Special." It begins:

> *Yes, as far as I can remember*
> *She'll remain the rose of my heart.*
> *Mam took sick along in December;*
> *February brought us broken hearts.*
> *The reason we've not called a fam'ly reunion,*
> *We knew she wouldn't be there,*
> *But since we've thot it all over, Mama*
> *We know that your spirit is there.*

If this is not wrenching enough, the song continues (with a line that
boasts one of the all-time great rhymes):

> *No, no, there's no need to bother;*
> *To speak of you now would only hurt father.*

This couplet just kills me, so to speak.

But modern country music is shiny and rich and rather shallow, and naturally it speaks less of desperate loss. The dead have all but disappeared, though they occasionally surface. Back in the '80s, George Jones's "He Stopped Loving Her Today" had everyone swooning with morbid joy. Babies are more likely to be celebrated in birth than in demise (as in Loretta Lynn's "One's on the Way").

Still, the family faded in country as sexual heat began to obsess most singers and songwriters, just as it does in pop music. Anyone who has listened to old honky-tonk knows that this has always been a theme of country, but today it is *the* theme: The airwaves are soggy with songs about romance, desire, longing for love, love that got away, love gone wrong, standing up to or by your man or woman, loneliness, frustration, carnal passion, lovers' quarrels, and on and on. It's all real stuff, certainly, and good fodder for song, but the hormonal flushes of love affairs are not the only thing going on in a life. Lost from view are the other potent relationships, forged of blood and shared history, rich with emotional content, ripe for exploration. As Bruce Springsteen— one of the most family-inspired songwriters of the past two decades— said in "Highway Patrolman," "Nothing feels better than blood on blood." Certainly that has informed my own writing. I've written about my children in "Carrie," "Child of Steel" and "Mid-Air"; about a baby I lost in "Just Don't Talk About It"; and about my dad in "My Old Man."

I owe you, Mom.

As I was writing this, I called my dad to ask him about the old songs. I asked him about songs about mothers, babies, brothers and sisters, fathers and grandparents. He gave me titles, years and the names of the recording artists, and then sang them to me over the phone, verse by verse, more excited by each new recollection. Out of time, he told me to call back the next morning so we could talk about the songs "for a long time."

"I know *all* of them!" he said happily. I thought about those old songs all night and called him back first thing the next morning so he could sing the entirety of "Sweeter Than the Flowers" to me. He paused at the end as I scribbled down the lyrics.

"There's a whole other group of songs, if you're interested," he said. "About who?" I asked.

"Dead dogs," he answered, solemnly, and rattled off a list of titles. I laughed. But what I was thinking about was that bakery truck and how I had lied to the driver. We do take our deliveries home at night, and everything comes inside, and we're not shy about getting our fill.

JAY BABCOCK

Fela: King of the Invisible Art

Fela always knew the power of a name.

If you are African—and especially if you work with music, which shares a link of common invisibility with the spirit world—you must have a spiritually meaningful, beneficial name. Without the correct name, Fela explained, "a child can't really enter the world of the living."

He didn't like the name he was given when he was first born, in 1935: his Nigerian parents had followed a local German missionary's suggestion. So Fela died and was born a second time, on October 15, 1938; this time his parents called him Fela.

"Bear the name of conquerors?" he asked Carlos Moore, author of *Fela, Fela: This Bitch of a Life*, in 1981. "Or reject this first arrival in the world? The *orishas* [spirits] they heard me. And they spared me. What can I say? I wasn't Hildegart! It wasn't for white man to give me name. So it's because of a name that I've already known death."

In 1975, at the height of his popularity and power, Fela changed his middle name. "I got rid of 'Ransome.' Why was my name 'Ransome' in the first place? Me, do I look like Englishman?" Fela's full name was now Fela Anikulapo-Kuti, which meant in whole, "He who emanates greatness, who has control over death and who cannot be killed by man."

14

That same year Fela also started to cheekily call himself Black President, eventually releasing an album bearing the same title in the midst of a thwarted campaign. And sometime in 1986, following his release from Nigerian prison after serving 20 months on trumped-up charges, Fela began to call himself the *Ebami Eda*, which translates roughly as "the weird one," or more delicately, as "the one touched by divine hand."

Fela was touched, all right. Not only was he a visionary musician who created a whole new style of music—Afrobeat—and left behind an incomparable body of recorded music. No. Fela also *simultaneously* spoke truth to power, and then recorded it as a 12-minute dance-funk song, with a title like "Government Chicken Boy" or "Coffin for Head of State." He endured brutal physical punishment and constant imprisonment. In the end, he died from complications associated with the AIDS virus. His heart was broken: he had sung so much, fought so hard, amassed such popularity, and still, hardly anything changed for the better in his beloved, heart-shaped continent of Africa. So: the following is the story of that big, generous, humorous, creative, divine heart that Fela had: from its early heartbeats, to Afrobeat, to the beatings it took, to its final, slow heartbreak.

Fela was born into a family of discipline and disobedience—two qualities he would absorb and exploit later in his life. His father was the strict Rev. Canon Israel Oludoton Ransome-Kuti, an ordained minister, grammar school principal and first president of the Nigerian Union of Teachers. Fela's mother Funmilayo, beside being the first known female car driver in Nigeria, was a leader in the country's nascent socialist-nationalist and suffragette campaigns: she even traveled to Russia and China, where she met Mao.

"My mother was quite heavy politically," remembered Fela. "And ohhhhhhh, I liked the way she took on those old politicians, all those dishonest rogues."

As a teen, Fela was already playing the role of witty rebel against authority that he would later refine and perfect. "In school I formed a club when I was sixteen, the Planless Society," he said. "The rule of the club was simple: we had no plans. You could be called upon to disobey orders at any time. Disobedience was our 'law.'"

Like many children of the Nigerian middle class, Fela was sent to London to study at university. But Fela, now a trumpet player, wasn't interested in the professional careers in medicine and law that such students (like Fela's brothers) usually pursue; instead, in 1958, three years after his father's death, he enrolled at the London Trinity College of Music.

Fela was joined in London by his childhood friend J.K. Braimah, who jokingly told Moore, "Fela was a nice guy, a really beautiful guy. But as square as they come! Whenever we would go to parties he would fill up on cider first. Then he would start challenging the others to dance. He didn't smoke cigarettes, let alone grass. He was afraid to fuck! We had to take his prick by hand, hold it and put it in the cunt for him. I swear!"

Fela eventually met, and married in 1961, his first wife Remi there in London. With some West Indian and Nigerian friends, he started a jazz band called Koola Lobitos, but had trouble finding gigs. Fela sat in at jazz gigs around town; one of the musicians in the scene at the time that he hooked up with was Ginger Baker, who would be one of Fela's life-long friends. Meanwhile, Fela and Remi had their first two children—daughter Yeni in '61 and son Femi in '62—and Fela graduated from Trinity with certificates in practice and theory.

Fela and his family returned to Nigeria in 1963, where Fela took an unfulfilling job as a music producer with the Nigerian Broadcasting Corporation, which he eventually quit. He had already formed a new Koola Lobitos band, but was finding it difficult to gain momentum in Nigeria's economically depressed nightclub scene. A 1967 tour of neighboring Ghana, where the "highlife" style of music was booming, greatly impressed Fela. "The whole country was swinging so much that I said to myself that this is the right place to come and play," he told Mabinuori Kayode Idowu in his 1986 book, *Fela: Why Blackman Carry Shit.*

But before long, Ghana's Pan-Africanist president Dr. Kwame Nkrumah was deposed in a military coup. The Nigerian government was engaged in a bloody, ridiculous civil war with Biafran secessionists. And mid-'60s James Brown–style Soul music, especially the version played by Ghanian Geraldo Pino, was gaining favor in both countries.

Fela was getting pushed out. "Everybody was playing soul, man, trying to copy Pino," he told Moore. "That's why I said to myself, 'I have to be very original and clear myself from shit.'"

So in 1969, when Fela was given an offer to tour America with his band, he took it.

The band was wowed by New York City. "I said to myself: 'Look those motherfucking tall buildings! Africans ain't shit! Just savages, man!' Oh I was so impressed by America! So blind, man!" Fela recalled. "Today I'd say 'Skyscrapers go up that high? To scrape what? Jo, make 'em scrape dirty streets of Harlem!'"

In a weird coincidence, Fela had met famous South African singer Miriam Makeba on the plane en route to the U.S.; she gave him the name and address of her agent in New York. But the agent refused to represent an unknown like Fela. Previous logistical arrangements began to fall through.

Fela: "Nigeria was now three months behind us. And we weren't *in* the America we'd dreamt of. No, man. We were *in* trouble! No gigs! No bread! No shit! Nothing! And our visas finish-o! I said, 'Now we're illegal immigrant motherfuckers! No visa, no work permit . . . Stalemate!' Terrible times, man."

The band ended up driving all the way across the country in search of gigs, finally bottoming out in Los Angeles in August, 1969, without a permanent residence.

"It was kind of difficult at first but ended up okay," Fela's drummer Tony Allen told Mean about life in L.A. "We got some friends that offered us places. There was one guy, he gave us a whole house, without heater! No hot water! One day the Gas Company man, just passing by, saw us. We say, 'Our problem is we don't have hot water or heater.' He came in, and he saw that in the chamber outside, the control was broken. Dead long time ago! So he just went into his car and took a brand new one, bring it up, took off the old one there, fixed it up and opened the gas for us."

Some band members took factory jobs while Fela tried to hustle up live gigs and a recording contract. A local musician and drum maker

named Juno Lewis saw Fela's group perform and heard that they were
to play at an NAACP function at the Ambassador Hotel.

It was at this gig that Fela's life changed.

Sandra Smith was a young Los Angeles anthropology student radical
who had recently joined the Black Panther Party for Self-Defense and
was interested in all things African: history, contemporary politics,
dance and music. On her friend (and troupemate) Juno's tip, she went
to see Fela's band play at the Ambassador in August, 1969.

"I walked into the Hotel's Ballroom, wearing this blue bellbottomed
jumpsuit and I just happened to look up onstage," Sandra told *Mean*.
"And Fela was looking down. It was like a simultaneous connection, a
beam that connected just the two of us. And I felt some energy like I
had never felt before. At the intermission, Juno said somebody wanted
to see me at the bar. And there was Fela."

The two quickly became lovers, with Fela moving in with Sandra at
her parents' house. Sandra: "As we spent time together, I got to know
the musicians, I got all involved in their business. They needed help,
and I just got involved.

"He'd play at the club, we'd party, and then he'd come home," remembers Sandra. "Until 3 o'clock in the morning, we were up, we're
talking. I remember him telling me how Africans are so stupid. Huh! I
had never gone to Africa, but then I was coming into the knowledge of
Self, and I believed that Africa had queens and kings and everything. I
was *intense*. Then I started introducing him to things. I guess he was
quiet and listening to me, but I thought I was learning from *him*."

Fela started reading the books that Sandra was enthused about: history books, Eldridge Cleaver, and what would become his favorite, *The
Autobiography of Malcolm X*.

"Sandra gave me the education I wanted to know," Fela told Moore.
"She talked to me about politics, history, about Africa. She taught me
what she knew and what she knew was enough for me to start on. She's
beautiful. Nothing about my life is complete without her."

The band got a regular gig playing at Citadel de Haiti, a struggling
nightclub run by Bernie Hamilton (who would later feature in the

Starsky & Hutch TV series) in a red brick building at 6666 Sunset Boulevard.

"We played there for about five months, six nights in a week," remembers Tony Allen. "Bernie gave us a house and we played in his club. It was grooving, you know."

"Anyone that was anybody—John Brown, Melvin Van Peebles, H.B. Barnham, Esther Phillips—came to see Fela," says Sandra. "It was all word of mouth."

Sandra was singing onstage with the band, who were playing a mixture of Fela's jazz compositions and his unique arrangements of contemporary soul favorites like "By the Time I Get to Phoenix." On his nights off from the Citadel, Fela would sit in around town at jazz gigs, or play private parties (including one where a drunk Frank Sinatra got in a heated exchange with Fela). Fela was busy writing and arranging music on a piano in the living room at Sandra's house. The band would rehearse using acoustic equipment in Sandra's backyard. Despite hardships—like Sandra having to take an extra job to buy a new trumpet for Fela when his was stolen—the arrangement was a good one, and allowed Fela to begin developing a new kind of music.

Sandra: "At that time, James Brown had 'Say It Loud, I'm Black and I'm Proud.' Fela was singing in Yoruba, you couldn't understand anything he was saying, but the music was getting better and better. He was getting deeper into his African roots. African music is about the chanting. Fela had all these rhythms and all these arrangements, and it was getting so dynamic! But when I asked him what he was saying, he said he was talking about what he likes in his soup! And I was saying, 'No. You need to sing some conscious lyrics. You can pass a message in the music.'"

Fela took Sandra's words to heart and began composing his first conscious music: songs like "My Lady's Frustration" and "Black Man's Pride."

Afrobeat had been born—in America.

Fela and his band were ratted out by somebody in L.A. Their visas had expired, and they headed back to Nigeria.

"We got real funky then," remembers Tony Allen.

Fela changed the band's name to the Nigeria 70. He wrote his first hit record, the humorous "J'eun Koku" ("glutton"). He bookended his performances and public appearances with the Black Power clenched fist salute he had learned in America. He started holding "Sunday Afternoon Jump" dance concerts at a venue modeled after similar shows he had seen years ago in Ghana. The club itself—two stories, no roof, packed with dancers, trays of very cheap "Nigerian Natural Grass" (marijuana) *everywhere*—was now called the Afro-Spot. It quickly became *the* place to see *the* happening band. In 1970, even James Brown's band came to the Afro-Spot, visiting each night after they finished one of their series of gigs downtown [see Bootsy Collins below]. Singer Vickie Anderson wanted to know who had written the brilliant arrangement of "Phoenix" that she heard at the club (it was Fela); Tony Allen claimed that Brown's people sat by his kit each night, attempting to chart his drum patterns.

With Remi and the children now settled in their own house, Fela went about creating what was essentially a hippie commune—with an African twist.

Fela: "I'd think to myself, 'Ah-Ah! What is this city shit-o? One man, one wife, one house isolated from everybody else in the neighborhood? Is an African not even to know his neighbors? So why all this individualism shit? This "mine." This "yours." That "theirs." What's that shit? Is it African?' That's how the idea of setting up a communal compound—one like Africans had been living in for thousands of years—came about."

So Fela moved into a large house at 14-A Agege Motor Road in the Surulere district of Lagos, bringing with him his band's female singers, roadies and anyone else involved with his organization. "It was only two floors and there were 100 people, but we were happy," Fela said. "It was beautiful, no problems."

The singers—who also danced onstage—were Fela's lovers. He now carried himself as a traditional African village king, or tribal chief, and his women were his "queens" . . . but they were more than that. He also called them his witches.

Sandra visited Fela in Nigeria during that year. "I had a great time, being with Fela. But at the same time, there was a lot of jealousy and animosity towards me by his wives."

Sandra was poisoned by one of the girls, becoming so ill that she had to take refuge at Fela's eldest brother's house; Koye was a doctor and he and his wife looked after her. But even far from Fela's jealous wives, she was attacked.

"I had a dream that this ghastly-looking thing was hovering over my bed, clawing me with lots of hatred and anger," she remembers. "And I thought it was just a dream, until I saw my body the next morning, covered with claw marks. Koye's wife was a witness to it. That's when I knew African witchcraft was *real*."

Sandra returned to the U.S. soon after.

In the next three years, Fela's music exploded in vision, quantity (an incredible six to eight albums a year) and popularity. He changed his club's name to the Shrine, saying that he wanted it to be "some place meaningful, of progressive, mindful background with roots. I didn't believe playing any more in nightclubs." He told England's *Independent*, "We smoke in the Shrine, all the time. The shrine is not a club, man. It's a place where we dance, we get high, we play drums to evoke the spirit. The power of the Shrine is very strong—the spiritual power . . . this is why we can smoke dope with impunity."

Fela had become a marijuana smoker of epic proportions. Besides smoking giant joints filled with *igbo* (Indian hemp), Fela had now developed his own marijuana recipe, which he called *goro*.

"He cooked a bag of grass about [two feet long], which cost just two pennies for like two weeks, soaking it with spices, honey and oils, cooked it right, right, right down til it was *thick*," says Fela's son Femi. "Very thick! All that came out was about [an amount that would fit in a small coffee cup]. You're only allowed to take about a spoon, and then, in maybe two or three hours, you are just so high, it's unbelievable. It lasts the whole day, two days, three days. Fela trained a couple of people to cook it, and for six years, man, I was the only one who had authorization (except for him), to serve it round the house, to give it to anybody who wants it.

"He just wanted to get higher!" laughs Femi. "He even did cocaine for a while, a month or so, but he said it stopped his sexual desires so he didn't like that. So he made *goro*. When they were traveling, he al-

ways made sure the embassy gave him a note, saying the *goro* was medicine. Which it was. He said that was the main reason he took it: It
helped his sexual desire and his creativity."

Fela's commune was beginning to attract all sorts of folk, from
street hooligans and runaways to the nation's political underground.
According to writer Bayo Martins, "A radical left wing organization
known as the Nigerian Association of Patriotic Writers and Artistes
formed a think tank around Fela for the ideological development of
Pan-Africanism with his Afrobeat Music, and to organize mass rallies
and publicity strategy which made sure Fela was constantly in the
news. It worked. In no time Fela had become a national household
word in Nigeria. Contracts for international concerts were starting to
flow in."

Fela's confidence knew no bounds. He would ride a donkey across
the street from his compound to the Shrine before each night's performance, stopping traffic up for miles. He purchased his own printing
press and started publishing fearlessly inflammatory broadsides against
the dictatorship in the name of his new youth organization, the Young
African Pioneers.

Fela's neighborhood became a hotbed of anti-government activity.
Finally, the military could take no more.

On April 30, 1974, the commune was raided and Fela was arrested for
possession of marijuana. Released on bail, he returned to his compound and re-named it "Kalakuta Republic" ("Kalakuta" being the
name of the prison cell he had occupied for two weeks), erected a ten-
foot barbed wire fence, declared that the Republic was its own nation
wholly independent of Nigeria, and recorded a hit album ("Algabon
Close") that chronicled the arrest.

The police raided the house once again, this time attempting to
plant weed on Fela. He asked to look at the evidence—and ate it, right
in front of the surprised officers. Once again, Fela was hauled off to
jail, where the prosecutors demanded that he produce feces containing
the marijuana. Fela wouldn't. He was set three days in Timbuktu, a
floating cell anchored in the Lagos Lagoon behind the prison. Eventually he defecated the weed in secret, and provided "clean" shit to the

authorities, who rushed it to the lab for analysis. The results were negative. Fela was released, and immediately wrote another hit album—entitled "Expensive Shit"—detailing his experiences.

At this point the Nigerian Establishment was so upset with Fela's continuing attacks on their corruption and lampoons of their efforts to stop him that he was safe nowhere—not even in other countries. Out on bail, Fela embarked on an international tour, only to be cut short in Cameroon when Nigerian police came across the border and arrested three of his Queens for not reporting to their parole officers in Lagos.

Then, on November 23, 1974, Kalakuta was raided for a third time in one year. This time the police weren't interested in arresting people so much as physically punishing them. Everyone in the compound was beaten; Fela himself ended up spending nine days in the hospital, being treated for a broken arm and receiving eleven stitches. Of course he wrote a song about the whole affair; and of course "Kalakuta Show" was another hit.

"Fela went through the entire gamut of our criminal system, from unlawful assembly to sedition to incitement to the highest of offenses," one of Fela's attorneys recalled in the 1999 TV documentary, *Femi Kuti: The New King of Afrobeat*. "So virtually all the time Fela's cases were politically motivated and therefore there was no cause to consider withdrawing from defending him. We always believed that Fela would come out of jail stronger, and that was what happened."

By 1977, Fela's every move was an embarrassment and affront to Nigeria's corrupt ruling class and military government. His hit records named names in both the songs' ridiculing lyrics and triple-vibrant, meticulously detailed sleeve artwork. He gave sensational press interviews. He declared Kalakuta an independent state. He claimed that he would be voted President of Nigeria if fair elections were held. It was all too much, and another government attack was inevitable.

So Fela installed a 65-kilowatt generator to electrify Kalakuta's fence. "You see the type of shit I was forced to do then?" he said. "Just to protect myself and my people, not from robbers, but from the authorities!"

The government invited Fela to participate in an image-conscious music and arts festival called FESTAC 77—but he refused. "One big hustle! A rip-off!" he retorted. Instead, Fela played concerts each night in his shrine; in attendance each night were many international artists and journalists (including, most famously, Stevie Wonder) who came to see the most popular African musician of all strut his stuff. Fela took full advantage of the situation, condemning the government generally and in particular its "Operation Ease the Traffic" program, which involved soldiers whipping drivers during the "go-slow" (rush hour traffic jams). The authorities were infuriated by Fela's actions, and after FESTAC concluded, the military took direct action.

On February 18, 1977 about 1000 soldiers surrounded Kalakuta and began a 15-hour siege. There was mortar fire. The generator exploded and the house caught fire, at which point Fela and his people surrendered. Fela's 78-year-old mother was thrown from the second-story. The Queens and other Kalakuta residents were beaten; some were raped and tortured. The compound itself was burned to the ground, as was the free clinic run by Fela's younger brother Beko. Beko was seriously injured. Fela himself went to the hospital and was then imprisoned on typically ludicrous charges.

Although the incident received plenty of attention from the international press (including a lengthy account in the *New York Times*), the Nigerian government's probe of the event concluded only that a residence at 14-A Agege Motor Road had been burned by "unknown soldiers."

Out of jail, with one arm and one leg in a cast, Fela reacted to this latest injustice as he always had: by making hit records. This time it was two albums, entitled "Sorrow, Tears and Blood" and "Unknown Soldier."

Homeless and penniless, Fela and his 80-person entourage lived in a hotel [see Lester Bowie below], and then for a short while in his brother Koye's garage. Fela was now encountering difficulties with his record company, the Nigerian branch of Decca, which had changed management hands and was now hostile to releasing Fela's inflammatory records, no matter how popular he was. It was a plain breach of contract, and Fela wanted the money he was contractually owed if such a breach occurred. The label refused, so Fela and his people went to the Decca offices. And stayed. For seven weeks.

"The Decca offices has very big sitting room and thick carpets everywhere, so we laid our mattresses down and stayed there in comfort," he explained.

Fela finally left for Ghana, where, by 1978, his anti-police "Zombie" had become a big hit, especially with the students. He returned to Nigeria briefly on the one-year anniversary of the assault on Kalakuta, playing a show at Ogbe Stadium in Benin City. During the festivities around the event, he married all 27 of his singers simultaneously in a traditional ceremony.

"A man goes for many women in the first place," Fela said later, defending his polygamy. "Like in Europe, when a man is married, when the wife is sleeping, he goes out and fucks around. He should bring the women in the house, man, to live with him, and stop running around the streets!"

Later he told the *Washington Post*, "When I do things, I do things honestly. I didn't sleep with any women outside my marriage." And he revealed to the *Lagos Weekend*, "Me, I fuck as often and as long as I can-o!"

Fela returned to Ghana with his band, but the popularity of "Zombie"—and Fela's habit of preaching the Pan-Africanist philosophy of Ghana's former leader, Kwame Nkrumah—made the Ghanian authorities nervous; before long Fela was deported from Ghana for being "liable to bring about a breach of the peace."

On April 13, 1978, Fela's mother died, having never fully recovered from the injuries she sustained in her fall during the Army's rampage at Kalakuta. Outraged that Olusegon Obasanjo—the ruthless military dictator who had never apologized for the sacking of Kalakuta (and who in 1999 is Nigeria's democratically elected leader)—was leaving office with full honors as the country transferred to supposedly democratic rule, Fela plotted his revenge.

"I just couldn't let him get away like that," Fela said. "*Obasanjo's soldiers had killed my mother.* That man will have to answer to that one-o!"

Fela had a life-size replica of his mother's coffin built, which he delivered to Obasanjo's home in the Dodan Barracks on the morning of

October 1, 1979. Accompanied by his Queens, his son Femi and others, Fela drove the bus through roadblocks towards the barracks.

Fela: "Oh, my wives, those women are courageous-o! The sentries lifted their machine guns and rifles. I told them, 'My brothers, will you also shoot my women?' They lowered their weapons. We arrived at gate. We lowered coffin to ground. We turned round. And we left. At that same moment it began to rain. Heavily! Oh, that rain-o!"

The seeming end of military rule in Nigeria in 1980 gave Fela new hope of finally being elected president. He formed a political party called M.O.P. (Movement of the People) and attempted to get listed as a candidate on the ballot.

"If I can take [Nigeria], then Africa is settled," Fela argued. "All of Africa will be liberated. If there is only one good government—a straight and progressive, clean government that knows what it is doing. No compromises, no Marxism-Leninists, no capitalism. Africanism."

During Nigeria's '80–'81 academic session, he gave more than 60 lectures at universities; one such lecture is printed in its entirety in *Fela: Why Blackman Carry Shit*. In his lectures, Fela related an ancient history of Africa grounded in pioneering Afrocentric Egyptologist Yosef Ben-Jochannan's *Black Man of the Nile*. His critical history of colonialism was principally based on the influential thinking of Dr. Kwame Nkrumah, the father of Pan-Africanism. Fela's acerbic criticisms were relentless.

"What America has done to Africa is bad," he said. "Bringing in arms, bringing Christianity, turning the people's minds upside down, bringing in fertilizers, doing shit, wanting to bring western civilization here. America and England are trying to brainwash Africans."

Fela criticized "reactionary African puppets [who] go about condemning apartheid South Africa while they go about killing innocent citizens in their countries to sustain them in power."

He preached in favor of traditional African home remedies and against the medicine of the multinationals: Cow urine, for example, was a cure for convulsion, and Africans need "synthetic tablets" to cure themselves of malaria. He argued that UFOs existed; that Nigerian government leaders should consult spiritual oracles; that there were "people in this country with enough knowledge of Africa's perfect system of government to guide us."

Finally Fela argued against industrialization, saying "the future of this world is based on nature, not the machine. Science means complications. When science brings out a new gadget it costs more than the others. People have to earn more to buy it. So science makes people run more. What we need is to rest more, talk more, walk more, fuck more and enjoy things in life more."

Fela told Moore, "When people say America, Russia, China are great powers, I say: 'No!' Oppressors, destroyers, massacrists can never be great people. Creativity, not destruction, should be the yardstick of greatness. If you cannot create anything that will make your own life, or that of your fellow human, happier, then get out of the way. Split! Disappear! And give others a chance."

"After Fela's mother died, it was a very difficult time for Fela," remembers Sandra. "It just went all downhill from there."

Besides his mother's recent death, Tony Allen, who had helped Fela develop the Afrobeat sound, had left the group in 1979; Fela's wives were slowly leaving him; and it didn't look like the M.O.P. would succeed in getting Fela on the ballot. But what seemed most important to Fela was establishing some sort of contact with his mother.

"He knew that in the African religion that the ancestors play a very important role," says Sandra. "They believe that once a person transcends to the other side that they're there to help you."

Fela had begun to solicit traditional African spiritual mediums, witch doctors and witches. "There were certain people in the house that claimed to be in communication with his mother," says Sandra. "And he was listening to them."

"I knew about the spiritual aspect of the African traditions, and I was getting very involved as a teenager," remembers Femi. "And I told him, 'Fela, this aspect of life does exist.' But he kept going out to look for traditional powers, and I was like, he has the greatest power, spiritually speaking, from an African man's point of view: to be able to create sound and make people think, make people cry, and to gather over

10,000 people because of his music. I was trying to make him see his spiritual power he had in his possession and he did not have to look anywhere else, but just look inward.

"One group of [witch doctors] came with a jacket, saying if Fela wore it and they shot him with a bullet he will not die. They tried it on a goat and the goat did not die. Lucky they got his brother to bring a shotgun and someone says try the jacket on the goat before you put it on. They pulled the shotgun out, put bullets in it and *pow!* The goat's head just falls off. That would have been Fela's head, man."

In the spring of 1981, Sandra received a call from a hotel in Paris. It was a very shaken Fela, asking her to come see him immediately.

"He felt that they were trying to kill him," she recalls. "He wasn't specific. I just jumped on a plane. I went to Paris for three days. The scene at that hotel was unreal. He had some heavy, wicked people around him at that point. I don't know how he could have remained sane in such an insane environment.

"I believe that was the weekend when Fela contracted the AIDS virus [that would eventually kill him]. I felt it. This is something that I can't explain, but it's real."

On his return to Nigeria from Europe, Fela had a spiritual revelation, in which he was possessed.

"I saw this whole [world] was going to change into what people call the Age of Aquarius," he told writer Roger Steffens. "Musicians were going to be very important in the development of human society and that musicians would be presidents of different countries and artists would be the dictators of society. The mind would be freer, less complicated institutions, less complicated technologies. It was in that trance that I saw the whole human race were in Egypt under the spiritual guidance of the Gods."

Fela immediately changed the name of his group to Egypt 80, and began to perform Yoruba rites in the middle of his performances at the Shrine at an altar decorated with images of luminaries like Malcolm X, Dr. Kwame Nkrumah and Fela's mother. The uncle of his old friend J.K. Braimah made spiritual incisions in the center of Fela's head. And finally, a witch doctor named Professor Hindu arrived from Ghana, claiming he had the power to "kill and wake"—to kill a man and bring him back to life.

Fela said, "That night he performed at Shrine. I wouldn't have believed it if I hadn't seen that shit with my own eyes. 'Kill and wake!' He's the man who started showing me the way to truth, to myself, to my mission and to . . . my mother! He revealed to me that one has to put this white spiritual powder on the face to communicate with spirits. He tells me what to do, what not to do, who my friends are and who are my enemies."

Femi was more skeptical. "Yes, Hindu performed a lot of magic," he says. "And I have no answers for some of the things he did. But when he said he killed somebody, and he did not let my father's brother [Beko] investigate properly, [almost] everybody became suspicious."

In December 1981, Kalakuta was once again assaulted—this attack was captured on still camera by the French TV crew that happened to be there filming the documentary later released as *Music Is the Weapon*. Police raided the compound, plundering the buildings and teargassing and beating everyone, including pregnant women and children. Once again Fela returned from jail, beaten but defiant—and as charismatic as ever.

"I'm getting stronger," he boasted to the film crew. "In fact I'm surprised at how quickly I've recovered, considering the beating I got."

"Something tells me that I am right, that I *will* be president of this country one day," he said, cheekily. "Don't worry!"

But once again, Fela was prevented from even running for election; instead, he became embroiled in a new host of absurd charges—this time for sabotage, murder and armed robbery—that would eventually be dismissed.

Over the next few years, for various reasons, Fela's domestic popularity began to dwindle. In 1984, he agreed to co-produce (or mix) his next album with the American producer Bill Laswell. But on September 4, as Fela was leaving for the U.S. to mix the album with Laswell and do a short tour, he was arrested once again. This time Fela was accused by Nigerian Customs officials of trying to smuggle Nigerian currency out of the country.

Fela was sentenced to five years in jail after a trial that was such an obvious procedural sham that Amnesty International declared Fela a Prisoner of Conscience. A "Free Fela" movement was born, with popular musicians like Stevie Wonder and David Byrne signing on.

On Sept. 24, 1985, the case's judge visited Fela in jail and apologized; he said the ruling government had forced his decision and made him jail Fela. But it wasn't until April 23, 1986—after 20 months in jail—that Fela was released, when news of the judge's secret prison visit finally began to circulate in the popular press, embarrassing the current government. Fela was not the same when he came out of prison.

"I can still see all the marks on his body from the bayonets of the guns and all that," remembers Femi. "He got beaten so. His whole body was kind of broken. Head injuries, his hands. He was in real pain for a long time. When people were around, he would try to hide it. I think what saved him was the grass, at the end of the day. It helped him handle the pain. He wouldn't have done it, normally. No human being could do that.

"There will never be another man like him. He started calling himself *Ebami Eda*, which means 'the weird one,' after he came from jail. He believed he was protected by something, by spirits, by the supernatural. Because he did not know where the music came from. It comes from somewhere else, something else that you cannot see. And music is related to that, because music is the one artform that you cannot touch, that you cannot see. You can see the instruments and you can plan in your head the music you will make, but you cannot say how it will sound."

"Music is a spiritual thing," Fela said in 1982. "You don't play with music. *If you play with music, you will die young.* Because when the higher forces give you the gift of musicianship, it must be well-used for the good of humanity. If you use it for your own self by deceiving people or doing this, you will die young. And I have told people this many times. So, I'm gonna prove them wrong and prove myself right. I'm getting younger! I can play music for ten hours. I'm never tired . . . because the spiritual life of music that I've lead *rightly* is helping me now."

"You tap into something—or, it taps into you," says Femi. "You have some say, your creativity, in arranging it, in making it your own. But you are still a medium for something, for whatever . . . message . . . they want to put out. He was a medium for it."

"Fela's career continued to go, but another type of realization had come in," says Sandra. "Fela told me there was nothing else to sing about, nothing else to talk about, because he'd said it all [and nothing had changed]. He was very sad. This was a man who had been very jovial-type person. He became a recluse. Fela was caught in his own world of Kalakuta. He was the king there, and he surrounded himself with a bunch of 'yes men.'"

"He knew what he wanted in the '70s," says Femi. "He knew what he was up against. He knew he could die. He was ready. In the '80s, I think he was now getting frustrated. Fela's problems started when he went spiritual. Cuz now he wanted an answer, from traditional medicine, he was looking for African technology. For all these years he has been fighting for the African people. Why are Africans not doing anything about what he has been talking about?"

Nevertheless, Fela continued to compose and perform (if not record) some brilliant music, as well as give sensational interviews to the Lagos press.

Fela told the press that his recent skin rashes were spiritual in origin—he was "changing skin," with a new skin scheduled to appear on January 1, 1992. He claimed he was still making love three hours a day—as well as brushing his teeth for an hour and taking 45 minutes in the bath, during which he would do "a series of body-building exercises." He dismissed as "junk" the 11 members of his band who left him during his 1991 US tour, instead emphasizing that he had a great time: "I had sex with all my girls in my band, and I got two extra American girls. Also I had a regulation that any Nigerian who wanted to see me [backstage] must give me present, and the only present I like is *igbo* [Indian hemp]."

By 1993, Fela was telling the press that "Kalakuta is not an ordinary place, it is the center of the world"—that his witches (who were no longer his wives, as he had divorced all of them following his release from prison) were directing what was happening in the country.

"If they want this country to be in total confusion in the next one year, they can do it," Fela told the *Lagos Weekend*. He claimed that the recent misfortunes of his longtime nemesis, ITT and Decca business-man Chief Abiola, was caused by his witches. "Abiola paralyzed be-cause he wants to sell Nigeria to America. It can never be. Abiola himself is just beginning to get what is coming for him. This country is witch country. World is witch world. I have said it before."

Smoking one of his 15-inch-long *igbo* joints, the 56-year-old Fela even claimed he was immortal: "I will never die; my ancestors have told me so."

But Fela's health had begun to deteriorate. It was obvious to those close to him that something was seriously wrong. The sexually promis-cuous Fela—who had refused to use condoms his entire life, on the grounds that they were synthetic, non-African and a conspiracy against black men experiencing full pleasure—had AIDS. He refused anything but traditional African folk remedies.

"I think he thought he could not catch the disease," says Femi. "I don't know why. But back then, nobody has really taken the disease very seriously. So many people have died from the disease in Nigeria and we don't hear because nobody comes out to say 'Yes, he died from AIDS.' Everybody believes that it's a shameful disease."

"Fela did not have to die from AIDS," says Sandra. "People don't have to die from AIDS in the '90s. That was the choice Fela made.

"When you start to mature, you start to question the way things are. You know, Fela talked about everything. And some people heard it, and a lot of them didn't. It was very, very disappointing. You wonder if death is better than life. I think Fela reached the point where he prob-ably didn't want to live. Fela stayed and died in Nigeria, when he could have came out of Nigeria and lived a better life."

There were, of course, final indignities. Fela was arrested again for drug possession and paraded before the TV cameras in handcuffs. Femi had to beg the authorities to release Fela on bail, arguing that al-though Fela had been arrested more times than any Nigerian in history, he had never jumped bail. Fela was typically defiant, saying, "It is not drugs. It is grass."

Fela, who had stopped eating and locked himself in his room, finally acceded to his family's wishes to visit a hospital. But it was too late.

On August 2, 1997, Fela Anikulapo-Kuti died.

Epilogue

Fela's heart had stopped, but you could still hear its beat.

The announcement in his final weeks that Fela had AIDS had done little to dampen the public affection for the man. On an early Monday morning, as Fela's body was taken by his family to an arena to lie in state, a million people—silent, crying with their fists in the air—lined the Lagos streets in an unorganized show of respect.

"For two days, people didn't do any work in Lagos!" Femi remembers, laughing. "This is the first time in the history of Lagos that they have not had a complaint of robbery, rape or anything. Because all the robbers, all the bad boys, they loved him, you know? Everybody was busy at the funeral!"

Today, Kalakuta still stands. The old Shrine has been demolished; Femi has plans to dedicate a new Shrine as early as February, 2000. Seun Kuti, Femi's younger brother, continues to perform Fela's songs with the remaining members of Egypt 80; Femi himself has his own career. Fela's brother Beko was finally released from jail after serving 40 months on typically bogus charges. And 2000 sees the launch by MCA of an ambitious program to issue Fela's albums (many for the first time) in the U.S.

"He saw all these things going wrong, and he felt he had to talk about it," said Fela's first wife Remi in a 1999 TV interview. "Fela had a mission, and people should have listened to what he was saying. Instead, they just said he was crazy."

•   •   •

Bootsy Collins

Bootsy Collins is one of the greatest bassists of all time, a member of the baddest version of the JB's, a funk-force with the Parliament-Funkadelic empire

*in the '70s and leader of his own impossibly stanky group, Bootsy's Rubber
Band. Currently at work at his home studio (which he jokingly calls "the
Bootzvilla Rehab") on multiple projects—including a new Rubber Band album, a new Funkadelic album and a reunion with all of the surviving members of the original JB's—Bootsy took a few minutes to speak with* Mean
about the JB's' famous visit to Nigeria in 1970.

Everybody was talkin' about Fela when we got there, and about how
he was like the African James Brown. And everybody was tellin' us he
was *the* man. So after we did one gig in Lagos, Nigeria, we all just
went over. Me, Bobby Byrd, Vicki Anderson, Jabo.

What was getting to the club like?
Oh man, that was wild! Cuz you know their police force was the
Army. They were *serious*. You know, everybody treated us really good
from the day we stepped off the plane. But this Army, they didn't
take *nothin'*. I mean, they didn't care who you were. It was like *everybody* was scum of the earth, man. [laughs] So we were on the way, and
the Army just stopped us out of the clear blue and then they started
asking who were we, and where were we goin'. And of course we
were *dirty*, you know? We'd just played and we was out havin' a little
fun. So we had a few dirty thangs on us. And it was like, "Well what
do you have in the boot? What's in the boot?" And what I had just
done, I had just put my dirt in my sock. And I thought the guy was
talkin' about you know what's in my boot, like what's in my *shoe*.
[laughter] I was through, man! I thought I was gonna be gone *forever*.
But luckily Vicki Anderson figured it out, that he was talking about
the *trunk*. Cuz I had my dirt and everybody else's dirt in my boot,
man! [laughs] So they didn't check nothing but the trunk, then they
let us through.
     We went on to the club and as we was pulling up, I'd say about a
mile and a half, two miles before you got to the club, you could hear
these drums, you could hear this rhythm goin' on. And as we were ap-
proaching, you just moved, you just started movin'. We didn't even see
nobody yet, we just heard the music, because the club that he had was
roofless. And when you start gettin' in the area, you just start vibin',
cuz I mean, those drums and the music that they had goin' on . . . !

And the things that you're told about Africa—we had no idea that they had electric guitars, you know.

You thought they'd be playing folk music . . .
Yeah, we had no idea! And we pulled up and all this was goin' on, man. They came and got us and we went to a room. This was when . . . Fela, he hadn't went on yet. He was still in the dressing room. And man, we walked in the room and the smoke knocked us down! [laughter] They was handing these cigars around that was like . . . We was in heaven! So we vibed with him, we talked, and we went out to see the show. He came out and did his thing, man, and we had never seen *nothin'* like that, or *felt* anything like that, you know. It was *amazing*, and I guess by going there and seeing that, I kind of *absorbed* whatever I was hearing and whatever I was seeing. I just brought it back with me, and it became a part of me.

Now when you guys went to the club, James didn't go, right?
No. We tried to get him to go but he . . . you know, he's always into his thang, you know. And he probably didn't want to see somebody, you know, other than him on the stage. [laughter] But you know, that's the way he is.

Did you all go there more than one night?
It had to be two or three nights. Because we played there. It had to be two or three nights that we played right there in Lagos, the capitol. Everybody loved us. It's the James Brown show, everybody was there. We played in a stadium. It was amazing, man. Uh-maze-ing.

So you'd finish playing at the stadium and go over to Fela's—
Oh yeah. We had to go, man. And we developed a real good relationship, man. It was like . . . the way he spoke, we understood what he said and he understood what we said. It was more of a *vibe* goin' on. And man, when these cats hit the stage and when the drums started, I mean . . . whatever you was doin', you just stopped doin' that and your body just start movin'! [laughter].

See, at that particular time in my life, I was so *amazed*, period. I mean, about *everything*.

You were young—
Yeah! I was over in Africa when I was 17 years old—

... you're 17, you're touring Africa with the greatest band in the world, and you're going to a club and seeing another one of the greatest bands in the world—
Well actually I thought *they* were the greatest, period. Even before I got into James Brown's band, the James Brown band was number one to me. But once I got there and saw Fela and them, then I had second thoughts about it. I mean, seriously. The James Brown band reminded me of that same non-stop groove, you know: You gotta move. And then when I heard these cats, it was like another dimension of that. A dimension that I had never experienced before. And it had a *deeper* feel to me. I couldn't explain it, you know, but it was something I had been involved with but not as *deep*. When I heard them, that was the deepest level you could get. That's the only way I can explain that. Not that I'm doggin' myself along with the rest of the guys, but that's the way I felt. When I heard that, it was like, "Man, this is IT. We gotta try to be like this!" [laughs] And I knew we couldn't! We had to be what we were, but at the same time, that was some helluva inspiration. When I got with Parliament and Funkadelic, if you listen to "Stretchin' Out," that was me playin' drums. And that was my version of what I had picked up. [laughter]

Wow. Thanks for taking the time to reminisce with us ...
It digs up some great memories, man. And a lot of times if you don't talk about that stuff, it's there, but you don't really experience it again. And it's a good feeling, man, just to rap. That sparked a whole 'nother ... Now I gotta go back downstairs and make sure I can do that beat again!

• • •

Ginger Baker

Best known for his work with Cream, Ginger Baker is one of the all-time great drummers, a versatile master at ease in a number of the world's drumming traditions. He also has a reputation as an imposing interview subject.

Still, at his wife's recommendation, Mean called Ginger at his South African home at 7 A.M., apparently interrupting his bath. Here's how the conversation went.

When did you meet Fela?
I knew Fela since the very early '60s, when he was at the World College of Music. He used to play trumpet, and come and sit in the all-night jams which I played in . . . 1960–61 . . . I went to Nigeria in 1970, that's when I saw Fela again. I [inaudible] there from 1970 to 1976 . . .

I'm sorry, did you say you were living there during that time?
[voice rising] I lived in Nigeria from 1970 until 1976!

[pause] Uh. Okay. What can you tell me about making the record with Fela?
Absolutely nothing. [pause] That was a combination of a lot of things before it, that we made the record, and a lot of things after it. It wasn't just a one-off thing, I mean I did a five-week tour with Fela's band when Tony Allen was ill.

Oh, okay.
"Oh, okay." Yes. ISN'T THAT FUCKING AMAZING? "How extraordinary!" Fucking, man . . .

When did you do that?
During the period I was in Nigeria! Do you think I keep a diary and write things down?!?

No, I'm just trying to get it straight—
Between 1970 and 1975! That five-year period.

Okay . . . um . . . some people say . . . How much of Fela's sound, do you think, came from James Brown, and how much of it was his own thing?
100% of it was his own thing. Completely his own thing. Absolutely nothing to do with James Brown.

Really?
Fela blew James Brown off the stage when he came to Nigeria.

What . . . did they—
"Whu-whu-ohmygawd—whoa—have I got a story here!" Fuck, man.
You're talking to someone who [inaudible] here.

**[pause] Um. When did they play together? Do you remember
the circumstances? Was it a big stadium show—**
I can't remember, exactly. You'll have to check it out. I'm sure you've
got records you can check out.

Um . . . so how did [drummer] Tony Allen work with Fela?
Tony Allen tuned the band up. Virtually in charge of the whole situation. [pause]

But the arrangements for the songs were Fela's?
That was Fela.

So you were there in Nigeria when Fela had an incredible band.
That was the best band he ever had. The very first band had a tenor
player called Igo Chiko . . . before Fela played tenor, Igo Chiko was
the tenor player, who was pretty fucking cool. He had a row with Fela
and left the band and that's when Fela took up tenor saxophone.
[pause] The band with Igo Chiko was *the* happening band.

And that's the band you recorded with?
That's the band I toured with too.

So Tony was ill and you filled in for him?
Yeah, Tony was sick.

How did that work out?
It was terrible, I got fired every night, they threw eggs and bottles at
me and told me to fuck off cuz I was a white man.

Ah . . .
What do you think?!? No, of course it was FUCKING ALRIGHT!
OTHERWISE I WOULDN'T HAVE DONE IT!

[pause] Well. I mean, had you been sitting in with the band much prior to that?
Yes I had, I used to sit in regularly with the band because people used to ask me to, especially Fela. Fela and I were very, very good friends. You know . . . Fela got very political. His music, instead of being humorous, became very political and he upset the Nigerian Army, which is not a good thing to do. [long pause]

Right. I'm pretty familiar with the politics, as much as I can be from reading these books and—
No, I don't think most people know everything that went down that led up to that event. I know more of it than most people. I mean, there were a whole load of events that lead up to it. It wasn't suddenly . . . The Nigerians got very, very worried about Fela. The Kalakuta Party held a political rally in Lagos City Stadium and got 250,000 people there!

That's the thing that's so hard to grasp, isn't it, how extremely popular he was, and how radical. But was it simply an anti-corruption thing for him, or was he a socialist—
No. I blame the people who were around Fela at the time. Fela himself was an incredibly humorous, wonderful fellow. Some pretty radical people got very close to Fela. I think they misadvised him some. I really believe Fela could have become president. . . . How good a president he would've been, I don't know. I mean, how good a president would I be? [laughter] He took a couple of wrong turns, that, to me were very un-Fela-like. It really wasn't like Fela. It was the committee . . . We used to sit round a table the shape of Africa. Called The African Table. And I was on that committee for two years.

So as Fela got more popular—
They got over-confident. Several of Fela's people heavily provoked the military, yes. Not a very good idea in a place like Nigeria.

Bill [Laswell] told me Nigeria was one of the most corrupt, evil places on the face of the earth . . .
Absolute rubbish. Absolute rubbish. When I mentioned this, when I was in Ghana, about the corruption, the reply I received was, "Where do you think we learnt it?" The British government is the most corrupt government in the world. Or it used to be. I think the American government is now the most corrupt government in the world. And if you don't think that, if you can't see that, then there's something wrong with you. [pause] Corruption in Africa is on a finer scale compared to the corruption in the United States or the United Kingdom. They cover it up pretty well, they're not quite so open about it. That is the fact.

Well . . . um . . . what about the harassment by the military, by the police?
Harassment of Fela? [chuckling] The harassment was a two-way thing.

Really? What do you mean?
Well, you know, Fela won a court case against the Nigerian police where he won a lot of money, when his house was first raided, when they came to arrest the underage girls that Fela had just married . . .

. . . And there were other times when he embarrassed the police?
Pretty much so, yeah. Some of it was very cleverly done. After the police thing, Fela got really angry about the Army being on traffic duty with whips. And he brought out a record called Zombie. That was the period when things started going awry. I think I had left Nigeria by this time.

Oh. Right.
See, Fela was in the same position I am. There's an awful lot of stories, exaggerated, done by people like you . . . [laughs] . . . tend to get things arse about face, you've probably got everything I've said arse about face . . .

[Nervous laugh] I'm getting it all on tape, Ginger, I don't want to misquote you . . .

Yeah, but when you edit the tape, you could come up with . . . I've had it done to me so many times. Fela has, too. Really Fela was a wonderfully nice fellow, you know, who was *extremely* popular. He was far more popular than James Brown in Africa by a country mile. I don't mean slightly. Fela was an incredibly popular fellow, and his music was incredible, especially, you know, in that period of the early '70s.

What did he have that his competitors didn't?

He didn't have any competitors. [laughs] There was nobody doing what Fela was doing. It was just . . . heh . . . you had to go to Fela's club to see that. You didn't see anybody that wasn't moving. The whole place was jumping. He had several clubs—the Afro-Spot, the Shrine, various places. One stunt he used to do . . . when the Shrine was on the opposite side of the main Lagos road, they would close the road before the gig, and cause a traffic jam for miles in both directions. [laughs] Completely block up Lagos. When Fela was ready to go to the gig he'd go across the road on a donkey, with all the girls and the band in a procession. And every time he did a gig they'd stop Lagos' traffic from moving. Completely. The whole of Lagos. This was a couple of times a week. The shows would go for hours. Two sets a night. If I was around, they insisted that I sat in. The favorite number everyone wanted me to play with Fela was "Gentleman." You ever hear that? That was when Fela was at his peak! It was humorous stuff. Fela had an incredible sense of humor, and [it was when] he was doing his tongue-in-cheek humorous stuff was when he was really hugely popular. He then started to get too political in his music . . . Well, it upset a lot of the band. Cuz the band were all, they were just like musicians. They were getting scared, is what happened. A lot of those really good players, you know, gave it up eventually because it was getting very heavy. Ask Tony Allen. [laughs]

In the movie you made, when you meet up with Fela, he just looks like the most generous, sweetest, good-humored person

. . . **when he comes out the door and is greeting you all in his underpants—**

[laughing] Fela lived in his underpants. He used to get dressed to go onstage, but most of the time Fela walked around in his underpants.

It just looked like he was always in his underpants. And always smoking something.

Yeah, well, that was the whole thing of the Kalakuta Party, it was a smokers' party, which is why the government was so anti the thing.

What did he smoke?

Marijuana. Natural Nigerian grass. NNG. You know, most people in Africa—most of the population smoke—but it's illegal.

I've seen a few videos of Fela live . . . he's really yelling at the band, making sharp motions—

Fela was . . . ah . . . Have you ever been to Africa?

No.

Well, you need to. [laughs]

Yeah, see, I don't know if he was being playful, or if he was serious—

Fela could get very, very angry. All musicians get pissed off, eventually. Fela was a very nice man is what I'm trying to tell you. Very humorous fellow, just great fun to be around.

● ● ●

Tony Allen

Tony Allen is the original funky drummer. As a member of Fela's '60s high-life group Koola Lobitos, Allen traveled with Fela to the U.S., where Fela developed Afrobeat. Allen's complex, seemingly eight-armed and eight-legged drum parts—an encyclopedia of inventive groove spread over dozens of albums—were the only parts of Fela songs not composed by Fela himself. Allen released an incredible series of solo albums in the late '70s and early '80s, three of which featured Fela and the Africa 70. Allen left Fela's band in the

early '80s; his first post-Fela album, the beyond-essential No Discrimina-
tion, *featured on its title track this pivotal, sensible lyric of goodwill and good
humor: "Black or white, we are all from the same universe/ . . . We have
plenty of things to do with each other." With the help of French label Comet
Records,* Mean *spoke transatlantically with Tony from his home in Paris on
the eve of the American release of his extraordinary, don't-call-it-a-comeback
late-nite dance-funk album,* Black Voices.

Everybody's interested in Afrobeat again. How come?
Well . . . I'm wondering too myself, you know. Wondering. What is
going on. These are things, I've done them for years, back a long time
ago. I never changed my style, y'know, just kept on playing Afrobeat
all the time. So maybe they just decide to start listening to it now. I
don't know . . .

It's good to hear a live drummer again on the dance floor.
[laughs] Yeah. On the dance floor, yeah. You know, I like play dance
music all the time. I love playing dance music. I play other things, but
when it comes to me, myself . . . I don't have big band really, 'know? I
already tried big band before [in Europe], but it never worked before
because this place is not like Africa, where you have cheap labor and
those other things, you know. So this time around, I'm playing with
. . . it ranges from . . . it depends on the project. From quartet to
quintet, sextet. But sometimes me myself, I just play with DJs. I
choose the records and then we play like that. I just know how to
play music. I've created something, the way of my playing. I would
want people to copy it. That would give me more good feeling,
pleasure.

That's not so easy. Your stuff is so complex—
I play like four drummers, normally. [laughter]

**Bootsy was telling me about when the JB's visited Fela's club and
saw you all perform.**
The musicians were always with us every night when they finish their
gig. They end up in our own club. They really had a good time there.
But not James Brown himself. He never moved his ass to the club.

Ginger [Baker] said Fela's musicians grew tired of the harassment by the government that was the result of Fela's provocative music and political stands. Was that why you left the group?
For me, a little bit of that. I was tired of that. I just wanted to play music and not have anybody harass me just for doing nothing, you know. That was a few times. But it had to stop because I could not stand the bullshit. I just take care. I just want to play my music. And when it was getting too tough, I just relaxed. It's useless, for one month, we are fighting about 20 people at a time. It's useless. And it's not 20 people talking about, it's a whole government. You know how many people make up the government there. Cannot fight them.

Even when Fela was at his most powerful, he still couldn't . . .
[That was] the main reason why they didn't shoot. Be careful, you know. They want to make sure that not anything goes wrong because they afraid of the weapon this guy has: the music, and he has a microphone, and he has a record. He was getting too much for them . . .

Did you see Fela after you left the band?
Oh yeah, yeah. We stayed friends, although there sometimes there was something like misunderstandings between the journalists and me and he, kind of like, misquotations sometimes come from the journalist. We just kept on going like that, everything. Then when I am in Nigeria, I go to his house, I go to his Shrine, sit down, say, "It's a nice day." And when he is here in Europe, he always called me, "I'm at the hotel." The last time I saw him, the last concert was in '92. I was sit with him.

●   ●   ●

Bill Laswell

Bill Laswell is a bassist, producer and, having worked with countless important musicians from dozens of countries, is one of the vortex points around which the musical universe revolves. Mean spoke with Laswell about his controversial work with Fela.

When did you first get into Fela's music?

When I started listening to Cream and stuff, I started to read interviews with people like Ginger [Baker] about where they were getting their stuff from. Just like Clapton was getting ideas from blues guys, I realized that rhythm musicians were getting a lot of information from Africa. I immediately started looking for the records, especially Afrobeat. Just that syncopation, the up feel. You get ideas about putting rhythms together. Those early bands Fela had were really tight. Just like when this African guy told me James Brown had just "messed him up." Fela had bands that were almost like that. I don't think as aggressively tight, but it had a feel, an Afrobeat, African feel, with a modern sound.

How did you end up producing *Army Arrangement*?
At that time in Paris in '84 or '85, Celluloid was the label that all African or West African, everybody was going to them for some reason. And they got a hold of Fela's contract and his catalog and they just started calling the shots. Fela was on his way to New York to come and we were going to mix the record when he came. On the way to New York, getting on the plane in Nigeria, he had something like ten grand in cash in U.S. dollars, I think. He was immediately put in jail, the tapes arrived, and the Celluloid people were like, "Well, great, go ahead and mix it. Let's capitalize on the fact that he's in jail, we'll get more press." But the tapes I received weren't really musical or necessarily well-recorded. So we felt that if we just mixed it, it wouldn't bring anything new to what Fela's legend was. So we added Sly Dunbar, Bernie Worrell and Aiyb Dieng from Senegal.

Did you ever meet Fela?
[When he got out of jail,] Fela did a press tour in the States. He was at the Gramercy Hotel in New York. I went there and he was sitting around his room wearing a shirt and some underwear and sitting in a lotus position on the couch, a bunch of people coming in and out, and we spoke for a few minutes. He was kind of amazed that I would come because he had said that he didn't like what I had done. There was an African magazine where I was quoted as saying, "It's much better to mix an artist's work if they're in prison." Some really stupid shit. And

that freaked him out. And he was saying that there was a sound that wasn't African that I put on the album. [But] it was a Senegalese drummer, so of course it's African.

It's very interesting because everybody thought I wouldn't go meet him, so I just went in anyway. By that time he had started to deteriorate, he wasn't as strong. You could feel he wasn't the person he was. He just wasn't the presence that he was before. And it showed in the music too, because in the '70s Fela had a really strong band and then he just got kind of more lighter and lighter. And then a lot of weird shit came into that scene. That was a heavy scene. They were around some heavy people. Cuz he was the *biggest* thing happening in Nigeria, and there's some heavy stuff in Nigeria—not all positive.

• • •

Lester Bowie

Lester Bowie, who died November 8, 1999, of complications from liver cancer, was one of America's most acclaimed trumpet players and jazz composers. He is best known for his work with the adventurous avant-garde troupe Art Ensemble of Chicago [see Art Ensemble of Chicago: Great Black Music —Ancient to Future *for more info]. Less than two months before Lester joined the great orchestra on the other side, I was privileged to visit the great labcoated trumpeter at his Brooklyn home. As we shared half a watermelon, Lester recalled his 1977 trip to Nigeria.*

Lester Bowie: I'd always wanted to go to Africa. The Art Ensemble of Chicago had been trying to get to Africa for years. So after one of our European tours, I had enough money for a one-way ticket to Nigeria and I think I had a hundred dollars. I didn't know anybody there, no idea about anything. The hotel in Lagos where I ended up staying at, the restaurant's waiter found out I didn't know anyone, and he says, "Well what you need to do is go see Fela." And I told him I ain't never heard of this Fela before. And he said, "Well just get in a taxi cab and say, 'Take me to Fela.' Everybody knows where Fela is."

So the very next morning I get in a taxi cab and tell him to take me to Fela. The guy takes me to this Crossroads hotel where Fela had really taken over. The cab pulled up into the courtyard and I got out. I had my horn with me and a couple of photos and records and so on, and this little guy comes up to me and said, "Well, you're a musician?" I said, "Yeah." He says, "What instrument do you play?" I says, "Trumpet." He says, "Well, you must be pretty heavy. What kind of music do you play?" I says, "Jazz." He says, "You must be pretty heavy then." I says, "Well, you know, a little bit." He says, "Well you come to the right place." I say, "Why is that?" He says, "Cuz we the baddest band in Africa!" [laughter]

Fela was asleep. So he took me to a room and said, "We'll get Fela up." Fela got up and we talked for a minute. He said, "Ah, Lester Bowie, you're from the Chicago Art Ensemble." I say, "Yeah that's right." And then he tells this guy to bring in a record player. And he tells this other guy, "Bring me my horn." The record was one that just had a rhythm section, so he figured we'd play along with that. So I just blew. I didn't know anybody in the town. I was playing my heart out there! So after I play about two [verses], Fela says, "*Stop!* Stop. Go get his bags. He's moving in!" [laughter] And I stayed there I think for about six months.

I stayed as an honored guest, so I was treated with the same respect as Fela was treated with. He said, "I'll show you how to be an African man. You want to be an African bandleader? I'll show you what it's about." And he showed me what it was about! They'd bring us food. Nobody else could eat until we finished. Which I wasn't used to, but I just played it off like, you know, "Cool with me too!" [laughter] He showed me about all the wives. He had eight wives at that time. At that same time, I was believing I should have more than one wife. At the time I was getting divorced. I was between marriages. I thought the best thing for me to do was have a couple of wives. But after I stayed with Fela for that time, I saw that one was better! [laughs] And I told him, "Fela, you've got too many women. You don't have time to put into practice. You want to get into jazz, it takes time, you know. You've got to practice. You can't just be mediating arguments about who get the clothes or who get to drive this or do that."

Fela had about 50 people around him, and he was responsible for 'em. He was the chief, so they would come to him with *all* their problems. Anything, he'd have to solve anything. There were people comin' in off the streets asking for money all the time. And Fela, you have to realize, there was always 10 to 15 people around him. But him and I were sitting there having a private conversation like you and I are right now. He always had a court around him. But me and him were . . .

He was like the village chief. He showed me what that was like and I was helpin' him with the music. I was with Fela the whole time—I [even] used to go to court with him when they were giving him a lot of problems . . . Fela's house was burned down, they burned down the free clinic he'd established for the people. I don't remember if he was in a cast at the time, but he was *hurt*.

So during those six months, was he performing live?
He'd do performances in the courtyard of the hotel where we stayed. And we did mostly studio work. We were in the studio a lot at that time. A lot of the time Fela was just kinda showing me around. Fela would ask, "Lester, you feel like playing tonight?" I'd say, "Yeah." So he'd find where a band was playing, and then he owned a bus, about 30 people would get in the bus and we'd sit in and play, you know. [chuckles] We'd get to the club, the club owner would have a big table set up for all of us. It was something else. His band, all the guys were really great, the whole band . . . and they really treated me well and I had a good time. We played all the time, I'd go around and hang out with all the different cats, show cats different things about the music. Rehearsing with them a lot. It was quite educational, believe me.

What did you learn?
It's a way of learning how to adapt what you know and fit it into what's being played at that time, and seeing what works and what doesn't. It broadens you, anytime you play in a different set of circumstances. I've tried to play in just about any kind of situation. I could play with a bus. A motorcycle. A baby crying. You learning how to deal with all these different sounds. It's all about sound. You don't play bebop licks with a truck going down a highway, you have to have something that works. [laughter]

Fela and I just hung out. Fela was interested in music, he was a jazz fan! [laughs] He liked jazz . . . Like I said, he'd heard of me before. So most of the time, we talked about the music. Music and its ramifications. What it implied. What is it. What can it be used for. It's about

... Basically, I always believed art is functional. It's not just something you put in museums, it's better for it to be used for something functional: educational usage, therapeutic usage. But it should be *used*. Music should be used, not just as entertainment. I'm not saying it's *not* entertainment. It's *everything*. It's entertainment, it's religion, it's a lot of things. That's what most of what our conversations would be about. The spiritual aspect to the music, what binds all these different types of musics together. That's why we say great Black music. I think Black music is the only music that can be subdivided down into ten subdivisions, and each division is like world astounding–type music, you know what I mean?

What was it like being in the studio with Fela?
When Fela was in the studio, we were either learning the tunes or playing the tunes or recording the songs. He was very serious about the music, and he was serious in a way I can respect. He would do a lot of parts on the organ or keyboard or something. He would maybe write something out for his own reference, but after that he would go play it. He always created our songs in the studio. He'd do a part and show it to the horns and say, do that. He'd work 'em out on keyboard. I just did what he wanted me to do. If he'd suggest something, I'd suggest something, we'd just do it. But he had kind of the same work ethic as me. Like when I work, I'm going to work. If I'm gonna play, I'm gonna play. If I'm working, I'm working. If I'm making a record, I'm making a record. So we got on great.

Why did you leave?
After seven months, I was starting to get migraine headaches. Between eight wives . . . seeing all that entourage Fela had . . . the police and the soldiers . . . When they suggested I leave, I was ready to go! [laughs] What happened was word came down that people were asking, "Who was this guy from New York? We heard he's a troublemaker. It'd be best for him to get out of town." Which I rapidly did, because I didn't want to end up in a Nigerian jail! And I had to bribe—this is the type of corruption going on there—I had to pay 50 bucks at the airport to a uniformed guy just to get a plane reservation! Later on someone gave me a tape of those same guys in the

band. And those guys were still playing like me, especially the trumpet player, still playing some of my stuff! We had a good time. I'd always try and see Fela when he came to New York [later on].

Ginger [Baker] said Fela was a truly humorous man.
Oh yeah, he was.

Always in his underwear.
In his underwear, smoking those big ol' joints . . . [laughter]

KAREN SCHOEMER

A Fragile Mind Bent in a Psychedelic Era

Like Bob Dylan's motorcycle accident or the sandbox Brian Wilson built in his living room, Alexander (Skip) Spence's freakout is the stuff of rock myth. In 1968, Spence, a guitarist for the San Francisco pop-psychedelic band Moby Grape, was in New York working on the group's second album. He hooked up with a woman who was known as a witch, and she gave him bad acid. Spence disappeared for a few days, and when he turned up again he was banging down the hotel room door of the band's drummer with a fire ax. The drummer wasn't there, so Spence proceeded to the recording studio in a taxi, ax still in hand. At the studio someone wrestled the ax away from him, but charges were pressed and Spence went to jail. He was given a choice: prison or a psychiatric hospital. He chose Bellevue, and he was there, doing penance, for six months.

Spence, who died in April at the age of 52, was well on his way to being another 60s casualty. But before he got there, he took a side trip. Upon his release from Bellevue, he asked his label, Columbia, for a small advance—under $1,000—and a motorcycle so he could drive to Nashville and make a solo album. In just four days in December 1968, Spence recorded *Oar,* an album of songs he had written in Bellevue. He produced it himself and played all the instruments himself. When he

was done, he got on his motorcycle and headed back to California. He
was 22 years old.

Released on May 19, 1969, *Oar* showed one of the bleakest under-
sides of the 60s. It was a snapshot of mental illness, a portrait of bitter
isolation in a time of communal celebration. Not surprisingly, *Oar* sold
only a few hundred copies. Columbia didn't promote it; it got no airplay, cracked no chart. A few months later, the critic Greil Marcus
wrote a prescient review for *Rolling Stone*. "This unique LP is bound to
be forgotten," he said. "Get ahead of the game and buy *Oar* before you
no longer have a chance." It was the perfect curse to lay on *Oar*. Mr.
Marcus knew that in rock-and-roll, nothing worthwhile is ever truly
forgotten. The harder it is to find, the more it is coveted. *Oar* was
bound for a particular cult doom: an album so obscure and neglected
that it could eventually be embraced by a different generation as something exceptional and brand new.

Thirty years later, it's finally *Oar*'s time. On Tuesday, Sundazed Music will reissue a remixed and remastered version of the album with 10
bonus tracks. That same day, the independent label Birdman will release *More Oar*, a lovingly compiled tribute featuring Tom Waits,
Robert Plant, Beck and Son Volt's Jay Farrar recreating the album's
songs in order. Tribute records are often obnoxious celebrity show-
cases, but *More Oar* is the rare case that really enhances the original.
Bill Bentley, a longtime record-company executive and the album's
producer, made sure that only performers who really cared about *Oar*
contributed.

"Once word went out that I was doing this, people started contact-
ing me," Mr. Bentley said. "Bands said, 'We love *Oar*. We have to be on
this.' We'd send people $500, and a few weeks later these DAT tapes
would show up in the mail. It was great."

The two albums work well in tandem. Each brings out strengths
the other doesn't show. Because of his fragility of mind, Spence's version is hushed and tentative. The songs are like hot, cramped rooms,
full of wandering thoughts and fragmented images. The vocals rasp
and quaver; the drums shuffle in a halting, folksy rhythm. It's the
sound of a man talking to himself. Some songs are nearly formless
psychedelic workouts; others, like "Cripple Creek" and "Diana," are
muttered depictions of characters at the end of their ropes. *Oar* also

has moments of joy: Spence relished childish singsongs and eccentric wordplay. "An Olympic super swimmer whose belly doesn't flop," he sings in "Broken Heart." "A honey-dripping hipster whose bee cannot be bopped."

More Oar sacrifices the singular, mind-bending intimacy, but it's more confident and accessible. In the hands of accomplished pros like Beck and Mr. Plant, the songs get room to breathe; the best interpretations reveal elegant structures and breathtaking melodies that Spence himself muffled. Spence's version of "All Come to Meet Her" feels like a pretty, half-finished thought; he hums and repeats the title line over and over, like a daydreamer musing on a place he'll never reach. Diesel Park West's cover brings out the pop brilliance at the song's core. The drums crash, the electric guitars ring out; it's nothing short of celestial, a hymn of fulfilled longing. A transcendence Spence could only imagine Diesel Park West brings to life.

Mr. Bentley is one of the faithful who bought the record in 1969. "I didn't have those kind of mental problems, but I wasn't doing too well," he said. "You listen to this and you go, well, there's people farther out and with bigger troubles than me, and they're still making art. Maybe there is a way to get through all this, and not just run and give up."

For Mr. Bentley, *More Oar* was a way to make sure Spence's work wasn't forgotten. When he began work on the project four years ago, he found that many musicians had been moved by *Oar* just as he had been. "'Books of Moses' reminded me of a Tom Waits song before there was a Tom Waits," Mr. Bentley said. "I thought, 'I'll just ask him.' He just said, 'Sure.' He cut it in his garage, played all the instruments himself. He's a guy that really taps into the mental space that a guy like Skip lived in. I think that's part of Tom's allure. He always, from the start, got inside the head of the have-nots and society's expendables."

What makes *Oar* and *More Oar* so compelling is that both records puncture many of the myths we've come to take for granted about the 60s. No other decade in rock has been so overhyped. From Dylan's plug-ins to Jimi Hendrix's guitar burnings, from the Beatles at Shea to Janis Joplin at Monterey, from Eric Clapton's solos to the Grateful Dead's endless jams, the era is stuffed way past capacity with icons,

masterminds, earth-shakers and ground-breakers. The last thing anyone needs is another 60s legend.

Spence was the antithesis of 60s heroism. He was of the era but apart
from it. He came from the Haight-Ashbury scene, but he did his best
work in solitude. Unlike Brian Wilson, whose mental instability became part of his mystique, Spence never parlayed his illness into
money or fame. "Skippy was not really in shape after '68 to ever come
back and pick up where he left off," said Peter Lewis, a Moby Grape
guitarist. "He couldn't be a show-business person. All that talent wasn't
something he could pull out of his hip pocket and use."

Spence was born in Windsor, Ontario, then moved with his parents
to the San Jose area. He migrated to San Francisco in time to spend a
year as the Jefferson Airplane's original drummer. In 1966, he helped
start Moby Grape, a slightly more garagey version of Buffalo Springfield, with rustic three- and four-part harmonies overlaid on snarly guitars. Moby Grape's closest thing to a hit was Spence's "Omaha," an
exuberant call-out to good times. "Listen my friends!" the song exclaims again and again.

"There's no way to describe the way he plays guitar, and the way his
chords work," said Mr. Lewis. "Him and the guitar, it was like a whole
orchestra. The way the melody moved and the chords moved was totally unpredictable but totally cool. Nobody else could do it. It's Skip."

After *Oar*, Spence worked sporadically with Moby Grape. He contributed to the 1971 album *20 Granite Creek* and to *Live Grape* in 1978.
But in between, Spence, a diagnosed paranoid schizophrenic, began a
cycle of living in halfway houses and state mental institutions. One
time in the late 70s, Spence wound up in a facility in Santa Cruz.
"They called us three days or so after they had committed him," Mr.
Lewis remembered. "They said, 'You've got to take this guy out of here
because he got lost and we found him in the women's ward with a
harem.'" Another time, Mr. Lewis added, he suffered a drug overdose.
"They took him to the morgue, tag on his toe and everything. And he
got up and asked for a glass of water."

Still, Spence was well enough during the late 70s to play gigs with
Moby Grape in northern California. Scott McCaughey, whose band
the Minus 5 contributed to *More Oar*, saw a few of them. "Skip would
sometimes be there, sometimes play, sometimes be there and not play,"

Mr. McCaughey recalled. One night after a show, Mr. McCaughey approached Spence. "He was kind of ambling about," he said. "My friends and I said, 'Do you want to come over to our house and have a beer?' He was like, 'O.K.' So he came over and sat in the middle of our funky living room. I said, 'Skip, what do you want to listen to?' He said, '*Rubber Soul.*' So I got it, and we listened to it, smoked some pot and just kind of talked. He was friendly but not super on the ball. You definitely got the impression he wasn't all there. After the record was over, I said, 'So, what do you want to listen to now?' He said, '*Rubber Soul.*' It wasn't like, 'Let's listen to it again.' It was like it never happened. So we listened to *Rubber Soul* again."

After *Live Grape,* Mr. Lewis lost track of Spence until the early 90s. Mr. Bentley said that Spence was never homeless, but that "he would panhandle money and drink quarts of beer all day." Around 1994, his life stabilized. He moved into a trailer with his girlfriend and apparently quit drinking. Spence played one last gig with Moby Grape in Santa Cruz in 1996. In the spring of this year, he was diagnosed with terminal lung cancer and hospitalized.

Mr. Bentley had spent the last few years of his life pursuing Spence's elusive legacy. He went to see him in the hospital and brought a copy of *More Oar.* But Spence was in a coma by then. On the day he died, April 16, Spence was surrounded by loved ones: his girlfriend, his ex-wife, his children, Mr. Lewis. They took him off his ventilator and played *More Oar* as he slipped away.

Peter Lewis sees his legacy in a slightly different way. "The thing that made Skip suffer in the end was he knew everybody loved him, but he couldn't come back," he said. "People had expectations for him to be well again and play music, and he just couldn't. I admire him as an artist and a human being, even though he was just a guy you'd pass by in the street, just another bum with a cup in his hands. But I guarantee you, he will become the Van Gogh of the 60s. This guy was peerless."

Me, Machine:
The Curious Case of
a Man Called Sean

Maybe we should start here:
"Do you think evil chases you?"

Sean "Puff Daddy" Combs pauses for the merest of moments to consider my question. Then he answers. In a blur.

"I don't know if it's some kind of evil that's chasing me, [but] you know how people say, like, you're going through pain 'cause you're getting prepared for something greater in the future? I be like, 'Damn, how much more painful is it gonna be in the future?' I'm such a strong human being it's to the point to where I get afraid 'cause I don't want to be cold, you know? So it's like I get hit and I get so many shots that bounce up off me, you want to be bulletproof and have that armor. But, at the same time, you want to be able to sometimes express your feelings—to yell or scream or do something."

Or here:
The church that Sean "Puff Daddy" Combs calls home sits on Liberty Avenue in East New York, Brooklyn, between Bradford and Miller. It

is known as the Love Fellowship Tabernacle. Puff Daddy is not with me. But I stand on this street nonetheless, staring at his church. I have come here to make sense of Puff Daddy. Or Sean Combs. And Sean Combs. It is not an easy undertaking. And after weeks and days with him on this story, not to mention a couple years of casual acquaintanceship, I still find myself wracked by the *inexactness* of it all. The lingering, conflicting questions. What the hell makes him tick? How can he be, by turn, so thoughtful and so tyrannical? How does he separate Sean, the man, from the machinelike, all-consuming drive of Puff Daddy? And why does he do it, still?

Murky answers. So, I stand here on a Brooklyn corner in the sweltering mid-July humidity. Staring. I don't really expect the stone veneer of this place to give me clarity. But maybe I'll find small clues by sheer proximity. The church that Sean "Puff Daddy" Combs calls home sits on Liberty Ave. in East New York, Brooklyn, between Bradford and Miller.

No. Here:
It is a steamy Sunday afternoon in New York City, June 13th, and I am looking for Puff Daddy's soul. No. That's not quite right. I am looking *at* Puff Daddy looking for his soul. He does this quite often these days. Sometimes it seems a conscious act. Him groping amongst the far too few rest moments in his life, seeking balance, searching for happiness. But most often the soul-search stays in passive mode, just an unconscious addendum to his talented and tortured trek through life.

Today he will be trekking along New York's 5th Avenue. Not quite yet, though. For this afternoon plays host to the Puerto Rican Day Parade and the P-Daddy float isn't ready to move. It sits amidst controlled madness: the cordoned off Bad Boy area on 44th Street between Madison and 5th. The float itself is a grayish, titanium-looking thing. Three ascending, circular platforms set atop a flatbed. From this stage Puff will roll into the heart of the New York Puerto Rican community's annual celebration, filming scenes for the Spanish (yes, Spanish) version of the video for his first single, "P.E. 2000," a remake of the Public Enemy classic "Public Enemy #1."

However, the filming will have to wait a moment, at least until the peculiar chaos that often affects Bad Boy productions reluctantly slouches aside in favor of order. Appropriately enough, the trailer that houses Puff sits in the heart of it all: frantic video crew, security hulks, visiting celebs, label personnel and the like. It is the nerve center of this organism, and it's protected as such. One zealous security guy sticks out a meaty arm to bar Puff's high-powered manager, Benny Medina, from entering the trailer, earning himself a look of incredulous venom and a few whispered, heated words. Unabashed, the guy lets Medina in, looks around, and shrugs his shoulders. Refusing to apologize for doing his job.

The trailer door creaks open one more time and Puff himself emerges, instantly generating a roiling wave of security, associates, camera-snapping types and sundry others, all seeking attention. It is a phenomenon that never ceases to intrigue me, no matter how many times I've seen it swirl around him. But for Puff, the wave is part and parcel of being the guru of hip-hop's cult of celebrity, an electric current snaking its way through the unstoppable Puff Daddy Machine.

After some 20 minutes, amplified voices ring out.

"Clear the street. Everybody clear the street!" The security chief keeps screaming. Someone from the video crew takes up the effort, and, eventually, a different security guy. They're trying valiantly to clear unnecessary folks from the immediate vicinity of Puff's float so things can, well, start.

Soon, chaos grudgingly begins to give way to order and the machine begins to hum. Puff carefully climbs to the top of the float. Instantly, a group of little kids standing to one side begin clamoring for him.

"Puffy. Hey. Puffy!" one determined little fellow hollers. Puff's attention is elsewhere. So the kid shouts again, insistently. This time Puff swivels his head left and down, spying the group of kids, waving. They react predictably enough. Wide grins. Open eyes.

Puff returns his attention to the business at hand, eyes intently surveying the scene 15 feet below him. He's quite a sight up there with his white pants, sleeveless leather vest festooned with the colors of the Puerto Rican flag, and the obligatory iced-platinum. He wears a lot of it, from the truck chains jangling around his neck to the sweatbandsized diamond bracelet on his right wrist. The entire collection winks madly in the high-afternoon sun.

Slowly, the procession rolls out. The float moves first. On it stands Hurricane G, who does the Flavor Flav type intro for "P.E. 2000," Flavor Flav himself, as manic at 40 as he was a decade ago, Daymond John, CEO of FUBU, Ed Lover, several Bad Boy staffers, the video crew, and, of course, Puff himself. To either side of the float marches a line of security men clothed in white uniforms. Just behind rolls a silver Lincoln Navigator, transporting Puff's main men, Bad Boy president Andre Harrell and executive vice president Jeff Burroughs, in air-conditioned comfort. Smart guys. And bringing up the rear are, literally, dozens of New York's finest on mopeds.

The screams come suddenly. And at shocking volume. The Puerto Ricans lining 5th Avenue have just caught sight of Puff Daddy, rocking the colors of their flag no less. And rhyming to them in Spanish over the ol' schoolish percussion of "P.E. 2000."

"Puerto Rico, Puerto Rico!" Puff shouts out.

And they scream right back. As I walk by the side of the float, a scant 12 feet or so from the sidewalk, the consistent roar buffets me with its sheer volume. Then I catch sight of the teenaged girls. Three of them. They stand at the curb; somehow they've slipped in front of the blue police barricades that pen most of the spectators in. And, between screams, they gaze at Puff with pure rapture on their faces. Almost on cue, all three begin to cry. Big, heaving sobs, all the while fixing those wide-open eyes on Puff. One little girl just stands there in shock, her left hand covering her mouth. Her right, the one holding the flag, hangs limply by her side. A friend grabs the dangling hand and raises it in the air so the flag can be displayed. But, as soon as the neighbor removes the supporting hand, the little girl's right arm plummets back down. And the tears keep falling.

What do you know of Puff Daddy? Probably a lot. You know the oft-repeated tale of his professional arc, his own pauper-to-prince fable. The way he used to break out of Howard University to come to New York for his internship at Andre Harrell's Uptown Records. The way he went from intern to A&R whiz kid in mere months, shaping the careers of acts like Jodeci and Mary J. Blige, birthing that whole R&B/bad boy/urban swagger thing. The way his frenetic youth and ambition eventually played him out at Uptown, causing his boss and mentor Harrell to put him—and his fledgling Bad Boy idea—out on the sidewalk. The way he walked into Clive Davis' Arista conference room, boldly outlining his plan for a label called Bad Boy Entertainment and a rapper named Biggie Smalls. The way he proceeded to tear up the urban music market, becoming a top-flight CEO, producer, and, eventually, artist.

You know how controversy and tragedy have dogged his every step, from the 1991 concert he promoted at New York's City College that left nine people dead after a stampede, to the still unsolved '97 slaying of The Notorious B.I.G., to his own headline-grabbing assault of music big-wig Steve Stoute this past spring.

You know he's a lightning rod for polarized opinions. Hate. Love. Adulation. Disgust. He's a brilliant producer and talent spotter. Or an unabashed rip-off artist and manipulator. He's an inspiration for hardworking, entrepreneurial folks everywhere. Or the chief proponent of a glitzy lifestyle so out of reach and over the top for most adherents of hip-hop, it ceases any pretense at aspiration and becomes debilitating, hollow and soulless.

What do you know of Puff Daddy? Probably not enough. You may admire his position, his status. But what it took for him to get there? And what it costs him to remain there? Those are the thousand-dollar questions. To even begin to answer them you must understand one simple thing about Puff: He wants to win. More than me. More than you. And more than anyone you know. I asked several of Puff's associates and friends to put that idea in context. All of them gave fascinating anecdotes and observations, but Ron Gillyard, Bad Boy's VP of marketing and a man who has known Puff since Howard, put it most succinctly.

"He's driven, and he's focused. He's clear about what it is he wants; he has a clear understanding of getting there and nothing is going to stop him from getting there, short of death."

Gillyard really meant that. And I think he's right. Puff's been talkin' about "he won't stop" on records for years. And most of us have danced and sung right along, never regarding those words as anything more significant than trite, pop music utterances, a cute little refrain. But they were true. Though probably not as true as my own little remix of that phrase: "He *can't* stop." Put it this way: He's like Jordan in the fourth quarter—all day. Ever read Peter Benchley's *Jaws*? Remember how the Great White Shark only died when it stopped moving, when the cessation of motion kept precious oxygen from sloshing through its gills?

But that type of obsessive-compulsive focus—and I would hazard a guess that most hyper-successful people share the trait—does not come free of charge. Bill Gates must pay it. Bill Clinton pays it. Puff pays it. And few people are in a better position to even begin to estimate that bill than Andre Harrell.

"I think when a person is driven by achievement in that way, a certain part of their own inner peace is always at risk," Harrell told me one afternoon in late June, sitting behind his desk at Bad Boy's new offices in the BMG building in Times Square. "'Cause there's no time out to think about [certain] things; moments that happen every day and how to appreciate and take advantage of those moments. Those moments at his age in life might be in the way of what he thinks his goals are. And maybe, in his mind, he'll get to those moments after he's achieved his goal."

Los Angeles. June 16th. The Whiskey Bar. One of those "LA places," populated by a certain high society element culled from music and film. White. Black. Others. Nightcrawlers all at this 1 A.M. hour. Leaning over drinks, flashing pearly whites and the occasional intoxicated leer. There's sex here. Money. Hollywood intrigue of the most banal sort.

Puff Daddy is here too. And he wants to talk. He really wants to talk. Chalk it up to the challenging year he's had. Or, better yet, attribute it to this particular place he's at. Not simply the eve of an album release, his sophomore project, *Forever*, but that soul-search moment. That nanosecond where he can pull away from the machine and find his soul. Of course the machine isn't just connected to him, doesn't just surround him. He is the machine. But he must try regardless.

So he sits with me in the Whiskey Bar. We're on a couch set off from the main area of hub-bub, slouched down, staring at the patrons. MC

Lyte is over there. And a few other folk of note. All of whom want to chat with Puff. He smiles. Makes quick small-talk when someone breezes by. But he's much more interested in unloading. The need is palpable. So we talk.

"Tell me about this year."

He doesn't even pause.

"This year has really been crazy. It's been blow after blow. I look back on my shit [and] I be like, 'This has been so fucking dramatic, just constant twists and turns, like a saga.' This year was like so much personal life stuff, having a baby; working so hard to keep everything afloat business wise, more than afloat, to keep everything successful, to that successful peak that everyone expects when you sell as many records as a label like Bad Boy has sold. Your personal life suffers a lot. That right there hurts you. You be getting pulled this way and that way, like, 'Damn what I'm supposed to do?'"

"How did the label do anyway?"

He sighs.

"The label has done better with the acts [whose] albums have sold more this time than they sold the previous time. It's just that when you up there in the ranks and you on a streak, people are trying to knock it. People are trying to compare the sales of Biggie, Mase and myself to the sales of Mase [*Double Up*], Total and Faith. It's ridiculous, it's like apples and oranges. You can't put out Biggie, Mase and Puffy in the same year all the time."

"So what about Mase?"

"I got a call one day that Mase didn't want to rap no more. I was like, 'What the fuck? Where did that come from?' He just renegotiated our deal, we had just finished an album. Me and Mase, we never really had bad times. The shit just came out of nowhere, and then he was on the radio like, 'Yeah I'm retiring.' I'm like, 'Oh shit,' and I felt confused, I felt like damn, like I put in a lot of time, the label—everyone put in a lot of time and we wish we could have talked about it. But it was a situation where God told him this, and I would never second guess that or judge him against that.

"Honestly, it kinda like hurt me. I never went and like pressured him or offered him money or told him to do anything that went against his feelings. I just let it be, but also there was a point where I understood, too. Sometimes *I* feel like taking a break from this. Sometime it feels overwhelming. I feel like he definitely had his calling from God, but also it could have got overwhelming for him."

"You gonna let him out of his contract? Doesn't he owe you a bunch of records?"

"I'm not going to force him to make a record. I'm not going to sue him. I'm supportive of him if that's what he wants to do. If he wants to make records, then we have a contract; it's just business."

We both stop for a minute. Perhaps to reflect on what's been said. To anticipate where it may go. To peer around the room again. To humor the drunken white girl now planted before us, profusely apologizing for breaking our cipher, stubbornly refusing to move until she's told Puff how dope he is. He thanks her graciously, and with just a touch of amusement. I glance at him. Then at her. Increasingly mortified, but still trying to make some obscure point, she hops from hip to hip, drink sloshing around, until, at last, she moves on.

"How are you doing spiritually these days?" I continue.

"Spiritually I am as strong as I have ever been," he replies in that steady, yet animated, tone of his. "Going through a certain amount of pain just makes you stronger. I made a lot of mistakes in my life, and I've had a lot of successes, and I've learned from both sides of it. I've nothing else to turn to. I chose the life that I was going to lead. It took a lot of sacrifices: I wasn't able to give people a lot of time; I wasn't able to hold a relationship with a woman; I wasn't able to be a good friend to somebody; I wasn't able to give that time. The only person I had after all was said and done, after losing my girl, after not being able to keep certain friends, was God. [I'm] trying to just be a better person every day; watch the way I talk to people, watch the way I make people feel, try to control my emotions. Sometimes I slip off the horse, [but] I gotta get back up no matter what."

Speaking of slipping off the horse . . .

"So how do you feel now about the Steve Stoute incident?"

"I feel like I played myself. But it gets to a point where you get tired of putting up with the bullshit. What made me upset was that it was emotional for me. It was my religion that was involved. I was not trying to portray Jesus, but when I saw the new video I felt like it [looked that way] and I don't feel comfortable with that. And that's the only thing that I got. Money gonna come and go. Women gonna come and go. Friends, some of them, are gonna come and go. God will always be there. He gonna love me no matter what. And that had me so scared to death, 'cause no matter what I do, I can always go to church. If I disrespect God and make a mockery of God, I can't even go to church."

The typical day of a machine begins, appropriately enough perhaps, in the workout room. But Puff's trainer has his job cut out for him today. His client's mind is elsewhere. And he's just a tad irritated. Nevertheless, the machine that houses the soul of Sean Combs does not quit for anything, or anyone. He plows through the workout.

Afterwards, he walks slowly along the outdoor path that leads to his private bungalow at the Beverly Hills Hotel. Blue Sean John pants and sleeveless white tee drape his frame. His omnipresent phone sits on one hand, the connecting wire with the mic and earpiece lodged in his ear. From afar, it looks like he's talking into thin air. His bodyguard leads him by several feet, and members of his entourage trail him: Shyne, his next big thing, whose first order of business is to remain attached to Puff's hip and observe; D-Mac, his road manager; and Ari, his bespectacled trainer.

Next, the machine will run to Universal Studios where scenes for the "P.E. 2000" video will be shot. There are already tons of people milling about the studio lot. Bad Boy staffers. Members of the video crew. All of them minute levers in the machine, aiding its progress.

Puff drifts over to an adjoining parking area, a place he will consistently head to when the day's phone conversations get intense, as they so often do. Mere distance, however, provides no buffer from the workings of the machine. He still has to flip gears rapidly: from the hustler cajoling or browbeating over the phone, to the artist approving wardrobe choices, to the CEO shooting down budget questions.

A machine's day unfolds with agonizing slowness—from without. From within it obeys its own rhythm. Herky jerk one moment. Lightning fast the next. All according to the dictates of Puff. I do my best to maintain an observer's distance, but the machine, Puff the entity, Puff the phenomenon, will suck you up if you enter its sphere. So even I find myself taking a message for Puff, letting Puff know the director's calling him. Like everyone else, I'm subject to the machine's charisma, its maddening drive.

The day of a machine ends at SRI studios, just before midnight. Well, it doesn't really end. More like it shifts into a different drive. For this is dance rehearsal time. Puff has to master the choreography for his special dance sequence that will be filmed tomorrow. And master it he does. For near two hours, he pushes himself harder and harder. Until the sweat pours from his body, thoroughly soaking the gray tank-top he wears. Leaning against a back wall, I have to fight to keep my eyes open. Not because the length of the day is unusual, but because hanging with Puff, trailing in his wake, can drain you in a way I find inexplicable. Even his trainer is mystified by Puff's ability to tap into energy. A week later, Andre Harrell will attempt to explain this internal fuel to me:

"I think in his mind he's gonna work twice as hard as anybody else so he can be ahead of the game. Most people think about eight hours, some people think of it as a 10-hour; but, for him, he thinks of it as a 16-hour workday. He's driven by tasks. He puts things in front of him that he wants to complete. I think he gets fulfillment out of that."

Tonight, however, all I can think about is *external* fuel. The things that the machine sucks up and uses to power itself. I visualize one particular, giant-sized tank: The Notorious B.I.G. Whether you ascribe to the cynical viewpoint that says Puff launched his own career on the back of his dead friend, or take the more benign angle whereby the senseless tragedy of B.I.G.'s murder simply pushes Puff on, the fact remains: B.I.G. is fuel for the machine, perhaps the most potent one available.

Later that night, after the dance rehearsal, after the trip back to the hotel, I ask Puff about it.

"Talk to me about Big."

He sits back in a chair in the master bedroom of his bungalow. With his plain black T-shirt, white shorts and no phone, he is clearly in a rest moment. A moment when the machine recedes, and Sean ascends.

"I still can't believe it," he answers. For the first time in our conversations, I actually hear weariness in his tone.

"I still see how depressed the whole family still is. Speaking to his mother, seeing his kids grow up. The shit is just so senseless and it's also so scary. Somebody could just die 'cause mufuckas is jealous.

That's the reason he died. He didn't die cause he did nothing to some-body. He didn't die 'cause he was East Coast. He got killed 'cause he was just the hottest mufucka. And niggas just couldn't take it."

"Has it been frustrating over the past two years with the case being open?"

He casts his eyes at the ceiling for a second.

"That part of it hasn't been frustrating for me as much as him not being here has been frustrating and painful. Like a couple of weeks ago, we was celebrating his birthday, and it just hurt so bad when you got to really face the reality. Like onstage, I get upset every time I rock onstage 'cause that's when I come to the realization that he's not there. We all try to block it out, [but] it still has not totally digested. He just got killed on some hate and shit. That shit is fucking foul. I could just go on and on about Biggie. Shit just ain't the same. It will never be what it could have been to me."

"Did it hurt you, the whispers that your becoming a star wouldn't have happened if Biggie was alive?"

"I think that I would have had a certain amount of success, but even that success was because of Biggie believing in me. [But] another part of the success of the album [*No Way Out*] could definitely be attributed to the unfortunate situation. I had to go on because there was nothing else for me to do. Either I was going to die or keep going."

Let's slip forward just a bit:
I haven't been to Howard University in, like, 10 years. Not since I was a college freshman barreling down I-95 to go to the mythical Howard homecoming. I still carry a lot of impressions from those days: the flood of well-dressed Black students; the parties; and the women, of course. Today those impressions ring true. It's Saturday afternoon in Washington, DC, June 26, several days since I've last seen Puff. Tech-nically, I'm in DC for today's Caribbean Carnival. But since the carni-val's route takes it along Georgia Avenue, smack dab into the middle of Howard, the reporter in me can't help but peek at this shaping cru-cible. Machines are assembled somewhere, after all.

The students walking in and out of Howard Towers on Sherman Av-enue look much like their counterparts from a decade ago. And the parking lot of the McDonald's on the corner of Sherman and Georgia still resembles an auto show–meets–fashion spectacle. I wonder what Puff's legacy means to these students. How many of them aspire to be like the Pied Piper of Howard?

"What I noticed about [Puff] was the fact that he always had a lot of people around him," Ron Gillyard told me. "Everybody was just following him. He had a Gumby back then [and] he danced in a Stacy Lattisaw video, and people who had cable, they were treating him like the guy who danced in the videos. [One day] during our homecoming [he had] a party. He had a whole list of celebrities that was gonna be there, Slick Rick, Doug E. Fresh, Guy, Heavy D, and damn near all those people showed up. And ever since that first party everyone made it a point to go to Puff's parties."

Of course, the components of the Puff machine didn't simply spring into existence in college. Howard merely provided, for the first time, a full-sized test venue, if you will. The shaping goes much further back, and much deeper, for Puff. One day, on the video set, I deliberately tried to catch him off guard after he had just watched footage for his album's promotional video, footage that included very intimate, and painful, family recollections—like his father's murder in 1973, four years after he was born.

"Tell me about your father."

He looked at me in disbelief.

"Oh my God! Not right now," he shook his head, a tad exasperated. "I be running from that. A lot of times I face all my tragedies, but then I try to not keep on facing it 'cause they hurt so much."

I steeled myself, because Puff can be unpredictably temperamental, and pressed him anyway.

"In what way? You don't talk about, don't think about them?"

He just sat in his little director's chair, eyes sweeping the set, hand clutching the tiny phone he carries everywhere. Then, almost, imperceptibly, he seemed to relax a bit, answering quickly, in tangents, but with wistful sincerity.

"I think about him. I don't talk about him. My pops, he was a hustler and I can be looking at a picture of myself and I say, 'Damn, I'm really starting to look like duke.' Lots of times I be looking in the mirror and I be like, 'I wonder if he acted this way or he did that.'"

"Do you remember him at all?"

"I remember him throwing me up in the air. That's one thing I do with my kids, I always throw my kids, I hold them up in the air."

"What about your mom, did she talk about him?"

"Nah, my mom, because he was killed, she hid that from me."

"How did you find out?"

"I found out when I went to Howard. I did some investigation. I looked in the paper around the time he died."

"So what did you think happened to him when you were younger?"

"She [mom] had told me he had died in a car accident."

Let's slip back:

Los Angeles. June 18th. I hadn't the energy to meet Puff on the video set for the 7 A.M. call. So I straggle onto the Universal lot around midday and head to his trailer, just in time to catch one of the most heated phone convos I've witnessed him have since I've been shadowing him.

"Dog, that little stunt ain't help matters at all," he snarls into his phone. Then, as if remembering he's not alone, he gets up, walks into the bedroom section of the trailer and closes the door. His voice still creeps through. Minutes later, he opens the door and bounds out of the trailer.

"Ask me about that Lox shit; that'll be good for the story," he tosses over his shoulder. I stare after him curiously. This isn't the first time he's suggested themes or lines of direction to me. And I can't decide whether it's part of his impulse to control or his desire to open his soul.

So I dial up a friend in New York to find out that The Lox, Bad Boy's only hardcore group, were on Hot 97 FM complaining about being on the label and asking Puff to let them go. I set off to find Puff, tracking him through rolling cameras that look like *Star Trek* weaponry, equipment laden tech-types, and visiting camera crews from MTV, BET and Entertainment Tonight. No pinning him down now. I've got to bide my time.

Two hours later, he looks relatively free. I nod at him. He nods back. We move to the same parking lot that's served as conference call central. Puff's been turning up the charm for the press folk, but I can tell he's still brimming with anger and frustration. I figure I might as well be blunt and direct.

"So The Lox wanna be off the label. How did things get there?"

And, like before, the floodgates open:

"Basically, The Lox want to be rich and there is nothing wrong with that. [But] it takes time to get to that point. I build with all my artists a long-term career. I didn't make no money off The Lox in any way. [The Lox] basically SoundScanned 750,000 albums. We shot a couple of videos. We went on tour. It's profit and loss. Artists get a record deal, and they think that they gonna be rich overnight.

"Me, I'm a different story. I been working at this shit for 10 years," he continues in exasperation. "A lot of times you have this big 'Puffy is worth 60 this million dollars.' People don't understand that, at the end of day, a lot of that is hype. People can't understand your worth versus how much you have in the bank. I'm not just sitting there in my house with $60 million floating around me."

"Is it more difficult being a fledgling artist like The Lox or Shyne on Bad Boy, and want to make that money because this is a place that champions the whole high lifestyle?"

"Yeah. It's definitely harder. And maybe we set ourselves up for that [with] the stuff we put in our records and the lifestyle that we live and all that, but the lifestyle that I live, I got from working everyday, 20 hours a day, for 10 years. And I tell you, if you do that shit, you will be somebody."

He stands in the high afternoon sun. Shades just containing the flash in his eye. I'm not sure which has him more heated. The Lox demanding to be released from his label, or the fact that they did it so publicly. It's the same "laundry in the streets" thing that hurt him where Mase was concerned.

Of course, it's plenty ironic. 'Cause Puff's had his own shit in the street of late—the Steve Stoute thing. So if his artists aren't adopting his all-consuming drive, maybe they're picking up on other things. Or maybe that very drive is what entices then pushes them away. Lotsa people think they wanna be Puff. But few find the work—and cost— attractive. Perhaps it scares them.

And since this man's also a father twice over, I can't help wondering about his sons, his obvious love for them, and the cost they too pay for the machine that houses their father's soul.

"What about your sons? Have you thought about how you're going to not have them grow up with just the famous father who is never there?"

"To be honest, I'm still trying to figure that out," he replies. "I got a lot of shit within myself that I'm cleaning out. My mind is not on worrying about this, or the frustrations of that, as much as it is as, 'Yo, the way you handled that situation right there was cool. The way you made them people laugh and feel good; the way you didn't flip out; the way you took time and spent more time with your kids, the way you spent time with your mother; that time when you turned off your phone and said fuck the business.' I need more of that."

"Was there a trigger or a point that made you realize that you had to get on that path?"

"Yeah, I went through . . . during the end of the tour, during the end of the album, I just went through a massive state of depression. I was like, I ain't happy in this shit, I ain't got Biggie, they don't like me, they don't appreciate what I do. Mufuckas don't understand me, like, 'I hate this shit right here, what the fuck am I doing in this shit?' It was like, 'I don't even like the way [I am] right now. I don't like the way I'm moving. I'm bringing everybody else down.' I have a certain type of energy that if I want to make you mad, I can make you and 5,000 people mad right now. I can walk into a room and just fuck up the whole mood of the room just by the way I feel."

He's not kidding. I've seen that infamous temper of his in action. I've seen his employees walk on eggshells when he's in *that* mood. I've heard him yell out, "Make me happy, damn it, or I'll fuck everybody's day up!" when the video crew ignored him while arguing among themselves.

Still, few of his traits can be boxed and labeled easily. Even his temper. Those tantrums often have reason beneath them, calculation even. And his good mood, his positive emotional largesse, is just as contagious.

I just have to recall those kids in New York at the parade. The grins won by his glance. The tears spurred by his passage.

Maybe we end here:
". . . think evil chases you?"

Sean "Puff Daddy" Combs pauses for the merest of moments to consider my question. Then he answers. In a blur.

"I don't know if it's some kind of evil that's chasing me, but you know how people say, like, you're going through pain 'cause you're getting prepared for something greater in the future? I be like, 'Damn, how much more painful is it gonna be in the future?'

"It's like you keep getting stronger and stronger to a point where you get tired of getting stronger. And that's the point I've gotten to. Just as a person going through all that stuff, it makes you weary; it makes you pray that you don't have to go through none of it again. It makes you look at the mistakes. It makes you search for answers. At the end of the day some of the things aren't explainable, a lot of the things are God's will and you have to stay strong, no matter how tired you are, you have to keep doing it and you just have to wait to see what He has planned for you."

No. Here:
The church that Sean "Puff Daddy" Combs calls home sits on Liberty Avenue in East New York, Brooklyn, between Bradford and Miller. It is called the Love Fellowship Tabernacle. Puff Daddy is not with me. But I stand on this street nonetheless, staring at his church. It has a different air in the daytime. Its outline burns the retina more sharply, as if God's rays were not merely providing illumination, but searing cobwebs from the eye.

I still can't claim to see Sean Combs clearly. He's still a soul that hovers within a construct called Puff Daddy. Still a man subject, in part, to the demands of a phenomenon, a machine. I do not know if Sean can ever separate himself from that machine. I do not know, even in his obvious search for *something*, if he truly wants to.

DAVID MOODIE AND
MAUREEN CALLAHAN

Don't Drink the Brown Water

Friday: July 23, 1999

Liz Pruitt arrived at the third coming of Woodstock by bus. The recent high school grad was hot and tired after a five-hour ride that began before dawn in a New Haven, Connecticut, parking lot and ended at a defunct Air Force base in upstate New York, but she was with three friends, and she was excited to be on site by 10:30 Friday morning. The dark-haired, willowy 18-year-old would have time to pitch her $30 Wal-Mart tent and walk more than a mile to the main stage before the first act played a note.

Her bus had "express entry" into the compound, so she wouldn't have to wait in the idling line of autos that stretched down into the streets of the rusty burg called Rome. It dumped her by the gates, and she waited 20 minutes to have her bags searched and exchange her $150 ticket for a wristband, and then she was inside. It became clear to her right away, though, that no matter how much fun she was going to have during the next 72 hours, the ride might get a little bumpier. The $100 Woodstock travel package that had lured her from Norwich, Connecticut, included "preferred camping"—if she could find it.

[With additional reporting by David J. Prince, Mark Spitz, and James Jellinek.]

"It became apparent that the staff from the bus didn't know where anything was," she says. "They said, 'Just look for the yellow flags.'" Pruitt and her friends wandered aimlessly, before chancing on the flags and plopping down under some trees, becoming the four newest residents of an instant city of 225,000. "I was kind of disgusted with the staff, but it wasn't their fault. It was the fault of the people who hired them. They hadn't informed them."

The lines snaking outward from the entry gates at the former Griffiss Air Force Base that Friday morning were so deep and vast that they resembled nothing so much as a supplicant stream of refugees—albeit refugees who paid $150 to rock, and who were about to be charged $12 a pizza and $5 a beer. The gates and the surrounding three-mile-long plywood fence at Griffiss were bracketed by a phalanx of security guards who wore loud yellow T-shirts with the words PEACE PATROL on them.

Inside the base, the sun, the concrete, and the ever-expanding mass of human bodies jostled in perpetual competition for concertgoers' attention. Woodstock '99 was held in a triangular-shaped section of the former air base, the surface of which was mostly concrete. Two paved ex-runway tarmacs met on the north end of the site at a point that abutted the main gate. During the daytime the concrete became superheated by the blazing sun, an unavoidable feature of the hottest July New York had ever seen. Unlike the verdant, shady rusticity of Saugerties, New York—the site of Woodstock '94—Griffiss offered no relief. Any spaces not taken up by vending booths, trucks, beer gardens, political-action tents, ATMs, and Port-a-Sans were deemed campsites.

As tens of thousands of people streamed in, it became increasingly difficult to stay oriented. A look in any direction across the flat landscape was blocked by the 10,000 sweaty faces closest to the viewer. The only usable landmark inside the base was the 50-foot control tower. Even the five-story-high East and West Stages, located one mile apart, weren't visible from the campgrounds. The space set aside for the crowds in front of the East Stage alone was the length of three football fields. Above it droned a squadron of helicopters and an ever-present plane trailing a streamer that read, WOODSTOCK '99—CD AND VIDEO AVAILABLE THIS FALL!

The festival officially began at noon Friday. On the East Stage, Tibetan monks chanted, and then MC Brother Wease yelled, "Show us your titties!" James Brown requested 30 seconds of silence for JFK, Jr. He got ten. Then he played "Sex Machine" and "It's a Man's Man's Man's World," two 30-year-old songs that would prove to be up-to-the-minute timely.

By 1 P.M., hundreds of people began to strip down in the oppressive heat. Public displays of affection quickly gave way to public displays of copulation. "Nudity was all over the place, and so was public fornication," said 18-year-old Gary Rushnick. "But you really got used to it." At least 100 kids dove into a shallow mud puddle near the row of Port-a-Sans closest to the East Stage, largely unaware that they were slathering themselves in human waste. Men who encountered backed-up stalls relieved themselves in public, in what they took to calling "the piss pool." Meanwhile, the Mud People, who quickly tired of hugging passersby, picked up chunks of mud and violently hurled them at the people drinking expensive warm lager in the adjoining beer garden.

Wearing an elaborate white feathered headdress, Jamiroquai's Jay Kay took the East Stage at 3 P.M. He was the first performer to tell the crowd to throw shit. They did. At him. Word got out that teenage sanitation workers, frustrated that the area was rapidly becoming one huge compost heap, were quitting. They said they had been given no instructions—and no water.

As the day wore on and the heat intensified, garbage cans overflowed. Paper, plastic, and pizza remnants smothered the wood mulch that smothered the concrete and dirt. Clifton Property Services, the sanitation firm hired by Woodstock, would later complain that the festival organizers hampered cleanup efforts. Woodstock failed to provide adequate plumbing for the vendors, so they had to build their own. Vendors were also at the mercy of Ogden Corporation, the firm that partially owns Metropolitan Entertainment (which is co-owned by promoter John Scher) and set the prices for soda and water. According to vendor Frank Cristiano, water sold by Ogden to the subcontracted vendors cost a whopping $70 a case, more than $3 a bottle. Fans paid $4. Attendees who didn't want to pay for bottles could drink from the free water spigots, most of which were located vast distances from the stages.

At the Action Lounge—an extreme-sports arena situated between the East and West Stages—attendees were charged $15 to skateboard, mountain bike, or in-line skate on, yes, a flat slab of concrete. A planned half-pipe had not yet arrived. The main attraction was a 10,000-square-foot "Shag-a-Quarium," which included extreme-sports heroes, ESPN announcers, 20 cheerleaders, and a disco. To compete with the crowd-pleasing flesh on display outside, nude competitions—rock climbing, BMX racing, wet-T-shirt contests, bridge—were hastily organized. "We were cautious to make it more comical and less sexual," said Action Lounge manager David Pelletier, "but people were getting naked anyway. We just gave them a forum."

A few weeks before Woodstock, promoters John Scher, Michael Lang, and Ossie Kilkenny, three longtime concert promoters, were found in violation of a 1970 law that was passed in the wake of the chaos at the first Woodstock. The promoters averted $1.5 million in fines levied by Oneida County for failing to meet deadlines the law set for transportation and security; they convinced the county to waive them, promising a staff of approximately 1,200 guards. Locals hired directly by Woodstock were promised $12 an hour, and subcontracted guards from around New York State earned $6 to $8 an hour. Starved for bodies, the promoters hired a number of workers from the local unemployment office. Upon arrival, the guards were told they'd work 12- to 14-hour shifts and get two meals a day. They were housed in on-site barracks with only cold water and slept on air mattresses. Some guards charged that other guards were looting each others' quarters. "There was a lot of robbing in the Peace Patrol houses," said guard Charles Knapp. "We chipped in to have our own security person."

By Thursday night, a hundred guards had already quit. Friday, the undersized force was primarily deployed outside the gate; it mostly seemed concerned with getting concertgoers inside the base without drugs, alcohol, weapons, and important contraband like sandwiches and bottled water—stuff Ogden could sell. The searches were random, quick, often ineffectual, and stopped altogether once people had set foot on the base. But people caught with drugs on their way in were often offered alternatives by some security guards. "They'd say, 'Okay, you can bring it in for . . . '" said Art Reid, a security supervisor. "They could make more money that way."

"If the [kids] had mushrooms," said guard Dawn Jones, "they'd let them keep 'em if they paid $20." Body-searches were common, especially for women. "Girls who had been body-searched were complaining [about harassment]," said Jones. "They were visibly upset."

Only one drug arrest had been made on Friday, and that was off-base: Nineteen-year-old Brooke Young was caught by DEA agents with a staggering 11,000 tabs of LSD. Young had tried to sell 6,000 hits to an undercover agent and had planned to sell his remaining 5,000 at Woodstock. He thought he'd make about $55,000 and probably could have if he'd gotten through the gate. According to staffers, the Peace Patrol had been instructed by promoters to ignore everything but on-site physical violence. "They said in orientation that there will be nudity and drugs, and you're going to turn your heads," said a security guard named Mark, who did not want his last name used. "'Turn your head unless somebody is hurting somebody else. You're in a different world, no holds barred.' That's what led up to Sunday."

The MTV crew had been setting up since the day before in the media tower to the right of the East Stage and the control tower in the middle, where the sound engineer operated. As MTV producers scoured the grounds for material, VJ Carson Daly mostly hung with the kids to get their thoughts. They were happy to share with him. "You're a fag!" yelled one. "I could fuck Jennifer Love Hewitt better than you could!" heckled another. One sated MTV viewer threw a cup of water in Daly's face, and the beleaguered VJ mumbled, "Just tell me, man, that that wasn't your piss." The mob of dirty, thirsty teens yelled, "Let's get him!" and Daly and his crew fled. Pursuing garbage traced lovely parabolic arcs through the air but failed to hit its mark.

As evening fell, the medics in the first-aid tent behind the stage had treated hundreds of cases of heat exhaustion, dehydration, and bad trips—nothing too serious. It wasn't till the Offspring took the stage at 7:30 that the crowd truly responded with abandon, and the first sprawling, brawling mosh pits took amorphous shape. Dexter Holland whacked the Backstreet Boys in effigy with a baseball bat. Nineteen-year-old Justin Brake relished every minute of it, despite jamming up his own shoulder while slam dancing. "It was more than I bargained for," he said enthusiastically, "an experience I'll never forget."

Since most of the 200,000 on base were by now firmly settled at the East Stage, waiting for Korn to start, anyone looking to take a breather could retreat to the campsites, which were quiet and empty, if rank. There was a definite sense of camaraderie. "Everyone was so friendly," said Renee Carter of Fultonville, New York, "that we didn't even worry about padlocking our tent." The sun had set, cooling the concrete tarmac. Airborne debris, seemingly equipped with Daly-homing devices, found its way onto the lofty perch of the MTV tower.

For all the shit-slinging, drug-taking, VJ-abusing, and spontaneous garbage-hurling, the real action didn't get under way until Korn strode onstage at nine. The center-stage mosh pit raged with a concentrated ferocity. Britt Abbey, who was watching from his post at his vending tent adjacent to the stage, saw five boys emerge from the mosh pit with blood-soaked T-shirts. "The crowd was hectic," said Abbey, "but it wasn't too bad at all."

Chaos erupted immediately in the backstage med tent. "When Korn came on, people were coming in every three minutes on stretchers," said Rachael Hoke, a medical volunteer. The medics had prepped for the expected bruises, lacerations, broken bones—but Hoke was stunned by what she saw. "Every single person in our tent was OD'ing. A lot weren't conscious. One girl freaked out and broke the cot she was on. Seven EMTs tried to hold her down. She broke the restraints— they ended up having to duct-tape her to a backboard." The EMTs loaded her into an ambulance. "She tried to bite the EMTs," said Hoke incredulously.

Dave Schneider, who was volunteering at Woodstock's Crisis Intervention Unit, watched Korn from the edge of the main pit. By now it was around 9:30, and the moshing was even harder than before. Suddenly, Schneider saw a crowd-surfing woman get swallowed up by the pit; when she reemerged, two men had clamped her arms to her sides. "She was giving a struggle," said Schneider. "Her clothes were physically and forcibly being removed." Yet no one nearby seemed to react.

Schneider said that the woman and one of the men fell to the ground for about 20 seconds; then, he said, she was passed to his friend, who raped her, standing, from behind. "The gentleman's pants were down, her pants were down, and you could see that there was clearly sexual activity," he said. Finally, the woman was pulled from the pit by some audience members, who handed her to security.

Schneider said he watched in horror as five more women were pushed into the very same pit throughout Korn's set. "They were holding [the women] down and violating them. Maybe not everyone was raped, but the first one was, I'm sure." The pit broke up before Schneider left for his 11 P.M. shift at the on-site ER, but since all the women had made it to the arms of security, he assumed the crimes had been reported. At the ER, Schneider watched as a 15-year-old girl who had OD'd on an estimated ten hits of Ecstasy was brought in unconscious. She was unconscious the next day, when he left. The only death of the day, officials said, was a 44-year-old Woodstock '69 veteran who had had heart surgery 11 days earlier. He succumbed to the heat.

The girls took over two hours later, at 10:30, when they pushed their way to the front for Bush. By now, a tacit rule had been established: If you were a girl, and you were topless, you were going to get groped. If you were a girl, and you weren't topless, you were going to get yelled at for not being topless. "There were naked women all over," said Pruitt. "I got so sick of it. I was like, 'Put those away!'" Bush singer Gavin Rossdale gazed out at the sea of half-naked women and said, "This is the best thing I've ever seen."

Around 2 A.M., at the Rave Hangar, 25,000 people seemed determined to outperform the day's communal hedonism. They pulled it off, ingesting a staggering amount of drugs and engaging in a staggering amount of public and/or group sex as first Liquid Todd, then Moby, provided the soundtrack. "There were a bunch of naked dudes, and girls were just taking turns riding them," said rave promoter Matt E. Silver. "There were girls having oral sex with each other in the DJ booth. We had a topless girl dancing, and people were pouring orange juice on her and she was licking her titties. We were calling it Titty-Stock." A 30-year-old man tried to pick up the fully clothed Pruitt, to no avail.

There was a large contingent of security at this event. But most had removed their badges, stripped off their T-shirts, and started partying like regular unlawful Americans. They were oblivious to the observant kids who quickly seized upon their discarded laminates and made their way backstage. "In the dance area, where there were no rock bands, the vibe was terrific," said Moby. "Unfortunately, I didn't get laid."

Saturday: July 24, 1999

On Saturday morning, Joel Ferree was waiting outside a Rome bowling alley. Yellow school buses were ferrying latecomers to the former Air Force base, because full parking lots prevented anyone from driving anywhere near the site. The bus rolled up, and Ferree took a seat. He was met with a musky combination of body odor and pot smoke. The passengers were shouting "Metallica!" while they banged their heads to a boom box blasting "Enter Sandman." Someone suggested that the bus driver indulge in a bit of smoke, and everyone agreed that this was truly a fine idea. They tugged on her arms until she turned and yelled, "Get off me, you cocksuckers! I'm driving." Soon the bus passed a barricade lined with police officers, and a quick-thinking passenger yanked his shorts down and pressed his ass against the glass. The bus occupants cheered.

At the morning's press briefing, Woodstock copromoter Scher was detailing his priorities for the festival. "You can have a Woodstock, and it can be a safe and secure environment," he said. "We're going to try and make a profit on this one."

That morning the sewage conditions at Griffiss were even worse than the day before. Port-a-Sans were clogged up and overflowing, and waste streamed into the field; several campsites were suddenly awash in rivers of human waste. A few campers, seeking relief from the sweltering temperatures, had unscrewed the nozzles from nearby water spigots to keep the flow constant—which meant: 1) a lot of those water sources had dried up; and 2) some of the water that was still running had been contaminated with E. coli bacteria, which was flourishing in the omnipresent "mud." Now, in addition to the kids who were dropping from heat exhaustion and dehydration, there were just as many who were uncontrollably vomiting or doubled over with stomach cramps. These ailing concertgoers were faced with three options: use a feces-splattered Port-a-San, which would likely make them sicker; run for it and hope they made it to a medical tent in time; or squat down in the dirt and add to the overall squalidness. Many chose the latter.

At noon, the Canadian band Tragically Hip played the first set of the day on the East Stage. The Canadians were representing. There were faces painted with maple leafs and Canadian flags worn like superhero capes. They began singing "O Canada." At which point patriotic American audience members drowned them out with their version of "The Star Spangled Banner" while pelting the Canadians with rocks and bottles.

Also at noon, the beer gardens opened for business. Surrounded by tall wire fencing and elevated stations from which security could monitor the perimeter, and devoid of anywhere to sit, what the promoters called gardens were more akin to prison yards. The one near the East Stage had been packed to capacity the day before, but this afternoon it was mostly empty. The beer-drinking crowd had already migrated to the East Stage in anticipation of Kid Rock's set, and patrons of the garden were only allowed to buy two drink tickets at a time without exiting and reentering the garden—so they weren't sticking around for very long. In response, panicked workers abandoned the two-drink-maximum rule and handed out chunks of drink tickets—sometimes 20 or 30 at a time—to get things going.

One hour later, an enterprising local radio station, WEDG, put two naked women on top of its RV and used the loudspeaker to recruit willing females. Britt Abbey, who worked the vending tables closest to the right side of the East Stage, says packs of shirtless, sweaty guys clambered atop the tractor trailers behind him and yelled "Show us your tits!" at passing women. Their friends on the ground would block women's paths, swarming around them like ants. Some women would laugh and deliver the goods; others were unamused and picked up their pace. One woman charged men $20 (an Andrew Jackson, please; no change) to watch as she inserted the rolled bill in her vagina.

At a quarter past one on an 88-degree day, Kid Rock took the stage wearing a full-length white fur coat. He told the crowd to say, "You want my balls in your mouth?" instead of fighting if they got in a confrontation with someone. A few songs in, Rock's sidekick, Joe C., came out dressed in a hysterical Jimi Hendrix costume. Then he changed into a T-shirt that read I'M NOT A FUCKIN' MIDGET, smoked a joint, and cursed himself sweaty. The crowd had unmitigated love for Kid Rock and showed it by throwing their bottles in the air like they just didn't care. Some who forgot to duck got their scalps ripped open.

Around 3 P.M., Wyclef Jean performed a fairly embarrassing Hendrix imitation, in which he attempted to set his guitar on fire. He burned his hand. Dave Matthews took the stage just before 5 P.M. Far more girls than boys were up front. But this was Woodstock after all. Dave Schneider, who had witnessed the rape during Korn, saw a crowd-surfing girl's clothes get ripped off during Matthews' set. By the time she was passed off to security, the only piece of clothing to remain intact was the collar of her T-shirt.

Alanis Morissette arrived onstage a little before seven. She was hit by a lot of shoes. A woman (who asked that her name be withheld) said that although she had been assaulted while watching Tragically Hip earlier, she was sure that the pit for Morissette would be much safer. She surfed her way to the front of the stage. "I don't know how they got me," she said. "There were about three guys on each arm and each leg, and then three or four right inside me with their hands. One guy put his hand inside my anus. Another guy was yelling, 'Rip her apart!'" The woman finally managed to extricate herself from the pit by kicking some of her assailants in the head. She sat on the ground and cried. Some passersby tried to ask her what was wrong, but she couldn't even talk. "All I wanted to do," she said, "was kill somebody."

In the 20 minutes between the end of Morissette's set and the beginning of Limp Bizkit's, there was a sea change in the crowd. Boys pushed forward and prepared to mosh. Girls, for the most part, ran for their lives. By Saturday afternoon, kids without tickets had split open small gaps in the Peace Wall, the wooden fence that bordered Griffiss, and broken in to the grounds. Security was unable to keep up. One yellow shirt noticed a boy with pierced nipples and a mullet climbing over a still-standing ten-foot-high section of Peace Wall. It was painted with a portrait of Jimi Hendrix that made him look like an Ewok. The guard yelled at the boy to get down. "Fuck you," said the boy. "Fine," shrugged the security guard, and he walked away.

In all, only 175 security guards showed up for Saturday night's shift. And that's who signed in, not who actually stayed. The bosses made a call to prisons and jails looking for correction officers willing to work on short notice for supervisors' pay. Forty materialized.

While the guards were disappearing, the crowds were growing. Another 25,000 fans had arrived late Friday night. With fewer guards on the gates, more contraband began to seep in, especially nitrous-oxide tanks and beer. Soon, a small fleet of entrepreneurs were selling nitrous-filled balloons from the tanks. A short time later, the med tents began to see people who were sick from inhaling too much nitrous.

There were just minutes to go before Limp Bizkit took the stage, but the crowd was so worked up they began throwing stuff with an inventiveness and dedication not seen before. At this point, hurling shoes and mud was an amateur pursuit. People moved on to batteries, disposable cameras, and rocks the size of hockey pucks. The media tower to the right of the stage, the camera platforms to the left, and the control tower in the middle of the airfield were swarming with kids who peeled off each structure's protective plywood like worn Band-Aids. Someone found an uncracked watermelon and hurled it at the MTV tower, where crew and talent were now huddled, many with their heads in their hands to deflect flying detritus. The MTV crew canceled their plans to tape Limp Bizkit's performance and decided to go live at 10 P.M. from the backstage first-aid area. "The MTV people were kind of shocked and overwhelmed," said an MTV staffer. "I mean if you have 250,000 kids bent on destroying you, you're gonna get rattled."

At 7:45, hippie totem Wavy Gravy appeared on the East Stage and said, "Enough of the mellow shit."

Not long after, Limp Bizkit singer Fred Durst yelled, "How many people have ever woke up in the morning and just decided you're going to break some shit?" before tearing into—what else?—"Break Stuff." Many in the audience took the song literally: They broke arms, legs, teeth, noses, collarbones. Scalps were lacerated by flying, half-full bottles. One mosher suffered a compression fracture of the spine. Another broke two ribs and prodded the medic treating him to finish quickly so he could return to the pit. Yet another boy's shoulder popped right out of its socket. As he stumbled toward security, his fellow moshers yelled, "Pussy!"

The first-aid tent, located behind the East Stage, was now seriously overflowing. EMT workers had trouble getting to kids who went down in the pit because the crowd wouldn't part for them. An estimated 200 people per hour were treated in the two med tents near the stage; ambulances took about a dozen people to local hospitals for examination. The MTV crew watched as the bodies piled up in the first-aid area, all the while dodging the rocks and bottles that the watchful crowd had retargeted at their hideout. Unfortunately, their aim was off, and they hit some kids who were, respectively, hooked up to IVs, vomiting blood, and OD'ing. "It looked like the *M*A*S*H* triage unit," said MTV producer Tim Healy. "The only people missing were Hawkeye and BJ." The EMTs were caught off guard by the level of casualties. "The busiest time for us," said Dr. Phil Vuocolo, Woodstock's medical director, "was Saturday night into early Sunday morning." Drug-related cases—resulting from Ecstasy, mushrooms, LSD, Ruphinol—plagued the medical units as well. At one point, a weary medic walked over to Healy and said, "Dude, do me a favor. Just tell everyone you know to stay away from the liquid Ecstasy."

Meanwhile, Durst was exhorting the crowd to "get all your negative energy out." People soared through the air with as much frequency as garbage; a few were flung skyward on bed sheets. Between songs, Durst made an announcement: "They want to ask us to ask you to mellow out. They said too many people are getting hurt. Don't let nobody get hurt, but I don't think you should mellow out!"

Around this time, an overzealous spectator fell from a sound tower. Soon after, the band lost all sound, and Durst stormed off the stage. By some accounts, a sound engineer thought a grave injury had befallen the spectator and had cut the sound feed.

Less than three minutes later, sound was restored, and Limp Bizkit tore into "Nookie." Durst tried to body-surf through the audience using only a sheet of fan-liberated plywood. The attempt failed, and security shepherded him back onstage. The band played their cover of "Faith," and the crowd went nuts.

Women who were sitting atop their boyfriend's shoulders were smothered by hands. Tops were torn away like tissue paper; girls fought valiantly to keep their pants on as boys tugged them down around their knees. Crisis-intervention workers who watched Limp Bizkit's set saw numerous sexual assaults in the mosh pits; one woman later reported to police that she had been raped, then had surfed her way out. She said that the size and mood of the crowd stopped her from yelling for help—she was afraid she'd be beaten up.

Still, a lot of the younger girls never felt threatened, whether or not they were near mosh pits. "From where I was," said Liz Pruitt, who stood near the front of the crowd, "it seemed like any other show, cause all I saw was people with their hands in the air. I felt safe." There was little pity for those who were unprepared for what they found in the front rows. "If you didn't want to be in a rough situation there, you shouldn't have been in the mosh pit," said reveler Doug Calahan. "I'm tired of people making excuses for their own fucking stupidity. Limp Bizkit equals mosh pit. Duh."

Forty-five minutes later, Rage Against the Machine started playing "No Shelter" from the *Godzilla* soundtrack, an appropriate song, all things considered. Behind the band was a large amp draped with an American flag. Bassist Tim Bob set it on fire when they exited the stage. Rage toned down their set in an attempt to keep the post-Bizkit crowd from actually transforming into a new species. Those in the mosh pit nonetheless got a workout. One man pulled off his shirt and set it on fire, then waved it around in a circle.

A 100-foot section of the west wall between gates two and three came down during the night, perhaps as early as 11 P.M. Security put out a number of small fires in the campground. There were a few minor attempts at looting. Near the center of the compound, in the beer garden, about a hundred people were chanting "Fuck the police!" This coalition of oppressed music-loving beer drinkers was organizing to rush the two security guards who wouldn't let them leave with their beers. Hundreds of people chanted in unison but nobody stormed the gate.

Rain threatened Saturday's final performances. On the East Stage, the members of Metallica all wore black and didn't say much to the crowd beyond, "Thank you, friends," and, "You motherfuckers want some more?" They played furious speed-metal oldies like "Seek and Destroy" and a head-exploding version of "One." But the rear-speaker delays were fried, and the crowd thinned appreciably. After the first encore, around 1 A.M., Kid Rock appeared and handed a salutatory Corona to drummer Lars Ulrich.

"We turned it up to about 11 that day," said Ulrich later. "We've been through this shit for so long, we fuckin' know how to deal with these situations—what to do and what not to do. If there's that kind of energy in the air, you just go out, shut the fuck up, play your music, and get on with it. You don't want to further ignite it."

Halfway through Metallica's set, at 12:36 A.M., 24-year-old computer analyst David DeRosia had walked into a first-aid tent complaining of heat exhaustion. His friend David Vadnais—who had last seen DeRosia at midnight, right before Metallica began—said that he seemed fine. But when he couldn't find him later that night, he got worried. On Sunday afternoon he was told by medics that DeRosia had been evacuated by helicopter to nearby University Hospital.

On the West Stage, where the Chemical Brothers were spinning, the music paused momentarily while 150,000 frenzied dancers were informed of the impending storm and instructed to hit the ground if lightning struck. In response, everybody threw their hands in the air.

"It was our favorite gig of our whole tour," said the Chemicals' Ed Simons. "It was a cool vibe. It was more like what Woodstock was meant to be, as opposed to what was happening on the other stage."

Wet and exhausted and not sated, tens of thousands of people, including Simons, strolled over to the Rave Hangar, where Fatboy Slim spun until 3:30 A.M. Ecstasy and acid were brazenly offered, sold, and dropped. As she walked through the maze of people, 23-year-old Lara Buthfer stumbled upon five girls having sex with one another. One woman won herself a free nitrous balloon by standing on the vending table, shedding her thong, and lowering her booty to within inches of the stunned face of the guy selling the balloons. But still, this was Woodstock. Spencer Tunick, a photographer who specializes in large stills of naked people, saw a woman being violated as she sat on a man's shoulders. "She must have been on some substance," he said, "she was so passive. It was just unbelievable how many hands went up there. She was surrounded by 20 guys in khaki shorts."

In the beginning of Fatboy's set, someone who had been hired to install the half-pipe in the Action Lounge drove a 14-foot U-Haul truck, with five guys dancing on top, straight through a hangar in an attempt to get to the stage. Though the driver was promptly arrested, he politely backed the truck up before being taken into custody. The unincarcerated joyriders then walked back to the Action Lounge and lit a fire in a garbage can, inspiring others to douse hay bales inside the Lounge with gasoline and set them ablaze. The fires were quickly doused. "Another 45 or 50 seconds of this would have been very dangerous—I mean, extremely dangerous, causing the loss of life and stuff," said David Pelletier, the Action Lounge's manager. "There's rock'n'roll and skate culture, but when people start getting hurt in the spirit of fun, that's not fun anymore."

Sunday: July 25, 1999

Allison Mann woke up early on Sunday morning. As she was enjoying a Fluffernutter sandwich, some kids from the Monkey Sex Cult came around.

The Monkey Sex Cult was a group of guys and girls—okay, mostly guys—who were trying to meet people—okay, mostly girls. "It has to do with a mating thing that monkeys do," said Mann. "How monkeys scare each other before having sex. They came up to people and were, like, 'Join the Monkey Sex Cult!' and they'd say 'uh huh' and keep walking. But it was a lot better than saying 'Show your tits!' like everyone else." Other people must have thought so too. About 20 of them joined.

Around the Monkey Sex Cult compound, the campgrounds were wrecked. Garbage was strewn everywhere, collecting in fetid piles that began to resemble landscaping in some of the less desirable neighborhoods in Manila. The flooded Port-a-Sans clusters were seeping their contents at an ever-faster rate. Small lakes of fecal matter slowly but relentlessly invaded several of the camping areas. Some of the shower facilities were either turned off or the water pressure was shot. Small groups of naked, dirty, and often bruised concertgoers stood around in a daze using pools of dirty water to exchange the dry filth on their bodies for new, wet filth from the puddles.

Earlier that day at a press conference, Scher admitted that the previous days' events were "a frat party to a large degree." Ken Donohue, the head of Metropolitan Entertainment security, said, "I think the event has been a great success from a security point of view." Copromoter Michael Lang said, "We've lost 15 to 20 percent of the security force. Some were let go. Through shift changes, I think we're having the right level of security." But actual security guards, like Mark, the guard who didn't want his last name used, described it differently. "At this point, they were kissing our feet to get us to work." Scrubs had been quickly promoted to supervisors as the ranks thinned. Units of 14 had shrunk down over the days to two or three.

At 9 A.M., the depleted security force repaired the 100-foot hole in the wall near the main gate, which had been gouged the night before. By 10:30 A.M., the wall started coming down again.

According to Art Reid, a security supervisor on the South Gate, "They had an incident sometime around noon where 200 security guards quit." The head of supervision for the security guards held a quick meeting and said he placed another emergency call to the correctional facilities to try to get 200 correctional guards to replace them. No one came.

Ogden had run out of water on Saturday, and some local vendors who bought their own supplies sold water for $2 and $3. They had wanted to drop prices anyway when it got hot, as had the medical staff. Ogden told them to keep the price at $4 or they'd close them down. Individual vendors who tried to reduce prices on sandwiches got shut down or were threatened with fines.

At 1 P.M., Willie Nelson was playing on the East Stage and Mike Ness on the other. Very little trash had been picked up for the duration of the festival, and the entire field before the East Stage was dotted with garbage. Fans picked through the refuse to find a clean pizza box upon which to sit. The crowd had thinned substantially from the day before, and there was a conspicuous absence of security. Pot clouds began to amass over Nelson's audience.

By 2 P.M., Reid's unit had to abandon the gate and watch as beer and other contraband poured in. Around the compound, security guards were taking off their shirts and melting into the crowd. Two tractor trailers full of bottled water, condoms, and gum fell prey to looters by the West Stage. The Robin Hoods sold the water for $2 a bottle.

A few hours later on the East Stage, Everlast covered Marvin Gaye's "Trouble Man" as a helicopter drew lazy circles above the base. The crowd was thicker by this point, and the usual stuff began to find itself airborne: bottles, trash, toilet paper. Many audience members were hot and pissed off. Some shoes were thrown. Everlast paused and addressed this. "Karma's a bitch," he said. "You better recognize that and act accordingly."

After the concert, Everlast added, "People are trying to blame bands for what the kids did and say what a reflection it is on this generation. All those people are nostalgic for something that happened 30 years ago. I don't think anything real came out of that first experience—it was just three days of sex and drugs and 'Oh, the world is such a great place!' Then they went home, became yuppies, and fucked the whole country up."

By mid-afternoon, rumors circulated among the security staff that they would be attacked if they didn't take off their yellow shirts, and that the vendors would be next. "There was a weird aura on Sunday," said Dave Bobela, 19, a student working in the vending tent closest to the West Stage. "People were getting cranky. The vendors were getting a lot of trash talked at us. If you weren't cutting deals with the customers, you were basically shit. I cut some deals, just to be nice. By then, I didn't give a damn if the person I was working for made any money."

Lots of kids were seriously blitzed, mostly on beer. Three days of being wasted in the broiling sun was beginning to have profound neurological effects on the crowd. The camping areas were full of strange sounds: moaning, screaming, various expulsions of gas. Some attendees, exhausted or attempting to beat the postconcert exodus, or both, packed to leave. But those who stayed appeared to be digging in.

Standing on the side of the path that led to the back of the tents was a 19-year-old brunette holding a bottle of Johnny Walker. "Free Scotch! Free Scotch!" she called out. As people drew from the bottle, a man who she had just met repeatedly lifted her shirt to lick her nipples. The boundaries and established social conventions that had been assaulted all weekend now seemed completely breached.

At the perimeter of Griffiss, the fence had also been breached—not by people trying to crash the concert but by the concertgoers themselves. Most wanted a piece as a souvenir. Others wanted fuel. Small blazes were starting across the base, initiated with symbolic-yet-conveniently-flammable chunks of plywood mural tossed into a heap and set afire. The first appeared to have been started at the rear of the campsite, near the West Stage. About 30 people stood peacefully around a medium-size bonfire cheering the flames, drinking beer, and passing joints. A fire crew and state troopers appeared quickly, but they seemed to take the whole thing as a joke. They sprayed out the fire, then turned the hose in the air for the crowd. As kids realized that there was very little consequence for their actions, small fires burned through the late afternoon.

While more concertgoers discovered the joys of dismantling the Peace Wall, the police contemplated the proper response. A state trooper Chevrolet Tahoe cruised the access road next to the wall and pulled over. The crowd ignored it. One of the officers called out to the wall-dismantlers on his PA, "Hey, bring us a piece, would you?" A man brought the officers a choice fragment. The cop placed the plywood in his trunk. As the police drove away, one of the men stopped atomizing the Woodstock Peace Wall long enough to yell, "Thanks, man! You guys rule!"

Dressed in a black tank top and tight capri pants, Jewel took the stage around 5 P.M. A sign in the audience read JEWEL: FUCK ME NOW. Jewel was unfazed. Jewel yodeled. The audience was unfazed.

"The crowd was really weird," she said a week later. "Generally when you do big shows like that it's always a bit weird, but here people seemed real strung out. Real tired. But I was pleased cause people really seemed to listen."

Soon after, it rained.

Although they were brief, the showers managed to cool down the entire area for the rest of the evening, the temperature settling into the comparatively sub-arctic mid-80s. Concertgoers perked up almost immediately. People ran back and forth, jumping up and down, yelping unintelligibly. A group of boys took over one of the food tents in the camping area and distributed its contents to passersby. The girl who worked the tent was helpless, so she joined the crowd.

"This," she said, "is the best time I've ever had."

At a 6 P.M. press conference, the promoters were already discussing the success of the festival. "All is well," announced Scher. Oneida County Executive Ralph Eannace, Jr., exalted the promoters' deft handling of the enormous crowd. "They said the wall wouldn't hold, and it did. They said security wouldn't work, and it did. It was a wonderful concert."

Of course, the wall had long been breached, and the concert was far from over.

Around 7 P.M., as Ice Cube unleashed a brutal version of "Fuck Tha Police," a thick line of thunderheads approached from the northeast. The sky turned a deep violet-blue. Lightning danced.

During Creed's set, someone drove a stolen white Mercedes-Benz through one of the many gaping maws in the Peace Wall up to a sound tower about 80 yards from the stage and ditched it. Security guard Tom Supernault—a 21-year-old local who says he reported to work Friday to find himself suddenly promoted to supervisor—got on top of the car and tried to stop the mob from rocking it back and forth. He was hit with bottles and fists from all sides.

The crowd gathered before the East Stage had swelled to an estimated 150,000. To the right of the stage, scaffolding, upon which about 100 people had been illegally climbing, collapsed. "It was suggested at this point," said Charles Knapp, a moonlighting corrections officer, "that security turn our shirts inside out so they didn't say PEACE PATROL anymore." The youth-activist group PAX distributed candles to be used in an antigun peace vigil, a noble if egregiously underthought gesture. "There was very little security," said Buthfer. "I saw maybe eight of them. They were looking at girls."

At 8:40 P.M., Red Hot Chili Peppers singer Anthony Kiedis came out dressed like a punk-rock schoolboy. Bassist Flea was naked. Perhaps in the spirit of things, and perhaps mocking the spirit of things, Kiedis requested that any menstruating women close to the stage throw their tampons at the band. There were no discernible takers. About halfway through the set, during "Under the Bridge," all the PAX peace candles were supposed to be lit, a hundred thousand points of light espousing the professed ideals and virtues of the original Woodstock.

Instead, the fires began in earnest.

Two hundred yards behind the left side of the stage, a medium-size pile of a former mural was transformed into a medium-size pile of combusting cellulose. Within minutes, a second and third fire ignited in close proximity to the first. For most of the audience, only a glow was visible at first, but as the show progressed, the flames began to dance above the heads of the crowd. As the Peppers played an encore, Kiedis said, "Holy shit, it looks like *Apocalypse Now* out there." They broke into Jimi Hendrix's "Fire."

At this point, there were five large and swelling bonfires in the immediate vicinity of the stage. Smaller fires sprouted like weeds at more distant points on the field. The Mercedes was flipped over and set aflame. Via radio, security personnel were ordered by supervisors to retreat to security headquarters at Building 100. The band finished the song, and immediately afterward, a short multimedia Hendrix tribute played on the various Diamond Vision screens surrounding the stage. One hundred fifty thousand people waited to see what was next.

Throughout the day, there were rampant rumors of a secret grand-finale act. In the quiet after the Hendrix tribute, the crowd became restless and agitated. Would it be Pearl Jam? Prince? Bruce Springsteen? "Word got around that the surprise band was either the Rolling Stones or the Who," said 19-year-old Justin Brake, "and people grew angrier!" Soon John Scher took the stage, but not to announce a special guest band. "[Something] is on fire, as you can see," he said. "It's not part of the show. It really is a problem, so the fire department's going to have to come in with a fire truck to put the fire out. Everyone needs to cooperate."

The fire truck didn't come. No surprise bands took the stage. The concertgoers at the East Stage wanted more. And within the formerly walled confines of the former Griffiss Air Force Base, it was as if the top was ripped off the world.

About 200 people surrounded the area illuminated by the flickering yellow light of the largest bonfire. Athletic-minded crowd members jumped through the fire and yelled, "Fuck you! I won't do what you tell me!"

Under attack, medical personnel near the East Stage abandoned their posts and took off their shirts. Security officially gave up the ghost. Those who hadn't fled the site already were ordered to take refuge near the Woodstock management offices.

State troopers rolled in on four-wheel ATVs and attempted to push people away from the largest fires. After computing the police-officer-to-fire-appreciating-concertgoer ratio, the officers quickly retreated. On the PA system, promoters started playing Rage Against the Machine, which had precisely the opposite effect on the crowd as intended. Though most of the audience headed for the tents to leave, those who remained, five to ten thousand people, were determined to tear the entire site apart. On the West Stage, Megadeth were screaming through "Peace Sells."

At 10:30 P.M., state police and a fire engine attempted to approach a bonfire but gave up when the crowd unleashed a missle attack consisting primarily of bottles. Ten kids rocked the 50-foot speaker tower next to the East Stage, shaking it violently. The cables snapped as steel bolts popped from their fittings. At 10:45, the tower came lurching down with a cacophonous thud. Young men climbed the remains of the scaffolding and banged on it like a victorious troop of chimps. Speakers and lighting equipment were hurled into the fire and exploded. A noxious cloud engulfed the area.

Around 11 P.M., the rebel army surged toward the center of the village. Police and security personnel were largely absent. The sound of yelling and chanting was everywhere. Almost 200 formed a drumming circle, banging on overturned garbage cans with their hands, chunks of wood, a sledgehammer, an ax. Cardboard and wooden pallets were added to the fires in the vendor area. Several storage trailers were set ablaze. "There was one kid with a megaphone," said 19-year-old Catrinelle Bartolomew, "who was saying, 'Will everyone please pick up one piece of garbage and throw it into the fire?'"

A mob amassed on top of a beer-garden tent and collapsed it. A hundred people fell 20 feet but none were hurt. The tent burned. At some point, jocular rioters took control of a PA system long enough to declare: "Woodstock is now under martial law. Anyone here who has a good time will be shot. Anybody with a Woodstock MasterCard will be spared."

Steel tent poles were used to break the locks securing several food-vendor semis. Kids tossed provisions to the crowd, mostly pretzels and snack food, which precipitated an extensive food fight. "It was raining pretzels and bread," said Bobela. The looting continued, spreading to the Ace Hardware trucks near the campgrounds. "People got in and basically started raping us for all we had," said Bobela. "There was no physical violence, but it was all about stealing and vandalizing. All we could do was walk away. It was kind of like watching your house go down and there's nothing you can do." Even so, many vendors continued to do brisk sales in pizza. In the Rave Hangar, about 15,000 kids were still dancing.

The growing blaze of vendor tents, now fed by cardboard boxes, foodstuffs, and assorted camping supplies, sidled up to the closest semi and engulfed it. Burning wood was tossed into the trailer, which was outfitted with refrigeration units consisting of volatile generators, propane, and coolant. The truck quickly exploded, shredding the sides and roof of the sheet-metal trailer and igniting other vehicles nearby. Miraculously, no one was seriously injured in the blasts. "Just imagine 12 tractor trailers on fire," said Bobela. "From where I was standing in the parking lot, it was almost like watching a sunset—it was that bright." Kids began throwing unoccupied tents and Port-a-Sans into the flames. Shit was literally burning. Women stripped for the crowd.

Someone stumbled upon a massive cache of glow-sticks looted from Ace Hardware. Kids cracked them open by the thousands. "We ran into these people who were having a glow-stick war," said concertgoer Matthew Farrington, "and decided they were gonna throw glow sticks at the cops. So we go over there and they're throwing them at the state troopers. This one guy was like, 'Follow us, we're gonna go kill the cops with glow sticks!'"

By 11:45 P.M., 500 to 700 state troopers in riot gear had arrived on site, some wielding pepper spray. They successfully pushed the crowd away from the East Stage, but the campsite-area chaos continued unabated. There were an estimated 30,000 to 40,000 kids in the center of the base; some threw garbage at the police. The officers yelled at them but were not making any arrests.

"It looked like fucking *Lord of the Flies*," said MTV's Healy. "Kids were shouting, 'Let it burn!'" The drumming continued. A teenage photographer paused to shoot some film of a young man being fellated by his girlfriend as a bonfire licked the sky behind them.

Near the vending areas, wild-eyed capitalists decided to make a withdrawal from the ATMs. "I saw people gathered around the ATM," said Farrington, "and I just thought they were breaking into it—with their bare hands! They didn't even have any tools." One minorly hobbled concertgoer attempted to use the blunt edge of his crutch to punch a hole in the metal casing.

After about 45 minutes, the kids successfully cracked open the ATMs only to discover what dozens had learned the easy way on Saturday: They were out of cash. As they walked away disappointed, people were smashing the little refrigerators in vending booths because they were there.

Mat Robin, a slight, brown-haired 22-year-old art-school grad from Toronto, had finally finished an hour-long rubbernecking trek through the fires to the Rave Hangar, where he and his friends hoped to see Perry Farrell spin. Security guards from the Rave Hangar had retreated to the ramp near the Woodstock offices at Building 100. Some of them began stealing boxes of CDs from the Rave Hangar, but they were halted by more virtuous guards.

Robin wound up on a raised patch of cement near the Rave Hangar in a group of 20 people. Nearby were some bales of hay, and not too far away were the ATMs, where the burgling horde had been joined by a few men clutching bats and steel poles. "I was trying to stay away from that stuff," said Robin. Someone tried to light the bales on fire. Robin heard a voice from the ATM yell, "Hey, put the fire out, we're doing something Federal over here!"

A stranger handed Robin a five-by-three-foot flag on a seven-foot pole, and he began to wave it. He had no idea what the yellow sun on it meant. "It may have said RUSTED ROOT on the other side," he joked. "I don't know." There were almost two dozen people with him, and they were talking, yelling, exchanging happy banalities.

The troopers were coming, several hundred of them, clad in riot helmets and shields, and they saw a man on a cement block waving a flag, yelling, near burning hay and the looted ATM area. They gave chase. It took him a day in the county lockup to figure out why, and how deeply he'd stepped in shit. He faces charges of being a ringleader in the riots and of pelting the cops with rocks and bottles. The police wanted to charge him with arson, but the lack of matches or a lighter on his person prevented that. Of the thousands rioting at Woodstock, and the couple dozen transported to county lockup with him, he was one of only seven officially arrested. He goes to trial in September.

"They're trying to find some individuals [to blame], and there aren't any individuals," he said upon his release from jail. "It's just the lemming effect, what happened. No one was in charge."

Elsewhere, looting of the Ace Hardware trucks continued. Boys and girls ran around, loaded down with every imaginable type of camping gear. "Hey everybody," one of them shouted, "it's Christmas in July!"

"When things were really raging," said Bobela, "we saw a couple guys strip naked and start doing indigenous dances as if their whole life had led up to that moment. One guy climbed on top of a display speaker. He was giving a sermon like Christ!—as if he was the chosen one, with his hands up in the air, yelling, 'Praise me, I'm God.'"

Just before midnight, the all-night dance party scheduled for the Rave Hangar was canceled by the promoters. Perry Farrell was scheduled to spin. "Perry looked like he couldn't believe it," said Justin Hirschman, a booking agent. "Everyone was so disheartened. The DJs were like, 'Why is this happening?'"

A phalanx of troopers, with a small contingent of moonlighting correctional officers who worked for Metropolitan Entertainment, managed to push the rioters back to the campgrounds. They cleared a third of the mile-and-a-half-long field. Every time they encountered a drum circle, resistance stiffened.

At 3 A.M., people continued to feed the campgrounds' fires. Police let the rioters tire themselves out before attempting to fight the blazes. As a result, the Rome fire department did not gain control of the fires until well after dawn broke. At 4 A.M., the drumming circles finally broke up. As a haze of fog and smoke blanketed the area, most of the remaining revelers staggered back to their tents or vehicles, mentally preparing themselves to rejoin the quotidian pursuits of modern-day America.

Feet black with dirt, hair matted and smelling of smoke, Pruitt got on her bus a little before 6 A.M. for the five-hour ride back to Connecticut. The next morning, Scher characterized the night's events as "an aberration." A week later, he floated the theory that a cult of indeterminate origin had orchestrated the rioting.

In the immediate aftermath, two concertgoers were confirmed dead, including DeRosia, who died of hypothermia on Monday; 5 rapes and sexual assaults were reported. "I was really surprised to hear that," said Pruitt. "All the guys I was around were cool." A supervisor of two state troopers who had posed with naked female attendees was suspended; a New York State prison guard was charged with sodomizing a 15-year-old girl during the riots; 253 people had been treated at area hospitals. The official numbers of fans treated on-site is between 4,000 and 4,500, yet Dr. Richard Kaskiw, one of the few area doctors who worked in the medical tents, says that he was told by Vuocolo—who issued the official stats—that the numbers were far higher, in the 8,000 to 10,000 range. Forty-four concertgoers had been arrested. Damage and insurance estimates were still being compiled.

"Burning stuff isn't the nicest thing to be doing, but it was justified," said Pruitt. "They took advantage of us. I know they said the free water was fine, but I wasn't going to drink it after getting sick on Saturday. I was forced into paying $50 for water that cost $1 in the supermarket. It was a way of getting back at them." Pruitt said she never thought about what she was doing, or what could possibly happen. "The only time I thought someone could die was when the tower fell," she said, "And yeah, I'd feel bad if someone did die, but I wouldn't feel responsible. I only threw paper and plastic on small fires that were contained. It was a thrill. I got to do anything I wanted to do and felt comfortable doing it. It's like you're a little kid doing something bad, but you're not gonna get in trouble because nobody's around."

"I'll tell you what, man, it's a generation of ambivalence," said the 19-year-old Catrinelle Bartolomew. "We'll all take a chance to live it up but we're intelligent enough not to hurt each other. Older people will never get it. When you look at Kurt and Serena on MTV, how scared they are—they'll never get it."

Mat Robin has no regrets. "It was insane—I'd never seen anything like it before in my life," he said. "Our generation ain't stupid. We're going to get our money's worth, *then* riot."

Pruitt is nothing short of wistful. "It was an amazing, incredible experience," she said. "Just to say that I saw all those bands. And all those fires."

LESTER BANGS:

INTRODUCTION BY

JOHN ROCKWELL

An Instant Fan's Inspired Notes: You Gotta Listen

Lester Bangs, who died in 1982 at the age of 33, was widely regarded as the great innovative, comic poet of rock criticism, a writer who sought to emulate in his rambunctious prose the spirit of the writers (William S. Burroughs and Hunter S. Thompson come to mind) and music he loved. Greil Marcus, who edited Bangs' selected work in the book Psychotic Reactions and Carburetor Dung *(Knopf, 1987), called him "rock's essential wild man, a one-man orgy of abandon, excess, wisdom, satire, parody."*

Bangs grew up in El Cajon, California, moved to Detroit in 1971 (some of his most characteristic work appeared in that city's Creem *magazine) and to New York in 1976, where he also led two punk bands. His death was partly drug-related, although he had cleaned himself up considerably in the preceding year.*

The Comedian Harmonists were a German pop vocal sextet; three of the original members were Jewish, and the group broke up in the mid–1930s under Nazi pressure. Within the last year a film and a Broadway show have celebrated their careers.

In 1980 Joe Boyd, the founder of Hannibal Records, planned to release a recording of the group drawn from 78 r.p.m. disks and asked Bangs to write liner notes for it. Boyd deliberately withheld factual information about the group to capture Bangs' immediate response to the music. That disk, delayed for business reasons, has now been issued under the title "The Comedian Harmonists" (HNCD 1445), but without the Bangs notes, which have remained unpublished.

Bangs' writing style changed when he moved to New York in 1976. "In Detroit," Mr. Marcus wrote, "he published mostly first drafts, hewing to the Beat line of automatic inspiration; in New York he began to work more slowly, writing a piece again and again, chasing a theme through 5, 10 times its publishable length, then cutting back or starting over." What follows is my amalgamation, with slight cuts, of two early drafts, a fragment and a fuller version.

Hi there. Right now I bet I can read your mind. You're standing there holding this album, your curiosity perhaps mildly piqued, but wondering (and probably more dubious than not) whether an album as off-the-wall as this one appears to be might actually be a worthwhile addition to your collection that you'd play often because you actually liked to listen to it, just like a lot of rock or jazz albums or anything else. I know, because I've been in the same position so many times, and I'm actually sick of all the dreams I keep having about it. The alternative outcome, of course, would be that you just paid hard-earned money for some oddball novelty item that might be good for one play, maybe another at Christmas when the relatives are over, a couple lame Nazi jokes and then "Get it off!"

Most records, as we know all too well, aren't worth the vinyl they're stamped in. Who the hell wants a bunch of by-now-probably-dead Germans from the mid–1920s singing harmonies that're some weirdo combination of music hall, rathskeller, Alpine folk strains and, most important to me and perhaps you as well, American black blues, gospel, ragtime and jazz influences. Which makes it more than just another novelty right there. Because when these guys sing Duke Ellington, they mean it. Do they ever.

Still reading? Good. Don't feel sorry for Hannibal Records if they end up taking a bath on this passel o' cheery Jerries—feel sorry for yourself if you don't buy it. Because I'm gonna lay it on the line right here and now: I have never heard anything like the contents of this album before in my life. Which is saying something, because over the years I've become something of a musicologist with around 5,000 albums covering everything from Mamie Smith and Her Jazz Hounds to Teen-age Jesus and the Jerks. I may well have bad taste (for instance, I truly like Teen-age Jesus and the Jerks), but at least I know the territory pretty well.

Now, the more I listen to this record, the more I'm impressed by two qualities it has in abundance: one is soul, and nobody has to tell you how hard that is to find in anything new being put out these days; the other is that, near as I can tell, this record does not fit into the territory. It creates its own turf and holds it masterfully. It's too steeped in jazz and gospel to be truly "German," but of course it's still European through and through, enough so that more than one listener has laughed out loud. But they were laughing with pleasure.

What's more, I'll admit in front that I have a special affinity for things that don't quite fit into any given demarcated category, partly because I'm one of those perennial misfits myself by choice as well as fate or whatever. By profession, I am categorized as a rock critic. I'll accept that, especially since the whole notion that one somehow has a "career" instead of just doing whatever you feel like doing at any given time has always amused me when it didn't make me wanna vomit. O.K., I'm a rock critic. I also write and record music. I write poetry, fiction, straight journalism, unstraight journalism, beatnik drivel, mortifying love letters, death threats to white jazz critics signed "The Mau Maus of East Harlem" and once a year my own obituary (latest entry: "He was promising . . . "). The point is that I have no idea what kind of a writer I am, except that I do know that I'm good and lots of people like to read whatever it is that I do, and I like it that way.

These notes may seem discursive but bear with me, we're going somewhere, and you're going to like it. This "career" business, like whenever somebody sees me playing music and says, "Is this going to be your new career?" always reminds me of an old Charles Bukowski story

called "Would You Suggest Writing as a Career?" It's about how he gets
up one morning with a terminal hangover, vomits, staggers off to make
some godawful dawn flight to some Bo-Weevil U located in the Lower
Left Dustbowl corner pocket where the li'l Cessna now verging on
Aeroflot vomitorium is about to touch down in one of the quaintest,
cutest, most dilapidately rustic little burbs in America: We Eats Out-
landers, Utah, our nation's last remaining dry college town. After showing the great poet (it is a fact that both Genet and Sartre have called
him the best writer in America) his lodgings for the evening (a gunny
sack in the bottom of a defrosted ice chest), they usher him with all
proper pomp, circumstance and puncturing of left eardrums with
Ticonderoga pencil lead into the Main Hall, where he commences to
befoul the lobes of these assembled pilgrims who never progressed by
reading about an hour and a half's worth of deadpan monotone descrip-
tions of cunnilingus, fellatio, missionary positions (well, of sorts) with
80-year-old landladies blind in one eye and palsied on the knee and one
little 4-year-old lass who I hope fervently was a product of his imagination rather than reminiscence, as well as every kind of drug-sex-drink-
orgy and an exhaustive catalogue of various methods by which one may
so Stradivarize the heartstrings of the L.A.P.D. that those dapper gentlemen will actually consent to put you up in a quite exclusive private
club they have established for the edification of just such connoisseurs
of the Cabernets and Beaujolais of Life as yourself.

The audience, who had never been past the outer rim of the Bowl in
their lives, were properly appreciative of these picaresques set in such
exotic locales as Pismo Beach, Hialeah and the East L.A. Blood
Donors' Center. Mr. Charles Bukowski, America's greatest living poet,
born in Andernach, Germany, around the time these recordings were
made, the toast of France since he went on its version of the Dick
Cavett show drunk, refused to wear his translator's headphones, asked
a literary critic there if he could slobber all over her calves on national
TV, and told the assembled frogmatik culture vultures that they should
have dropped a hydrogen bomb on themselves the day in 1961 that
Louis-Ferdinand Celine died inasmuch as they had not produced a single writer above Peugeot ad-copy level since; this man, author of 33
published books so far, including *Confessions of a Man Insane Enough to*

Live With Beasts, Poems Written Before Jumping Out of an Eight-Story Window, Notes of a Dirty Old Man, The Days Run Away Like Wild Horses Over the Hills, Doing Time With Public Enemy Number One, Nut Ward Just East of Hollywood, A .45 to Pay the Rent and *Twelve Flying Monkeys Who Won't Copulate Properly,* now sat back in his worn swivel chair, relit his stogie, unpopped another Colt .45 and surveyed his audience. Dustbowl residence apparently did not do too much to encourage proliferation of barefoot boys with cheeks of tan. But that was all right; enough master races already. No, these sandlocked little lubbers looked positively bloodless, not unlike the specimens one may observe any day of the week buzzing, beeping, chirping and peeping through the tubes traversing Greater Boston (if there is such a thing)—they don't call 'em WASPs for nothin'! But these were not wasps. These were chiggers. And at length one of them raised one of his bloodless yet febrile and oddly clawlike little hands.

"Mr. Bukowski?"

"Yes?"

"Um . . . we . . . uh, um . . . would you suggest writing as a career?"

That's your punch line. Just imagine asking Archie Shepp, "Would you suggest free jazz as a career?" Charles Bukowski worked in the post office, with unpaid overtime, for 14 straight years. Eventually he got desperate enough that one night he stopped off on the way home and bought a fifth of whiskey, two six-packs of beer and two packs of cigarettes; as he himself put it later, "I wanted to be a writer and I was scared." That night he got dead drunk and wrote 30 pages. The next night he got dead drunk and wrote 40. Most of what he found on the sofa in the morning, a good deal of which you may be sure he had no memory of composing, was not only usable but good. Literature, even. Many writers try to duplicate experiences like this, since they've bought the myth that to write well you must be a drunken wretch. I'm glad they bought it because most of them are terrible writers who will end up on skid row instead of bothering the rest of us in some capacity or other. Bukowski wrote a novel called *Post Office* in 21 nights. It has been in print for 10 years and gone through several editions. I've read it five times. It's not one of my favorite works of his. Charles Bukowski does not have a career.

You may wonder what all this could possibly have to do with the Co-median Harmonists. Aside from shared national/geographic origins, which is pure chance, and the fact that I suspect Bukowski would like this record very much, the point I am concerned with here is that there are certain types of creative productions: records, books, plays, mono-logues, jokes even, call them what you will, but one of the most signifi-cant things about them for me is that they fit into no genre. Why? Because they are too original. Or too prescient. Or just plain quirky.

But let me ask you a few questions. What is *Sketches of Spain* by Miles Davis and Gil Evans? Is it jazz, since Miles plays on it and even (gasp!) improvises? Is it classical, since it does include awesome renditions of works by the Spanish (all this arbitrary nomenclature is going quotes from here on out) "classical" composers Joaquin Rodrigo and Manuel de Falla? You haven't a clue. Good. That's the way I like to see you. O.K., let's try something in rock, not too arcane—say, *Astral Weeks*, by Van Morrison. On it, Van plays acoustic guitar and sings original songs in an outpouring of poetry that as far as I'm concerned would do Walt Whit-man proud, and kicks ass on anything Allen Ginsberg's managed to come up with in upward of 20 years. Musical accompaniment is provided by the likes of the drummer Connie Kay of the Modern Jazz Quartet, the bassist Richard Davis, who played with Eric Dolphy, and the guitarist Jay Berliner, whose only previous LP exposure to my knowledge was Charles Mingus's ultimate masterpiece, *The Black Saint and the Sinner Lady*, itself yet another unclassifiable work, featuring flamenco guitars, Duke Ellington horn charts, yearning waltzes, gutbucket NYC streetlife blare like a fusillade of lava: taxicabs honking, babies being born, people crying, dying, making love, tenderly comforting the wounded beloved one . . . It's all life, is what it is, which is what I think all the best music is, or writing, for that matter, or anything. Mingus made a point on the front, back and inner sleeves of *The Black Saint and the Sinner Lady*: where the usual logo read, "The New Wave"—that's what they called it!—"of Jazz Is on Impulse!" Mingus saw to it that all over that album the word "jazz" was deleted and "Ethnic Folk-Dance Music" emblazoned instead. A trifle clunky, maybe, but it gets at least part of the point across. And, babe, if you've ever heard that record, you sure do know you can dance to it. Across the crest of the sun.

As I may have said earlier, over the years I have noticed that the music that has meant the most to me, whether in terms of plain old garden variety association (you know, romance and all that stuff), the deeply personal identifications that occur when that magic confluence causes a certain piece of music to come along at a certain time, and—guess what?—it turns out to be better medicine for heart/soul-ache, balm for shredded nerves, them jetstream tropic mambo rumpus when spring breaks out in you lubricious unto delirium in any old time of the year—somehow, always, I end up with music, the soundtracks to whatever latest escapades ('cause I am truly obnoxious, carry armloads of albums with me everywhere I go), refusing to fall into your generic categories which, by the way, have you noticed in the stores they getting 'em ever-narrower defined till one day we're gonna wake up and the only way to tell *The Heartbreakers Live at Max's Kansas City Vol. VII* from *Chuck Mangione Plays Rupert Holmes Gorillas For Unicef* will be by dat big old black-n-white PRICE CODE slapped right on the front of every album? Cover art? Who needs it? We gotta veritable New Hebrides among computer filing systems what don't give diddley iffen you think y'all just gonna barge in here splitting whocares hairs such as por exemplo Judy Holliday and Billie Holiday now wasn't they sisters somewhere backthere in the corncrib we'll file 'em together anyhoo they're both dead after all.

And that's the present and future state of the art of the music business, which is why I am more than merely proud to be associated with this set. I'm honored because, friends, if you'll just take my little words here on good faith, buy this sucker, take it home and slide it on that turntable, I guarantee you gonna have a listening experience like unto you never previously suspected existed in this galaxy at least. And they didn't even have to fall back on no *Star Wars* synthesizer gimcracks. Nope. This music sounds like it was recorded in the ballrooms of Heaven, and that's right, I'm talking about that place where all those peculiar emanations plop theyselves on stray cloudlets and Hendrixify just a tad now and then on all them golden harps. Here, you have one too, easy to play, ain't it?

But, I still hear you screaming, where in God's name did this stuff COME FROM? The answer is that I don't know. Haven't the foggiest. I do know that it was recorded in Germany pre-Hitler, mid–20s to

early 30s, that everybody in the band is white, that they've absorbed
black soul, gospel, blues, ragtime and SOMETHING ELSE
AFRICAN that really sproings the chilly willies up your spine (eat your
hearts out Byrne 'n' Eno, these kraut kats only beatcha by about 55
years!). Also you'll hear plenty purely Germanic trills bitten and uvular
shimsham, often corkscrewing through at the oddest moments convey-
ing palpable deja views of secondary blears from the most vintage car-
toons made in the same era and neck o' the glove this music was.
Which is another good thing about it, its completely unexpected diver-
sity of appeal. Why, you could slap this on the box and sit some
dopesmokin' ponytailed Grateful Deadheads right knee-to-knee with
the brittlest herringbone-cheeked SoHo artiste nouveau-punquelettes
and they wouldn't even claw blood and de-snaggletooth each other!
Not one hincty snoot lanced for drill even. Comedian Harmonists promote Peace & Love wherever, whenever they play!

And if you want to know why I'll tell you. Because of what I was talking about before: what you are holding in your hands ain't no career.
These guys didn't record, say, "Creole Love Call" (my far-and-away
absolute favorite cut; I think this truly sounds like it could have been
recorded on some astral plane) because they'd heard Duke Ellington
was hip and maybe moving some product in the States so they'd cover
it quick cross the pond. They recorded it because they loved Duke
Ellington so deeply and were so moved by the original that they just
had to say thank you some way and this was fortunately for us the best
way they knew how. I can't speak or read German—almost all music
I've heard from that country since these sides were cut makes me nervous at best. But I've been listening to music and at least trying to keep
my ears open for the real thing amid the tides of dross long enough
that I think I can still tell when something is done not only professionally and technically up but with pure hearts collectively welling for a
long-awaited outpouring of love for their mentors, their accompanists,
each other, whatever audiences (and of whatever kind!) they may have
had, and most of all, for their music. When was the last time you heard
someone sing for joy? Unalloyed.

What I'm interested in is people with musical obsessions they're driven to work out. In the cases of the Comedian Harmonists, I just kinda
suspect they were a bunch of nice, unsuspecting German guys who

some smartass slapped upside the head with their first blast of black American music one day, which musta been some kinda religious experience for them (I know it was for me, and I was born here), after which they were never quite the same again. Admittedly, it musta been more than a little schizo at times. Because there is, all delicate political questions aside, a certain emotionalism in American music, a passion of a particular kind, and I am not even just talking about black music, that seems absolutely antithetical to everything German music is about structurally, conceptually, attitudinally. But believe me, there is something deep in the, well, soul of that society, national identity or whatever, that shoots off a hotline emergency interrupt call straight down to the gut every time that big American beat starts up again, the Voice of Control, where it issues from sepulchrally intoning booty-defamations leaden with dread, fear and God knows whatall else.

One of the things I like best about this album is the way it transcends the usual inevitably somewhat sickly trappings of "nostalgia"-oriented disks. I'm sorry, but I had one childhood, one adolescence, and (particularly re the pube phase) once was more than enough. Maybe it's my age, but I have absolutely no referents for this music. Yet it sounds somehow familiar. There's nothing creepy about it, don't get paranoid you're gonna look up all rosy-cheeked and blanch at Hitler leering in the wings. It has nothing to do with "Cabaret"-style decadence chopped 'n' channeled into mass-marketable kitsch, either (always hated that play). Like I said, this music is from outer space. That's just about the only way I can begin to convey the effect it has on me. Brian Eno once said the same thing about his first exposure to American a cappella doo wop groups of the early '50s he heard when he was a little boy growing up near an American military base in the Midlands in England. So maybe even in a curious way it's tit for tat: we gave them the Five Satins, and they gave us this; but whatever on earth are we going to do with it?

Like those old doo wop records that made li'l Eno's wig flapjack, these recordings serve perhaps their most important and heartening message in reminding us yet again that they can invent all the synthesizers, computers, phase shifters, distortion boxes, 980-track boards and what have you they want—I use all that stuff myself, whenever somebody's foolish enough to let me get my hands on some of it—but there never has been and never will be any substitute for the pure soul and directness of the human voice, rolling up outta that throat so tremulously glad to be the official megaphone for that temple of un-ending mysteries and delights simply known as you and me. So spend those few bucks on this (if ever there was) one-of-a-kind platter, check in on these sauerbraten bashos' stopsout pearlpure whoopup, then let yourself loose, throw back your head and yawp out a joyful noise unto the Lord or whoever else you wanna annoy. I'll be right there beside you.

JONNY WHITESIDE

Merle Haggard's Twin Oracles

Induction into the Country Music Hall of Fame is as high an honor as any country performer can attain, a validation reaching far beyond engraved-plaque prestige and industry recognition. When California singer Merle Haggard got the Hall of Fame nod in 1994, he took the stage, slick and dignified in a beaded, black-on-black outfit. With an intense gaze into the audience, Haggard produced a thick roll of paper, announcing that it was a list of all those deserving thanks. It unscrolled, hit the floor and kept rolling a good six feet across the stage. Behind him, horror froze the gleaming smile on presenter Marty Stuart's face; Nashville held its breath. "First of all," Haggard solemnly intoned, "I'd like to thank Andy Gump, my plumber—you're doin' a great job keepin' my toilets workin', Andy . . ." Haggard stared into the camera. A pause, a wicked grin, the briefest of acknowledgments, and he walked off the stage.

That moment of potential chaos—carried live on network television—made it clear that while Haggard may have been pardoned by the state of California, he has certainly never reformed. After almost 40 years in the business, stacks of awards, dozens of gold records (38 No. 1 hits), he remains a musical and social renegade, beholden to none. Part jailbird, part sensitive troubadour, all-around rugged individualist, Haggard stomps to his own distinctive, internal syncopation.

Without doubt, Haggard rates as one of the greatest artists the Golden State has ever produced, a folk-song chronicler and outspoken crusader trafficking in generally ignored subject matter. From dustbowl émigrés to itinerant Chicano field laborers, much of his music is born of and reflective upon life in California. Haggard has managed it on such a grandly sweeping and successful scale that he's wholly unrivaled. Yet today, at age 62, with all his considerable talents intact, he operates in a strange, cloudy netherworld.

For the past few years, Haggard has avoided almost entirely the conventional trappings and obligations of the music business. He has no binding recording contract and is in no hurry to sign one. (*For the Record*, Haggard's current RCA set of remakes of his hits, is strictly an open-ended option deal and, with duets featuring hot country duo Brooks & Dunn and pop pinup Jewel, rates as simple exploitation.) The public's only access to his music—since radio has not played a new Haggard release since 1994's *In My Next Life*—is at personal appearances. Haggard just doesn't give a damn about the hustle and hype, and, since being released from his contract with Curb Records in 1996, has been between tours that tend to favor outlying sub-suburban venues, steadily recording and writing—stacking up, by his count, a total of some 130 unreleased tracks.

Thus Haggard's Shadetree Manor studio has become his focal point and spiritual center. Tucked among the rolling hills of Palo Cedro, in the middle of an expansive nowhere flanked by Mount Shasta and active volcano Lassen, the sprawling, razor-wire-walled compound is Haggard's own empire. Entering the studio on a cold, rainy morning, one first notices a reverently displayed series of photographs and memorabilia that represent the singer's idols and tribal history: an on-set group shot from Buck Owens' pre-superstardom Washington TV show, featuring Buck's then-wife, Bonnie Owens, Haggard's longtime horn player Don Markham and a very young Loretta Lynn; a portrait of the cast from the Bakersfield hillbilly TV show *Cousin Herb's Trading Post Gang*, depicting cohorts Bonnie Owens, Roy Nichols and Fuzzy Owen. There's a huge enlargement of a color snapshot of influential California country singer Wynn Stewart, and a framed 45 r.p.m. record with an engraved plaque that reads, "The last recording ever made by Wynn Stewart." There's a framed portrait of Bob Wills, and scattered throughout are gold records, dozens of BMI song awards, an assortment of other trophies, honors.

The second thing one notices is the tangy aroma of freshly burned cannabis ("Son," Haggard said in 1974, "Muskogee is the *only* place I don't smoke it"), and the third is Haggard's eyes, dark and unblinking. That gaze—probing, intimidating, curious—is like staring down into a vortex. The ruts and wrinkles lining this face seem to suck up all the available shadows.

In the studio, Haggard is working on a series of gospel duets with Al Brumley Jr., son of the gospel songwriter who penned "I'll Fly Away" and a friend since he and Haggard worked together in Bakersfield, circa 1961. The pair is immersed in anecdotal repartee that shifts, just like the set list of a well-rounded country show, back and forth from hilarity to misery.

The between-takes conversation twists from subject to subject, first to Dr. Gene Scott, the maverick Los Angeles televangelist (on whose Sunday-afternoon KDOC broadcasts Haggard and his band, The Strangers, appear every few months); for the past several years, Scott has been irritating fundamentalists with videotapes of his frolics with buxom, miniskirted, er, bodyguards. "I heard a rumor that he had to get rid of most of 'em," Haggard says. "Ol' Doc found out they were actually private investigators sent to spy on him, hired by the government or somebody . . ."

Talk meanders to Marty Haggard, the troubled son whose erratic behavior, general malfeasance and two-part *National Enquirer* "Daddy Dearest" hatchet job led Haggard to seek a restraining order against him last year. "He went on that radio show, told that story 'bout me locking him in the trunk," Haggard says. "And Cash, man, he's really angry. He said, 'God may forgive him, but I won't.'" Brumley blinks at that one: "Cash said *that?*" "Hell, yes. Marty went down to Nashville, took money from Cash, took money from just about everybody I know down there. I'd paid off a $65,000 note on a house of his. Honestly, I think it was that head injury—he was in a terrible head-on collision, you know."

Haggard, clad in a shiny black track suit and a pair of those corny running shoes with built-in blinking lights, shakes his head and swigs off a handy half-pint of George Dickel Tennessee Whisky. Haggard doesn't drink much these days, swore off cigarettes over a decade ago, but right now, like a bebop jazz cat, he's using the juice, breaking free, kick-starting his brain up into a loose, uninhibited musicality. They get back to work on the vocals. Haggard studies his verses, singing them two or three times, giving each run-through entirely different readings, phrasing the notes in distinct modifications within each bar of music. It's an impressive display of technique, and once he settles on the preferred approach, he nails it. One take.

As engineer Lou Bradley rewinds for playback, Theresa, Haggard's (fifth) wife, and a couple of the kids drift in. She's a slim blond in her mid–30s, a quiet yet forceful presence. "I've got some potato soup and corn bread for your lunch, Merle," she tells him. Haggard, giddy from his just-concluded performance, shoots back, "Well, that's fine, but did you make enough for Al and Lou and Jonny? Here, listen to this . . ." Bradley rolls the tape of Brumley Jr.'s "Marching Across Jordan," and at the close Theresa opines that "it feels just like church." Haggard ponders that a moment, tilts the bottle again and shouts, "Yessir, the devil's gonna get pissed off when he hears that!"

A peck on the cheek, a pat on the head, and the family withdraws. Haggard sends Brumley into the booth for his part on the next tune, riding him with merciless glee until every syllable is satisfactorily delivered. It's clear that Haggard is never as happy as when he's in control, and that the object of that control is nothing less than perfection—and that goes for his lunch, too. Not long after the family departs, he suddenly says, "I'll be right back," and disappears for 15 minutes. An hour or so after his return, the phone rings. It's Theresa. Haggard gets on the phone. "What?" he cries. "Someone put bacon in your potato soup? Who in the world'd do that?" Evil grin. "And keep on cookin' it. Potato soup's no good unless it's really cooked well."

Haggard's back in the booth now, pipe in hand. *Flic-CLICK*. *Sssssssssssssss*. A long draw. A huge cloud of blue smoke, a hand signal to Bradley, and he's singing—charged and transported. Haggard's voice flows with understated, hypnotic style, drawing as much from precise doses of theatrical emotion as it does from breath control and intonation, the set of the jaw and the distance between mouth and microphone.

It's another one-take job. The song is a Brumley Sr. composition. "Al's daddy wrote it," Haggard explains, "and it was one of my daddy's favorites. I remember him singin' it to me when I was a kid, us sitting together on the living-room couch." Hearing Haggard deliver "I Dreamed I Saw Mama and Daddy"—in which the protagonist encounters the spirits of his deceased parents, who whisper, "Oh look, it's our little boy"—is chilling.

Much of what made Merle Haggard the mile-high artistic figure he is can be found in this particular subject, for it was the death of his father that scarred and shaped his psyche, introducing the disarray that would become a recurring and perversely sustaining element in his life. Without his beloved daddy's anchor, Haggard drifted into a series of ill-advised misadventures that eventually got him thrown in prison. This almost entirely self-imposed strife has led Haggard to refine the art of playing both ends against the middle in virtually every aspect of his personal and professional life, and is, perhaps, the key to understanding his character and successes.

Oildale, a tough little burg just across the Kern River from Bakersfield, was Haggard's point of entry, born there to Oklahoma immigrants James and Flossie Haggard on April 6, 1937. Nine years later, James suffered a stroke and soon died, leaving Flossie to raise Merle and his older brother and sister. By the time Merle was in his early teens, he was already roaming as far off as Texas, getting stomped by misanthropic rednecks, picked up by police cruisers, and winning friends via an uncanny ability to sing just like Lefty Frizzell, the Lone Star honky-tonk god who'd made history in 1951 by dominating the *Billboard* Top 10 with four concurrent hit songs.

As a youth, Haggard had knocked around the joints, as fan and performer, and been in and out of various juvenile detention facilities, accruing both considerable musical skill and a not-insignificant criminal rap sheet. Eventually, the latter dominated his life, and after he was caught fleeing a break-in scene with a heisted check machine, the ensuing federal charge and his history as an incorrigible landed him in San Quentin, his home away from home from 1957 until 1960.

By 1961, Haggard seemed, despite his evident talent, like just another Bakersfield screw-up, striving to stay out of trouble and make enough money to raise his quickly growing family. The launch of his music career was fortuitous: One day at KERO television, which broadcast *Cousin Herb's Trading Post Gang*, producer Al Brumley Jr., then 23, got a phone call from a stranger asking if he'd be willing to listen to his brother-in-law, whom he described as "a pretty good singer." "I said, 'Well, bring him in,'" Brumley recalls. "I always kept a guitar in the office there, and so he walks in, and he was Merle. I could tell right off the bat that he had it, so we put him on the show. He started at two nights a week, and then he was on three nights a week, and everything started from there."

At that time the cast of *Cousin Herb* included Roy Nichols, the former Maddox Brothers & Rose and Lefty Frizzell guitarist who was, as Brumley says, "idolized by everyone." Other regulars were a young Bonnie Owens, who'd caused a sensation as a singing waitress at several local nightclubs, and Fuzzy Owen, a respected Bakersfield singer-songwriter who'd recently partnered with California honky-tonk hero Lewis Tally to found Tally Records, an indie label operating out of a nearby garage. It was not long after Haggard's first appearance at KERO, Brumley says, "that Fuzzy began making statements to the effect of 'I'm going to make him a star.'"

Owen made good on the promise, succeeding to a far greater degree than anyone at KERO had imagined and igniting one of the most complex and longest-running dramas in country-music history. In '61, Merle Haggard was a charismatic and beautiful young man, the shadow of his recent incarceration casting an air of melancholy mystery about him. With the young singer's clear-toned voice, natural proclivity for curling a phrase in all the right spots and desperate need to find a steady job that he would not loathe, Owen had found a prospect worth developing. Haggard had found a man to trust; not long after Tally began recording him, Capitol hitmaker Ken Nelson, who had already made Buck Owens a major star, approached Haggard and offered him a deal—the ticket out of Kern County and onto national stages. Haggard did not hesitate. "No," he answered. It didn't take long to outgrow Tally, however, and the Owen-Tally-Haggard team eventually, and gladly, signed on with Capitol. By 1965, Haggard's carefully crafted sound was a commercial smash.

As a writer, Haggard radically expanded the psychology and themes of country music. Cheating songs gave way to tales of revenge and cruelty, even bald misogyny ("I'm Gonna Break Every Heart I Can"); celebrating the underdog took on unorthodox new proportions ("I'll Be a Hero (When I Strike)"). In Haggard's hands, flag-waving became an aggressive, accusatory affair, and an ongoing theme, from the late '60s' "Fightin' Side of Me" to 1988's "Me and Crippled Soldiers." His sound, often with deep acoustic guitar rhythms and angular, tricky steel- and electric-guitar fills, was austere, stark, and his voice slid through the mix as a rich counterpoint of tradition and audacity.

In the Shadetree studio, where the gilded Hall of Fame plaque seems to loom over Haggard's shoulder, the high-hog dreams seem long since past. Finally, Haggard shoots a direct question: "Just what exactly is it you came up here to find out?" The answer is obvious: Why in the hell are you recording hundreds of new songs with what seems like not a chance that anybody will ever hear them?

"Well," he says, "we got some real good possibilities. We got some record contracts. But what we're findin' out is, everybody since Gene Autry—including Bing Crosby and Bob Wills, all the people who pioneered modern recorded music—they never got paid! And people are *still* not gettin' paid. And I started realizin' it, and the minute I did, they started thinkin', 'Uh-oh, got a problem here.' So they tried to murder me, musically, tried to put my music in a casket. Curb did."

Scowling, voice even-toned, Haggard sounds like the old campaigner regrouping between skirmishes, assessing casualties, surveying the replacement troops: "It's a lot easier to bullshit the young boys and young girls they're signing to these fantastic record deals that aren't worth the paper they're written on. Oh, they might get paid the first two or three checks, but it's a fraction of what they've got comin' and it'll be the last money they get, and if they want any more they're goin' to have to hire a law firm to go after it."

Both Haggard and Johnny Cash are currently auditing Sony, the bitter fruit of dealing with an international corporate beast. "Sony, Epic and CBS own the masters," says Haggard, "and Sony, who owned Epic, went and bought [Nashville song publishers] Tree, so they own all my copyrights. Well, you can't get an honest report out of any of 'em, 'cause their attorneys are scratchin' each other's backs, playin' footsie under the table. So I wanted out of it.

"And now they come to me and they want me to re-record 16 songs. I asked 'em, 'Why do you want me to redo "That's the Way Love Goes"? That was a Grammy performance.' And they said, 'We lost it.' They lost several masters in some legal deal—in between themselves. I said, 'You mean it's easier to pay me and lease the recordings from me?' I said, 'You gave me a good idea—I'm gonna make the 16 songs, but I'm gonna keep 'em for myself.'" (These became the cornerstone for Haggard's current *For the Record* release—a project finished only after a deal was struck for an accompanying pay-per-view TV special, forcing him, in typical jumbled style, to return to Palo Cedro between road dates and record more than 30 songs in 72 hours.)

Ultimately, wayward business dealings have led Haggard to a shocking loss—giving up a huge chunk of his song catalog. It's a veritable mother-lode-in-perpetuity of publishing and performance money (his "Today I Started Loving You Again," for instance, has been recorded by 400 artists), but by the early '90s, after four marriages' worth of settlements and alimony, on top of a large collection of antique automobiles, his short-lived Silverthorn resort and nightclub, and various properties and construction costs from Shasta to Bakersfield, Haggard was $5 million in debt. The catalog deal, with Sony Tree paying a very substantial up-front sum, was essentially a bankruptcy bailout (Haggard filed Chapter 11 in 1993).

He's not thrilled with the way it has all played out. "I've been very bitter, and there've been times I've been on the brink of closing down and walkin' away, disappearin' into the woods," he says. "But you can always quit. I'm 62, people still like my music, I've still got friends . . . and I've still got enemies, so I think we should continue to try and do something, because it's gonna be over before you know it anyway. And I'm writing good songs. I got a stack of stuff this high up at the house that'll probably never be recorded."

The prospect is at once tragic and intriguing. At his peak, every successive Haggard album seemed to take fresh new turns, and found him journeying into wild territory, while looking back to his predecessors; his Bob Wills tribute album and re-formation of Wills' surviving Texas Playboys (amazingly, this involved teaching himself to play the fiddle in six months) was one of the great homages in country history. He's worked overtime to keep the music of Jimmie Rodgers alive, and has displayed a tendency to co-write songs when his collaborator was most in need of a boost.

Haggard has also made outsmarting others' expectations a major element in his life. At about the same time that Johnny Cash began to deliberately court the disaffected hippie-folk crowd, Haggard went the other direction with equal success. His biggest hit, "Okie From Muskogee," the flag-waving redneck anthem of 1969, was, of course, a gag, and he wanted to follow it up with "Irma Jackson," an interracial love story blasting intolerance. Capitol refused to release it.

Through the years, Haggard's psychology, along with the timbre of his voice, has significantly deepened. He began probing intensely personal zones with his 1979 *Serving 190 Proof* midlife-crisis album, and by the mid–'80s, many of his songs were fraught with an air of depression that reached dirgelike extremes. When 1990's *Blue Jungle*, his first Curb album, hit the bins, Haggard was clawing at the lock on his cage with venomous, self-castigating rage ("Sometimes I hate myself and wish I could scream . . . there's a curse on my heart . . . I'll never love again"). For all the broad scope of his art, he's also a man with a shocking record of strife involving those closest to him, invariably brought on by that relentless need for control. He brawled bare-knuckled with his late mentor, Lewis Tally, on streets from Bakersfield to Belfast; when he and singer Bonnie Owens decided to marry in 1965, Haggard telephoned guiding light Fuzzy Owen—it was a ghastly sucker punch for the Bonnie-smitten Fuzzy ("How could you do this?" the distraught Owen cried. "You know I've loved her for years!").

As important (and forgiving) as Fuzzy Owen and Lewis Tally were in Haggard's life, it was another, Wynn Stewart, without whom he might never have gotten off the ground. Stewart gave Haggard not only his first professional job, but also his first hit, "Sing a Sad Song" in 1963.

"Wynn's sound was what influenced Buck and me both," Haggard says, "and in a strange twist of fate, his band was the heart of the old Frizzell band—Roy Nichols was part of the Lefty band, and he went to Wynn Stewart and ran into Ralph Mooney, who played the steel, and they were the basis of the modern West Coast sound."

When Haggard first made his mark with Tally Records, it was during a turning point for country music. The hillbilly corn of the 1940s and '50s had little context in the jet age; Nashville reacted by pouring sweet string syrup over the same themes and messages. But there were a handful of renegade stylists actively mapping out new territory, and introducing subtle but deeply influential new approaches. The distinction of being a modern country artist is important to Haggard, and important when one attempts to begin to understand the man's complex inner workings. That modern upshift was easily the idiom's single greatest artistic leap, and Merle Haggard became the most creative and successful practitioner in its development. But it's equally important to remember that the nightclub culture that produced Haggard, Owens and Stewart was wide-open, as much pop and rock & roll as it was hillbilly—a tradition reflected by Haggard's numerous inclusions of pop and show tunes on his albums ("It's All in the Game," "Thank Heaven for Little Girls"), and Owens frequently throwing "The Macarena" and "Play That Funky Music White Boy" into his current stage show.

Haggard, who has graced the cover of jazz bible *Down Beat*, seems weary of being labeled as anything at all. After all, he'd invented an artistic persona, a sort of hillbilly Frankenstein: "I thought, 'You know what I'll do? I'll take a little bit of Lefty, a little bit of Elvis, a little Wynn Stewart, a little bit of Ernest Tubb and the other influences I had—Jimmie Rodgers, Chuck Berry, Grady Martin and Roy Nichols, Bob Wills—and just be honest with it, try to make somethin' out of what I was.' Well, it worked. It was a new pie.

"It really wasn't part of the Nashville sound. It came from Texas and all over the West. I thought, if I combine all that, maybe I can come up with something sustaining. And it started happening, even as early as when Wynn was kind enough to give me 'Sing a Sad Song' and it went into the charts. And from that day, from 1962 until 1991, we were never absent from *Billboard*, *Cashbox*, *Record World*—we were never out of the charts for almost 30 years."

Those days are behind him now. Haggard settles deeper into a chair behind the studio board, tugs the brim of his ball cap down low: "The music is a way of takin' it out of them. You can cuss 'em out in the song, or you can just lump it and say nothin'. I've been fortunate enough to take out my political and personal convictions on the public in a song, and it's sure bound to release some tension. It's a great feeling, it's something wild, being a writer. It's a body of work, and you keep tryin' to kick that same height on the wall. Because you know where your best is at, more than any of the people around you, and you know how hard it was to get to that."

It's been a remarkably circuitous route, marked by a tendency toward self-imposed burdens; by the early '80s, Haggard's band, the Strangers, was dazzling, a hillbilly jazz orchestra featuring not only Nichols, but former Texas Playboys Eldon Shamblin, Jimmy Belken and Tiny Moore, players who exuded an epic magic that no other country band since has been able to approach. But Haggard managed to screw even that up—the angry departure of Nichols and the firing of Moore coincided roughly with an ugly, litigious falling-out between Haggard and his longtime friend and business associate Tex Whitson; Haggard even temporarily fired Bonnie Owens last year.

Haggard is an odd one, with his own unique sense of logic; once, a pair of young pickers recounted the troubles amphetamines had caused them, telling Haggard they were quitting for good. "Bullshit!" he snapped. "What if you had to drive to Alaska—right now?" But he's sharp—any particular date, any subject's age, Haggard's got the correct answer, which, in the road-weary, pill-happy upper echelons of country music, is a rare quality. None of this is downplayed; at a recent Southern California appearance, he playfully crooned, "Since I was a little kid/everything I did/ I did on marijuana."

"I think the '90s is a modern, technical version of the '70s with the freedom extracted out of it," he says. Or, veering wildly, "They're reportin' high-altitude airplanes with contrails—they're sprayin' us with somethin', and people are comin' down with these terrible respiratory problems. I seen 'em myself, and I'm thinking, 'Damn! Could it be that they're tryin' to exterminate us?' I've got an office in Arizona, and they're bringing into our National Guard people from the United Nations Guard—they're comin' into Arizona by the thousands, and as to what they're expecting over there, I don't know. The most disturbing thing I've read is, when you sign on as a serviceman in the United States, the last thing you agree to do is gun down your own people if necessary. So there's some serious things happening. . . . "

One moment he seems backed into a corner, the next he's perfectly at ease, and precisely where he wants to be. Haggard doesn't have to prove anything, yet he seems as desirous of recognition as ever. One reason he refuses to sign a long-term deal with any company is because he knows they won't provide the full-bore promo push an artist such as Haggard expects. "He wants to be able to walk into Kmart and see a bigger-than-life statue of himself alongside his latest album," Brumley says, "and that's exactly what should be happening."

In the studio, conversation between Haggard, Brumley and engineer Lou Bradley always swings back, like a compass point, to a handful of subjects and country personalities. There's talk of Lefty, it flows to Wynn Stewart, and it ripples gleefully to ribald slap-bass renegade Fred Maddox. Haggard sends Bradley to dig up the tape of a recording Maddox made at Shadetree Manor one day. En route to sister Rose's home, Maddox had telephoned out of the blue: "Merle? You got a studio out there, don'tcha? I'm gonna come over and cut this song." Bradley cues the tape. It's "Give Me Back My Fifteen Cents (and I'll Go Home to Mommy)," a typically strange Maddox statement on love and marriage framed as a novelty romp. Maddox's nasal drawl floods the studio, singing about a pretty little girl, tying the fatal knot, playing the devil. Haggard is beaming, then roaring with laughter, clapping his hands, stomping his feet. Maddox's is a voice from beyond the grave.

Talk shifts to another key Haggard ally, the great songwriter Tommy Collins, who's been fighting emphysema. Haggard happily announces that when he recently telephoned Collins, "he sounded like a kid again—got a new woman, says he's crazy about her." The temporal aspects of life suddenly loom; out of the blue, Haggard launches into "The Four Dogs," an unrecorded Collins song. Told from the viewpoint of a mountain hermit, it's part religious allegory, part secular introspection. The four dogs—Love, Hope, Faith and Pure Hell—lead their master on a surreal journey, leaping over a steep precipice and landing, unharmed, in Paradise, where, of course, things sour. Haggard bids engineer Bradley to dig out the demo Haggard made of it 15 years ago, delivered in a weird brogue. The four-minute recitation winds to a close—it turns out that Love and Pure Hell are twins, and then the tape segues into a stunning Haggard original, "Love and Hell" (". . . are never far apart").

Haggard is soaking it up, lost in the rich, haunted wordplay—the essence, in effect, of his life and career. "Ain't that the truth, though?" Brumley muses. "They really are twins, and it can go either way in an instant—it's just which choice you make."

"That's absolutely right," Haggard says. "That's it . . . "

SASHA FRERE-JONES

Run-D.M.C.

SINCE KINDERGARTEN I ACQUIRED
THE KNOWLEDGE: INTRO

April 1983
I'm a 16-year-old rap devout and it's Friday night, so I gotta go to
church. Thursday nights Afrika Islam preaches very late at night on
WHBI, but the weekend nights belong to Mr. Magic's Rap Attack
on WBLS and whoever is spinning on WRKS 98.7. I have Maxells on
hand, always. I greet my friends by saying "super super blast blast
PKKHWOWW!" like Magic does.

Saturday morning, my friend Tom calls me.

"Yo, you going to Kealy's party tonight?"

"Yeah, I guess."

"Did you hear that 'Sucker MCs' song?"

"No. I fell asleep."

But I've got Friday night on tape, so I go back to the C-90 and cue
up the second side. After a long, super-super-mega-blast exclusive intro, Mr. Magic indeed plays "Sucker MCs," by something called Run-
D.M.C. I stare at the meters on my tape deck. They look OK. The
tape isn't distorting. What's up? Where's the rest of the music? It's just,
like, one crazy drum machine beat and these guys yelling. It's not really
a party tune, it has no hook, and it's all jumped up. The music is alien

but the words are easy to understand, specific. One guy says he went to St. John's University. I don't know what to think.

I walk over the Brooklyn Bridge to J&R Music World and buy the 12". The red and black Profile generic sleeve. Run-D.M.C. "It's Like That" followed by "Sucker MCs (Krush-Groove 1)," neither listed as A or B sides. Mixed by Kurtis Blow, music by Orange Krush? Even after I listen to it some more, I can't figure it out. It doesn't even have a bass line. And what the hell is "Krush-Groove 1"? Will there be another?

That night, most of my high school is at the party. I ask a fellow rap fiend what he thinks of the song. He likes it. I am troubled. It's the first time my love of rap music has been shaken. Suddenly, the song starts playing on the stereo and whatever is left teetering inside of me falls over the edge. It's the first really hard beat in rap, sounding aggressive before the words have a chance to announce it. As much empty space as music, it's abstract noise compared to the smiley funk retreads and synths on the radio. The rhyming style isn't singsongy, suave, or part of any known continuum. Run and D.M.C. shout, basically, but the rhymes go back and forth like beach balls between sea lions, with one finishing the other's line, a strategy that—requiring rehearsal—hasn't been heard since battle crews like Cold Crush Brothers ruled in 1980 and 1981.

That summer, there's a squad of four or five breakdancers with some cardboard and a boombox dancing to "Sucker MCs" on every corner of Fifth Avenue between 47th and 53rd Streets. Even after hearing it 20 times a day, I go home and cue up the 12" to "really" hear it again. Whole sections of my body and mind are unlocked by this ragged stack of electric Legos and blunt language. The world is slightly tilted from then on.

BEATS TO THE RHYME: THE ALBUMS

Run-D.M.C. put rap music through its first overhaul. In 1983, rhymes were mostly bragging and boasting tales of partying and being your bad self. The backing tracks were still largely live renditions of obscure '70s funk tunes, played by Pumpkin and friends at the Enjoy label and the Fats Comet band at Sugar Hill. Some TV themes got recycled, some happy souls let the Roland TR-808 boom a little, and there was some light scratching here and there.

"Sucker MCs" upended that. Run (born Joseph Simmons, November 14, 1964), D.M.C. (born Darryl McDaniels, May 31, 1964) and their DJ, Jam Master Jay (born Jason Mizell, January 21, 1965), made music that was as weird and hard as New York was supposed to be but with rhymes as direct as a cabbie standing in front of you, chewing you out. The fact that the band was from Hollis, Queens, which felt like Brussels to us, just made it more unbelievable. (Hip hop only came from the South Bronx, right? And didn't middle-class people go to St. John's University?)

Run-D.M.C. launched their cannonballs with the significant help of Run's well-known brother, Russell Simmons—coproducer in name, manager, and already rap's most significant *macher*—and the criminally unknown musician/coproducer Larry Smith (a.k.a. Orange Krush), who arranged and played the backing tracks for everything from the first single through *King of Rock*, their second album.

We saw pictures, eventually. They weren't wearing those wack Village People costumes the Furious Five wore or those dopey matching red leather outfits the Treacherous Three and Fearless Four wore. They looked street in their matching Adidas suits (a style swiped from breakdancers), big Cazal eyeglasses, and those weird black fedoras. Sometimes they wore matching black leather suits. That was even cooler. (That summer, lots of people got their Cazals "vicked on the subway by hard rocks." It says so right here in my diary, slang verbatim.)

I had no idea where Hollis, Queens, was, and I assumed it had to be pretty hardcore, since Run-D.M.C. looked a lot tougher than that Deney Terio style the Furious Five were kicking. It eventually emerged in interviews that Hollis wasn't exactly Beirut and that the band was solidly middle class. Rap, like the blues, had gone missing and then been found miles away from its origin point (South Bronx, Mississippi Delta). Rap had been reread, reinforced, and made more itself by "outsiders." Eventually De La Soul would drop the other shoe and make hip hop with clearly visible middle-class roots, but for now, rap's capacity for blunt confrontation and ghetto attitude was being expanded by guys who had been to college, for heck's sake, but were definitely not

trying to make anyone feel more comfortable about using rap as entertainment. Perhaps their distance from ghetto aesthetics allowed Run-
D.M.C. to pull off something their less advantaged forebears were too
deep inside to see. Either way, rap was no longer folk music; it was now
a portable, formal conceit and whoever could do it best would win.

The second Run-D.M.C. single was both a step down and a step up.
"Hard Times" was just a retread of "It's Like That"'s man-on-the-
street reportage but not nearly as casual and straight ahead and, hence,
less powerful. The B-side, "Jam Master Jay," was some other shit—a
song about their DJ, woo-hah. Not since "Wheels of Steel" had we
heard some good good wikky-wikky scratch madness. The group
seemed cooler and more unknown than ever. They were on *Soul Train*
but I missed it. I almost cried.

The third single, "Rock Box," tore the crowd in half and began the
social part of their revolution. Behind some top-shelf rhymes, Eddie
Martinez played a Godzilla metal guitar riff over a huge, slow, not very
syncopated beat. It was total apostasy after the Protestant revolution of
"Sucker MCs." My friends, the white rockers, didn't like it, generally.
Lots of black folks hated hated hated it. I thought it was cool, but I was
worried my favorite group was going to flame out trying to run faster
than the average beat. The single only appeared on the Dance charts;
R&B wouldn't touch it. The night-time rap shows played it a few times
but the daytime black shows didn't know what to do with it.

In May of 1984, Run-D.M.C.'s debut album came out, mostly the
singles compiled with a few goodies. I loved it like the Second Coming
but, man, the artwork was lame. I thought the album would look
Bauhaus and sleek like their music and not all cheeseball like other rap
LPs (all ten of them), but it was a harbinger of much wack rap artwork
to come. (How come punkers could have cool art but rappers couldn't?
I wanted to know.) No matter. Run-D.M.C. had eaten from the Tree
of Knowledge and now anyone could rhyme about any subject over any
beat.

Around that time, a guy I knew to say hello to named Adam
Horovitz came to my school one day talking excitely about how he'd
been one of the background party people on this new record, T La
Rock's "It's Yours." T La Rock had something to do with the Treacherous Three, somebody's brother, I think, and the record was the first re-

lease on a label called Def Jam, Adam told me. Adam was in a band called the Beastie Boys with a guy named Mike from my school. They had done this rap parody called "Cooky Puss," roundly dismissed by all the Islam and Magic devotees. Mike had a lot of cool punk rock records, though, and Adam went out with my friend Samantha. When I bought "It's Yours," catalog number JAM 1, it had the Partytime and Streetwise logos on the label. I figured I'd never see JAM 2.

The second Run-D.M.C. album, *King of Rock*, came out in '85 (the same year they served as the only rap act to step on stage at Live Aid), and was the most massive sophomore slump bummer I had experienced to date. Why was the title track just a copy of "Rock Box"? "Jam-Master Jammin'" didn't, and the drum machines and scratches on "Darryl and Joe (Krush-Groove 3)" kept falling out of time, egregiously so. None of which changed the fact that the group was no longer even paying lip service to black music rules or the vague guidelines established by three or four years of rap charting. Russell Simmons's Def Jam label, started with Long Island longhair Rick Rubin, had already parlayed his brother's stark drum machines and shouting style into a successful market niche, leading with a record by a young kid named L.L. Cool J, a one-man Run-D.M.C. with better chops and deeper wordplay.

My friend Tom told me that the Beastie Boys were hanging out with Rick and had even been signed to Def Jam. Huh? Russell also seemed to be managing every rap group who put out a record. Weird. Ultimately, the kid from my school and Russell Simmons would simultaneously elevate Run-D.M.C. and make them redundant.

Run-D.M.C.'s third album, *Raising Hell*, came out in 1986 and restored my faith in the band, full stop. At a party I threw around then, some guy named Tod Ashley from a great, scary band called Dig Dat Hole kept taking off my party mix tape and playing "Perfection," over and over. It was a measure of the group's position in a fold in pop history that groovy ghoulies who only listened to the Stooges thought Run-D.M.C. were cool while frat boys were simultaneously warming up to them through the baldly crossover track "You Be Illin'" (a kind of blackface anthem that queasily made light of Black English) and the corny product placement "My Adidas." But "Perfection" and "Peter Piper" were astonishing hip hop monster-pieces, their back-n-forth style honed to Wimbledon-like levels. "Is It Live" translated go-go, my obsession of the day, into a fairly credible drum machine pattern, and "Proud to Be Black" was the fierce return of the band's social eyeball—and not a moment too soon, considering who started pumping them at football games.

"My Adidas," Run-D.M.C.'s first Top Ten R&B single, paved the way for their Frankenstein remake of "Walk This Way" with Aerosmith. The first rap single to reach *Billboard*'s Top Ten, it peaked in the fall of 1986 at No. 4 and stayed on the chart for a total of 16 weeks. It made *Raising Hell* the first rap album to reach No. 1 on the R&B charts, the first to go multi-platinum, and the first to go Top Ten Pop. They even appeared on the cover of *Rolling Stone*—the first rappers to do so—but that was largely because of a notorious show that summer in Long Beach, California, when L.A. gang members, outside their usual turf for the concert, went on a rampage before the group even took the stage, forever linking the words "rap" and "violence" for mainstream America.

Coproduced by Rick Rubin and Russell Simmons, *Raising Hell* was making a crossover in a specific direction. It was lots of fun to see Run, D, and Jay on MTV every five minutes but I feared the possible punch-line: that rappers would eventually court white rockers on their turf, if pushed. What the heck did that have to do with "Sucker MCs"?

And then, all of a sudden, the meatheads of America found a way to have their cake and own it too—the Beastie Boys. Although it read to me as a great, snotty, funky inside joke about rap and all the music it could legitimately envelop, *Licensed to Ill* (also produced by Rubin) became, and possibly remains, America's favorite party record. Sure, Run did the backward 808 beat on "Paul Revere" and Run and D wrote "Slow and Low," earning them a "special knowledge" shout-out on the record sleeve, but the torch had been passed. Or grabbed—once the unexpected commercial juggernaut of *Licensed to Ill* began to sail, everything in rap, including *Raising Hell*, became flotsam in its wake. Yup, Run-D.M.C. were rap's Moses, parting the pop waters simply, but profoundly, to reveal that hip hop was there. They made Top Ten hits, tours, and platinum records part of the rap career curve, but in 1987, the aesthetic ante was upped above their heads.

PAUSE: THE DEADLY HIATUS

Two years after *Raising Hell*, Run-D.M.C. could barely get someone to answer the door at Hip Hop Central, much less let them stay overnight. They failed with an unusually great record, an unusually terrible movie, and some unusually bad timing and luck. Fighting with their label Profile for two years, Run-D.M.C. sat out the game until 1988, when they released what could generously be called a blaxploitation homage directed by Rick Rubin and an album, both called *Tougher Than Leather*. All the acronymic bands they had let into the park—BDP, L.L., PE—had taken Run-D.M.C.'s aggressive style way beyond its parents' perimeter.

After BDP's 1987 debut *Criminal Minded*, the "otherness" of crime and poverty became another weapon in the arsenal of Afrocentricity. A powerful one too, as N.W.A.'s *Straight Outta Compton* in 1988 proved it to have more commercial appeal to white listeners (via some pretty dodgy role-playing, but hey, it's all going into the coffers of the revolution, right?) than the classroom caveats of "It's Like That" or "Proud to Be Black." And where BDP's attitude immediately deputized every underclass black person as a soldier in a war against, er, someone, Public Enemy revitalized the classroom approach with music so intense that everyone who didn't sympathize at a street level could still join the revolution simply by cheering on the loudest, densest, angriest black music ever heard. Legible, populist minimalism had lost its mandate.

Tougher Than Leather "only" went platinum but didn't deserve to get lost between the tectonic plates of rap's second and third waves. There was some badass sampling on "Run's House," "How'd Ya Do It, Dee," "I'm Not Going Out Like That," and the stellar Road Runner funk of "Beats to the Rhyme." The corny, stiff stuff—"Mary, Mary," "Papa Crazy"—was more entertaining than last year's cheese, and the only duff track, the clubfooted "Miss Elaine," didn't get in the way of meaty, aggressive hip hop that sounds prescient now.

But that was it for history's window. Life got hard beyond the aesthetic hurdles; Run spent ample time and money in court fighting a rape charge that I really didn't want to know the truth about, while D.M.C. and Jay were rumored to be having some kind of Betty Ford moments, which I also didn't want to hear. Then Jay got into some hellafied car accident and I became officially Sad for My Heroes.

To keep their hand in and see if they could play by someone else's rules, Run-D.M.C. released *Back From Hell* in 1990. While probably their weakest album due to an unconvincing attempt to court the gangsta demographic (they curse!), talk tough (several times!), and generally disguise their voice, it wasn't the dog everyone judged it. In the midst of 1998's received thugisms, it sounds river deep and, except for some lame new jack jacks, it moves, thanks to unsung production by Jam Master Jay and longtime Run-D.M.C. collaborator David (Davy D) Reeves. (Big up for crossing the color barrier again, without fanfare, on "What's It All About," which sampled the Stone Roses' excellent "Fool's Gold.")

Another extended hiatus on the charts followed, even though the band continued to tour, building up a core audience they would eventually call on again. The King became God, and Run became a Reverend. *Down with the King*, in 1993, found the band wearing crucifixes instead of Cazals and riding the super-fine Pete Rock–produced title track to their highest chart position since *Raising Hell*. It was my favorite song for about a month and I marveled at how great it was to hear someone rapping hard and loud without some off-the-rack psycho profile or ghetto sob story. I even dug the Christian angle for variety, but the album wasn't consistent in either musical style or quality, so it confused b-boys of all ages, stumbled on the pop charts and, once again, the group dropped out of sight.

Run popped up as a radio personality delivering daily homilies on New York's Hot 97 and, in late '97, a white techno producer named Jason Nevins turned the beat around yet again. His dopey but effective house remix of "It's Like That" was a minor hit in the U.S. but a global smash, going to No. 1 in several countries. Big Beaters like the Chemical Brothers, meanwhile, were reviving legible, crunchy beats and signifiers of the b-boy era like scratching, boomy sounds, and shouted catchphrases. In early 1998, hip hop obscurants Company Flow sampled "Beats to the Rhyme" for their "End to End Burners" single and every time somebody asked him, Chuck D would remind us that Run-D.M.C. were his favorite live group ever. Run-D.M.C.'s essentially populist vision was back in popular consciousness.

I pulled out all the albums after I heard Red Alert play "Beats to the Rhyme" on Hot 97's "Old School at Noon" one day. I was shocked at how great they sounded, how little they did wrong. And when they did slip—*cf.* "Mary, Mary"—it was the kind of risk you wish hip hoppers took now, if only to change the pace.

Go ahead and lean on their songbook: no bitch rhymes (unless you count "Dumb Girl," quaint by post-Snoop standards, or using "nagging wife" as an insult), no gun talk, early turntablism, and a rock-in-my-rap Reese's that still bangs. With very little cursing but loud as anything, local but weird, spare but as expansive as foam, Run-D.M.C. disregarded history and helped make hip hop the most resilient popular music of my brief lifetime.

Now, What's My Name?:
Bonus Resurrection Beats

October 11, 1998:
Tramps, NYC
I am surrounded by lots of the frat guys who made me, in a display of disloyalty, forget about my heroes the first time around. But there are also lots of old school black guys in their 40s with dates in the house, all dressed up, good church style. After waiting long enough to foment a little catcalling and booing, the group throws us a bone and makes us ask for the meat. Jam Master Jay comes out in black leather, black fedora, black T-shirt. There is no distance between me and the meatheads. My hands are in the air. Yes, I will yell loud enough for Run and D to hear me. Yes, we want to see Run-D.M.C. When they come out, time dissolves in the roar.

Hell, how old is 31 anyway? I'm an oldie?

Run's a little heavier but D.M.C.'s looking super buff, and the show is, if possible, louder and faster. Nobody's lost their fastball; Run even does some kinda Twista-style speed a capella, and gets oddly generous applause when he name-checks *Krush Groove*. The show moves fast, everyone hitting their marks, songs dropping and stopping on the one. It's only an hour and I don't love the medleys, but man, do I feel all scrubbed-down and groovy.

Run says they've signed to Arista—"We aren't on Profile anymore. We went from the pit to the penthouse." They leave, too early, and return to do "Peter Piper" and "Down with the King." Run says: "As sweaty and tired as we are, we're going to go over there and sign T-shirts for you, shake hands, and say what up. You know why? There's only one reason we would do this. It's three words. We love you."

TONY SCHERMAN

On Song

When I was in my early teens, my father and I spent countless Sunday afternoons driving around the Hudson Valley in his Volkswagen Beetle. We often sang—rather, he sang and I sometimes joined in.

I didn't know many of the hundreds of Tin Pan Alley and Broadway show tunes in his repertory; besides, their shapely melodies, full of sharps, flats and key changes, were daunting. If I ventured to add my voice, my father quickly left the melody in my quavery custodianship to improvise a flawless harmony. Hitting an especially piquant interval, he would turn to me and say something like, "Flatted sixth," his feigned complacence masking the pleasure he took in the sharpness of his ear. I wouldn't have known a flatted sixth if it had come crashing through the VW's roof and knocked me on the head.

My father was unusually musical, but that's not the point. He grew up in an America whose pop tunes, the music he and his friends imbibed as youths, were often highly sophisticated pieces of work. (My mother is from a musical culture, too, but that's another story; she's Viennese.) My father's generation, raised on Berlin, Gershwin, Porter and Kern, developed a harmonic acuity, a suppleness of ear, that mine lacks.

I grew up on the three chords of rock-and-roll, on Phil Spector, Bob Dylan and the Rolling Stones (and The Beatles, of course, but they were an anomaly, their chord progressions unpredictable, their melodies hard to harmonize to). Music meant as much to my friends and me as it had to my father and his contemporaries—more, I think, for it was the emblem of our resistance to the conventions we considered our parents trapped in. Lyrically, our music was more interesting than all but a few show tunes. That was Dylan's significance, after all: to give pop lyrics the resonance of literature. But Dylan's harmonies are crude compared with Gershwin's and Porter's. We and our musical heroes were, and are, stuck in the blues, in simple triads and major keys that would have bored Gershwin to tears. I'm not saying that everyone who grew up in the '30s can sing perfect harmony and identify tricky intervals; I'm saying that music fans today have a less intuitive grasp of two of music's essential building blocks, harmony and melody, than they had 50 years ago.

I can't marshal much hard evidence for my argument. But given the millions of hours of piano lessons my father's generation collectively squirmed through, once as standard a feature of middle-class family life as the upright in the parlor; given the harmonically rich tunes that once floated daily from Times Square office buildings out across the nation; given that America's favorite dance hits once had enough intellectual meat to pique the improvisational genius of a Charlie Parker or a Lester Young—given these facts, these vanished aspects of everyday American life, it's hard not to suspect that the average pop-music listener, circa 1940, was more alive to the full range of musical expression than his or her baby-boom offspring.

Forty-five and graying, almost as old as my father was when we took those drives, I eye my future uneasily. Am I going to spend the rest of my life listening to rock-and-rollers chase threadbare melodies across three chords? And what about the generation after mine, the Tone-Def Generation, reared on music in which melody and harmony are even more attenuated? It would be easy to argue that the last five decades represent a wholesale dumbing-down of America's musical public.

Culture's path is never that simple. My father's hummed bass lines may have been harmonically ingenious, but their four-to-the-bar uniformity always irked me. In rock and its spawn, rhythm has supplanted harmony and melody as the creative motor. You don't need to be a hip-hop fan (although you do need a good sense of rhythm) to hear the skill and creativity of more than a few rappers, deejays and remix artists. Is it possible that the young people who flock to today's dance clubs are developing an awareness of rhythmic nuance equal to an earlier generation's harmonic sophistication?

Rhythm's new prominence reflects a seismic cultural shift. As the world shrinks, Euro-America is awash in influences once beneath its notice. The rhythm-rich sounds of Africa and the African diaspora, whether Nigerian juju, Brazilian samba or African-American funk, now pervade pop music. Today's musicians draw on, and today's listeners absorb, rhythmic riches that were unimaginable 40, or even 20, years ago.

Still, how excited can you get about pop's expanding rhythmic possibilities if our awareness of harmony and melody is atrophying? Nor am I at all comfortable with some of the social implications of rhythm's hegemony. When the *New York Times* critic Jon Pareles recently wrote that in an era of overload, rhythm organizes time and information in manageable, pleasurable ways, he touched on a troubling state of affairs: the enervating sensory glut that makes serenity all but impossible today. And Mr. Pareles' judgment that contemporary pop's reduced melodies are the victims of shrinking attention spans—well, it's a chilling thought.

My father and I weren't just tooling around the suburbs, of course; we were traversing the century, navigating its currents. He died 20 months ago. As the months lengthen into years, I miss him more and more. A small part of that ache, I think, is that his death severed my living connection to an already faraway place: an America whose pace was leisurely enough for its pop music to be elegant. My father's ear thrived on the music of those centenarians Gershwin and Ellington, whom my generation may admire but does not love. Our souls belong to Elvis, and we pay the price.

SUSAN ORLEAN

Meet the Shaggs

THINGS I WONDER (2:12)

Depending on whom you ask, the Shaggs were either the best band of all time or the worst. Frank Zappa is said to have proclaimed that the Shaggs were "better than The Beatles." More recently, though, a music fan who claimed to be in "the fetal position, writhing in pain," declared on the Internet that the Shaggs were "hauntingly bad," and added, "I would walk across the desert while eating charcoal briquettes soaked in Tabasco for forty days and forty nights *not* to ever have to listen to anything Shagg-related *ever* again." Such a divergence of opinion confuses the mind. Listening to the Shaggs' album *Philosophy of the World* will further confound. The music is winsome but raggedly discordant pop. Something is sort of wrong with the tempo, and the melodies are squashed and bent, nasal, deadpan. Are the Shaggs referencing the heptatonic, angular microtones of Chinese *ya-yueh* court music and the atonal note clusters of Ornette Coleman, or are they just a bunch of kids playing badly on cheap, out-of-tune guitars? And what about their homely, blunt lyrics? Consider the song "Things I Wonder":

> *There are many things I wonder*
> *There are many things I don't*
> *It seems as though the things I wonder most*
> *Are the things I never find out*

Is this the colloquial ease and dislocated syntax of a James Schulyer poem or the awkward innermost thoughts of a speechless teenager?

The Shaggs were three sisters, Helen, Betty, and Dorothy (Dot) Wiggin, from Fremont, New Hampshire. They were managed by their father, Austin Wiggin, Jr., and were sometimes accompanied by another sister, Rachel. They performed almost exclusively at the Fremont town hall and at a local nursing home, beginning in 1968 and ending in 1973. Many people in Fremont thought the band stank. Austin Wiggin did not. He believed his girls were going to be big stars, and in 1969 he took most of his savings and paid to record an album of their music. Nine hundred of the original thousand copies of *Philosophy of the World* vanished right after being pressed, along with the record's shady producer. Even so, the album has endured for thirty years. Music collectors got hold of the remaining copies of *Philosophy of the World* and started a small Shaggs cult. In the mid-seventies, WBCN-FM, in Boston, began playing a few cuts from the record. In 1988, the songs were repackaged and rereleased on compact disk and became celebrated by outsider music mavens, who were taken with the Shaggs' artless style. Now the Shaggs are entering their third life: *Philosophy of the World* was reissued last spring by RCA Victor and will be released in Germany this winter. The new CD of *Philosophy of the World* has the same cover as the original 1969 album—a photograph of the Wiggin girls posed in front of a dark-green curtain. In the picture, Helen is twenty-two, Dot is twenty-one, and Betty is eighteen. They have long blond hair and long blond bangs and stiff, quizzical half-smiles. Helen is sitting behind her drum set, is wearing flowered trousers and a white Nehru shirt; Betty and Dot, clutching their guitars, are wearing matching floral tunics, pleated plaid skirts, and square-heeled white pumps. There is nothing playful about the picture; it is melancholy, foreboding, with black shadows and the queer, depthless quality of an aquarium. Which leaves you with even more things to wonder about the Shaggs.

SHAGGS' OWN THING (3:54)

Fremont, New Hampshire, is a town that has missed out on most everything. Route 125, the main highway bisecting New Hampshire, just misses the east side of Fremont; Route 101 just misses the north; the town is neither in the mountains nor on the ocean; it is not quite in the thick of Boston's outskirts, nor is it quite cosseted in the woods. Fremont is a drowsy, trim, unfancy place, rimmed by the Exeter River. Ostentation is expressed only in a few man-size gravestones in the Fremont cemetery; bragging rights are limited to Fremont's being the home town of the eminent but obscure 1920s meteorologist Herbert Browne and its being the first place a B–52 ever crashed without killing anyone.

In the 1960s, when the Wiggin sisters formed the Shaggs, many people in Fremont raised dairy cows or made handkerchiefs at the Exeter textile mill or built barrels at Spaulding & Frost Cooperage, went to church, tended their families, kept quiet lives. Sometimes the summer light bounces off the black-glass surface of the Exeter River and glazes the big stands of blue pine, and sometimes the pastures are full and lustrous but ordinary days in southern New Hampshire towns can be mingy and dismal. "Loneliness contributed to severe depression, illness and drunkenness for countless rural families," Matthew Thomas wrote, in his book "History of Fremont, N. H. Olde Poplin: An Independent New England Republic 1764–1997," which came out last year. "There may have been some nice, pleasant times . . . but for the most part, death, sickness, disease, accidents, bad weather, loneliness, strenuous hard work, insect-infested foods, prowling predatory animals, and countless inconveniences marked day-to-day existence."

When I was in Fremont recently, I asked Matthew Thomas, who is forty-three and the town historian, what it had been like growing up there. He said it was nice but that he had been bored stiff. For entertainment, there were square dances, sledding, an annual carnival with a Beano tent, Vic Marcotte's Barber Shop and Poolroom. (These days, there are weekend grass drags out near Phil Peterson's farm, where the pasture is flat and firm enough to race snowmobiles in the summer.) When the Shaggs were growing up, there were ham-and-bean suppers, boxing matches, dog shows, and spelling bees at the town hall. The hall is an unadorned box of a building, but its performance hall is actually quite grand. It isn't used anymore, and someone has made off with the red velvet curtain, but it still has a sombre dark stage and highbacked chairs, and the gravid air of a place where things might happen.

In a quiet community like Fremont, in the dull hours between barn dances, a stage like that might give you big ideas.

WHO ARE PARENTS? (2:58)

Where else would Austin Wiggin have got the idea that his daughters should form a rock band? Neither he nor his wife, Annie, was musical; she much preferred television to music, and he, at most, fooled around with a Jew's harp. He wasn't a showoff, dying to be noticed—by all accounts he was an ornery loner who had little to do with other people in town. He was strict and old-fashioned, not a hippie manqué, not a rebel, very disapproving of long hair and short skirts. He was from a poor family and was raising a poor family—seven kids on a mill hand's salary—and music lessons and instruments for the girls were a daunting expense.

And yet the Shaggs were definitely his idea—or, more exactly, his mother's idea. Austin was terribly superstitious. His mother liked to tell fortunes. When he was young, she studied his palm and told him that in the future he would marry a strawberry blonde and would have two sons whom she would not live to see, and that his daughters would play in a band. Her auguries were borne out. Annie was a strawberry blonde, and she and Austin did have two sons after his mother died. It was left to Austin to fulfill the last of his mother's predictions, and when his daughters were old enough he told them that they would be taking voice and music lessons and forming a band. There was no debate: His word was law, and his mother's prophecies were gospel. Besides, he chafed at his place in the Fremont social system. It wasn't so much that his girls would make him rich and raise him out of a mill hand's dreary métier—it was that they would prove that the Wiggin kids were not only different from but better than the folks in town.

The girls liked music—particularly Herman's Hermits, Ricky Nelson, and Dino, Desi & Billy—but until Austin foretold their futures they had not planned to become rock stars. They were shy, small-town teenagers who dreamed of growing up and getting married, having children, maybe becoming secretaries someday. Even now, they don't remember ever having dreamed of fame or of making music. But Austin pushed the girls into a new life. He named them the Shaggs, and told them that they were not going to attend the local high school, because he didn't want them travelling by bus and mixing with out-siders, and, more important, he wanted them to practice their music all day. He enrolled them in a Chicago mail-order outfit called American Home School, but he designed their schedule himself: practice in the morning and afternoon, rehearse songs for him after dinner, and then do calisthenics and jumping jacks and leg lifts or practice for another hour before going to bed. The girls couldn't decide which was worse, the days when he made them do calisthenics or the days when he'd make them practice again before bed. In either case, their days seemed endless. The rehearsals were solemn, and Austin could be cutting. One song in particular, "Philosophy of the World," he claimed they never played right, and he would insist on hearing it again and again.

The Shaggs were not leading rock-and-roll lives. Austin forbade the girls to date before they were eighteen and discouraged most other friendships. They hadn't been popular kids, anyway—they didn't have the looks or the money or the savvy for it—but being in the band, and being home-schooled, set them apart even more. Friday nights, the family went out together to do grocery shopping. Sundays they went to church, and the girls practiced when they got home. Their world was even smaller than the small town of Fremont.

This was 1965. The Beatles had recently débuted on American tele-vision. The harmony between generations—at least, the harmony be-tween the popular cultures of those generations—was busting. And yet the sweet, lumpish Wiggin sisters of Fremont, New Hampshire, were playing pop music at their father's insistence, in a band that he di-rected. Rebellion might have been driving most rock and roll, but in Fremont Dot Wiggin was writing tributes to her mom and dad, with songs like "Who are Parents?":

> *Parents are the ones who really care*
> *Who are parents?*
> *Parents are the ones who are always there*
> *Some kids think their parents are cruel*
> *Just because they want them to obey certain rules. . . .*
> *Parents do understand*
> *Parents do care*

Their first public performance was at a talent show in nearby Exeter, in 1968. The girls could barely play their instruments. They didn't think they were ready to appear in public, but Austin thought otherwise. When they opened, with a cover of a loping country song called "Wheels," people in the audience threw soda cans at them and jeered. The girls were mortified; Austin told them they just had to go home and practice more. If they thought about quitting, they thought about it privately, because Austin would have had no truck with the idea; he was the kind of father who didn't tolerate debate. They practiced more, did their calisthenics, practiced more. Dot wrote the songs and the basic melodies, and she and Betty worked together on the chords and rhythms. Helen made up her drum parts on her own. The songs were misshapen pop tunes, full of shifting time signatures and odd metres and abrupt key changes, with lyrics about Dot's lost cat, Foot Foot, and her yearning for a sports car and how much she liked to listen to the radio.

On Halloween, the Shaggs played at a local nursing home—featuring Dot's song "It's Halloween" in their set—and got a polite response from the residents. Soon afterward, Austin arranged for them to play at the Fremont town hall on Saturday nights. The girls worried about embarrassing themselves, but at the same time they liked the fact that the shows allowed them to escape the house and their bounded world, even if it was just for a night. At that point, the girls had never even been to Boston, which was only fifty miles away.

The whole family took part in the town-hall shows. Austin III, the older of the two sons who had been seen in Austin's future, played the maracas; the other son, Robert, played the tambourine and did a drum solo during intermission; Annie sold tickets and ran the refreshment stand. A Pepsi truck would drop off cases of soda at their green ranch house, on Beede Road, every Friday night. Even though, according to one town-hall regular, most people found the Shaggs' music "painful and torturous," sometimes as many as a hundred kids showed up at the dances—practically the whole adolescent population of Fremont. Then again, there really wasn't much else to do in Fremont on a Saturday night. The audience danced and chatted, heckled the band, pelted the girls with junk, ignored them, grudgingly appreciated them, mocked them.

The rumor around town was that Austin forced his daughters to be in the band. There was even talk that he was inappropriately intimate with them. When asked about it years later, Betty said that the talk wasn't true, but Helen said that Austin once was intimate with her. Certainly, the family was folded in on itself; even Austin's father and Annie's mother, after they were both widowed, became romantically involved and lived together in a small house on the Wiggin property. The gossip and criticism only made Austin more determined to continue with the band. It was, after all, his destiny.

I'm So Happy When You're Near (2:12)

"Through the years, this author as town historian has received numerous requests from fans around the country looking for information on 'The Shaggs' and the town they came from," Matthew Thomas wrote in his section about the band. "They definitely have a cult following, and deservedly so, because the Wiggin sisters worked hard and with humble resources to gain respect and acceptance as musicians. To their surprise they succeeded. After all, what other New Hampshire band . . . has a record album worth $300–$500?"

The Beatles' arrival in America piqued Austin. He disliked their moppy hair but was stirred by their success. If they could make it, why couldn't his girls? He wanted to see the Shaggs on television, and on concert tours. Things weren't happening quickly enough for him, though, and this made him unhappy. He started making tapes and home movies of the town-hall shows. In March, 1969, he took the girls to Fleetwood Studios, outside Boston, to make a record. According to the magazine *Cool and Strange Music!*, the studio engineer listened to the Shaggs rehearse and suggested that they weren't quite ready to record. But Austin insisted on going forward, reportedly telling the engineer, "I want to get them while they're hot." In the album's liner notes, Austin wrote:

The Shaggs are real, pure, unaffected by outside influences. Their music is different, it is theirs alone. They believe in it, live it. . . . Of all contemporary acts in the world today, perhaps only the Shaggs do what others would like to do, and that is perform only what they believe in, what they feel, not what others think the Shaggs should feel. The Shaggs love you. ... They will not change their music or style to meet the whims of a frustrated world. You should appreciate this because you know they are pure what more can you ask? ... They are sisters and members of a large family where mutual respect and love for each other is at an unbelievable high ... in an atmosphere which has encouraged them to develop their music unaffected by outside influences. They are happy people and love what they are doing. They do it because they love it.

The Wiggins returned to Fleetwood a few years later. By then, the girls were more proficient—they had practiced hundreds of hours since the first recording session—but their playing still inspired the engineer to write, "As the day progressed, I overcame my disappointment and started feeling sorry for this family paying $60 an hour for studio time to record—this?"

I once asked Annie Wiggin if she thought Austin was a dreamer, and after sitting quietly for a few moments she said, "Well, probably. Must have been." If he was, it no doubt got harder to dream as the years went on. In 1973, the Fremont town supervisors decided to end the Saturday-night concerts, because—well, no one really remembers why anymore, but there was talk of fights breaking out and drugs circulating in the crowd, and wear and tear on the town hall's wooden floors, although the girls scrubbed the scuff marks off every Sunday. Austin was furious, but the girls were relieved to end the grind of playing every Saturday night. They were getting older and had began to chafe at his authority. Helen secretly married the first boyfriend she ever had—someone she had met at the dances. She continued living at home for three months after the wedding because she was too terrified to tell Austin what she had done. On the night that she finally screwed up the courage to give him the news, he got out a shotgun and went after her husband. The police joined in and told Helen to choose one man or the other. She left with her husband, and it was months before Austin spoke to her. She was twenty-eight years old.

The Shaggs continued to play at local fairs and at the nursing home. Austin still believed they were going to make it, and the band never broke up. It just shut down in 1975, on the day Austin, who was only forty-seven years old, died in bed of a massive heart attack—the same day, according to Helen, they had finally played a version of "Philosophy of the World" that he praised.

PHILOSOPHY OF THE WORLD (2:56)

Shortly after the newest release of the Shaggs' album, I went to New Hampshire to talk to the Wiggin sisters. A few years after Austin died, Betty and Dot married and moved to their own houses, and eventually Annie sold the house on Beede Road and moved to an apartment nearby. After a while, the house's new owner complained to people in town that Austin's ghost haunted the property. As soon as he could afford it, the new owner built something bigger and nicer farther back on the property, and allowed the Fremont Fire Department to burn the old Wiggin house down for fire-fighting practice.

Dot and Betty live a few miles down the road from Fremont, in the town of Epping, and Helen lives a few miles farther, in Exeter. They don't play music anymore. After Austin died, they sold much of their equipment and later let their kids horse around with whatever was left. Dot hung on to her guitar for a while, just in case, but a few years ago she lent it to one of her brothers and hasn't got it back. Dot, who is now fifty, cleans houses for a living. Betty, forty-eight, was a school janitor until recently, when she took a better job, in the stockroom of a kitchen-goods warehouse. Helen, who suffers from serious depression, lives on disability.

Dot and Betty arranged to meet me at Dunkin' Donuts, in Epping, and I went early so that I could read the local papers. It was a soggy, warm morning in southern New Hampshire; the sky was pearly, and the sun was as gray as gun-metal. Long tractor-trailers idled in the Dunkin' Donuts parking lot and then rumbled to life and lumbered onto the road. A few people were lined up to buy Pick 4 lottery tickets. The clerk behind the doughnut counter was discussing her wedding shower with a girl wearing a fuzzy halter top and platform sneakers. In the meantime, the coffee burned.

That day's Exeter *News-Letter* reported that the recreation commission's kickoff concert would feature Beatle Juice, a Beatles tribute band led by "Brad Delp, former front man of 'Boston,' one of the biggest rock bands New England has ever produced." Southern New Hampshire has regular outbreaks of tribute bands and reunion tours, as if it were in a time zone all its own, one in which the past keeps reappearing, familiar but essentially changed. Some time ago, Dot and her husband and their two sons went to see a revived version of Herman's Hermits. The concert was a huge disappointment for Dot, because her favorite Hermit, Peter (Herman) Noone, is no longer with the band, and because the Hermits' act now includes dirty jokes and crude references.

The Shaggs never made any money from their album until years later, when members of the band NRBQ heard *Philosophy of the World* and were thrilled by its strange innocence. NRBQ's own record label, Red Rooster, released records by such idiosyncratic bands as Jake & the Family Jewels, and they asked the Wiggins if they could compile a selection of songs from the group's two recording sessions. The resulting album, *The Shaggs' Own Thing*, includes the second session at Fleetwood Studios and some live and home recordings. Red Rooster's reissue of *Philosophy of the World* was reviewed in *Rolling Stone* twice in 1980 and was described as "priceless and timeless." The articles introduced the Shaggs to the world.

Three years ago, Irwin Chusid, the author of the forthcoming book *Songs in the Key of Z: The Curious Universe of Outsider Music*, discovered that a company he worked with had bought the rights to the Shaggs' songs, which had been bundled with other obscure music publishing rights. Chusid wanted to reissue *Philosophy of the World* as it was in 1969, with the original cover and the original song sequence. He suggested the project to Joe Mozian, a vice-president of marketing at RCA Victor, who had never heard of the band. Mozian was interested in unusual ventures; he had just released some Belgian lounge music from the sixties, which featured such songs as "The Frère Jacques Conga." Mozian says, "The Shaggs were beyond my wildest dreams. I couldn't comprehend that music like that existed. It's so basic and innocent, the way the music business used to be. Their timing, musically, was . . . fascinating. Their lyrics were . . . amazing. It is kind of a bad record—that's so obvious, it's a given. But it absolutely intrigued me, the idea that people would make a record playing the way they do."

The new *Philosophy of the World* was released last March. Even though the record is being played on college radio stations and the reviews have been enthusiastic and outsider art has been in vogue for several years, RCA Victor has sold only a few thousand copies of *Philosophy* so far. Mozian admits that he is disappointed. "I'm not sure why it hasn't sold," he says. "I think people are a little afraid of having the Shaggs in their record collections."

While I was waiting for the Wiggins, I went out to my car to listen to the CD again. I especially love the song "Philosophy of the World," with its wrought-up, clattering guitars and chugging, cockeyed rhythm and the cheerfully pessimistic lyrics about how people are never happy with what they have. I was right in the middle of the verse about how rich people want what the poor people have, and how girls with long hair want short hair, when Betty pulled up and opened the door of my car. As soon as she recognized the song, she gasped, "Do you like this?" I said yes, and she said, "God, it's horrible." She shook her head. Her hair no longer rippled down to her waist and no longer had a shelf of shaggy bangs that touched the bridge of her nose; it was short and springy, just to the nape of her neck, the hair of a grown woman without time to bother too much about her appearance.

A few minutes later, Dot drove in. She was wearing a flowered housedress and a Rugrats watch, and had a thin silver band on her thumb. On her middle finger was a chunky ring that spelled "Elvis" in block letters. She and Betty have the same deep-blue eyes and thrusting chin and tiny teeth, but Dot's hair is still long and wavy, and even now you can picture her as the girl with a guitar on the cover of the 1969 album. She asked what we were listening to. "What do you think?" Betty said to her. "The *Shaggs*." They both listened for another minute, so rapt that it seemed as if they had never heard the song before. "I never play the record on my own anymore," Dot said. "My son Matt plays it sometimes. He likes it. I don't think I get sentimental when I hear it—I just don't think about playing it."

"I wonder where I put my copies of the album," Betty said. "I know I have one copy of the CD. I think I have some of the albums somewhere."

The Wiggins have received fan letters from Switzerland and Texas, been interviewed for a documentary film, and inspired a dozen Web sites, bulletin boards, and forums on the Internet, but it's hard to see how this could matter much, once their childhood had been scratched out and rewritten as endless days of practicing guitar, and their father, who believed that their success was fated, died before they got any recognition. They are wise enough to realize that some of the long-standing interest in their music is ironic—sheer marvel that anything so unpolished could ever have made it onto a record. "We might have felt special at the time we made the record," Dot said uncertainly. "The really cool part, to me, is that it's thirty years later and we're still talk-ing about it. I never thought we'd really be famous. I never thought we'd even be as famous as we are. I met a girl at the Shop 'n Save the other day who used to come to the dances, and she said she wanted to go out now and buy the CD. And I saw a guy at a fair recently and talked to him for about half an hour about the Shaggs. And people call and ask if they can come up and meet us—that's amazing to me."

Yet, when I asked Dot and Betty for the names of people who could describe the town-hall shows, they couldn't think of any for days. "We missed out on a lot," Betty said. "I can't say we didn't have fun, but we missed a social life, we missed out on having friends, we missed every-thing except our music and our exercises. I just didn't think we were good enough to be playing concerts and making records. At one point, I thought maybe we would make it, but it wasn't really my fantasy." Her fantasy, she said, was to climb into a car with plenty of gas and just drive—not to get anywhere in particular, just to go.

We ordered our coffee and doughnuts and sat at a table near the window. Betty had her two-year-old and eight-month-old grand-daughters, Makayla and Kelsey, with her, and Makayla had squirmed away from the table and was playing with a plastic sign that read CAU-TION WET FLOOR. Betty often takes care of her grandchildren for her son and her daughter-in-law. Things are tight. The little windfall from their recordings helps, especially since Dot's husband is in poor health and can't work, and Betty's husband was killed in a motorcycle accident six years ago, and Helen is unable to work because of her depression.

For the Wiggins, music was never simple and carefree, and it still isn't. Helen doesn't go out much, so I spoke with her on the phone, and she told me that she hadn't played music since her father died but that country-and-western echoed in her head all the time, maddeningly so, and so loud that it made it hard for her to talk. When I asked Betty if she still liked music, she thought for a moment and then said that her husband's death had drawn her to country music. Whenever she feels bereft, she sings brokenhearted songs along with the radio. Just then, Makayla began hollering. Betty shushed her and said, "She really does have some kind of voice." A look flickered across her face. "I think, well, maybe she'll take voice lessons someday."

Dot is the only one who is still attached to her father's dream. She played the handbells in her church choir until recently, when she began taking care of one of Helen's children in addition to her own two sons and no longer had the time. She said that she's been writing lyrics for the last two years and hopes to finish them, and to compose the music for them. In the meantime, Terry Adams, of NRBQ, says he has enough material left from the Fleetwood Studio recording sessions for a few more CDs, and he has films of the town-hall concerts that he plans to synchronize with sound. The Shaggs, thirty years late, may yet make it big, the way Austin saw it in his dreams. But even that might not have been enough to sate him. The Shaggs must have known this all along. In "Philosophy of the World," the song they never could play to his satisfaction, they sang:

> *It doesn't matter what you do*
> *It doesn't matter what you say*
> *There will always be one who wants things the opposite way*
> *We do our best, we try to please*
> *But we're like the rest we're never at ease*
> *You can never please*
> *Anybody*
> *In this world*

Madonna

The interview took place on August 25, 1998, in the living room of Madonna's duplex apartment on Central Park West. The space is large and imposingly formal, with oversize deco armchairs and a plush sofa across the room from a fireplace flanked by shelves that are empty save for a few deco vases and some art books. There are paintings by Tamara de Lempicka on two walls, a small, exquisite Dali canvas near the fireplace, and some framed photos of her child, Lourdes, on a sideboard. A book by the Peruvian photographer Martin Chambi sits on the coffee table, where an assistant has placed a tray with a china tea service, but the room feels like a public space, a meeting room for guests rather than an integral part of the apartment's regular domestic life. Madonna, fresh from emergency root-canal work, says she's a bit groggy from the gas, but she looks just fine in all black, and she moves quickly from subdued to playful to witty woman of the world.

V: I found a quote from your interview with Bill Zehme, when you said, "I'd rather own an art gallery than a movie studio. Or a museum. I'd rather be Peggy Guggenheim than Harry Cohn." Where did your interest in art and photography start?

M: My interest in art started as a child because several members of my family could paint and draw and I couldn't, so I was living vicariously through them. And from going to the Detroit Institute of Arts, which is how I got into Diego Rivera, which is how I found out about Frida Kahlo and started reading about her. Then, if you go to enough Catholic churches, there's art everywhere, so you get introduced to it that way, from a religious ecstasy point of view. And then just coming to New York and dancing. As an incredibly poor struggling dancer, you could get into museums for free, so that was my form of entertainment. It was just something I was interested in. And then you get into it, and when I started collecting, I started reading more and more about the artists themselves, and names would keep popping up—you know, Peggy Guggenheim. And of course I started reading about her and she was just—

V: She was definitely a character.

M: Oh, my God! What a life she led! Just the idea of being in contact with all those great artists and nurturing them and giving them a place to show their work and being their patroness is, to me, fabulous.

V: It's the one great thing to be.

M: Totally! I mean that's real art. And to be able to be a part of that and to nurture it—it's a very enviable and honorable position.

V: I've always collected images and torn pages out of magazines and put them up on the wall—

M: Totally.

V: And one picture that's been up on every dorm room or apartment wall I've ever lived in was this Richard Avedon photo of Lew Alcindor from Harper's *Bazaar*. I wondered if there was anything like that in your life early on. Was there an image that you've carried with you?

M: The image that always struck me was one that I ended up using as an inspiration for one of my videos, and that's a really sort of Cubist photograph—I forget who the photographer is—of a man working on some big, huge piston-shaped cylinder.

V: The famous Lewis Hine photo.

M: Right. Well, that ended up in my "Express Yourself" video; that was totally the inspiration for that. Every video I've ever done has been inspired by some painting or some work of art.

V: That's what I was wondering. Obviously "Vogue," with the Horst references, which I know you got into some trouble for.

M: Well those were all pretty obvious. I consider them to be homages of course. And I didn't get into trouble, the director did. Fortunately, I owned the Tamara de Lempicka painting that I used for the opening of "Open Your Heart." That one over there. Only we put lights on her nipples.

V: What else? Most of the others aren't quite so—

M: Obvious? Well my "Bedtime Story" video was completely inspired by all the female surrealist painters like Leonora Carrington and Remedios Varo. There's that one shot where my hands are up in the air and stars are spinning around me. And me flying through the hallway with my hair trailing behind me, the birds flying out of my open robe—all of those images were an homage to female surrealist painters; there's a little bit of Frida Kahlo in there, too. What else? The "Frozen" video was totally inspired by Martha Graham—I have a lot of photographs of her dancing: the big skirts and all the iron shapes and stuff like that.

V: I thought that the "Vogue" video was especially terrific because those were all pictures that—

M: We brought to life.

V: Yeah, and it angered me that Horst couldn't see that as a tribute. What could be better?

M: Yeah, and those images are really powerful, and it's great to remind people of them and to bring it into pop culture and not keep it so outside where people are never going to be exposed to it.

V: When did you start collecting?

M: When I got my first paycheck, $5,000 or something.

V: Do you remember what you bought?

M: This is a good question for my art dealer. I bought a Leger and I bought a Frida Kahlo self-portrait, but I don't know which came first. But I remember buying it and I had just gotten married and it looked completely out of place in my house in Malibu. (*She laughs in a light, breathy burst.*) But those were my first paintings.

V: And were those things that you had always wanted—always hoped to have?

M: Well I've always been kind of obsessed with Frida Kahlo, so I was really into the idea of getting something that belonged to her. And then from Frida Kahlo I found out about Tina Modotti and then I started collecting her stuff and Edward Weston, and one person always leads to another person with me, because for me it started with Diego

Rivera, then it went to Frida Kahlo, then it went to Tina, and Edward and . . . (*She trails off.*) Also, if you're into Picasso, and you want to find out about him and that whole area of art and European culture, then you start reading about Man Ray and the surrealists and Andre Breton, and all of a sudden you're in that whole world and you start having interests in other people. It's like a disease.

V: Of the best kind.

M: Lately, I've gotten more into newer photographers. I'm really into Guy Bourdin right now; I've got a couple of his photographs in my bedroom that I wake up to every morning. I just move all over the place, really.

V: That's been my impression whenever I read about the art that you have; it seems to be very wide-ranging.

M: It's more that a sensibility appeals to me. I'm really interested in two things in art. One is suffering, and the other is irony and a certain bizarre sense of humor. And that you can find everywhere.

V: Who else beside Guy Bourdin would you consider somebody new for you?

M: That I love? Well I love Nan Goldin. She's amazing. Now I'm into color photography—don't get me wrong, I still love black and white—and I like a lot of the really young photographers. I interviewed Mario Testino for his show in Naples and Rio, and he has a new book—it's great! Fantastic book—I love it. And I did a piece for him for the book and we had a lengthy discussion about young photographers that we really like right now. Like Mario Sorrenti—people that are considered fashion photographers. For instance, I love Inez van Lamsweerde. She photographed me for *Spin* magazine and she is unbelievable. She's Dutch.

V: What is she like? I'm really curious about her work.

M: She's so interesting. She's tall; she's got really long black hair; she looks like a Modigliani painting. She and her boyfriend [Vinoodh Matadin] work together and he does all the art direction. They make such beautiful photographs, and they do a lot of campaigns for a lot of young designers.

V: A lot of their work looks very computer-altered. Did they do that with you?

M: Not that I know of, because I don't like that. I knew I was going to get it with . . . what's his name? I'm sorry I had too much gas and I can't remember anyone's name right now. David LaChapelle! Because you can't work with him without being computerized.

V: It's part of the look.

M: Yeah. Anyway, I just love [van Lamsweerde's] photographs, but I'm into Sean Ellis and Mario Sorrenti. Their photographs are very cinematic and they're like a whole new wave, I think, of photography that transcends fashion and Steven Meisel, Patrick Demarchelier—that whole school of photographers, who I think were really inspired by Avedon and Helmut Newton.

V: You brought up Mario Testino. I'd been wondering who would be the official photographer of your baby and he's not the person I would have expected.

M: Why, who would you have expected?

V: Someone you had worked with before, like Herb Ritts or Stephen Meisel.

M: Herb Ritts did take photographs of my daughter that are quite beautiful, two days after she was born, and those are all framed and in my house in L.A. But more like the classic, black-and-white; there are some beautiful, beautiful shots of her foot in my hand—incredible. There are some shots that look like photographs Man Ray did of Lee Miller, too. My hair was really blond and I had red lipstick on and they were black and white; just the way he processed them, they look very Man Ray–ish. But Mario's really one of my favorite photographers right now, which is why he ended up taking the official portrait of me and her together. And when she had a real personality; I mean, babies don't have personality when they're two days old. I suppose some people think they do, but they're just amoebas. They can't even focus on anything.

V: I thought Testino's pictures were wonderful.

M: Believe me, there's a lot more. He captured something about her. He has a real, natural kind of journalistic style of photographing that I like, which I think is better for a baby who's running around and can't stand to sit still. It's not about lighting or anything, it's about capturing her doing something, and he took some fantastic pictures of her.

V: It was those pictures that convinced me he was more interesting than I'd thought.

M: Have you ever met him? He is a scream. He's so much fun. He's the kind of guy who will photograph you, and if he doesn't like the way you're standing or something, he'll kick you. And he's constantly singing and moving around the room and he's so full of life, and I feel like his photographs are, too. He creates an atmosphere, a relaxed atmosphere, and then he just starts taking pictures. Which is very, very different than someone like Steven [Meisel], who is really precise. (*She says this last phrase with a deliberate pause between each word.*)

V: I suspected that.

M: He has a very specific aesthetic. But because I worked with him for so long, I felt like I needed to get away from it.

V: Let's talk a little bit about him, because I'm very curious about him and your relationship with him. It did seem like you two formed one of those bonds that a subject and a photographer can form.

M: Muse?

V: Yeah. And that you brought out very interesting things in each other.

M: Yeah, well, first of all I have to feel like I'm friends with a photographer and that we enjoy the same things, like the same movies, have the same sick sensibility. And I felt that with Steven, which is why we just kept working together and working together and finally the idea of doing a book together came up. You really have to feel like someone's part of your family to work on a book like that, where you're just like hanging out. And not only did we photograph everything, we also filmed everything on a Super-8 camera—everything that we did.

V: Really? What's happened to all that stuff?

M: Oh, it's around. It's in the archives. It'll be unearthed after I die. It'll be playing at the Film Forum.

V: What drew you to Meisel in the first place, and what clicked between you?

M: Well, first of all, he just really, really appreciates beauty, and he knows how to photograph a strong female. He's a diva himself. And he, like me, is sort of a scavenger who picks stuff out of things, whether it's old movies, old Warhol films. He's interested in street fashion. He picks up stuff from all over the place and puts it in his work and so do I. And he likes a lot of the same things I like. I don't know—we just clicked. He's one of those people who will call you and go, "You've gotta see this movie or rent this movie." It's always movies you have to go and rent or buy somewhere; it's nothing that's out, nothing modern.

V: He fascinates me because there's always what's there on the surface and then there's all this stuff behind it. I know he has this incredibly broad range of things that he pulls from, and they're never what I'm expecting next.

M: No, and that's the great thing about Steven. He'll take you down a road and then he'll completely throw a curve ball. I wish he'd do more outside of *Vogue* magazine. I suppose he can't. Because that's certainly working within a serious restriction, and unfortunately *Vogue* has turned into a *Speigel* catalogue.

V: I hardly pay attention to his work in American *Vogue*, because—

M: It's all about Italian *Vogue*.

V: That's so great, and it does seem that he can get away with just about anything there. But I am curious about the *Sex* book and how that came about. A lot of the visual influences there seem to be Man Ray and experimental European work.

M: Man Ray and every movie that Visconti ever made starring Helmut Berger and—did you see *The Damned?*—Ingrid Thulin. I mean I *was* Ingrid Thulin for several of those photographs. And the book was inspired by all kinds of things: those old Warhol films, where people did nothing and just sat there and peeled bananas and stuff, to all the Visconti stuff, especially the stuff we shot at the Gaiety when I'm dressed in an evening gown and I've got all the men on leashes and I think Udo Kier is even in the photographs. We had to bring Udo Kier back—he's incredible.

V: Was the book something you concocted together or something you decided you should do and then you pulled Meisel into it?

M: We were always fooling around and doing stuff anyway—stuff that never made it into any magazines—because we were always working together on so many things. I guess it was my idea and then I pulled him into it. I mean, we had talked about doing a book together, we just weren't sure where we wanted to go with it and what kind of a book, because I love taking on different personas and becoming and transforming and the whole chameleon thing with a twist on Cindy Sherman—something a bit more aggressive than that. I'm a big fan of hers, by the way. So originally it was going to be this thing of different guises, and then we used to go to the Gaiety all the time and we got onto the subject of sex and gender confusion and role playing and men playing females and women playing men and that's how the *Sex* book came about. Steven, like me, likes to fuck with people, so that was a big part of it, too.

V: With the public, you mean, or with the people who are his subjects?

M: Everyone, everything, at every level. It was about celebrating the ultimate taboo and also just having fun doing what you're not supposed to do. I mean, a pop star's not supposed to do those things. I'm telling you, I had the time of my life while I was doing it. Of course, I got the shit kicked out of me for it, so it's a good thing I had a good time doing it. And I had fun. I don't regret it. The whole thing was like performance art while it was happening and it was a real throw-caution-to-the-wind, devil-may-care time of my life.

V: Can you imagine doing something like that again?

M: I don't know . . .

V: There's no point in doing that again, obviously, but . . .

M: I never want to repeat myself. I like the idea of doing something political and provocative, but I don't know what it would be. That's one of those things that you can't plan, you just have to let it happen.

V: I suspect that if you meet another photographer who inspires you in the way that he did . . .

M: Or maybe I'll do it with film; maybe it won't be photography.

V: In a sense, you did it with *Truth or Dare.*

M: This is true, and I like that confusion of is it real or is it not real? Is it life imitating art or is it art imitating life? Is it something that we planned that we filmed, or is it something that we captured? Because I'm telling you, the line starts to get very blurred.

V: Even when you're in the middle of it.

M: Totally. And that's beautiful, too.

V: Let's talk about Cindy Sherman. I know that you sponsored her show of "film stills" at the Museum of Modern Art. What is it that appeals to you about her work?

M: Just her chameleon-like persona—her transformation. What she's able to evoke—the subtlety of her work, the detail. I just think her stuff is amazing.

V: Do you own work of hers?

M: No, can you believe that? I've always admired her work, but the images that were available to be bought I wasn't that crazy about. But I really respect and admire her.

V: What exactly was your involvement in the Modern show? Did you actually put up the money to buy that whole group of "film stills"?

M: Yeah. I was a patroness. (*She laughs at her own pretension.*)

V: I like that idea; I think it's important.

M: It's the best place to put your money, honestly. I know it's good to get involved in lots of charities, but I think it's really, really important to do things that inspire people in other ways. Because people need to have their consciousness raised in many ways, and sometimes it's too easy to just give your money to something that you don't have any connection to. It's much more gratifying for me to be able to give money to tangible things, like to help keep a theater open, to a school, to supporting an artist in getting a show together.

V: How did the Cindy Sherman arrangement come about?

M: My art dealer [Darlene Lutz], she has relationships with a lot of people at the Museum of Modern Art. They come to me a lot and ask if I want to get involved with different shows. The only shows I've been involved in in terms of financing have been the Tina Modotti show and the Cindy Sherman show—that's it. You know, we chicks have to stick together.

V: And you want to do something that—

M: That I love—that I love totally.

V: To go back to photographers that you've worked with, I wanted to ask about Herb Ritts. It seemed to me that you had an interesting, symbiotic relationship with photographers, both as a muse and as a great subject. And these people helped to create your image in a lasting way.

M: Yes, absolutely. And Herb Ritts was really a big part of that, especially in the beginning of my career.

V: What did he bring to the relationship that made those pictures so effective?

M: An innocence. Herb is one of those people who doesn't even seem like he's a photographer. It feels like he discovered it by accident in a way, and he has a real naivete about him. He doesn't really plan things; he kind of stumbles across things. He's got a real aw-gee-shucks vibe on him. He's a really innocent, geeky-nerdy type of a person, and I became friends with him. I asked him to photograph my wedding, and things went from there. Because I always have to be friends with them first, and they become part of my inner circle, and once I'm really comfortable with them, that's when things start to be created. And Herb was very much a part of my social circle. And Herb—Steven doesn't do this much, but Mario does it—they always have a little camera in their pocket. I mean, Herb and Mario must have a billion photographs of me in their archives—just of parties, hanging out at my house, coming to visit me on the sets of movies—that I'm sure will resurface someday, when I've been reincarnated as a camera lens. But there's a certain comfortability factor that came with Herb. And I'd never really been conscious or aware of photographers before, and, believe me, I'd been photographed a lot before that, but I wasn't really present. I didn't care. And, in fact, all the nude photographs that surfaced of me from my early days of modeling for art classes and photography schools and stuff, I so didn't want to be there that I removed myself from the whole process. I wasn't relating to the photographer, I wasn't relating to the camera, and it wasn't a relationship. I wasn't there—I was gone. It must be like what a prostitute does when they're with a john. I was not present. So, to me, the whole Herb Ritts thing was the first time that I realized that symbiosis, that exchange of energy and the creation of magic that happens from that exchange. A good photographer creates an environment for you to shine—for you to express yourself in whatever statement it is you want to make. And you do have to feel comfortable with people. I remember Robert Mapplethorpe kept asking to photograph me back in the day, but he scared the shit out of me.

V: Why?

M: I don't know why, he just did.

V: You seem relatively unscareable.

M: Yeah, but there was some energy that he had that I didn't feel comfortable with. And I couldn't even explain to you what it was. I was very young when I met him and I hadn't been living in New York that long. Anyway, Herb was the first photographer that I really had a relationship with.

V: And then Meisel after that?

M: Pretty much. I worked with other people, but nobody that made a difference. And then I worked with Steven. What was the first thing I did with him? I don't even remember. But I remember once I got more into fashion and started collecting more art and becoming a lot more aware of the intersection of art and fashion, that's when I got into Steven Meisel.

V: In a sense, you were more on his wavelength, then.

M: I sort of went into Steven's wavelength, and then that worked for a while, too, and culminated in the *Sex* book and all of that stuff. And then I didn't want to have my photograph taken for a really long time, and then I hooked up with Mario Testino. I worked with lots of photographers in between, but a sort of artist-muse relationship existed with those three photographers.

V: There are tons of other pictures of you—

M: But those were just one-offs.

V: —but those were the photographers who seemed to bring you out in a collaborative way. Is there one, definitive Madonna picture?

M: I think there is with each photographer, but there isn't just one, because I feel like I change and evolve so much that it's hard for me to put my finger on one.

V: I suspected that you'd say that, because if you chose one, you'd be pinning yourself down to just one moment and there is really no one moment. Are there other photographers that you'd like to work with?

M: Like to become the muse of? Well, I really wanted to have my picture taken by Helmut Newton, and I did. I love his stuff, too. But I didn't have a relationship with him; he's not available, or accessible. I also had my photograph taken by this other photographer who I adored, but the photographs never got used: Paolo Roversi, he does beautiful work. They were going to be pictures for my album cover—not this record but the record before—but the people at the record company were all too freaked out; they thought the pictures were too blurry, they weren't going to read well—whatever.

V: In all of photographic history, who would you wish to have photographed you?

M: Well, Man Ray—no question, no question. There are a lot of photographers that I admire, but I'm not sure that I would have wanted them to photograph me. Irving Penn, but not now—forty years ago. I can't think of anyone else.

V: Weston?

M: Yeah, yeah. No question; he was amazing. But I think that's it: Weston, Man Ray, and Irving Penn—not a shabby crowd.

V: Following that, who in the history of art would you like to have painted your portrait?

M: Wow! That's a good question. Well, Picasso would have been amazing. I've got a portrait of Dora Maar that's *un*-believable. It wouldn't have been a pretty picture, but we would have liked it anyway.

V: With Picasso it would have been so beyond just having your picture done.

M: He paints your personality, he doesn't paint your portrait; and he paints his personality, too. But I'm happy to share a canvas with Picasso. I would have loved Bouguereau to paint my portrait, because I would have looked really good. (*She laughs.*) He doesn't paint an ugly picture of anyone. Or Rembrandt, he would have been OK. (*Said with the feigned unconcern, and sly smile, of a princess indulging in high noblesse oblige. Then, after a long pause:*) Oh, I know who: Edward Hopper. Love his paintings.

V: With your photographs, your videos, and your performances you've had a real impact on our ideas about femininity and, I think, masculinity because of the way you've pulled that into it. I'm curious about what influences you've had on your ideas about femininity and masculinity over the years. What were the defining influences, if there are any?

M: I think a lot of the art that I have has influenced me in that way. I have a photograph in my office that Man Ray did of Lee Miller kissing another woman that I think is really powerful and that has really inspired me. I've also been inspired by—well, everything inspires me. A lot of the movies have inspired me—a lot of the movies of Visconti and Pasolini. With Pasolini, there's a lot of religious ecstasy intertwined with sexual ecstasy, and when I think of Visconti's films, I always feel sexually confused by them. For instance, did you see *The Night Porter?*

V: No.

M: You haven't seen it? (*She slaps a pillow like a disapproving school mistress.*) Anything with Charlotte Rampling you must see. She is genius! Images of women dressed in Nazi Gestapo uniforms—the vulnerability and fragility of a female but the masculinity of a uniform, and the whole sense of playing that out and performing, doing sort of cabaret—the movie *Cabaret*! The confusion: what's male, what's female? For me, David Bowie was a huge influence on me because he was the first concert I went to see. I remember watching him and thinking I didn't know what sex he was, and it didn't matter. Because one minute he was wearing body stockings—the whole Ziggy Stardust thing—and the next minute he was the Thin White Duke in white double-breasted suits, and there's something so androgynous about him. And I think androgyny, whether it's David Bowie or Helmut Berger, that has really really influenced my work more than anything.

V: You project so many facets of femininity very strongly so it's fascinating to me that androgyny is also part of the mix.

M: Absolutely.

V: That definitely comes out in the *Sex* book.

M: Yeah, but when you think of all the stuff that I did in my live shows with Gaultier and the costuming and having the two guys standing by my bed with the cone-shaped bras on. It's always been about switching genders and playing with that whole masculinity/femininity issue.

V: What do you find powerful about that—or intriguing?

M: I don't know—the most interesting people to me are people who aren't just one way. And obviously I'm attracted to it because I am a female but I have been described as being very male-like or very predatory or having a lot of male traits. But that's because I'm financially independent, and I have spoken about my sexual fantasies in the sort of frank and blunt way that has been reserved for men. And the more people have criticized me for behaving in an unladylike fashion, the more it's provoked me to behave in an unladylike fashion and say, I can be feminine and masculine at the same time.

V: It seems to me you've always been about blasting away old ideas about what is feminine and what is masculine. To say that you're not feminine because you take charge—that's an old idea about what femininity is.

M: And, by the way, artists through the centuries have been into role-playing. I mean Frida Kahlo always dressed like a man. And so did Lee Miller for a time. There are lots of people who sort of switched back and forth, but that was always reserved for fine art; in pop culture, you're expected to behave in a socially acceptable way.

V: In a sense it's easier for guys—from Bowie to Jagger to Boy George—to fuck around with that.

M: Absolutely. Because men feel safe about it. Men feel safe with men dressing like women; they do not feel safe with women dressing like men. You're not feeling intimidated by a guy who dresses like a female, but you might feel intimidated by a woman who walked around in a pin-striped suit with her tits hanging out, grabbing her crotch—who absolutely doesn't need you for anything. Except for one thing, but even then, you can leave after that.

(*Here, inspired by the film* Elizabeth, *which she'd seen in London, Madonna digressed into retelling the story of Elizabeth I, including her unconventional life, her ascension to the throne, and her eventual triumph as a queen. She led up to this point:*)

M: But she never had public favor; it was a bit like the Hillary Clinton thing. She did all the right things for her country, but she wasn't ultimately revered. So she had a conversation with her confidant-adviser. She asked him, When have they ever looked up to or idolized a woman? Only one, he told her, the Virgin Mary. So she said, Then I will become like the Virgin Mary, and she did. She created a facade for herself; she stopped having lovers; she became like a virgin. She became sexless, and painted her face in a white alabaster way, and turned herself into an icon that was untouchable and sexless, and then she had everybody's respect.

V: At what cost?

M: I know, but for me it was a very enlightening moment.

V: But it is a terrible cost—to give up everything in order to rule?

M: Right, but if you are a powerful female and you don't play the traditional role that you are supposed to play when you get married and have a family and everyone feels safe with you, then you are going to be intimidating to people. And that idea has always been running through my work. Accepting it, not accepting it; accepting it, not accepting it. And shoving it in people's faces. I mean that whole crotch-grabbing thing was just so like, OK every other rock star in the universe has done it, so I'm going to do it. And you know how freaked-out people got about it. Whatever. But we got off the subject.

V: Is there an early influence on your ideas about femininity and masculinity?

M: I think probably my earliest influences probably came from the world of dance, especially with Martha Graham, because I studied at her school and I read all about her and saw the movies of her dances and performances. She freaked people out, too, because she brought to life all of these Greek myths and she reenacted them in her dances. And she was always turning things around; she was always the aggressor who trapped the men. And her dances were very sexually provocative, very erotic, and very female-assertive, and I know that that really influenced me. And also ballet is such a female thing, and when I was younger, being surrounded by male ballet dancers—to me, that's gender confusion. I mean, a bunch of guys walking around in tights putting their toes up in the air, and they're incredibly effeminate men. Being surrounded by that on a regular basis when I was growing up—I mean, I wanted to be a boy when I was growing up because I was in love with all of the male dancers I knew and they were all gay. And I thought, Well, if I was a boy, they'd love me. So I got into role-playing then. That's where it began. I remember when I was still in high school, I had cut my hair off really short, and I was totally anorexic—I had no boobs—and I would dress like a boy and go to gay clubs and my goal was to trick men into thinking I was a boy.

V: Did it ever work?

M: It did actually, a few times. Yeah, it really started in the dance world.

V: And when you got into music, it wasn't in the rock-and-roll world, which is a lot more gender-defined, but through disco, which was much more fluid.

M: And I'm sure that's really influenced me, because from the dance world to the music world, my social strata was mostly gay men. That's who my audience was, that's who I hung out with, that's who inspired me. For me, it freed me, because I could do whatever I wanted and be whatever I wanted.

V: Knowing that your audience is ready to be fucked with.

M: Totally. Ready to be fucked with and certainly not intimidated by a strong female. So the problem arose when I left that world and went into the mainstream. Suddenly, there was judgment. But before that I was in my little gay cocoon.

V: But you certainly fed off the judgment.

M: Well, absolutely. As soon as you tell me I can't do something— And that's how I've always been, starting from when I was a little girl. The boys could wear pants to church and the girls couldn't. And I used to say, But why? Is God going to love me less if I don't wear a dress? It just irked me—the rules. So I would put pants on under my dress, just to fuck with my father. And after church, I would tell him I had pants on and I'd say, See, lightning did not strike me. And I guess I've been doing that ever since.

V: Do you have a feminine ideal? Is there someone who seems like perfection—and I mean totally in your own terms?

M: Well, a lot of the artists that I collect and that I admire: Lee Miller, Tina Modotti, Frida Kahlo—that whole group of females that kind of started off as muses and became artists in their own right and absolutely worked in a lot of different worlds and moved in a lot of different worlds and were artistic and political and still had their femininity about them. I can't think of anybody now. That's a tough one. I'm sitting here and combing all the areas: Is there an actress? Is there a singer? Is there an artist now? Help me!

V: For some reason, Liz Taylor came to mind, but most of the stars around today are complicated because they've made so many compromises along the way.

M: Hollywood is about playing the game, and I can't think of any successful actresses who didn't play the game. There's a lot more renegades in the music business, from Patti Smith to Janis Joplin.

V: So Lee, Tina, and Frida, but neither of us can come up with someone working now who could qualify.

M: It's lonely out there.

V: Is there a masculine ideal, either now or in the past?

M: I would say David Bowie, absolutely. I was terribly inspired by him and I still think he's an amazing human being. He keeps pushing the envelope in his way. I can think of a lot of male artists that I admire, but everytime I start to think about them, and how they behaved, they were all real shits. Fuckfaces. And the thing is, all those women that I named—I know a lot about them. I've gotten into their work and then read their biographies and really followed them and studied them, and they're women that I really look up to. Whereas the men, I haven't followed as much; I haven't felt the desire to know about them. I mean, everybody knows what a shit Picasso was. But all of those guys—they were all pigs. I'm sure Man Ray was a pain in the ass, too.

V: But is there an ideal image of masculinity, one that doesn't depend on biography?

M: I go back and forth. For me, a male image that I'm really moved by is somewhere between the kind of Oscar Wilde type of a male: the fop, the long hair, the suits, too witty for his own good, incredibly smart, scathingly funny—all that. But then my other ideal is more like the Buddhist monk—the shaved head, actually someone who sublimates their sexuality.

V: Not exactly like anybody you've ever been involved with.

M: I wouldn't say that.

V: I shouldn't assume.

M: No. Like one of my yoga teachers, for instance. He has a Jesus-like quality to him. I know he's a heterosexual, he wears earrings and he's got a very androgynous look to him and long hair. But he has an aesthetic and a humility about him that I think is very appealing and something to aspire to.

V: Interesting. When I think of you and males, I think of all the guys in your videos, most of whom have been like thugs.

M: Hunky boys? Yes, I am attracted to a thug. I like that quality, but I like the other side of it, too. Because all guys who go around behaving in macho ways are really scared little girls. So you have to look beneath the surface. There's a difference between my ideal man and a man that I'm sexually attracted to, believe me. Therein lies the rub.

V: What is your overriding visual inspiration?

M: The crucifix. It's the first image that sticks in my mind from childhood. I've used it a lot in my work; I've used it in my videos; I've used it onstage. The whole idea of the crucifixion and the suffering of Christ is all kind of intertwined with masochism, and Catholicism is a huge part of my upbringing, my past, my influence. And it's a very powerful image.

GEORGE W. GOODMAN

Sonny Rollins at Sixty-Eight

On a summer day in 1960 I lugged my tenor sax up a flight of wooden stairs in an old building in midtown Manhattan where a stubby little man named Jake Koven rented out practice rooms to musicians. Jake was a nice guy with a democratic attitude toward his clientele. For a few bucks a guitar-toting teenager with no ear for music could strum away the afternoon in a room sandwiched between a flutist from the New York Philharmonic and a songwriter tinkering with the finale of a Broadway show. I was playing the minor-sixth intervals of Thelonious Monk's "Misterioso," thinking I sounded cool, even a little intimidating, when the first four notes of the 1930s hit "Three Little Words" came through the wall like shots from a nail gun.

The saxophonist in the other room began splintering the notes into partials, and then constructed arpeggios that swirled up from the bottom of his horn, spiraling out beyond the legitimate range of the instrument and into the stratosphere of the piccolo. He restated the notes, played them bel canto, made them waltz, turned them upside down and inside out, and ran them up-tempo in 4/4 time, taking outlandish liberties with meter and intonation. It was pure passion, power, and precision. It was pure Sonny Rollins.

I put down my horn and considered my prospects for jazz greatness, which lay at my feet like a granite slab. Sonny Rollins was my hero, in so many ways everything I wanted to be. In January of 1959 *Esquire* had published the now famous Art Kane photograph of fifty-seven musicians in front of a Harlem brownstone, an astonishing congregation that covered the depth and breadth of American jazz as its golden age was coming to a close. Rollins was the youngest star in the picture, too young to have been so *bad*. Having begun his career in seven-league boots, he'd cut his teeth in the company of the legends Bud Powell and Thelonious Monk before finishing high school. His improvisational genius had earned the respect of Babs Gonzales, Fats Navarro, J. J. Johnson, Art Blakey, Tadd Dameron, Charlie Parker, Miles Davis, Coleman "Bean" Hawkins, Dizzy Gillespie, Clifford Brown, and Max Roach even before his career had begun.

The power and the complexity of his solos—improvisation as composition, like the ordered madness of a Jackson Pollock canvas—were at the core of his appeal for me. But there was also the man himself: Mr. Cool. The shades, the Pharaonic bush on the chin, the walk, the talk, the imperviousness to everything uncool. For many black men of my generation, coming of age in the late 1950s, before the new breed of race men like Malcolm X and Stokely Carmichael came to the fore, the young lions of jazz were our cultural revolutionaries—rebellious, angry, but always cool. The music we called "our thing" was steeped in ethnicity. Playing it with authority meant you were at home in your own skin. Cool was defiance with dignity in the days when white cops could beat Powell and Monk for minor offenses with impunity. Miles Davis was clubbed with a nightstick outside Birdland after one of his sets. He was photographed leaving jail the next day with a bandaged head wound and a blood-splattered jacket. He was the essence of cool, and we were in awe. The lurid stories of his and others' drug use enhanced the gritty existential mystique that actors like James Dean and Marlon Brando were projecting for white America in the movies. Brando and Ava Gardner studied Davis at Birdland the way Norman Mailer and Jean-Paul Sartre absorbed the noir atmospherics of exotic expatriates like Bud Powell and Dexter Gordon when they performed at the Blue Note and Club Saint-Germain, in Paris.

By the time of my encounter with Rollins in 1960, "our thing" was all over the city, but when Rollins was coming of age, there was 52nd Street, the cluster of clubs that thrived in the Forties, and Harlem. If "The Street" was the jewelry showcase, Harlem was the mine that supplied it.

"Harlem was my conservatory," Rollins told me one day not long ago as we sat in his music studio, miles and light-years from all that, in the farm country of Germantown, New York, near Rhinebeck, where he has lived for twenty-six years. Rollins's hair is thinning and turning snowy, like his beard, but his eyes are clear and their gaze is penetrating. With broad shoulders and stone-cut features, he is a muscular six foot two, thicker in the trunk and just as imposing as he was forty-three years ago, when a critic called him the Colossus of the saxophone. He has the bearing and gravitas of a Cushite king, even if the tunic, woolen scarf, and cap (it was a chilly afternoon) added a touch of mujahideen. I was struck by his gentility though I sensed he was not a man to be trifled with.

"Music, *our* music, was everywhere," he said in a voice of raspy sonority. "You could hear it from the best players of every style. Kenny Drew and I used to go down to the Apollo to see Tiny Bradshaw and Louis Jordan. Duke Ellington lived around the corner from me." So did the singer and actress Ethel Waters; Ellington's principal composer, Billy Strayhorn; the pianist Teddy Wilson; and the Renaissance poets Countee Cullen and Langston Hughes. So did the premier jazz tenorist of all time, Coleman Hawkins. His definitive recording of "Body and Soul" was (and still is) the cross that every jazz saxophonist has sooner or later to take up. If he was not Rollins's first hero, he probably had more to do with shaping the young Rollins than anybody else.

Rollins's mother, Valborg Rollins, a domestic who came to New York from St. Thomas, in the Virgin Islands, bought him his first saxophone when he was thirteen. (His father, Walter William, came from St. Croix, and was a career Navy sailor who helped to support his family but was rarely at home.)

In the Rollins household learning an instrument was one thing, playing jazz was another. Many middle-class blacks were fearful of what they saw as the social stigma of the music. "All West Indian parents wanted children who could entertain by playing something at teatime on Sundays," Gloria Anderson, Rollins' older sister, says, "but no one wanted them to think of becoming a jazz musician." Rollins' older brother, Val, was studying classical violin, but on his way to medical school. Once it was clear where Sonny was headed, he became, in Anderson's words, "the black sheep of the family." (Anderson wasn't overjoyed when, years later, her own son, Clifton, decided to follow in Uncle Sonny's rather than Uncle Val's footsteps. Clifton has played the trombone with his uncle for fourteen years.) Still, his mother paid for the twenty-five-cent lessons at the New York Academy of Music. Rollins was grateful, but says, "Twenty-five cents didn't get very much. I consider myself largely self-taught, but not well enough." A nagging sense of deficiency, Rollins says, is one of the things that drive him even now. "I've always tried to push myself to make up for it."

His first band was composed of kids from the environs of Sugar Hill—in Rollins' time the city's most prestigious black enclave, which overlooked the Polo Grounds and the central plain of Harlem. There was a wealth of talent to draw on. Andy Kirk Jr., the son of the bandleader and a promising saxophonist who would die young, was already making a name for himself. Jackie McLean, the founder of the Hartford Artists Collective, is a passionate altoist famous for an exquisitely dissonant pitch and a raw tone and gusto reminiscent of Charlie Parker's. He was one of the band's early members, and takes credit for introducing Rollins to the airy nonchalance of the tenor legend Lester Young.

Other alums include the pianists Kenny Drew and Walter Davis Jr., the drummer Art Taylor, and the bassist Percy Heath, a onetime Air Force fighter pilot who became the rhythmic mainstay of the Modern Jazz Quartet. The periodic presence of the piano wizard Bud Powell, who also lived in the neighborhood, set a standard for polish and authority. Davis and the percussionists Max Roach and Art Blakey would come up to hang out and also played with the band in local clubs—the 845 Club, Bowman's Lounge, the Celebrity Club, the Audubon, the Savoy, and Minton's Playhouse, Harlem's always-happening hot spot whose manager, the saxophonist and ex-bandleader Teddy Hill, presented a bottle of whiskey whenever Billie Holiday, Lester Young, or other notables took a table.

"They called them the Sugar Hill Gang," says Johnny "Little Dynamo" Griffin, the hard-driving Chicago-born saxophonist, who lives abroad but still tours the States. "They all had a respect for the masters, and they were—how can we say it for print?" He pauses and then whispers, "Bad motherfuckers! They could *all* play." They were the progeny of the passing bebop era, the young vanguard of what would be called the modern-jazz movement. With a prizefighter's swagger in his sound, Rollins commanded attention. One of the most important musicians to take note was Monk, who quickly cultivated a collaboration.

Rollins says Monk was his guru. Musically they were soul mates. According to Steve Lacy, the Paris-based soprano player, Monk once said that Rollins was the best interpreter of his music. If the New York of the 1950s were to have a title track, my choice would be "Pannonica," Monk's tribute to his patron the Baroness "Nica" de Koenigswarter, on *Brilliant Corners* (1956), with the big, lush tone of Rollins' horn set off against the spare crystal tinkling of Monk's celesta.

Since the days at Jake Koven's I had wanted to ask Rollins what he learned from Monk. He answered me in a word: "Everything." What was it that Monk taught him? "Nothing." And so it was with Bud, Fats, Bird, Miles, and Dizzy. Rollins explained: "You were asked to come back or you weren't. If you were playing a gig and weren't cutting it, they might leave you alone on the bandstand."

"That's the way things went in those days," Percy Heath says, remembering the Darwinian rigors that only the fittest survived. "When the 'demon' [a guy who couldn't play] showed up, they raised the pitch a half step, and usually that was that. He'd get the message and move on."

Rollins's old friend Jackie McLean remembers musical encounters with Rollins that were sometimes brutal. "He and Miles gave me many a cruel lesson on the bandstand," he says. "In those days it was all about predators and their prey. And Sonny was the biggest predator of them all." Gil Coggins, a once-promising pianist who recorded with Rollins and Davis, used to warn other players about going up against Rollins: "If he doesn't blow you away in the first few bars, it's just the wolf talkin' to you before he eats you up."

Rollins has no memory of having been competitive. He remembers instead moments of insecurity and having at times felt as if he were the prey.

"Sometimes when I played with Miles and Coltrane, John would be taking a solo and Miles would sidle up to me and whisper something into my ear about how good I was. A little later, when I was playing, I would notice Miles whispering in *Trane's* ear." The memory ignited a thundering laugh that filled the room.

What Rollins didn't laugh about was the unflattering comparisons some fans drew between him and Coltrane after Coltrane's ascendancy.

"John and I had been so close, musically and personally. What happened was that as the guys began to praise Trane, they put me down. I went through a period where I resented Trane. For a minute. I was later very ashamed of myself for that. I would have been more ashamed had I thought Trane knew it. I had to work on myself to get past the fickleness in those people and in myself. There I was, acting like an ordinary human being. I finally got around to facing these things. We were never competitors in the way prizefighters are. We had too much respect for the music for that kind of thing. To be ranked in such a way was demeaning, reducing us to a spectacle when we were both striving to reach higher levels. We inspired each other when we played together. The excitement of playing together was focused on making better music, not trumping each other. In those days we were fighting against the established tenor style, a style that was heavily white-boy. We were still the rebels in those days, the outsiders."

To me, the difference in their sounds matched the difference in their backgrounds. Rollins was a big-city hipster. Coltrane was raised in High Point, North Carolina. He was a gentle man offstage, soft-spoken when he spoke at all, as if he saved himself for the bandstand. You could hear the rural black South in his sound, echoes of a world-weary soul crying out in the night. But in other ways they were kindred spirits. Unlike their idol Charlie Parker, whose poetic brilliance burst forth full-blown, Coltrane and Rollins acquired their mastery through exhaustive practice regimens that were obsessive if not fanatical. Coltrane's boundless researches took him into Nicolas Slonimsky's *Thesaurus of Scales and Melodic Patterns.* At the time of our encounter at Jake Koven's, Rollins told me about grappling with the high-register studies of Sigurd Rascher, the great classical saxophonist and the architect of Rollins' stairway into the stratosphere.

Rollins and Coltrane were unmatched in their worship of Parker, which led them nearly to self-destruction as they fell into some of the excesses of Parker's personal life.

"We used to get high on grass in a little park we called Goof Square," Rollins remembers. Soon they were experimenting with heroin. A former sideman and longtime friend says, "After the war the streets of Harlem were flooded with heroin. Musicians believed that the government gave the Mafia carte blanche to distribute narcotics in Harlem as a favor for Sicily's help against the Nazis. But the pressure to use came from the older guys we played with—though not Hawk [Coleman Hawkins] or others of his generation. They preferred booze."

"I thought at first that it helped me focus on music," Rollins says, "but then I realized it was a trick bag. Soon I didn't even own a saxophone anymore. Guys I knew were crossing the street when they saw me coming. I was even stealing from my mother."

Rollins says the worst night of his life was one he spent in jail for carrying a handgun, something he was "too stupid" to refuse to do when he and some fellow addicts trekked downtown to steal or rob so that they could afford drugs. They were desperate and looked it. "The police stopped us as soon as we got off the subway. They found the gun and took me off to jail. Going through withdrawal I wigged out and they threw me into a straitjacket."

It was not his only trip to jail, and he was rarely without the company of fellow musicians. During one stint on Rikers Island he was commissioned by officials of the Protestant chapel to write music, and produced "Oleo," "Airegin," and "Doxy," jazz standards that wouldn't have been commissioned on the outside in those days.

The bottom for Rollins was 1955. He was "carrying the stick"— homeless—and living in the Chicago subway system. Somehow he managed to make his way to Kentucky, where he checked into the Public Service Hospital in Lexington. Four months later he was back in Chicago, clean, working as a janitor, and practicing again. Like Coltrane, Rollins became a penitent of sorts, incorporating the artist's solitary confrontation with self and complete immersion in music as if they were both the ends and the means of a devotional calling.

Bob Cranshaw, the veteran bassist, lived in Evanston, Illinois, in those days. He says, "Musicians knew who [Rollins] was and where he lived,

and we would go by and listen to him practicing from the street."
(Cranshaw would later meet up with Rollins in New York and join his
band, which he has stayed with for the past forty years.) Max Roach
knew Rollins from the Sugar Hill days, and asked him to sit in with
him and the fabled trumpeter Clifford Brown. By the time they came
to New York, the band had jelled into what was one of the hottest and
hardest-swinging jazz quintets of the era. All were powerhouse players,
and they were soon drawing crowds at New York's Basin Street, the album title for one of their great recordings.

Rollins had a special affinity for "Brownie," because he was clean,
gifted, and humble. It was a devastating blow to him, and to Max
Roach, when Brown was killed in 1956 in an automobile accident.
Brown was twenty-five, two months younger than Rollins. After the
shock of it passed, Rollins would begin one of his most productive pe-
riods, when he made some of his most important recordings. *Dizzy
Gillespie With Sonny Stitt and Sonny Rollins*, the second of two albums
the three made for Verve in 1957, is a feat of blistering pyrotechnics.
Jazz in 3/4 Time, also from 1957, and *Freedom Suite*, from a year later,
both with Max Roach, have some of Rollins' best playing. *Night at the
Village Vanguard* (1957) is a live recording of bare-bones instrumenta-
tion featuring different drum-and-bass combinations, the best of
which, to my ears, was Elvin Jones and Wilbur Ware. Rollins helped
out a troubled Coltrane around this time by inviting him to play on
Tenor Madness, a definitive study of their contrasting styles.

Rollins was also having success performing and recording on the
West Coast. On *Way Out West* (1957), the first of two records he made
in California, he showed off his talent for making more from less by
using the simplest tunes as foils for displaying his creativity and technical brilliance. "Wagon Wheels" and "I'm an Old Cowhand" were
heretofore unheard of in the cool-jazz idiom. It was Rollins' idea to put
himself on the album cover stone-faced in a ten-gallon hat, posed in a
cactus-studded desert.

Steve Lacy, who used to live in New York and play with Monk, loved
this side of Rollins. "He was a very funny character," Lacy says. "He
went through many different phases and was always very critical of
himself. He kept trying to change his sound, his image, even his haircut. He went into the cowboy thing and then he started a thing about

the Native Americans, and that got divided into cowboys and Indians at the same time. He had a Mohawk haircut under the cowboy hat and he had everybody cracking up. But when he got up to play, nobody was laughing."

By 1958 Rollins was at the peak of his powers and reaping the rewards. He had an apartment on the Lower East Side, a new Cadillac (just like Coleman Hawkins), and, briefly, a wife, the actress and model Dawn Finney. But if the year began in triumph, it ended in sorrow. That November his mother died, sending him into an emotional tailspin. A year later, following his first European tour, he stopped performing. He was out of the public eye for almost two years, but the musicians knew where he was and what he was up to—woodshedding. Coltrane would come by, and so would Jackie McLean. Monk would arrive, and, sometimes without exchanging a word, he and Rollins would start to play.

Rollins also took his practicing outside. Steve Lacy remembers marathon sessions on the pedestrian walk of the Williamsburg Bridge. "Sonny was my idol and the idol of most jazz players everywhere," Lacy says, "and I tried to follow in his footsteps until I realized that what he did on the tenor was too strong for me to emulate. On the bridge there was this din, a really high level of sound from boats and cars and subways and helicopters and airplanes. Sonny played into it. I couldn't hear myself but I could hear Sonny."

In 1961 Rollins came back to a music scene that was about to be turned on its head. Between rock-and-roll and television, nightclub jazz would all but dry up. "Our thing" was becoming the "new thing," also called free jazz. Coltrane, the altoist Ornette Coleman, the pianist Cecil Taylor, and the woodwind player Eric Dolphy were playing outside the harmonic structure, outside the rhythm, outside everything. Typical of him, Rollins took on avant-garde figures like Coleman's sideman the trumpeter Don Cherry. He made a fine but "out" recording of duets with Coleman Hawkins and the pianist Paul Bley, *Sonny Meets Hawk* (1963). Unlike Hawkins, many of the old guard who couldn't make the change were dropping from view.

Toward the end of the decade Rollins was exploring new spiritual territory. Coltrane, before his death in 1967, had become drug-free and was exploring Christianity and Islam. Rollins was drawn to Eastern philosophical teachings. In 1968 he traveled to Japan to perform, and later studied Zen Buddhism. Then, taking his horn and little else, he spent four months in the Powaii Ashram in the Bombay suburbs, meditating on his life's mission and practicing hatha yoga. He came back to greet the seventies with floppy hats and a friendly smile, for many of us his most startling reinvention to date. His music was a lot more accessible too, taking on a new pop flavor that won him legions of young fans who had never heard of Bud Powell, Coleman Hawkins, Lester Young, or Thelonious Monk. His work for the next two decades left much of his original following behind and failed to draw the critical acclaim of his earlier years.

As the nineties come to a close, however, Rollins seems to be pulling it all together. The last two times I heard him, last year in Boston, where he packed Jordan Hall with mostly college kids, and in Lenox, Massachusetts, where he drew older and younger fans, he seemed to be weaving together disparate threads of his long career. In Boston he delivered a volcanic outpouring of standards and originals, doubling and quadrupling meters during his solos, tossing up quotations from other songs in other keys like so many sparks. He gave an old-style crooner's treatment to "Skylark," bending the notes, making little motifs, and then exploding them in a vintage-Rollins torrent of cadenzas.

Unlike the bigger, rounder, unamplified sound of years gone by, Rollins's sound has a gruff, grainy texture, and the bell of his horn is miked, a common practice among musicians nowadays. He's using a softer reed than the stiff No. 4s that he used to prefer and that require intense pressure from the muscles in the lips and the jaw.

In part the new sound may be age-related, but it's also artistic exploration. "There are people who want to hear the way I sounded on *Saxophone Colossus*," he says, referring to a 1956 album that drew widespread critical acclaim. "You don't go back over the same ground and stay creative. What I want is a sound that's more earthy, more unsaxophonely. I don't want to sound like a sax."

His appearance at the Berkshire Performing Arts Theatre at the National Music Center, in Lenox, was a powerhouse "show" (his word) with a peppering of Caribbean themes which ended with kids dancing in the aisles. The context was a crossover, accessible, international sound, but Rollins' solos at its heart were pure jazz, high-octane and straight-ahead, recalling the golden age as few are left to do.

Today Rollins is once again the most highly regarded saxophonist in jazz. The *Down Beat* critics' poll for 1997 named him jazz artist of the year and tenor saxophonist of the year. He works only when he wants to, and only when the travel arrangements and accommodations are up to snuff. He seems to be at peace as much as Sonny Rollins can be at peace.

His privacy is protected by his personal manager, the former Lucille Pearson, to whom he's been married for more than thirty years. She is a genial woman with a lovely smile that belies a flinty eye for business. "I've heard that some music-industry people call me Mrs. No," she told me as she drove us on a circuitous route to their house which I couldn't have remembered had I attempted it on my own. The bed of gravel in the horseshoe driveway was thick and fresh-laid. The teal-blue paint on their small farmhouse looked new, and so did their cars. But there was nothing that spoke of great wealth or ostentation. There is a swimming pool, but Rollins has never been in it, according to Lucille.

"I've come to appreciate my solitude," Rollins said as we talked beside a fireplace made of stones the size of bread loaves. Without a fire it radiates a chill, a reminder of the spartan regimens on which Rollins thrives. "I still love the city, though more from a distance. I'm up around six A.M. and rarely on my feet after nine P.M. They're the same hours I used to keep, except they're reversed. I don't smoke, I don't drink, I don't have hobbies, because music is everything for the remaining time I have on this earth."

"When I'm right and the band is right and the music is right," Rollins said, "I feel myself getting closer to the place where the sound is less polished and more aboriginal. That's what I'm striving for. The trumpeter Roy Eldridge once told a guy he could only reach a divine state in performance four or five times a year. That sounds about right for me.

"In India I renewed my commitment to music as my path. Protest is part of this. You can't have jazz without protest. Protest may be too narrow a word to apply to men like Basie, Ellington, and Hawkins. But by carrying themselves with pride, just by acting like men, the older musicians influenced younger guys like me. So did the Pullman porters, fighting for their dignity. We looked up to those guys and, when we were old enough, went a step further. It was a generational thing. The world was changing."

Even before his male role models there was Miriam Solomon, his grandmother, who took care of him while his mother worked. An activist in Marcus Garvey's Universal Negro Improvement Association, a back-to-Africa movement that swept Harlem in the 1920s, Grandmother Solomon took Sonny to the Abyssinian Baptist Church to hear the Reverend Adam Clayton Powell and his son the Reverend Adam Clayton Powell Jr. The younger Powell would become a U.S. congressman, but both were fiery champions of militant civil-rights campaigns long before the arrival of Martin Luther King Jr. Grandmother Solomon took Sonny to marches protesting hiring bias against black clerks in Harlem department stores. She took him to demonstrations against Italy's invasion of Ethiopia, on behalf of the Scottsboro boys, and in support of Paul Robeson, the baritone and social activist harassed and beleaguered during the anti-Communist fervor that began in the late 1930s. Years later Rollins' *Freedom Suite*, recorded in 1958, was inspired by the sit-ins in the South, just as *Global Warming* (Milestone), his most recent CD, is, in Rollins's words, "about how we're trashing the world."

"As for my spiritualism," he says, "it's more an amalgamation of my religious convictions, including my belief in reincarnation. I am trying to clean up my karma so that I can come back with the blessings of the Great Spirit."

EDDIE DEAN

Desperate Man Blues

Somewhere deep in the heart of the boonies, Joe Bussard, the self-proclaimed king of record collectors, was lost. A few miles back, he had made a wrong turn, and now he didn't know where in the hell he was. All he knew for sure was that he was in 78 r.p.m. country.

A native Marylander, Bussard was not a complete stranger to these parts. He had traveled many times to southwest Virginia to hunt for old records. It was the late '60s, and once again he was canvassing the coal region, a long, bumpy, gizzard-neck stretch that belongs more to Appalachia than to the rest of the Old Dominion. The cradle of country music, this area was then the best place in the world to find the 78 r.p.m. records made in the '20s and '30s, the golden age of early American recorded music. Even during the Depression, the people here—whether white miners earning steady wages or blacks who owned farms—had money for records, and they bought plenty of them, from local string-band music to blues from the Mississippi Delta.

In a little town called Tazewell, Bussard had launched the day's search as he always did, asking around about where he could find old records. He'd gone door to door holding a 78 so folks could see that he meant music discs and not dog-eared heating bills. He hadn't had much luck until somebody told him about a flea market out on the edge of town. In no time, Bussard had managed to lose his way—not a difficult thing to do in these mountains, where, as the late West Virginia writer Breece D'J Pancake once wrote, "road maps resembled a barrel of worms with St. Vitus Dance."

The places that Bussard usually staked out don't appear on any maps, so he had to let the rugged terrain take him where it might: One minute he'd be driving along some cheery stretch of green hills right out of a postcard, and the next he would find himself plunged down in some dark hollow where the sun refused to shine. All the better. The more remote the place, Bussard had long ago discovered, the better the chances of finding a stash of old 78s. So getting lost was all part of the endless quest.

Up ahead, Bussard saw an old man trudging along the road, so he pulled over to ask for directions. The man said he was headed to the flea market himself and would be happy to show Bussard the way. On the drive, a cassette of vintage string-band music (custom-taped from Bussard's vast collection) purred on the car stereo, and the geezer piped up, "Boy, I like that music." Bussard replied, "Yeah, I'm looking for records like that." The old man looked out the window at the hills rolling by: "Oh, I got a gang of them back at the house, a couple hundred or so."

The man's casual aside, spoken as if he were mentioning the weather, gripped Bussard to the very core of his being. The affable coot didn't know it, but he'd spoken the magic words that ruled the life of any hard-core 78 fiend. Somehow, Bussard managed to retain his composure: "Can I go look at 'em?"

Sure, said the old man; he'd let Bussard see the records after they visited the flea market, which was held every weekend in the empty parking lot of an abandoned drive-in movie theater. That was just fine with Bussard. He had all the time in the world. A trust-fund baby, he spent most of his waking hours in pursuit of old 78s. To call it a hobby would be an insult: It was his life.

At the flea market, there wasn't much in the way of records, and the only sign of old-time music was next to a dilapidated concession stand and projection booth, where an elderly blind man sat picking a banjo. Bussard listened to the bony grayhead pluck in an archaic style reminiscent of local legend Dock Boggs, who hailed from these music-rich hills. Before his death, Boggs was fortunately enshrined for posterity on those sturdy old 78s. All Bussard could think about was that he should have brought his reel-to-reel tape recorder. The banjo player droned on, and Bussard got back into his car, feeling those familiar pangs: another snippet of music history lost forever.

Twenty miles later and deeper into the mountains, Bussard pulled up to the old man's house, and from the first glance he knew he'd hit pay dirt. It was a little shotgun shack, no paint on the faded wood, junk scattered all over the yard, with a broken-toothed fence that remained standing through sheer stubbornness. A little ramshackle, but not too. Lived in. Perfect. He could almost smell the old records waiting for him inside.

In his years of canvassing for 78s, Bussard had learned the myriad signs—old lace curtains, flowerpots on the porch, smoke snaking from the chimney—that meant a home's current residents had been there for decades. These were the people who had long ago bought the records that Bussard was now after. And they would still have them, because mountain folks never throw anything away, whether it be a broken refrigerator, a tin coffee can, or old Victrola records they haven't played in years.

Long before the advent of vinyl, records were made of shellac. During World War II, millions of 78s were melted down for raw materials needed in the war effort. In those early days of the recording industry, there were no master tapes stored in record-label vaults, only metal discs, most of which were likewise destroyed during the war years— which made the 78s craved by Bussard all the more rare. Sometimes, only a single copy survived, a lone slab of shellac to prevent a song from disappearing into the black hole of silence.

Inside the sparsely furnished house, the old man shuffled to the bed and dropped on his knees as if preparing to pray. Instead, he pulled out a cardboard box, along with a cloud of dust—"as thick as whipped cream"—that filled the cramped, closed-off room. Bussard leapt on the box like some drug-sniffing dog on the scent, only to initial disappointment. On top of the pile were some typical records for this area: the Carter Family on Victor, Uncle Dave Macon on Vocalion, Charlie Poole on Columbia, and other old-time hillbilly 78s. Good—even some great—stuff, but for the most part as common as cabbage. Bussard had already amassed one of the world's most formidable collections of this genre. Sure, there was always room for more, but this find seemed like nothing spectacular.

Bussard had moved beyond old-time country. What he was really on the lookout for were the old jazz and blues sides that had lately captured his fancy. Bussard had begun to realize that it was all good, from jug band stomps to sacred-harp hymns, as long as it came from the '20s and '30s—that magical era. That was his philosophy, anyway.

Then, a few records down, something caught his eye: the lavish outspread tail of a peacock, its burnished-gold feathers resplendent— almost glowing—in a field of deepest purple. It was a Black Patti, one of the most obscure and coveted labels of the '20s. There had been only 55 records, mostly blues, jazz, and gospel, released on the black-owned label in its brief seven-month existence.

Like so many indies of the era, Black Patti (named for a turn-of-the-century African-American opera singer) was a fly-by-night operation that offered a modest output of its "race" records to a black audience before retreating into silence, shrouded in mystery. Little was known about the ultra-obscure musicians whose enticing names (Half-Pint Jackson, Blind Richard Yates, and so on) were emblazoned under the sheltering canopy of the peacock's tail. These were mostly limited pressings, sometimes just a few hundred per record, and their extreme scarcity had made Black Pattis dream finds for devout 78 collectors. Bussard had only glimpsed a few battered copies, until now.

Above all, a record canvasser must mask his emotions, but Bussard could barely contain himself. "'O my God,'" he recalls whispering to himself. "I was pissing and shitting little apples." The peacock seemed to be strutting, as if it were alive. The room felt oppressive. The dust hung in the air like some hallucinatory fog. Regaining his composure, he said rather coolly, "Oh, man, this is a nice label. I like that." His host chuckled, "You do? Well, there's a bunch more."

Indeed, there were many more, all the way to the bottom of the box, pristine and gleaming, black as coal and as shiny as store stock. Fourteen Black Pattis, the most ever found in a single place, now sat in a neat stack in front of Joe Bussard. "Some man gave 'em to my sister back in 1927," the old man was explaining. "We played 'em once, but we don't care much for blues and such, so we packed 'em away and they've been there ever since."

Black Pattis, damn near mint. Jesus H. Christ. So taken was he by the sight of the golden peacocks, Bussard had nearly lapsed into a trance. But he knew it was time to make a deal fast, before the geezer had a sudden conversion to the blues, or before some unseen harpy started shrieking from somewhere in the bowels of the house, as had happened so many times before: "Daddy, don't you dare get rid of them—those are Mama's records!"

Not this time, said Bussard to himself. He would have called on the Lord for help, but he wasn't a religious man. He was that most desperate of lost souls—a 78 collector face to face with his quarry—and he would do anything short of violence to get those records safely into the trunk of the car parked outside. Mustering all the nonchalance he could, Bussard slipped the 78s into their sleeves—copies so new they slid in as if they were greased—and put them into the box. "What do I owe you?" he asked. "Oh, give me 10 dollars," the old man replied, delighted to unload the junk for some cash.

Three decades later, one of those prize Black Pattis is now considered among the rarest blues records in the world. "Original Stack O' Lee Blues" by the Down Home Boys—Long Cleve Reed and Little Harvey Hull—is a strange, haunting, almost mournful take on the Stagger Lee tale, which has been covered by hundreds of musicians, from Mississippi John Hurt to Nick Cave. Recorded in 1927, this guitar-and-vocal duet version is something else altogether, harking back to the murky nineteenth-century origins of the blues; pre-Delta, racially mongrel, profound, and seemingly not of this world.

While its aesthetic merits are indisputable, it is its uniqueness as an artifact that makes it a treasure: Bussard's near-mint copy is the only one that has ever been found. He says he has turned down offers of $30,000 for the record; in fact, he laughs in the faces of prospective buyers. Now listen up, he says, and listen good: When it comes to those old 78s, nobody gets the better of Joe Bussard.

His narrative finished for now, Bussard puffs triumphantly on a $2 cigar in the basement of his modest brick rambler on a hill outside Frederick, Maryland. Through its telling, he can once again relish one of his greatest finds. The ritual begins when he pulls the record from the shelf and shows off its pristine surface to a visitor; it ends when he nestles it back among the other 78s—more than 25,000 at last count—

that line the walls from floor to ceiling. Most come with their very own war stories, starring Joe Bussard, record hunter. It's no accident that Bussard has failed to mention that he had a traveling companion on this trip; there's little room for accomplices in Bussard's record-canvassing adventures, always starring Joe Bussard.

In reciting the Black Patti saga, for example, he provides all the sound effects, including the good-natured bellow of the old man, the high-pitched screech of the archetypal harpy, and even the thumb-picking technique of the blind banjoist, all expertly rendered. It is a compelling performance, one that he has given countless times to those who make the pilgrimage here. They come to see (and hear) firsthand what many consider to be the most vital, historically important privately owned collection of early-twentieth-century American music.

"Bussard's got shit that God don't have," says collector and musician Tom Hoskins, an authority on pre–World War II Delta blues. "It is one of the great glory holds, probably the finest in the world. He was canvassing earlier than most, and he's been at it longer, and he took everything: He recognized stuff that he really didn't even like at the time, but he recognized it as being good, and he kept it."

"Joe, as a private person engaged on a practically full-time basis, has built up a really important private archive," says author, collector, and WAMU-FM DJ Dick Spottswood. "There are surviving examples of American music there that would not exist today had Joe not gone out and scoured for them."

Record dealer Mike Steward of North Carolina regards Bussard's hallowed hoard as an intimate reflection of its maker. "All those records are an extension of his personality," says Stewart, who has amassed his own respected stash of 78s. "I'd rather have Bussard's collection than anybody's. He's got four or five of the best Charlie Pattons, and a couple of Skip Jameses, and endless fascinating blues and country. He's got all the best early country music, basically."

Still, there are plenty of formidable collections out there. What makes Bussard such an undeniable force in old-time music circles isn't simply his collection but what he has done with it over the years. It is a bizarre fusion of obsessive, almost pathological hoarding and an equally strong impulse for rampant dissemination. He's got to have this stuff, yes, but he wants the whole world to hear it, too.

North Carolina archivist Marshall Wyatt paid a visit last spring to Bussard's basement in preparation for a compilation of black fiddlers, *Violin, Sing the Blues for Me*. Bussard had a dozen 78s Wyatt desperately needed, and he welcomed him into his home on short notice: "A lot of collectors, even if they're cooperative, tend to drag things out, but not Joe," says Wyatt. "If anything, he was rushing me. His collection is a great resource, because he makes it so readily available."

For 35 years, Bussard has taped a radio show that broadcasts on various AM stations throughout the South (locally on WTHU, 1450 AM out of Thurmont); and his house has been a hive of activity and a gathering place for musicians. In his makeshift basement studio, all sorts of future legends recorded their first songs. In the late '50s and early '60s, guitarist John Fahey, now toasted as a hero by alt-rockers like Thurston Moore, recorded under the blues nom de guitarre "Blind Thomas" on Bussard's Fonotone Records label, which featured custom-made 78s that Bussard traded on his canvassing expeditions. In the same era, Washington bluegrass pioneers John Duffey and Buzz Busby launched their careers singing into a $50 mike that hung from the ceiling. These 78s are now collector's items in their own right. Bussard himself made an album of old-time music, *Jolly Joe and His Jug Band*, that was released on the local Piedmont label.

A Johnny Appleseed spreading the old-time sounds far and wide, Bussard has seen his influence reach well beyond the D.C. area. For 50 cents a side, he makes cassettes of his rarities for a world-wide audience, ranging from Japanese businessmen to European archivists. It is the clean-sounding copies from his collection that form the cornerstones of two recent compilations that have helped launch a so-called new folk revival: The Smithsonian Institute's reissued *Anthology of American Folk Music* from '97 and this year's Dock Boggs retrospective on Revenant have been embraced and endlessly celebrated, not only as essential documents of bedrock American music, but as trendy CDs to show off to friends. Both are now critical darlings, appearing on rock critics' Top Ten lists from *Newsweek* to *Spin*. Wilco, Son Volt, Beck, and other hipsters worship this archaic racket, much the same way Bob Dylan and Fahey did back in the '50s.

Bussard himself remains willfully oblivious to most of these developments. The very term "folk music" rankles him: The music he worships was made by professionals—backwoods or no—and released on commercial records that were revolutionary in their day. He dismisses Dylan as "shit," but then again he despises all forms of rock 'n' roll, which to him is no more than the cuss-word verb of its original meaning, a blues double-entendre for fucking. He similarly rejects all country music made after '53, saying it was finished when Hank Williams croaked in the back of that Cadillac in West Virginia. As for jazz, well, that died out around '33, murdered in cold blood by the Depression and the arrival of the big bands. When told about the so-called swing revival, he nearly chokes on his cigar, incredulous that anyone would bother resurrecting the brassy dreck of the Dorseys and their ilk.

In his absolute negation of postwar American mass culture, Bussard is very much in line with his fellow 78 collectors. This rabid brotherhood is almost invariably made up of eccentrics who came of age in the '50s and '60s, rejecting everything around them. More than just hippie-haters, though, these men loathe the very idea of popular music, right back to the time of fox trots and Al Jolson, the Jazz Age cliches often mistaken for the soundtrack for their beloved era. They've got their own names for such million sellers as Vernon Dalhart: Vermin Dogshit and Vernon Stalefart. These are the enemies, the pop crooners on the crapola 78s that they've had to muck through to find the gems that never made it in mainstream America. Their Jazz Age is strictly the music of poor whites and blacks: wild-ass jazz and string-band hillbilly, surreal yodels and king-snake moans, lightning-bolt blues and whorehouse romps and orgasmic gospel.

It's all anti-pop, anti-sentimental: the raw sounds of the city gutter and the roadside ditch. Most important, it was captured on disc for all time at a crucial historical juncture. "What gives the '20s interest to 78 nuts like me and Joe and Fahey is you have the industrial process meeting a vernacular music, and initially meeting it purely on its own terms," says Spottswood, who has written extensively on the subject. Spottswood says the early record companies' objective was "to seek out the music, to record it, to disseminate it on phonograph records, primarily to the area from which it originates; secondarily, across the national spectrum to whatever extent the market will bear. But they're doing it in a way that doesn't really tamper with the music." As Bussard puts it, more succinctly: "the sound of American music before the modern world fucked it up."

The group's bible is a publication called *78 Quarterly*, an elaborate scrapbook of shared obsession featuring exhaustive articles on the old records and the musicians who made them—the more obscure and primitive, the better. Delta bluesman Charlie Patton is a particular hero, especially in the wake of Robert Johnson's unprecedented popularity in the '90s—a former god usurped by rock geeks. Above all, though, are the 78 records themselves—festooned with their hieroglyphic labels, secret talismans from the underground world: "My saliva thickens, my heart pounds, and my blood rises when I see some of the records pictured in *78 Quarterly*," confesses a disciple in a typical letter to the editor.

The philosophy of this underground cult is best summed up in a scene from the '94 documentary *Crumb*, about the misanthropic cartoonist Robert Crumb. Most of the movie details Crumb's twisted dysfunctional family, featuring his pair of tortured-genius brothers, cursed by their inherited artistic gifts. Only Crumb has been able to forge a livable existence (and a comfortable living) from his talents. In one scene, the irascible Crumb, brooding in his record room, puts a Black Patti 78 on the turntable and sits back on a mattress in reverie.

As he rhapsodizes about the power of this music, he vents his spleen in a nakedly revealing moment, and it becomes clear that behind the thick glasses and savage cynicism lies a hopeless romantic lamenting his own paradise lost: "When I listen to old music, that's one of the few times that I actually have a kind of love for humanity," he says, for once forsaking the trademark smirk that punctuates his conversation. "You hear the best part of the soul of the common people, you know—their way of expressing their connection to eternity or whatever you want to call it. Modern music doesn't have that calamitous loss—people can't express themselves that way anymore."

Among this pack of cranks, where nuts are not only tolerated, but a welcome part of the social landscape, Bussard is the odd man out of the oddballs: an unschooled and profane "pure cracker" (in the words of a fellow collector) among a bunch of mostly urbane Northerners. A horse trader and hustler besting the former frat boys at their own game, sprung from the very culture that he's hellbent on memorializing. "Out of all these city collectors, Joe was one of the only country boys out there canvassing," says Fahey, who hunted for records in his native Takoma Park and the District as well as throughout the South. "But behind all that, he is a brilliant intellectual. You just have to listen closely to him, because he speaks in parables."

Bussard is universally acknowledged as a breed apart, someone who has literally dedicated his life to his pursuit, family and friends be damned. "Joe is a bit overenthusiastic, sort of the extreme expression of the collecting mentality," says Spottswood, who has known Bussard for four decades. "It's when the collecting instinct overrides any other instinct of social equity or decency. . . . He has not led an unproductive life—I take my hat off to him. I just think that the personal cost is more than I would have cared to pay."

Fellow collectors talk about a man so driven by his passion that they have had to distance themselves from Bussard, lest they too be completely consumed. Bussard's wife, Esther, admits that the toll has been more than she reckoned on. A music lover herself, she long ago resigned herself to playing second fiddle to the 78s always beckoning from her husband's basement. "If I wasn't a born-again, spirit-filled Christian, who the day I married him made a commitment to God, I would have left long ago," she says somberly. "He's a very, very difficult person to live with. Our only daughter sometimes doesn't think too much of him either, because he was always so busy with his music, that he hardly had time for anything else."

Joe Bussard has a record in his hands as he sprints across the carpeted floor of his basement shrine. He's never had a steady job, and he doesn't have to worry about deadlines. He's in a frenzied rush because that's the way he does everything.

Despite his hyperactive verve, he looks as if he just got out of bed, and he did. It's mid-morning, and he's got on his usual working clothes: a flannel shirt, jeans, and worn-out slippers, white socks poking through the holes. His gray hair sticks out like a scarecrow's, and a cross hangs from his neck. He found it metal-detecting years ago—treasure hunting, as always—put it on, and has worn it ever since—not for any spiritual significance but because he likes the looks of it. He says he gets all the religion he needs from his old gospel 78s, heavenly quartets and crazed country preachers who shame the slick TV evangelists of today.

Despite his haste, he's careful to handle the record on its rim, so as not to soil the grooves. He crams the 78 right into a visitor's face, and then draws it away defensively just as fast. Don't even think about trying to hold it yourself. The only person allowed to handle the records in Joe Bussard's basement is Joe Bussard. There are warnings, pecked out on his manual Smith-Corona Galaxie typewriter, stickered all over the shelves of his collection: PLEASE DO NOT TOUCH RECORDS.

Throughout their 35-year marriage, Esther Bussard has honored this request. "I've never touched one of his records, or anything in his room, because I respect it—that's his room," she says. "Even though I sometimes feel resentful and bitter, I still respect him for what he has done. He has a fantastic collection, and I realize this because I appreciate music, and I appreciate his saving it for history."

Despite his fanatical protection of his records, Bussard usually has a lit cigar smoldering on his lips, and the ash end often droops dangerously close to the discs. Just before it drops onto some priceless 78, Bussard manages to react instinctively and put it in a nearby ashtray.

"Lemme play you one of the last real jazz bands, Joseph Robechaux and his New Orleans Rhythm Boys, recorded in New York City in 1933," he says of the record, *King Kong Stomp* on Vocalion. "You can hear it slip into the swing [he slurs this word as a ready-made profanity], but it's still good, one of the last really hot jazz songs. But that beautiful tone, that perfection, is starting to slide."

Then Bussard puts the record on a huge RCA turntable unit that he got from a radio station; it's as bulky as a bank safe, with an oversize tone arm as big as a fly swatter. "See, most collectors, they'll have a nice pile of records, but their turntable's a piece of shit, and they'll have Mickey Mouse speakers." He points to a massive wooden Altech speaker cabinet in the far corner of the basement. "I bought that speaker system in 1959 in Baltimore for $800," he says in a near-shout. "You could have bought a car for that! That was the sort of hi-fi that doctors and lawyers had. It weighs 300 pounds, and it'll run your ass out of here. This gives you an idea of what was really on these old records."

He dips the diamond stylus ("That's $90 worth of needle!") on the record. The volume is cranked almost to max, and the combo's tight rhythms fill the room, in a blast loud enough to knock RCA Victor mascot Nipper's furry little head right off. The sound is splendid, a resounding rebuttal to anyone who claims that 78s are scratched-up slabs meant to be played only through a wind-up in an antique shop. ("Steel railroad spikes," says Bussard of the Victrola styluses of old.) Throughout the song, Bussard dances his lanky-limbed jib, wielding his wet cigar like a trombone, and then taking it out to wag his tongue lasciviously. With his long, wolfish face contorted in exaggerated expressions of glee, he resembles some Tex Avery cartoon character come to life, complete with the original soundtrack. During the song, at least, he's 62 going on 16.

Like his stories of canvassing, this is another Bussard ritual, one that has astonished even the most jaded collectors who've made the rounds. Tom Hoskins visited the basement more than two decades ago, and he remembers the impression it made on him. "He's definitely certifiable," says Hoskins, who adds that this remark is meant as a compliment. "He'd go over to those shelves and pull a record from out of the green sleeve, and he'd hold the record with his fingers on the edge, and he'd shove it right into your face—'Look at the surface, look at that condition!'—and then he'd plop it on that turntable and drop the old fang of the cobra tone arm into the groove and—bingo!"

Spending time in Bussard's windowless, smoke-filled lair can be an exhausting experience. As he rushes around his immaculate archive, whose only index is in his head, he might as well be on an unmapped island. When the outside world intrudes by way of a phone call for his wife, he won't be distracted for more than a moment: He's rigged up a system to relay such messages without having to leave the basement, barking through a microphone hooked to an upstairs speaker.

Indeed, the records seem to have a narcotic effect on Bussard, a lifelong teetotaler. And for the visitor, the barrage of one Bussard fave after another—kazoos and cornets and tubas as deafening as techno dance music—blasting from the speakers is akin to being imprisoned with the guy in high school who played record after record for listeners whether they wanted to hear them or not. Marshall Wyatt's recent visit turned into a two-day marathon as Bussard played records for him both nights into the wee hours. "It's hard to get away," says Wyatt, who relished the experience. "He's always saying, 'Lemme play you one more—you gotta hear this one.' It's definitely like this adrenaline that keeps pouring out. It's very entertaining."

Just when it seems that Bussard has played every 78 ever recorded—from Tennessee string band Dr. Humphrey Bate and His Possum Hunters to a jazz combo called the New Orleans Feet Warmers—he flashes a maniacal grin, and he cackles through his cigar: "Now, you wanna hear some way-out *weird* shit?" Joe Bussard's always got one more you have to, *have to*, hear.

Back in the late '50s, Pete Whelan dropped by the Bussard basement archive for the first and only time. The publisher of *78 Quarterly*, Whelan is a Penn State alum and author whose collection rivals Bussard's. At the time, Whelan was returning from a canvassing trip down South, headed back up to New York; he was dog-tired and struck by his host's boundless enthusiasm. Most collectors play it cool, letting the records speak for themselves. Not Bussard. "He had sort of a brush crew cut; he reminded me of someone who belonged to the National Rifle Association," recalls Whelan. "He seemed to have this incredible energy, like it was sort of overwhelming."

What Whelan remembers most from that long-ago visit is that Bussard got the best of him on their first and only record trade. "I traded an E-condition record—it turned out to be the only copy of a white Cajun group on Paramount, Leo Soileau, doing a blues, 'East Rider Blues.' This guy was the best of the Cajuns," says Whelan. "I got an Irene Scruggs on Champion and a Tommy Bradley on Champion—16,000 series—at that time the only copy that had showed up. Then one popped up later in the same shape. . . . In retrospect, I made a bad trade."

Whelan says he and Bussard still keep in touch, and he plans to feature a color slide of Bussard's lone copy of the Black Patti "Stack O' Lee" on the cover of an upcoming issue of *78 Quarterly*. "That's a great record," says Whelan. "But I've got the only known copy of Skip James' 'Drunken Spree' on Paramount. And that's a great record, too." These are the sort of one-of-a-kinds that make Robert Johnson records—which are plentiful by comparison—seem run-of-the-mill stuff for moneybag dupes like Eric Clapton to invest in.

Bussard's basement walls are covered not only with record shelves but with the art deco sleeves of the era, which doubled as brilliantly designed ads for legendary labels like Champion and Gennett and Black Swan and Melotone and Paramount. On the wall above his turntable are some of his favorite collectibles: a Blind Lemon Jefferson Birthday edition of "Piney Woods Money Mama," Ma Rainey's "Lost Wandering Blues" on Paramount; in between the hallowed pair—Rainey is Bussard's favorite female blues singer—is a 78 from the KKK Record Company ("Best in Klan Music") out of Indianapolis. Titled "Mystic City," it's a Klan anthem, featuring the vocals of "100% Americans with orchestral accompaniment," according to the blood-red label, which boasts a burning cross. Bussard says the music is awful, but it's a historical artifact nonetheless, and he's got a bunch more; he's made cassette copies for various Klan chapters willing to pay.

There is a small row of books, mostly jazz discographies and record-label ledgers, as well as a biography of Jimmie Rodgers, but in general Bussard distrusts scholars and musicologists. Vintage photos of old-time musicians gaze sternly at the collection from the opposite wall. It's startling how many of these hillbillies are dressed in formal suits; in fact, there's barely a pair of overalls in the bunch. A different world, and not squat to do with *Hee Haw*: Charlie Poole, the Delmore Brothers, A. P. Carter, as serious as an undertaker. About the only smiling face on this wall of honor is a rail-thin, sharp-dressed Jimmy Rodgers before he died of tuberculosis in '33 ("Yodelingly Yours," the photo is autographed, supposedly by the Singing Brakeman himself).

The raucous "King Kong Stomp" rocks to a close, and Bussard bleats through his wet cigar. "All that in *three* minutes! Can you believe it? That's jazz, man, not this swing shit! How in the hell can anybody listen to anything else? That's what I want to know!"

It was swing that Bussard had to listen to while growing up in the '40s. His parents played big-band records on a Victrola that Bussard keeps in a corner of the room, exiled in eternal punishment. The experience left him with an undying hatred for this genre, especially now that he's hooked on the "real" jazz records of the '20s: early Louis Armstrong, King Oliver, Johnny Dodds. "*That's* the hot jazz," he says.

"Not like that shit that guy plays on WAMU [referring to Rob Bamburger's popular *Hot Jazz Saturday Night* program]. He doesn't know crap. Did you hear what he said about Dodds' playing? Said he didn't have any range—the greatest clarinet player ever! *Cold*-jazz Saturday Night, I call it."

The first singer to capture Bussard's fancy was Gene Autry, who starred in the cowboy movies that Bussard loved. But then, one day, the 10-year-old heard a Jimmie Rodgers song on the radio, and there was no turning back. "His voice just grabbed me," he says. Smitten by the Blue Yodeler, he went to a Frederick record store to buy a Jimmie Rodgers record; the clerk told him they'd all been out of print for years, but some of the old-timers in town might still have copies.

It is fortunate for him that Bussard was successful on those early canvassing expeditions around his hometown; he acquired his first 78s knocking door to door, and he caught the bug. By the time he got his driver's license in the early '50s, he was ready to branch out, and he began traveling in his Chevy all over the South in search of records.

Unlike many big-time collectors, Bussard acquired the bulk of his precious finds himself, through his own record hunting. Many of the Northern 78 addicts acquired their cargo through estate sales, auctions, large-scale trades, and buyouts. Bussard harvested most of his now-hallowed crop the hard way, and in fact, canvassing and collecting has always been his main occupation. (His grandfather ran a farm-supply store, and after its sale in the '60s, Bussard subsisted on family money.)

Bussard was most active during the late '50s and '60s, the salad days of canvassing. By then, he had some competition, not only from the Northern blues posse but from locals like Spottswood, Fahey, and Hoskins, who were keen on the Delta blues. As it turned out, the best place to find old 78s wasn't the Delta or the Deep South at all, but the Southeastern states, especially the mountain regions of West Virginia, Virginia, and North Carolina. This was Bussard territory.

Most canvassers were interlopers in an exotic realm, but Bussard was working familiar turf, not much different from his own area, which at the time was still strictly rural. He would simply ratchet up his Frederick drawl a notch or two and gab to the old-timers as if he were trying to wheedle some allowance money out of his granddad.

Mostly, Bussard just followed his instincts and whatever luck came his way. Once he was pumping gas in a small coal town in southwest Virginia, refueling for the long ride back up Interstate 81 to Maryland. He asked the attendant about old records, and the man told him there was a hardware store with racks of them: *Store stock*, thought Bussard to himself, as he roared across the mountain. "So we go into this little coal town which the highway had bypassed. It was dead. And we walk into the store, and it was like going back into the 1920s—old metal tile ceilings with designs and big ol' round bulb lights hanging down. I went in back and found the owner, this short little guy, and he said, 'Yeah, they're upstairs,' and we got on this freight elevator that moved about a tenth of a tenth of a tenth of a mile per hour. I thought we'd never get up to the second floor—a snail crawling up the wall could have beaten us up there. Well, we finally got up there, and there was a balcony that ran the whole length of the store. You could walk out along there, and halfway out was a shelf of records—5,000 records in the shelf—*store stock*, never been played. I just about *shit*. The sleeves were all black and dirty from coal soot, sticking out. So I reached up in the far left-hand top row, six rows high. The first one I pulled out was 'Sobbin' Blues' by King Oliver on Okeh—absolutely new—at least a $400 record. The next one I pulled out was 'Jack Ass Blues' on Vocalion by the Dixie Syncopators. New. 'Dead Man Blues' by Oliver. *Mint*. It was heavy on jazz, some blues; most of the country had been sold. I went through there—I was so nervous I had to pinch myself. O my God. There were Paramounts, Ma Rainey Bluebirds, Brunswick 7000s, Kansas City Stompers, and Jabbo Smith, you name it! I picked 'em out, four big stacks, each about 4-and-a-half feet tall, and carried 'em downstairs—it took me about a half-hour—and put 'em on a table, which is leaning from all the weight. 'What do you want for 'em?' I said. 'How bout $100 for the whole works?' The old guy takes his hands out of his pockets, and the coal dust goes flying. He says, '*Take 'em out of here!*' I was so high when I went out of that store I could have floated."

Such big scores were not uncommon, and Bussard even found his wife while he was hunting records in the early '60s. In those days, he often got on the CB radio to inquire about old 78s. He developed a cordial on-air relationship with a man from nearby Damascus: "One time he mentioned that his daughter had a bunch of records, so I went down there and met her, and she came up here, and we went back and forth for about a year, and then we decided to get hitched. I got her records that way, see? Her dad was a real nice man."

A bluegrass and hillbilly music fanatic, Esther helped make their home a gathering place for musicians and collectors. But after the birth of their daughter, Esther had a religious awakening and decided "to put God over bluegrass." Her husband continued down the music road. She still listens to her own records upstairs, but it's more likely to be John Denver than Dock Boggs. Joe Bussard, of course, despises John Denver's music, but he says he and his wife have a truce of sorts. "She plays her records, and I play mine," he says simply.

During the '60s and '70s, Bussard spent a great deal of time canvassing in the mountains, where some of the cabins didn't even have floors, much less electricity. Some people just didn't want to sell, for whatever reason. Not one to take no for an answer, Bussard found these refusals grating. What really infuriated him was the mountain folk who beat around the bush: "Down in North Carolina, some of the people acted funny. When you ask people down there about records, if they have 'em and they don't want to sell 'em or don't want to tell you that, they'll say, 'I reckon not,' or 'Not today.' They don't want to say they ain't got 'em, because that's lying. See, they're very religious. That's Bible Belt."

Bussard has a particular dislike for Seventh Day Adventists, who often had the records but refused to sell, depending on the day. One family told him they were in mourning for a dead relative, but they had some nice 78s, so Bussard kept returning. Each time, they told him that someone else had died, so he finally gave up. One woman told him she couldn't make a deal because it was the Lord's Day—Saturday—until Bussard made her an offer for her records she couldn't refuse: He put the money in her mailbox, so she wouldn't have to complete the transaction until Sunday.

Sometimes, Bussard veered close to outright robbery: "This one lady let me look through her records, but then she started hemming and hawing, and I couldn't stand it. These were beautiful records, so I finally just shoved $50 in her hands and grabbed the box and ran out the screen door down to my car and gone. I didn't even wait for her to say yes or no."

One of Bussard's record-hunting companions in the '60s and '70s was Leon Kagarise. The pair had met back in the late '50s, when Bussard bought his stereo speakers. Kagarise worked at the hi-fi store in Baltimore, and the two started talking 78s: A friendship was formed.

Kagarise accompanied Bussard on several expeditions all over the South; they usually split expenses, staying in separate motel rooms. After a few trips, he began to be wary of Bussard, whose volatile canvassing technique bothered him. One time in West Virginia, Kagarise sat in the car outside some mountain shack, waiting for Bussard to make a deal: "He's in there for maybe 15 minutes—a good while—and then I hear yelling, and they come to the door. Joe's yelling at her and she's yelling at Joe, and he shouts, 'I hope they put those 78s in your casket and bury you with them!' She was probably in her 70s or 80s. He could have given that poor lady a heart attack."

Still, the two remained friends; after all, Kagarise had been in Bussard's wedding. But in the early '80s, Kagarise struck out on his own. He says he was tired of Bussard's hogging most of the pickings on their many trips, including the Black Patti bonanza (Kagarise got none of the 14 Bussard bought); he claims that they'd agreed on a 50-50 split on everything, including records. Bussard says they had an agreement that he got first dibs on everything. The two men haven't spoken for nearly 15 years.

Bussard remains undecided as to what will become of his collection upon his demise. He definitely won't give it to the Library of Congress or any other public institution. Library officials say that Bussard's hoard has a reputation that precedes it. "We would love to have such a collection," says Sam Brylawski, head of the library's Recorded Sound Section. "It would fill a lot of gaps here, especially because of its emphasis on country music. It would fit in very well."

Bussard has heard horror stories about how entire collections given to institutions remain in boxes for years, unopened, forgotten, doomed to oblivion. That can't happen to Joe Bussard's records. Never. "I'm not giving it to any of those places," he says. "If you give it to them, they shove it back in some hole, and there it sits." Instead, he says he may leave it to his wife or his daughter and her husband; he's in no hurry, because he plans on staying around for a while. "It ain't no worry of mine. I don't expect to kick off that quick. I expect to be around another 20 years to enjoy it."

One thing is for sure: Bussard won't be parting with his records while he's alive, whether the whole hoard or even one single 78 (unless in a swap for another). "Before he would sell his records, he would literally live in a pigsty," says Esther. "He would have to be to the point of starvation and no way out before he would sell a record from that room. And I'm not even sure then whether he would sell any or whether he would lay down beside them and die."

It's odd seeing Joe Bussard in someone else's basement, but here he is, and he's not at all comfortable. He has driven 60 miles southeast to Ashton, a Silver Spring exurb not far outside Washington, and it's as close to D.C. as he ever cares to get. Bussard has brought over a box of 78s to the house of Jack Towers, one of the most respected sound-restoration engineers in the music industry.

They have gathered to make some digital transfers of Bussard's 78s for a Time-Life Music project on prewar blues. Since the advent of CDs, Bussard has been in great demand as companies such as Time-Life have reissued the old music. His collection has been tapped as much as any, especially by the Yazoo label (featuring the famous Black Patti peacock), which has put out such acclaimed sets as *The Roots of Rap* and *Jazz the World Forgot*. Thanks to these sorts of reissue projects, the sounds of the '20s and '30s have never been more accessible to the average record buyer.

"The important thing about Joe Bussard is that he has disseminated the music more than anybody else on earth," says Richard Nevins, head of Yazoo and its New Jersey-based parent company, Shanachie. "He has preserved and popularized the music more than anyone, and he's done more for the music than anyone—all the institutions are bogus nonsense. They don't do any good at all. . . . The asshole Library of Congress refuses to tape 78s for people, not that they have anything worth taping anyway, but here's Bussard: If the UPS driver comes to his house to deliver a package, he won't let him out of there 'til he plays 78s for an hour for the guy. There are people in Australia who have tapes of his entire collection."

Nevins, who also boasts a world-class 78 collection, is the only person whom Bussard will mail his records to. He has a custom-made reinforced wooden-planked box with special screws that he uses on these occasions. Usually, though, he accompanies his records wherever they go, as when he drives over a pile of booty on his frequent trips to Towers' studio.

During the session, Bussard is all over the place, doing jigs and getting into the music just as he always does. Towers, a dapper, silver-haired 84-year-old, mans the turntable and mostly remains quiet, intent on the task at hand. Towers is no fan of hillbilly and country-blues records, but he is polite and reserved about this judgment. He will only say he doesn't much care for it. He's strictly big-band, an authority on Duke Ellington and Count Basie and Ben Webster. Portraits of the jazz icons hang on a wall nearby, more like family photos than museum pieces. He once counted them, especially Webster, as dear friends.

Clearly, though, Towers enjoys Bussard's volatile presence. "Joe's music doesn't hit me so much, but when I'm around and he's playing it, I get a kick out of seeing his response," he says. "He's valuable to have in the system because he saves a lot of discs that probably otherwise wouldn't even be around."

Following the session, Towers decides to pick a choice item from his own collection, a sort of post-work treat for himself and his guests. In a sense, the gesture seems to imply, "Now let's listen to some *real* music," but he would never be so brazen as to actually say so. The shelves of jazz 78s—he has only a few hundred—are bound up in Towers's own life; he bought them as he grew up, went to college, and then moved on to work and marriage. This is the soundtrack of his life. He courted his wife to these big-band sounds, and now she's busy upstairs in the kitchen making sandwiches.

He puts on a test pressing of an Ellington 78 "Blue Goose" from the early '40s, the glory years of the Ellington big-band era. As the music plays, he nods his head to the arrangements, murmuring the names of the soloists as they take their turns in the spotlight.

Listening, Bussard looks as if he's about to climb the walls. The song ends, and Bussard can stand it no longer: "Duke went to hell in '33!" he growls. "This big-band stuff is Dullsville, Dullsville!"

Later, at a diner outside Frederick, Bussard settles into a favorite booth. The diner has been around about as long as Bussard; it features a fifty-foot-tall candy cane outside in the parking lot. It's the sort of place where nearly every customer is of retirement age and mashed potatoes come with nearly every dish. He comes here almost every day, and not just for the food. He likes it because it's one of the few public places left without piped-in music. He comes here to eat and drink in the silence.

The coffee isn't too bad, either: "They've got the best coffee in the state of Maryland or anywhere," he says. "As long as you get a fresh pot."

He's in a fouler mood than usual today—a potential deal has stalled, and it's driving Bussard nuts. He found out through a collector buddy that a local woman—just a couple miles away!—has a decent copy of a rare Robert Johnson record, *Crossroads* on Vocalion. He's been haggling with this woman since last fall, always on the phone—cajoling, pleading, everything except outright begging. It's a long way from the glory days of canvassing.

"I told her I'd pay her book-value price, if it's in good condition. It lists for $300." Then he grimaces. "There are a lot of weird people. The hardest thing to do is deal with these people who have some records, but they're not collectors. I keep telling her I want to go there and look at it, but she keeps putting it off. I'm going to call her one last time. I think the best thing to do is to show up on her doorstep. A lot of these people say they want to sell, and they keep putting you off. If it had been anything else, if it was her kitchen table, her bed, her washing machine, I'd have had it a long time ago. But let it be a record, and it's a whole different world. I'm close to saying the hell with it. I've got plenty of records to play if I never get another one. But there's never enough."

A Jeep packed with teenagers swings past the window on a shortcut through the parking lot, blaring bass-heavy rap that resonates for blocks around. "Listen to that shit," hisses Bussard. "*Boom! Boom! Boom!*" He begins to rail against the contemporary world anew, once again comparing it with the '20s, "the zenith of Western civilization." For architecture, movies, and especially music, he says, it was a shimmering decade of American excellence that will never be topped. That was back when musicians knew how to play their instruments, when the bands played together like families (and, in fact, many of them were families), when records were works of art from the performance right down to the calligraphy on the labels, when there were still regional styles, before modern communications—including the very 78s that Bussard treasures—began to destroy the "pockets of eccentricity," as one collector describes the long-lost American sounds.

Listening to Bussard rhapsodize about this lost age and its enduring artistry, you finally see a glimpse of the idiosyncratic intellectual that Fahey recognizes beneath Bussard's gruff manner. There is a whole philosophy underlying Bussard's love of old 78s, a worldview that leaves little room for faith in the future.

A waitress finally stops by the table, and he takes a break from his tirade to place his order. "Can we get some fresh coffee?" he asks. Then his gaze follows the waitress, who promptly goes to the coffee station and starts to pour from a pot that's been sitting there. "That ain't fresh, little girl," he murmurs to himself. "I'm watching you—I know what's goin' on—that pot's half-empty."

As she returns, Bussard doesn't complain and instead asks her about music: "Do you like the blues?"

The waitress, maybe 25, ponders his query for a moment and then says cheerfully, Sure, she likes the blues: Big Bopper and Chuck Berry and all that music her parents listened to. Her face brightens, as if she's just answered a difficult question rather well.

"That ain't the goddam blues," says Bussard, disgusted. "You ever hear of Charlie Patton?"

A Joyful Noise

It was a sunny Memorial Day, and as boats cruised up the river toward the spires of Georgetown University, a stiff breeze whipped across a temporary stage, perched on an outdoor balcony overlooking the Potomac River. Phil Campbell, a portly black man in glasses and neat gray slacks, stepped to the microphone, and said, "We'd like to do a number called 'I Feel Good.' It's not James Brown; we've got another one, because when we're in church, we feel good."

When the Am-Jam Festival, a one-time affair organized by the New Orleans Jazz & Heritage Festival, came to Washington's Kennedy Center last year, the big stage hosted rousing performances by the likes of Los Lobos and Arlo Guthrie. But the day's most exciting moment occurred on that small stage.

Campbell's song might as well have been by James Brown, for the Campbell Brothers gave this old hymn a funky, rocking groove. And when singer Katie Jackson—a short, stocky woman in a yellow-and-purple dress—started wailing, "There's something about the name of Jesus that makes me feel good," her big voice skated across the octaves with gravity-defying ease. Right on her heels was an eerie, quivering sound that slid through notes with equal agility but with a sharper, metallic edge.

Jackson's pursuer was a pedal steel guitar. Chuck Campbell, a forty-one-year-old utility serviceman in a trim afro and a brown plaid shirt, played the instrument as if he were Junior Brown tackling the Mahalia

Jackson songbook. Sliding his silver cylinder across his 12-string in-strument, Chuck and Katie engaged in a duet, tossing phrases back and forth, testing each other with melismatic glides up the scale. The middle-aged church women in the crowd knew just what to do; they were swinging their hips to the beat and shaking their arms to the shouts, and soon the rest of the observers had no choice but to join in.

Most of the audience had never heard anything like it, for the pedal steel guitar, the ultimate country music instrument, had been wrenched out of its usual context and turned into the lead instrument of an old-fashioned, testifying gospel group. The same instrument that sounds like a weeping balladeer or a turbo fiddle in a hillbilly band suddenly resembled a Delta slide guitar or an ecstatic choir singer. An instrument we thought we knew had revealed a whole new personality.

It was new to most of the world, that is, but inside the House of God (a.k.a. the Church of the Living God), the steel guitar has been the dominant instrument since the 1930s. They call it the Sacred Steel, and services in this African-American Pentecostal church are built around instrumentals where the steel's ringing tones are the lead voice and vocal numbers where the singer and steel trade phrases in a kind of duet. Seven decades of this has created a musical genre unlike any other and a set of virtuosos to rival the world's best steel guitarists. But few, even in other black churches, knew Sacred Steel even existed.

"The first time I heard that Sacred Steel," remembers Katie Jackson, who married into the church, "was in Nashville for a House of God Assembly, and I had never heard an instrument like that. That Hawai-ian guitar gives the service that extra pick-up it needs. I know a lot of country musicians use it, but not like Sacred Steel players, who have the Holy Ghost in them."

On the Campbell Brothers' album *Pass Me Not*, the old hymn "Walk With Me" begins with a bluesy Chicago stomp right off a Muddy Waters record. Phil Campbell and Chuck Flenory kick the song off with a regular bass-and-guitar figure before Chuck Campbell comes in with a slicing, slashing pedal steel solo. Jackson enters soon after with a gritty, Koko Taylor–like growl, asking the Lord to accom-pany her down the path of life. Chuck follows with another wild, octave-leaping solo; then the third Campbell Brother, Darick, jumps in with a lap steel solo that finds him running up and down the same string, rollercoaster-style.

"Oh my goodness," Jackson exclaims, "when I'm singing with the Sacred Steel, my voice reaches a certain peak it never reached when I was singing with organ and piano. I'll practice a song at one key and at one tempo, but when you get up there with the Sacred Steel, you start to feel it and the higher, faster notes just come out. And that steel guitar is so close to my voice that whatever I sing, they can play it, too."

"When I play with Katie," Chuck Campbell adds, "it's like a vocal duet. You try to make the strings sound like a voice, and you hear everything from a yell to a scream to a moan. You run into a lot of gospel singers who can have fun in church, but they haven't perfected their skills so they can hit particular notes. Katie has great skills and she makes me sound good, because she sets the stage almost like a point guard giving you the basketball in the right place for a slam dunk."

Sacred Steel might still be a secret locked away in the House of God if it hadn't been for Robert Stone. Working as a folklorist for the State of Florida, Stone is always on the lookout for unknown artists, and he was intrigued by a 1992 phone call.

"One of my jobs is to find folk artists all over the state," explains the 55-year-old Stone, "and it's a big state, so I rely on other people to be my eyes and ears. Mike Stapleton, a good friend of mine, co-owns the Banjo Shop, in Hollywood, near Fort Lauderdale. One day he called me and said, 'Bob, these black men are coming in and buying these lap steels; they say they play them in church.' He held the cordless phone up, so I could hear a little bit."

"That little bit I heard convinced me I had to go down there. The musicians had told Mike, 'Well, we can play a little, but you should really hear Glenn Lee and Aubrey Ghent.' So on my first trip I interviewed Aubrey and taped him playing three pieces unaccompanied. It was like nothing I had ever heard before; it gave me goose bumps. It changed the whole way I perceived the steel guitar, because it was so African-American.

"This is what folklorists dream of: coming across a vibrant tradition that no one has ever heard of. It was like discovering another species. I started playing Aubrey's tape for other people, and the reaction was universal—everyone loved it."

Stone got some money from the National Endowment of the Arts and the Florida Department of Historical Resources to press up 600 copies of a cassette called *Sacred Steel: Traditional African-American Steel Guitar Music* in Florida in 1995. Accompanied by a 32-page booklet, the tape provided a 20-track overview of Florida's Sacred Steel scene, showcasing live performances from Ghent, Lee, Sonny Treadway, Henry Nelson and Willie Eason.

One cassette went to *Guitar Player* magazine, which declared the recording its "Disc of Destiny" for 1995, beating out such competition as Sonny Landreth and Ani DiFranco. Another went to Chris Strachwitz, the founder/owner of California's venerable roots-music label Arhoolie.

"Like any folklorist," Stone explains, "I was aware of Chris and the wonderful work he has done, but I had never met him. So when he phoned me and said, 'I'm calling about this extraordinary album,' that was another high point of my life. That was a nice validation.

"It took him a while to get the rights from the State of Florida and to remaster the tapes, but he re-released the album in 1997 with only minor changes to the tracks and the booklet. The response was so positive that Chris called me up and said, 'I want to do some single-artist studio albums.' I told him it should be three albums: Aubrey, the Campbell Brothers and Sonny Treadway."

In the meantime, Stone had been doing more research and had discovered that Sacred Steel wasn't limited to Florida. At the House of God's annual General Assembly in Nashville, he had heard the Campbell Brothers from Rochester, New York; Katie Jackson from Baltimore, Maryland; Robert Randolph from New Jersey; and Calvin Cooke and Ted Beard from Detroit, Michigan.

The second wave of Arhoolie's Sacred Steel series, released later in 1997, included *Pass Me Not* by the Campbell Brothers, featuring Katie Jackson; the all-instrumental *Jesus Will Fix It* by Sonny Treadway; and *Can't Nobody Do Me Like Jesus* by Aubrey Ghent. This year saw the release of the series' fifth and best album, *Sacred Steel Live!*, with performances by the Campbells, Jackson, Eason, Cooke, Beard, Randolph and others recorded during actual House of God services. Here you get the full effect of Sacred Steel as it is used in its natural environment, Sunday church.

The album kicks off with Phil Campbell establishing a brisk, hand-clapping beat with his chunky, chicken-scratch chords. Jackson announces that "God is a good God," first way down low and then way up high, as Chuck Campbell dances all around her with his pedal steel notes. Before long, Jackson is shouting out exclamations and Chuck is repeating each one in a near-perfect mirror image on his instrument. Back and forth bounce their phrases; up and up goes the energy; soon Jackson is hollering without words, and Chuck is off on a heart-racing solo that would excite the staunchest Duane Allman fan. On and on it goes for eight blistering minutes.

"That song is about how you can sit around and complain about things," explains Chuck Campbell, "but if you stop and look around there's a whole lot more good going on than bad. What I'm doing is just letting that feeling flow through me. Because I don't have a voice like Katie, my best way of expressing it to you is through my instrument. I'm paying close attention to the words and trying to sing them on the steel.

"If you listen, first I play the backup, then I answer Katie like I'm the congregation, playing the same words she sings. Once she lets it go, I take over the lead. You can almost hear the words in what I'm playing. Then I'll just strike out where I'm screaming or hollering, because I'm so happy, because you realize it's such a blessing for us to have each other in this world."

"Chuck tells me that playing onstage is a piece of cake compared to playing at a service," says Stone, "because in church you never know who's going to get up and start singing; you don't know what key they're going to sing in and whether they're going to stay in that key. And the selections can go on for a long time, eight to 12 minutes. In a typical service, there's a real emphasis on the praise music, the hard-driving stuff, with a lot of spontaneous singing, clapping, tambourine-shaking, shouting and dancing by the congregation.

"The service usually begins with a reminder that the Bible says, 'Make a joyful noise unto the Lord.' Then there will be a praise hymn, with the steel accompanying the singers. Often the singing will stop and the steel will take over. Then there's a sermon, often as long as 30–45 minutes. During the call to the altar, people come up to be saved, to give themselves over to Jesus; that can be quite emotional and can go on for half an hour. There's also the offertory, where people come forward to make an offering to the church.

"These processions are accompanied by instrumental steel music—either 'The House Of God March,' which Willie Eason says he invented, or a medley of hymns such as 'When the Saints Go Marching In,' 'I'll Fly Away,' and 'Down by the Riverside.' When things really get going, you'll see church members do what they call the holy dance, where they fall out and go into a kind of trance. Sometimes even the musicians will get up from their instruments and do a holy dance."

In 1903, a Tennessee street preacher named Mary Magdalena Lewis Tate founded the Church of the Living God, the Pillar and Ground of the Truth Without Controversy. As a Holiness or Pentecostal Church, it emphasized a belief that the Holy Spirit can enter the soul of a true believer and change his or her life. When Tate died in 1930, a leadership battle broke out, and a 1933 court order divided the church into three parts, now known as the Jewell, Keith and McLeod Dominions. The Keith Dominion is also known as the House of God.

In the early '30s, even as the court order was being written, a Hawaiian guitar craze swept the United States; for several years, electric steel guitars outsold conventional electric guitars. Western swing and hillbilly bands embraced the instrument because it had the same legato qualities as the fiddle and dobro but with a broader range and more power. In the Keith and Jewell Dominions, however, musicians liked it because it so closely mimicked the note-slurring melisma of their vocal soloists.

In Philadelphia, Truman Eason bought a lap steel and took lessons from a local Hawaiian. Truman showed his little brother Willie how to play a few licks, and when the two brothers started playing the newfangled instrument in their local House of God church, the response was instantaneous.

"The congregation was thrilled when the steel came in," Willie Eason says. "It was amazing for us as musicians to see how thrilled they were. People liked it right from the start. The members in the church would be clapping hands, shaking their tambourines and doing the holy dance; that's how sanctified people rejoice."

Eason, now 71, defined the classic Sacred Steel sound on his six-string lap steel. Though he retained elements of the Hawaiian and hillbilly styles, he pretty much invented a whole new style for the instrument. He imitated the traditional gospel piano by strumming rhythmic chords, and he imitated wailing gospel singers by sliding up and down one string.

In the '40s, Eason took to street-corner preaching. He would plug his lap steel's extension cord into a nearby store, and he would preach, sing and play for anyone who walked by. He collected donations in an upturned hat and billed himself as "Little Willie and His Talking Guitar".

"If I said something, it seemed like the guitar could repeat it," Eason explained. "If you sang a song like 'Jesus Keep Me Near the Cross,' the steel guitar could make it sound like it was saying the words, too. I've heard people say, 'Listen to that; it's talking.' This is why they call it the singing guitar or the talking guitar.

"One time I was out on the street playing in Chicago, and I ran my extension cord into a cleaners that was owned by James Medlock, one of the Soul Stirrers. That's how the Soul Stirrers heard me, and they asked would I like to record? I was a little shy, but I thought that was a great thing; I didn't know I was that good.

"We made an appointment, and I went down there to record 'Pearl Harbor' and 'Why I Like Roosevelt.' At the time, the war was on, and I would take words from the newspaper and put them together into a song. Wherever you get a line that will rhyme and have some meaning, that's what you use."

Eason's two 78s with the Soul Stirrers were released on Aladdin in 1947. As Brother Willie Eason, he released "There'll Be No Grumblers There" and "I Want To Live (So God Can Use Me)" on Regent in 1951; these two are part of the CD anthology *Guitar Evangelists: 1928–1951*, available from either England's Gospel Heritage Records or Germany's Document Records. Far more important than his recordings, though, was his impact on a whole generation of Church of the Living God steel guitarists.

Eason's first wife, Alice, had a younger brother, Henry Nelson, who avidly imitated everything his older brother-in-law did. Nelson soon became known in his own right for his warm tone and subtle dynamics on the six-string table steel. When Mahalia Jackson heard him in 1959, she was so impressed that she invited him to play on her Columbia recording of "To Me It's So Wonderful." Nelson subsequently passed his knowledge on to his son, Aubrey Ghent.

"When my father and I played together," the forty-year-old Ghent says, "people liked it, because we were father and son. Our styles were closely related, and we could play together with no problem; it was almost as if we thought alike. It just enthused me that I was playing with my father; our personalities connected so well. The sound portrayed by Willie Eason and my father was the sacred sound, the true House of God sound."

Eason, Nelson, Ghent and the Campbells belong to the Keith Dominion, but one of Eason's most eager disciples was the late Lorenzo Harrison of the Jewell Dominion, who had gone to high school with Nelson. Harrison took the Eason style, slowed it down, added more chord changes and gave it a boogie-woogie rhythm. This became known as the Jewell sound, and Sonny Treadway is its greatest living practitioner.

"Lorenzo had a jazzed-up swing approach," acknowledges Ghent, "and that's the Jewell sound. He also learned from Willie Eason, but he developed his own style. The melodic tuning and the bluesy sound of the Jewell Dominion players made the difference. In the Keith Dominion, we weren't allowed to be that wild."

Lap and table steel guitars are very expressive instruments, but they're limited harmonically. In an effort to overcome this problem, Nashville guitarists started adding foot pedals and knee levers to their steels to enable them to change keys without retuning. Pioneers such as Bud Isaacs, Jimmy Day and Buddy Emmons soon made the pedal steel such a versatile, emotive instrument that every country record had to have one.

It was inevitable that the Sacred Steel guitarists would be drawn to this innovation. In the early '70s, two veterans—Calvin Cooke and Ted Beard of Detroit—and one teenage prodigy—Chuck Campbell—traded in their table steels for pedal steel models. It was the biggest thing to hit Sacred Steel since the '30s.

"When I was 14," Chuck Campbell recalls, "I went to our 1971 General Assembly in Nashville. While I was there, I walked into a music store and saw Jimmy Day playing 'What a Friend We Have in Jesus' on the pedal steel with a pick in one hand and a whiskey bottle in the other. It made me realize that the spirit wasn't only in church, that this guy also had a connection, and that maybe the pedal steel had something to offer.

"Although I was impressed by the precision and prettiness of his playing, the real reason I took up the pedal steel was I wanted to imitate all my Sacred Steel heroes—Henry Nelson, Calvin Cooke and Ted Beard. I wanted to be able to switch between tunings with a switch of the pedal rather than having to retune the whole guitar. In church, you don't have time to do that between songs. With the pedal steel, I could just press a few pedals and be in a different tuning.

"Lo and behold, that allowed me to play the chord progressions the country players used. And that allowed me to play with choirs. The new gospel writers like Andrae Crouch and Edwin Hawkins were writing songs that didn't lend themselves to a straight E tuning, but with the pedal steel, I could play their songs, too. At the same time I switched, Ted Beard and Calvin Cooke switched over too. They felt they had gotten what they could get out of the tabletop; they felt they were blocked from progressing."

Not every Sacred Steel guitarist jumped on the pedal steel bandwagon. Chuck's younger brother Darick stuck with the eight-string tabletop and continued to play in the classic style of Willie Eason and Henry Nelson. Nelson's son, Aubrey Ghent, continues to play the tabletop, too.

"Around '78–79, I bought a Sho-Bud pedal steel and fooled around with it," Ghent explains, "but it was a lot of work. Sometimes you got to the service, and it took so long to put in the rods and connect them to the pedals that the service was half over by the time you were ready. With the lap steel, you just took it out of the case, plugged it up and began to play. My dad plays six-string and Willie plays six-string, so I decided to keep that tradition alive.

"With the six- and eight-string, you can concentrate a whole lot on the spiritual without worrying about a lot of levers and pedals. We were encouraged not to play just for showmanship but to make sure it brought in edification for the congregation. We were encouraged not to be showoffs but to play in the spirit, so the playing lifted the spirit. That was implanted within us."

The younger generation of Sacred Steel players—especially whizzes such as Robert Randolph and Glenn Lee—is following Chuck Campbell's example with the pedal steel. They are borrowing tricks and licks from country musicians and applying them to the needs of House of God services. The two camps cross paths at music stores and on the Internet.

The country pickers, in turn, are fascinated by their Sacred Steel counterparts. Buddy Emmons has spoken to Chuck Campbell about a possible collaboration. Alt-country guitarist Dan Tyack is dedicating tracks to Chuck and Aubrey Ghent on his next steel album.

Meanwhile, Stone is finishing up a video documentary about Sacred Steel and just beginning a book on the subject. He promises there will be more recordings for Arhoolie as well. Inch by inch, the music is easing out of the insular world of the Church of the Living God and entering the public arena.

"What we do in a theater is the same thing we do in church," Katie Jackson claims. "Some people may not like it, but that's what we are, a gospel group. In Boulder, we played in a small theater, and people were so happy they didn't know what to do. A woman told me later that most of those people never go to church, but they loved the music. That let me know that I'll never reach these people unless we play outside the church."

"We had always wanted to record," Chuck Campbell admits, "but we were trying to use synthesizers and drum machines to be up with the times. When Robert Stone and Arhoolie came in and said, 'What you're doing in church is the greatest thing in the world,' we were both surprised and glad. We had loved what we did in church, but we didn't know anybody else would feel the same way."

Steve Earle

Steve Earle works from conflict—past and present, real or imagined. On an early spring afternoon he is sitting in a Chicago hotel lobby, dressed in a dapper gray suit and matching vest to honor the traditional bluegrass world he's living in. He looks like a turn-of-the-century train conductor, but he's talking about making a rock & roll record. At this moment, Earle speaks eloquently of bluegrass collaborator Del Mc-Coury, yet a couple of months down the road McCoury and Earle will have a falling-out.

Conflict has been a way of life for Earle, who would be the first to tell you he's surprised to have made it this far into the future. Earle turns forty-five in January. His life—personal and professional—has been filled with controversy. In 1995 he kicked a twenty-six-year heroin addiction that took him through Nashville slums and the county jail. He's been married six times, he's been on at least half that many record labels. He's released a number of albums and soundtrack singles, beginning with his obscure 1982 debut *Pink & Black*, followed by his 1986 landmark MCA release *Guitar Town*. Earle's late 1980s and early '90s releases—including *Exit O, Copperhead Road, The Hard Way*, and *Shut Up and Die Like an Aviator*—were marked by a more rocking drive and, behind the scenes, an alarming and escalating personal drug habit. His post-rehab CDs since the mid–'90s include *Train a Comin'*, *I*

Feel Alright, El Corazón, and his collaboration with the Del McCoury Band, 1999's *The Mountain.*

He is one of the most outspoken and restless voices in country music, or any genre for that matter, and can never be accused of tempering his opinions. He has thrown his celebrity behind controversial causes; most recently he emerged as an ardent opponent of the death penalty. He's also severed ties with Warner Bros. and is content making records for E-Squared, the production company and record label he owns with partner Jack Emerson.

Earle has dug swimming pools, worked on oil rigs, collected motorcycles, and part-owned a dirt-track race car. Although conflict has surrounded him, there are no conflicting reports when it comes to his output—Earle moves at a fast pace.

"At one time I believed there was something to the suffering artist thing," Earle says while smoking a pipe. "But the truth is I've been happier since I got out of jail and since I've been clean. There's less conflict. It's not like it's easy. There's always stuff going on. But I'm probably the happiest I've been in my life. I'm making an embarrassing amount of money for a borderline Marxist doing exactly what I want to do. I've managed to parlay my modest success into careers for a couple of bands [E-Squared recording artists the V-Roys and Six String Drag] that wouldn't have gotten heard otherwise. I'm really proud of that. And I'm in love." Earle pauses. Then he says, "Maybe I don't fish enough."

One of Earle's favorite fishing spots is at the Elk River, near the foot of Monteagle Mountain, about an hour southeast of Nashville. The peaceful river is often stocked with trout.

On a midsummer morning earlier this year, Earle assembled a fishing posse that consisted of his youngest son (twelve-year-old Ian), and his girlfriend Sara's two kids. They were joined by many other older and wiser fishermen. Nothing was biting.

"It was slow," says Earle, who doesn't like slow. "I was fishing with my fly rod. I had one fish come up, look at the fly, stick his tongue out at me, and disappear. A lot of people had left. I was just about ready to give up and all of a sudden here came the game department's truck. It backed up and dumped 2,500 good-sized rainbow trout into the water right in front of us. The water was literally boiling with trout. In about fifteen minutes, I caught five, my girlfriend's girl caught four, her boy caught five, my boy caught two." Life works that way sometimes. When in doubt, along comes the trout.

And Earle never gives up.

Steve Earle was born on January 17, 1955, in Fort Monroe, Virginia, and reared for the most part in Texas. Armed with an eighth grade education, he inherited an ample amount of tenacity from his father Jack, an air-traffic controller who was often transferred around the country and settled for many years in the San Antonio area. Earle is the oldest of five children. One of his sisters is singer-songwriter Stacey Earle, who named her back-up band the Jewels after grandmother Jewel Earle.

"My grandmother ran a halfway house for recovering alcoholic women," Steve Earle says. "Her neighbor across the street was Anita Court, Jimmie Rodgers' daughter [born January 30, 1921, to Carrie and Jimmie Rodgers]. So when I was a kid and just getting interested in guitar, her place was an open house for anyone interested in her father. I've held one of Jimmie Rodgers' guitars in my hands. I've heard a lot of recordings I don't think anyone else has heard. He is a real constant for me."

Earle studied Rodgers' guitar licks, notably his consistent, jazzy bass runs. "My acoustic guitar style is heavily rooted in the way he played," Earle explains. "I was fascinated with his style. It's running bass lines constantly. Leadbelly did it too."

Earle learned to play rock & roll guitar by listening to the Rolling Stones' 1967 compilation *Flowers*. "The first song I learned was 'Mother's Little Helper,'" Earle recalls. "One of the things that screwed me up was that I never learned to play a song in a minor key first. I did the same thing to my [seventeen-year-old] son Justin. When he was thirteen, his first song was [The Beatles'] 'Eleanor Rigby.'" (Earle has three children who range in age from twelve to seventeen.)

At age sixteen, Earle ran away from home to follow singer-song-writer Townes Van Zandt through Texas. Van Zandt died of a heart attack on New Year's Day, 1997. He was fifty-two years old.

"Townes was absolutely my primary teacher," Earle says. "He's the reason I do this. Artistically, he set the standard for me. I was lucky because he was one of the first people I saw who did this with a level of integrity that almost dictated they weren't going to get rich. Because no concessions were made. Now, he did a lot of other things I had to learn the hard way."

The Hard Way. That's the title of Earle's 1990 guitars-and-drums album, his sign-off before bottoming out. Earle had long looked to Van Zandt as an artistic mentor, but he had also taken Van Zandt's personal tribulations too close to heart. Townes was notorious for his extreme living. In a 1990 interview Van Zandt said, "I was real crazy for a long time. I had no address, phone, or anything. I lived in the mountains and drank all the time. I gambled. I almost died a few times, but I'm all past that. It's Grand Ole Opry material, right? I'd be too bashful to be anything else."

Remembering the fate of his late friend and mentor, and his own nights spent on the dark side, Earle's husky tenor trails off into the not-so-distant past. He says, "If I had those things to do all over again. . . . At one time I thought they were all part and parcel of the same way of living. I don't believe that anymore. I miss him. And I wish it could have been different because he would still be here. And he could still make me laugh and write those songs."

As much as Earle and Van Zandt were kindred spirits, Earle never wrote with Van Zandt. "Townes maybe co-wrote three songs in his life," Earle says. "And I don't co-write anymore. I used to do it from time to time, mostly with guys in my band, and it was mainly about a paycheck for them. It's like fucking in front of people anyway. The best stuff is never co-written."

As further evidence of his artistic drive, Earle has completed his first collection of short stories, titled *Doghouse Roses*, which has elements of the autobiographical soul of his *Guitar Town* album. "'Doghouse Roses' is the name of one of the [ten] stories," Earle says with an apologetic grin. "You know those roses with the stems in the little tube of water they have at a 7-11 for when you've fucked up? Those are doghouse roses."

Earle first wooed Nashville as a kid in the 1960s. His mother Barbara is from Nashville, and the family would take in the Grand Ole Opry during breaks when visiting relatives.

"Three things impressed me at the Opry," Earle says about his visits to the Ryman. "Tammy Wynette doing 'I Don't Wanna Play House.' It was dynamic. She was so tiny and the chorus would hit and wow! Then there was a guy [Walter Forbes] who worked for a carpet mill by Chattanooga. He made [a] record [released in 1962] called *The Cumberland Mountain Deer Chase* [an Uncle Dave Macon favorite], and my grandad heard that on the Opry. The guy had a doghorn that he blew in the song. [*The Cumberland Mountain Deer Chase* was also the first session for future Earle and Bob Dylan dobro, fiddle, and Hawaiian guitarist Norman Blake.] I remember walking across the street to Ernest Tubb's Record Shop and buying the single for my grandaddy.

"And the other thing that knocked me out was [Bill] Monroe. He did 'Blue Moon of Kentucky' and maybe 'Kentucky Waltz.' Even then it was obvious it was different from everything else on the Opry. Of course I didn't realize it then, but there was a dignity about it. The reason I wear a suit while playing bluegrass is that it was important to Bill. He prided himself on the fact they were the first band at the Opry to wear a coat and tie as opposed to overalls or a cowboy suit. He was intentionally trying to inject an air of dignity into music that people dismissed as hillbilly. He wanted his music to be taken seriously."

Earle maintains that the Nashville industry is seriously the Nashville industry's biggest enemy. "It's us," he says, shrugging his shoulders. "We are hillbillies. We're always trying to convince people we're not, but we are. And we're at our best when we admit when we are. Me making rock records in Nashville is no big deal. I didn't invent it. Nashville is just a cheap town to live in with a lot of recording studios."

Earle first moved to Nashville in 1974. After running away from home at sixteen and knocking around Texas for a few years, he came to Music City to play bass for Guy Clark. He hung around Clark and Van Zandt, who were part of the new breed of rough, harder-edged songwriters.

In 1981, after a second marriage which took place at the Take Five Bar in Nashville's Metropolitan Airport, Earle left Music City for what he described as "two tequila-drenched years" in Mexico. He returned to Nashville in 1982 when he was signed by CBS/Epic, where he made one neo-rockabilly album. Produced by Roy Dea and Pat Carter, it resurfaced in 1987 as *Early Tracks*, featuring workshop versions of "Continental Trailways Blues" and "Devil's Right Hand."

In 1986, Earle inked a seven-record deal with MCA. His critically acclaimed 1986 album *Guitar Town* was framed by power-twang chords and working-class themes which drew comparisons to Bruce Springsteen and John Mellencamp. Earle didn't shy away from the imposing rock shadows. He covered Springsteen's "State Trooper" during his *Guitar Town* tour, even performing it on the Boss' turf at the Bottom Line nightclub in New York City.

Guitar Town was an auspicious success for Earle. He was quickly hailed—along with Dwight Yoakam and Randy Travis—as a fresh voice in country music. Yet the making of that album—like Earle's subsequent tenure at MCA—was not without conflict. Earle clashed with the legendary Jimmy Bowen. A controversial record producer and big label kahuna, Bowen would also clash—in his later position as the head of Capitol Records—with the "eight-hundred-pound hillbilly gorilla" Garth Brooks.

"No one has ever told me what kind of record to make," Earle says. "Well, Jimmy Bowen did once. I went over his head. Bowen tried to fuck with me on album covers and what was going to be on my second record [1987's *Exit O*, which delivered eclectic tracks like the Tex-Mex "San Antonio Girl" and the Farm Aid anthem "The Rain Came Down"]. My relationship with MCA was like that."

More trouble followed the original critical success of *Guitar Town*. *Exit O* sold a paltry 135,000 in the months following its release, and MCA withdrew tour support.

In Bowen's 1997 autobiography *Rough Mix*, he wrote about MCA's plans to market Earle in its pop-rock division. At the time, Bowen was head of the label's Nashville division. Bowen wrote, "They took a terrific songwriter with a distinct, haunting voice and started pumping his head full of 'you're the next Springsteen.' They got him so worked up and confused between Nashville and L.A. that he wound up musically somewhere around Albuquerque. . . . He came to us pretty much fixed, and they broke him."

"Well, that's a bunch of bullshit and you can quote me," says Tony Brown, MCA Nashville president who signed Earle in 1986 when he was Vice President of A&R at the label. "What happened to him after that had nothing to do with what we did. His life took its own course. I still think he's one of the greatest writers this town has ever seen."

Brown said that Earle's gnarly vocals had a pronounced effect on Bowen. He recalls, "Before we cut the [*Guitar Town*] demos Bowen said, 'If you can make me understand a word he says, I'll let you sign him.' So me and [producer] Emory Gordy cut 'Good Ol' Boys (Gettin' Tough)' and I made Steve *eeee*-nunciate the words more than he normally would have. Of course he bitched and moaned the whole time. Then Bowen told me I had to have Steve's teeth fixed, too. Bowen put me through all the trials and tribulations of how to deal with an artist like that."

On the side Brown had been writing songs for the Oak Ridge Boys' Silverline-Goldline publishing company, which is how he met Earle. Brown and Earle were part of a little songwriting field trip from Nashville to Gulf Shores, Alabama.

"I went down with Steve in a van and he talked my head off," Brown said. "It sort of scared me a little bit. He had all these stories about hitchhiking and getting into fights and you'd think, 'He's making this shit up.' But he wasn't. Then he played me 'Fearless Heart' and he just started writing *Guitar Town*. It wasn't at all like the stuff he was doing for CBS. I was intrigued by the power of what those songs were doing to me. I thought, 'This is the next Waylon Jennings.'"

Earle's resemblance to legendary country rebels extended far beyond his songwriting. His volatile personal behavior was also becoming a matter of public record. After a 1987 New Year's Eve show, Dallas police choked Earle unconscious with a nightstick before arresting him on a charge of felonious assault against a police officer—a charge for which he was facing a possible five-year prison sentence if found guilty. Earle pleaded no contest to a reduced charge of resisting arrest, which carried a $500 fine and one year's unsupervised probation.

"We were beginning to work on *Copperhead Road*," recalls Tony Brown, who co-produced that record with Earle. "He told me what he wanted to do with certain things if he had to go to prison. There was a sparkle in his eyes, like he sort of hoped he'd go to prison. And it didn't happen. Conflict was a big deal with Steve."

Not only did Earle lock into the rock landscape, he further confused country audiences and radio by opening for acts as diverse as the Replacements, Dylan, and George Jones. Earle would play rock & roll clubs like the Roxy in Los Angeles at the same time Dwight Yoakam was holding court at the Palomino in L.A. But where Yoakam tweaked the Nashville machine from the West Coast, Earle continued to try and work within the Nashville industry.

"What I am doing is patently country," Earle told me in 1986. "But at the same time it may be rock. But the main point is the song, and great country music's main point is always the song."

On a steamy night in mid-July 1993, Earle stood alone with his acoustic guitar on stage at Schubas, an old-fashioned 200-seat music room on the north side of Chicago. With his voice bending and cracking like branches in a rainstorm, Earle sang Van Zandt's "To Live's To Fly": "Where you've been is good and gone / All you keep's the getting there / To live's to fly low and high / So shake the dust off of your wings / And the sleep out of your eyes."

By this time Earle had succumbed to the grip of heroin addiction. Over a handful of albums, Earle had held his career together despite his drug use. But on stage at Schubas, it was clear he was at last coming undone. His weight had tumbled to 125 pounds in January 1993, but by the time friends brought him to Chicago, Earle was up to 160 pounds. [Today he weighs in at 205.] He had been so inactive since 1990 that he stress-fractured a foot by constantly stomping his dusty black boot on the Schubas stage.

Chicago has long been a foundation of artistic and emotional support for Earle. He needed to perform at Schubas in order to regain a sense of place. Earle gave one of the most gallant, confessional concerts I've seen.

The standing room–only audience helped a weakened Earle with the otherwise steadfast anthem "I Ain't Ever Satisfied." Earle reached from deep within to sing "Close Your Eyes," his tender ballad that says, even with eyes shut, the world does not stop spinning. Earle told the audience, "Sometimes I think that was a lullaby to myself."

In a 1995 conversation from his Nashville home, Earle said he got away with heroin addiction "for reasons that aren't really important." In his trademark braggadocio rhythm, he added, "But in getting away with it, I accomplished more than most junkies. A lot of that's luck. But it got to the point where all the 'yets' happened to me. I stopped writing when it became a full-time job to support my drug habit. It's that simple."

The final yet happened in July 1994. Earle was sitting behind the wheel of his 1993 Mercury coupe when Nashville cops busted him with crack cocaine, a glass pipe, and ten syringes. Charged with misdemeanor drug possession, he pleaded guilty and was sentenced to a year in jail.

Earle began his sentence on September 13, 1994, at the Davidson County Criminal Justice Center outside Nashville, and his withdrawal pains were brutal. After a ten-day jail stay and a plea on Nashville television, Earle was transferred to the Lincoln Regional Hospital in Fayetteville, Tennessee, for detox. He was placed on methadone, a heroin substitute. By November 11, 1994, he was clean. All told, Earle ended up serving three weeks in jail and another thirty-three days in the treatment center. He spent almost three years on probation.

"I was a junkie when I made *Guitar Town*," Earle said. "I've been doing this since I was thirteen years old. *Train a Comin'* [1995] was the first record I made clean in my life."

Earle had burned many music industry bridges because of his cantankerous attitude. Other bridges collapsed during his darkest, drug-induced hours. "I was sort of a target in Nashville," Earle reflected. "There's a lot of people around here who always supported what I was doing, but basically they watched what I did, and if I got my ass shot off, they knew not to do that. But [while on heroin] I wasn't writing, recording, or anything. It was the last thing to go before the lights went out."

A few old friends remained. Johnny Cash wrote a letter to Earle, Emmylou Harris checked in, and Waylon Jennings sent word at every turn. While Earle was in treatment, Jennings sent Earle a picture of a state fair date he had done with a bandanna around his wrist, an Earle trademark.

In 1986 Jennings recorded Earle's "The Devil's Right Hand" in a session produced, ironically, by Jimmy Bowen. And in 1996 Earle produced his composition "Nowhere Road" for the Jennings, Willie Nelson, Jessi Colter, Outlaws twentieth anniversary record. Not surprisingly, Jennings and Earle argued over the vocal tracks. The two rebels are still not talking to each other today.

Chicago artist Tony Fitzpatrick is one of Earle's heartfelt friends. Fitzpatrick did the cover art for Earle's 1996 rebound record *I Feel Alright*, a Stones-like project shaped by love, hope, and redemption.

Fitzpatrick, forty, also did the cover for 1997's *El Corazón* (The Heart), which is inspired by the playing card in the Mexican bingo-inspired *Lotería*. And Fitzpatrick handled all artwork for 1999's *The Mountain*, Earle's bluegrass collaboration with the Del McCoury Band. In fact, Earle says Fitzpatrick will do his album art for the rest of his career. Fitzpatrick has also done album art for the Neville Brothers and Lou Reed.

"Is there an amount of anger that fuels what Steve does?" asks Fitzpatrick, who says he has known Earle for twenty years. "You bet. Does his music come out of conflict? Of course it does. Just months after he got out of the joint, *Train* comes out. Then a year later, *I Feel Alright* is out. That's art made out of conflict.

"But he is loyal. If you have Steve Earle for a friend, you have a very good friend. Steve has been considerably fucked with in the industry, and it makes one put on a little tougher armor all the time."

Earlier this fall, Earle and Fitzpatrick traveled to Galway, Ireland, where Fitzpatrick opened a show of his etchings. Earle introduced Fitzpatrick to Bernard Logan's gallery in Galway. Someday Earle would like to live in Ireland.

"I'm closer to leaving Nashville than I've ever been," Earle says. "I'd wait until my kids are grown. I'd move to Ireland. I'm buying a place there. I work well there. I came back from a [two-month stay in] Ireland with nineteen thousand words of prose, five poems, and four songs. In Ireland, I write one thousand words a day.

"And I'll be doing death penalty stuff in Ireland. I'm starting a campaign within the European Union to put the mechanism in place to bring economic sanctions against the United States if we don't get in line with the rest of the world on the death penalty. I'm trying to find at least one person in each of the countries in the European Union who will communicate with each other. I've changed my tactic. I've become more involved in a political solution to the death penalty."

Earle's profile as an outspoken opponent of capital punishment has been rising since 1990 when he wrote "Billy Austin," where the title character reflects upon his death sentence for killing a gas station attendant. Earle wrote, "As the final hour drags by / I ain't about to tell you that I don't deserve to die / But there's twenty-seven men here, mostly black, brown, and poor / Most of 'em are guilty; who are you to say for sure?" In 1996 Earle contributed the desolate "Ellis Unit One" to the *Dead Man Walking* soundtrack. That preceded his randy take of "In the Jailhouse Now" for the 1997 album *The Songs of Jimmie Rodgers: A Tribute,* on Bob Dylan's Egyptian label, distributed by Columbia Records. It was Dylan's idea for Earle to cover "In the Jailhouse Now," as Earle's coming out party, so to speak.

Earle has always had an affinity for the underdog.

He explains, "My music is either me saying something I want to say or me lending a voice to someone that doesn't have a voice for whatever reason. Besides Townes and Guy [Clark], I cut my teeth on Woody Guthrie and Utah Phillips, although Townes and Guy were apolitical.

"Guy and I were on stage a couple years ago at MerleFest [the annual Wilkesboro, North Carolina, festival held in honor of the memory of folk music picker Eddy Merle Watson] and I played [the Guthrie-influenced] 'Christmas in Washington' for the first time in front of people. Guy told me, 'Man, you're getting militant in your old age.' But it's always been there for me. I've gotten more outspoken as the years have gone on because the bully pulpit got a little higher and I had that opportunity. I'm pretty careful not to be too over-the-head with it."

In one of his most controversial moves, Earle earlier this year formed the national board behind "The Journey of Hope . . . From Violence to Healing," a series of anti–death penalty music events. The board is composed mostly of family members of murder victims. They speak of healing through reconciliation and call for alternatives to the death penalty. Earle, who also works with Amnesty International, was one of two board members who wasn't a family member of a murder victim.

In October 1998, Earle witnessed Jonathan Nobles die by lethal injection in a Texas prison. Nobles was executed for stabbing two women to death in 1986 while he was high on speed. He asked Earle to attend his execution.

Earle minces no words in his opinion. "We are the killers," he says. "No one in that place that day was any more responsible than I was. That's the main reason I'm opposed to the death penalty. I'm not willing to lie down and let the state make a murderer of me.

"He was thirty-seven when they killed him," Earle says. "Jon was probably a serial killer who got caught on his first crime. He had a really bad speed habit. He thought he would kill again. But he changed a lot in prison. He was a third order Dominican when he died and he was buried in a Dominican habit. I'm trying to get a death certificate out of the state of Texas to take his ashes to Ireland. The Dominican community in Galway has agreed to bury him. People say, 'Oh, that's a death house conversion.' I promise you, if there's any conversion in the world that's not bullshit, it's a death house conversion."

Pilgrims arrive from all walks of life. Acoustic bass player Roy Huskey Jr. played on Earle's *Train a Comin'* comeback record for Winter Harvest records. Huskey was part of a buoyant, bluegrass-oriented ensemble which also included Norman Blake and ex–Bill Monroe sideman Peter Rowan on mandolin.

Huskey died on September 6, 1997, after a fifteen-month battle with lung cancer. He was forty. Besides Earle, Huskey had recorded and performed with George Jones and Johnny Cash. He won a Grammy for his work with Emmylou Harris & the Nash Ramblers on the CD *At the Ryman.*

Earle was a pallbearer for Huskey and was asked to sing at his funeral. Earle wrote "Pilgrim" as a tribute to Huskey. (A lilting lullaby to wanderlust, "Pilgrim" is a standout track on *The Mountain*, Earle's critically acclaimed bluegrass collaboration with the Del McCoury Band. The backing chorus for "Pilgrim" includes Huskey's widow, Lisa, their two children, Emmylou Harris, Gillian Welch, and Tim O'Brien.)

"I couldn't come up with anything I felt like singing," Earle says. "I woke up at 8:30 in the morning of Roy's funeral and wrote the song. The funeral was at 1:00 p.m. I read it off a piece of paper taped to a microphone stand at the funeral. Making *The Mountain* was a constant reminder of Roy, because it would have been a natural thing for me to make another record with Norman, Pete, and Roy. We really thought there was a future for that band. Without Roy, I wasn't emotionally able to go on and do it again that soon."

Always counterpointing the past with the present, Earle wrote *The Mountain* bluegrass songs while keeping one ear on his eclectic record collection. "At the time I had [the Sex Pistols' 1977 punk classic] *Never Mind the Bollocks*, [the Rolling Stones'] *Exile on Main Street*, Springsteen records, and my real hard bop and Chet Baker CDs," he says. "I like melodic jazz. I always have a copy of solo [Thelonious] Monk. I have two CD cases. One holds twenty and the other holds ten. Out of those thirty records, there's usually seven or eight bluegrass titles in there anyway. One of them is *Blue Side of Town* [a 1992 Del McCoury Band record that includes Earle's 'If You Need a Fool']."

But it wasn't the CDs that bothered McCoury, or the reason for their falling-out after their critically acclaimed collaboration.

In a 1999 interview with Baker Maultsby of the Greenville, South Carolina, edition of *Creative Loafing*, McCoury complained about Earle's onstage profanity: "I kind of didn't want him in the bluegrass community because I always like to have a clean show, you know, and I think your music is what's carrying you—the songs you've written. And there's no place on stage, I don't think, for vulgarity, for anything like that."

Earle's response to the issue of his public use of the f-word is in keeping with his singular style. "Del may very well be uncomfortable with my language and probably is," Earle says. "So is Bob Dylan. And I did all of that [1989 Dylan] tour. After about three weeks they told me Dylan wished I wouldn't say 'fuck' so much and I said, 'Fuck it.' It got back to Bob, and everything was all right.

"I've never loved making a record or doing a tour in my life as much as I did with Del. I respect him, and I'm sorry if my language makes him uncomfortable, but I don't think that's what any of this is about. It became unworkable because at MerleFest they stuck Del on a smaller stage for his show. And I didn't give Del a spot on my show, which was on the main stage, because I had no idea he had been relegated to a smaller stage. His feelings were hurt, and I do not blame him one bit. That's reprehensible on the part of the organizers of MerleFest, and I'll probably never play their festival again. We played a date the next day in Nashville, and suddenly Del said he didn't want to do any more U.S. dates, he didn't want to go to Europe, he didn't want to do David Letterman."

The two camps ended up negotiating a compromise, which took McCoury and his band through the end of the spring 1999 European tour. But Earle and McCoury had to cancel their appearance at the 1999 Telluride Bluegrass Festival.

Earle's opinions on this aspect of his musical life are as candid and controversial as his views on the death penalty. "The truth is that MerleFest and Telluride are not bluegrass festivals," Earle declares. "They pay people like me more money than they pay bluegrass bands because we sell tickets, but they call themselves bluegrass festivals. And they treat the bluegrass bands—their real bread and butter—like shit. The whole bluegrass world has a tendency to treat itself like shit. And the people who run the bluegrass labels are criminals. They take a band's publishing, and the bands go out and sell their records at their gigs when they have to pay for them in advance. It's a racket. But I love bluegrass, and I love Del McCoury. And I'm going to make another bluegrass record."

This time Earle's collaborator is Tim O'Brien, the former lead singer and fiddler-mandolinist for the 1980s bluegrass band Hot Rize.

"I'm real lucky," Earle says as a calm rolls through the hotel lobby. "I've always known how lucky I was. I never felt sorry for myself. I would have been a drug addict had I been a carpenter. I had a habit, and I could afford more dope than most people could and so I got into a lot of trouble. It's just really important to me to remember how lucky I am to be able to make a living doing something I really love, exactly the way I want to do it."

And no one can argue with that.

KEVEN MCALESTER

Bad Teeth

McCabe's Guitar Shop, Santa Monica, 1/23/99, 10:30 p.m. Am sitting in back row of intimate and well-known auditorium. Am waiting for appearance by Ray Manzarek. Tall, skinny character. Old occupation: Doors keyboardist. Current occupation: former Doors keyboardist. Author of recent *Light My Fire: My Life With the Doors.* In which Manzarek goes baroque on pleasures and hazards of being former Door, pausing just long enough to caution readers against rampant consumerism and the like. (Strange—no mention of *Steal This Book* as potential title.) Tonight's performance promises "spoken word and music."

Am a bit puzzled by Manzarek. Always thought he was underrated member of overrated band. Always liked his keyboard playing. Thought it added at least as much distinction to Doors as Morrison's "poetics" or myth-making shenanigans. So despite evidence to contrary—including aforementioned book, certain recent public appearances, and post-Morrison Doors albums—am still willing to believe in one-percent chance that he might have something interesting to say. Translation: Am attempting to ignore 99-percent chance that self = complete, hopeless sucker.

10:45 p.m. Manzarek takes stage. Is wearing strange black-cape situation. Am not yet prepared to use image to evoke metaphor of vampire sucking air out of a bloodless corpse. Would be presumptuous and rude. Plus: Cape removed before spoken word begins.

10:46 p.m. Manzarek: "Just got back from Poughkeepsie, New York. Holy cow, is it cold there. Thank God we're not in Poughkeepsie. Boy, oh boy." Am distracted by sound of interesting-show odds ticking down from one percent to minute fractions thereof.

10:47 p.m. First mention of words "Jim Morrison." Elapsed time since start of remarks: 156 seconds. Approximate pause between completion of word "Morrison" and yelping from certain audience members: three seconds. Probable reason for unexpected length of pause: audience somnolence due to Poughkeepsie weather updates.

10:56 p.m. "We were trying to open *the doors* of perception. We wanted to *break on through to the other side.*"

11:21 p.m. After 36 minutes of rapt attention, have discerned pattern of tonight's spoken-word oeuvre:

1. Mention name "Jim Morrison" approximately every 36.2 seconds (= 99.45 Morrisons/hour).
2. Use words "pothead," "acid-head," "joint," and "God's good green herb" at will.
3. Extra points for combining above two objectives into one sentence. Example from 11:09 p.m.: "Jim was just horrible at editing film, but he could roll a perfect joint."
4. Add patina of relevance by occasionally mentioning longstanding desire to "change the world" by eliminating such ecological ills as "unclean air" and "hamburgers."
5. Every 19.1 minutes, say something that might genuinely qualify as retarded. Example from 11:20 p.m.: "If you're gonna get drunk and get in a car, you should be killed, too. If you're that dumb, fuck you."

and finally

6. Add levity by making fun of Oliver Stone. Call his movie *The Doors* "a fiction by a coke-head." Question his motives for serv-

ing in Vietnam. Accuse him of not wanting to change world.
(Potential reason: Has eaten too many hamburgers?)

11:55 p.m. Manzarek talking audience through writing process of
"Light My Fire." Memorable moment: when he demonstrates, con-
vincingly, influence of both John Coltrane and Sonny & Cher on song.
Not memorable moment: when he attempts analysis of few lyrics from
song. ("'And our love become a funeral pyre'—OK, your love is gonna
be inflamed by the flames of a funeral pyre, we've got some kind of Indian burial going on here . . . ") Really annoying/kind of sad moment:
While Manzarek plays parts of song on piano, two random guys in
back section take guitars off wall and start playing along with him.

11:56 p.m. Manzarek: "So I said to the guys, 'We need an orgasm in
this song.'"

Audience member: "Viagra!"

11:57 p.m.–12:25 a.m. Jim Morrison Doors Doors Morrison Doors
Jim "Riders on the Storm" Doors Jim Morrison Jim Morrison Jim
Morrison Doors let's change the world Doors Doors Doors Jimmy
Jim-Jim Doors.

1/26/99, 3:47 p.m. Q: "Is it ever frustrating to you that, after all this
time, you're still primarily identified as a former member of the Eagles?"

Manzarek: [Laughs] "Yeah, yeah. Member of the Eagles. You wise-
guy. You know, I'll probably always be known as a former Door. The
Doors were extremely successful, and that's probably the way it's always going to be. If people choose to see me that way, there's nothing
wrong with that. It's a convenient handle. I'd sure rather be a Door
than not be a Door. You've got to take the bitter with the sweet."

Q: "How much damage do you think Oliver Stone actually did with
his caricature . . . "

RM: "Well, he created another . . . "

Q: ". . . of Bill Morrison?"

RM: ". . . persona for Jim that is not the real Jim Morrison. Jim was
a funny, artistic, intelligent, witty human being who unfortunately had

a penchant for alcohol and ultimately drank himself to death. Oliver
Stone turned him into this sort of crazed, white-powder man. It's really
a white-powder flick, as opposed to a psychedelic flick. In a way, it's appropriate to today's way of thinking—today's linear, 1959 style of
thinking."

Q: "Do you think Morrison's legacy has adversely affected the career
of his daughter Alanis?"

RM: "No, you know I think it's been a very positive influence on
Alanis Morrison. The only problem is that we haven't been able to figure out who her mom was."

*Note to reader: please disregard opening ³/₄ of column. Have concluded that
Ray Manzarek = genius. Thank you.*

DAVID SAMUELS

Hip-Hop High

Def Jam Records, Kevin Liles likes to say, signs only stars. In his nearly two years as president of Def Jam, Liles has personally signed one star—a seventeen-year-old rapper from Teaneck, New Jersey, named Shanell Jones, who is also known as Lady Luck.

"I was on my way to work," Liles recently recalled, talking about the first time he heard her, one morning in February, in the back seat of his Lincoln Town Car. "Luck was on the radio, because she had just won five days in a row on 'Check the Rhyme,' on Hot 97." Hot 97 is the most listened-to hip-hop station in New York. Every weekday morning, starting at seven-twenty, the hosts of "Check the Rhyme" invite unknown rappers to call in and start rapping. The caller with the best verses is asked to phone in again the following morning. Anyone who wins the competition five days in a row is invited to the Hot 97 studios, on Hudson Street, to rhyme on the air.

Liles was listening to Hot 97's latest winner when his cell phone rang. The caller was Erick Sermon, the leader of a Def Jam rap group called EPMD. "Yo, do you hear this girl on Hot 97?" Sermon said. Liles was already impressed. The girl was rapping off the top of her head, lighting up the airwaves with the sorts of inventive rhymes and electric phrases that would stick in the heads of teen-age hip-hop fans as they rode the subways and buses to school.

"I said, 'Yo, she's ill,'" Liles recalled. "So he said, 'Yo, let's call up there.' So we call up there, and I said to one of the hosts, 'Yo, tell the girl and her parents to come directly to my office. Do not stop anywhere else.'"

When Shanell Jones walked into his office with her mother and stepfather later that morning, Liles saw a chubby girl with lively brown eyes, toffee-colored skin, and a pretty face, who was dressed in a sweatshirt, a pair of Nike Air Jordan sneakers, and a fitted baseball cap cocked to one side, just like thousands of other seventeen-year-olds in New York. A minute or two later, he saw something else. "A star can walk in and light up the room," he said. "And she did that when she came into my office and started to rhyme." When she finished rhyming, Liles called Lyor Cohen, the president of the label's parent group, Island Def Jam, and said that he'd found a star. The two executives took Shanell and her parents to lunch, and then to dinner. Two weeks later, Liles sent her a dozen red roses for Valentine's Day.

As word of Def Jam's interest in Shanell Jones spread through the tight-knit community of rap, executives at other labels, including Bad Boy, Atlantic, and Elektra, also became interested in her, and a bidding war ensued. Def Jam won. On March 3rd, Liles signed the girl who called herself Lady Luck to a new-artist contract with Def Jam. The contract obligated her to be the principal rapper on five albums, for which she would receive various payments and benefits, including rent money for an apartment of her own, college tuition, a car, and thousands of dollars' worth of jewelry—altogether, a package worth somewhere between half a million and a million dollars.

What Liles acquired was a bubbly seventeen-year-old who had wanted to be a rap star since the age of five, when she spoke her first rhyme. More important, he had found a performer who might fill a conspicuous gap in Def Jam's mostly male lineup of rap stars—self-invented urban superhero characters like L.L. Cool J, Jay-Z, DMX, Redman, Method Man, and Ja Rule, who rap about living large and keeping it real, about wearing platinum chains and driving Mercedes-Benzes, selling crack and murdering rivals. Liles needed a hard-rhyming female rapper who, with proper guidance, could become Def Jam's answer to superwoman rappers like Eve, L'il Kim, and Rah Digga, who record for other labels.

One's chances of commercial success as a rapper are determined, in large part, by the persona or character one projects, and how vividly it stands out from the personae of the other hot rappers of the moment. "When you think about Eve," Liles explained to me, "if Eve's man was in a gunfight and he got shot, she would pick up his gun and start shooting at the other guy. L'il Kim would fuck that other man. Rah Digga would stab that other man. Luck would have a great time with that man, and then hit him in the head with a bat. So all of them have their own special qualities."

For all of Liles's faith in his new star, though, Shanell's future is far from guaranteed. The apartment, the car, the jewelry come to her as, in effect, advances against royalties; if she fails to produce hits, the perks could vanish overnight. Moreover, if she does succeed in making Lady Luck a household name, there is a more insidious danger to worry about. "All too often, the character simply kills off the real person," Lyor Cohen told me. "It's easy to understand why. You can wake up tomorrow as Earl Simmons, a kid from a bad neighborhood whom no one ever gave a fuck about for the first twenty-six years of his life. Or you can be DMX"—Simmons' rap name—"a character who sells millions of records, and whom every kid in America loves, and behave like DMX does in his rhymes." It is no accident that Tupac Shakur and Biggie Smalls, rap music's two biggest stars of the nineties, were shot to death before the age of thirty. "You pray that that doesn't happen," Cohen said, "but often, much too often, it does."

One afternoon a few weeks before the start of Shanell Jones's senior year at Teaneck High School, she was camped out on a beige couch in the office of DJ Enuff, the executive at Def Jam who is responsible for guiding her career. She had spent much of the summer in the recording company's headquarters, on the twenty-seventh floor of the Worldwide Plaza office tower, on Eighth Avenue, getting to know everyone who would be involved in turning her into the street-talking rapper known as Lady Luck. Most mornings, she had worked out with a personal trainer named Pop, who was charged with reducing her thighs, waist, and butt. Most afternoons, she had been holed up in DJ Enuff's office listening to a vast assortment of CDs and DATs (digital audiotapes) for instrumental tracks that might mesh with her lyrics.

On this afternoon, Shanell looked nothing like the bat-wielding vixen of Kevin Liles' dreams. She was wearing a Cleveland Indians baseball cap, a yellow Iceberg T-shirt emblazoned with a cartoon of Fido the dog, jeans that stopped in the middle of her calves, and a pair of brand-new blue-and-white Nikes. Around her neck was a diamond-studded platinum four-leaf clover, which the label had given her after she signed the contract. DJ Enuff, a friendly, bearlike man who also spins records on Hot 97, was on the phone, asking a friend to pick up his laundry.

Earlier in the summer, Lady Luck had made her recording début, a thirty-second guest appearance on "Symphony 2000," a song on EPMD's last album, "Out of Business." When I asked how she was enjoying her first taste of fame, she sighed, then said, "I have a hundred boyfriends. They say, 'Lady Luck, she my baby mama.' I have brothers and sisters I never met before in my life. And I have eight bars on one song on someone else's album. So imagine what happens when I go platinum."

Her beeper went off, and she grabbed her cell phone. "All right, Mahogany," she cooed. "I love you with your pretty hair." She flirted some more, then turned to business: "I got a call from a movie person—a lady named Heidi, working on the 'Next Friday' sound-track. I need a song."

Mahogany is a young rap producer from the South Bronx who made his mark last year, when he produced an instrumental track on Jay-Z's quadruple-platinum album, *Hard Knock Life, Volume 2*. In rap, producers create the multi-layered instrumental tracks that provide the background—the beats and sonic atmosphere—behind the lyrics. Like Mahogany, most producers operate as free agents, going from label to label with their arsenal of tracks, hoping to make a quick sale with an up-and-coming rapper like Lady Luck and curious to see whether the label's faith in the newcomer's talent is justified.

A few minutes later, Mahogany appeared in DJ Enuff's office. He is a tall, well-built young man, and was wearing a gray T-shirt and a fitted Yankees cap; a cell phone peeked out from a pocket of his spacious jeans. Lady Luck frowned at the Yankees cap. "I told them all about your pretty hair," she teased. Mahogany responded with a shy smile, exposing a gold-framed tooth. He handed her a CD, which she popped into DJ Enuff's stereo, and then he sat down on the couch and began bobbing his head to the beat, glancing back and forth from Lady Luck to DJ Enuff, in a way that suggested he was confident in his work and only mildly interested in their reaction.

"You got some hot shit here," Lady Luck said, after listening to the third track. The music was paralyzingly loud. As the fourth track came on, DJ Enuff turned up the volume, and the faintest shadow of a smile appeared at the corners of Mahogany's mouth.

"I gonna spit," Lady Luck said, a few bars into the track, and she began improvising a verse: "I keep my gat in my bra strap . . . "

DJ Enuff nodded and grinned. Mahogany grinned, too. The mating dance between rapper and producer had begun.

Next, Lady Luck dropped in on her publicist, Gabby Peluso. Although the sounds in Def Jam's offices are resolutely black—rap music booms from behind closed doors and executives greet one another with expressions like "Whassup, dawg?" and "You my nigga"—the heads of the label's marketing, production, and distribution are a multiracial mix. Bounding into the publicist's office, Lady Luck spotted a picture of herself on the party page of an issue of *Vibe* that was lying open on Peluso's desk. "That's me!" she screamed.

"I love new artists," Peluso said indulgently.

Lady Luck's small talk with the publicist was interrupted by the arrival of Ron Robinson, the manager of Ja Rule, a Def Jam rapper whose latest album had just gone platinum. Wearing a white striped ENYCE baseball shirt, he entered with a smirk that suggested he'd come to give the publicist a hard time.

"I be trying to get Ja to come up here," he said. "He say, 'Man, fuck that.' Because the nigga be *tired*."

"Ron and Ja used to come to my office every day and eat," Peluso explained to Lady Luck. "That's when they didn't have any money. I'd say, 'Ja, I have an interview for you inside a black hole.' And he'd do it. And now . . . "

"The nigga freaks *out*," Robinson said, spreading his arms to indicate the magnitude of the situation. "It's the animal y'all created. Because the nigga was *never* like that before."

"And everything in his songs is 'murder, murder, murder,'" Peluso said, frowning.

"We makin' songs for *real* niggas, y'all," Robinson said. Then, catching Peluso's glare, he demurred, "Well, not *everything* is murder."

Peluso picked up a copy of Ja Rule's platinum album, "Venni Vetti Vecci," and began reading the song titles listed on the back: "'Murda,' 'Murda 4 Life,' 'The Murderers.'"

Robinson shrugged. "We're Murder, Inc.," he said.

Lady Luck listened to all this with the attentiveness of an A-student. When Robinson left, she reassured Peluso that even after she had sold millions of records she would always show up for interviews and be on time. The publicist nodded skeptically.

Outside Peluso's office, Lady Luck skipped down the tan-carpeted hallway, rhyming:

> *Lady,*
> *arrogant cat . . .*
> *y'all stay behind me like my backpack*
> *strap on the condom*
> *and stay riding to fame*
> *rock harder*
> *till the whole world is screaming my name.*

There is no shortage of teen-agers in hooded sweatshirts and baggy jeans who, like Shanell Jones, write down rhymes in their spiral notebooks, listen obsessively to hip-hop radio stations like Hot 97 and KISS FM, beg friends in the business for studio time, send demo tapes off to record companies, and dream of the moment when they will be signed to a million-dollar contract with a label like Def Jam and the larger-than-life character inside them will erupt into the world with blazing, digitally mastered clarity. For them, making it in a business that has transformed the insular experience of black urban life into a billion-dollar-a-year segment of the music industry is a way to stay true to their roots while living the American Dream. Shanell credits her success so far to the intervention of a higher power. "God told me to call Hot 97," she says.

She was born in 1982, in Englewood, New Jersey—the daughter of parents who had one foot in the suburbs and the other on the inner-city streets. Her mother, Donna, worked in the promotions department of Sugar Hill Records, a small label in Englewood which, in 1979, had released the first rap recording, the Sugarhill Gang's "Rapper's Delight." Shanell's father ran betting spots in Harlem and didn't spend much time with his wife and two daughters. (Shanell has a younger sister, Shaté.) When Shanell was nine, the relationship broke up.

Shanell says that in those days her mother used cocaine. "But she wasn't a crackhead," she adds. "She did her thing on the weekends. There was always money for rent and utilities and food. But it was scary. When we got saved, she left all of that behind."

As a child, Shanell was a frequent visitor to Sugar Hill's studio, where she recited her early rhymes for producers, engineers, and old-school rappers like Melle Mel and Master Gee. They called her the Sugar Hill Baby. "I always wanted to be a rapper," Shanell told me. "I remember once writing to a friend in the fifth grade about how I had met Russell Simmons"—then the president of Def Jam—"and how I had a contract with Def Jam. Which was a lie."

In 1995, when Shanell turned fourteen, her mother married a man named Kory Ward, who had dreamed of becoming a rapper, and who had performed briefly with a touring version of the Sugarhill Gang, before going to work in a sneakers store. That year, Donna Ward was saved. The family started going to church regularly, and two summers ago Shanell herself was saved when she spent a weekend at a Christian retreat. Since then, she has tried to balance her faith with her love of rapping and the usual temptations of teenage life. She doesn't smoke, and she recently swore off hard liquor. "That was me two weeks ago," she recalled with solemn conviction. In August, she and her parents bought a house in Teaneck—the first house the family has ever owned. Her parents are supportive of her career as a rapper, she says, but they both wish that Lady Luck didn't curse so much when she rhymes.

Shanell's day at Def Jam didn't end until six o'clock. That allowed her only a couple of hours to get herself home to Teaneck and into party clothes for a celebration of the latest release by the rappers Method Man and Redman, which was to be held later in the evening, back in Manhattan. Along for the ride, in a town car that snaked up the West Side Highway and across the George Washington Bridge, were

Shanell's second cousin Shan and her friend Saleem. They are both rappers and members of Lady Luck's backup crew, the Cuzones. Saleem, who is seventeen, is tall and good-looking, and has a shy, sweet manner. Shan, who is also seventeen, is stocky and likable, with a long, thin, intelligent face, a wispy goatee, and an enormous pair of Versace glasses.

The three of them carried on much of their conversation in rhymes inspired by what they could see out the windows. "A blacked-out Benz . . ." Shan began at one point.

Before he could go on, Shanell jumped in. "That's not good enough," she said. "Say you see two ads for a Benz in the paper. One just says 'black Benz.' The other says, '1999 model, custom-leather interior, with twenty-two-inch platinum hubcaps, and three television sets.' Now, which one are you going to cop?"

As the rapping continued, it became clear that the best verses—perfectly balanced, with a sense of narrative and a keen ear for internal rhymes that made the lines snap and bounce—belonged to Shanell. Listening to her was like watching a kid hit a tennis ball against a wall for hours and never miss once:

> *Rhymin' about your diamonds shinin'*
> *Nigga, please—I got these.*

"You can get an idea from a word or a phrase," she explained. "Like 'cash stacked up in Philly.' Whose cash is it? How did they get it? You can make a whole song off that one line."

She noticed a passing black Ford truck. "Driving across the bridge in your black Ford truck," she began, and almost before the line was fully out of her mouth she had envisioned the rhyme:

> *With your hand on the wheel*
> *While you're feelin' on Luck.*

She paused to register the line for future reference. Then her pager went off. The call-back number belonged to a boy she'd met last week in Washington, D.C. She punched in the numbers on her cell phone. When the boy answered, she said softly, "I'll call you after the party. I be home like two or three." Then, in a voice that held hints of the gangsta rapper inside the not totally secure teen-ager, she added, "Don't get bold now. Save your boldness for me."

The new house in Teaneck is a bluish-gray two-story clapboard on a quiet tree-lined street—in "the *white* part of town," as Shanell was quick to point out. She led Shan and Saleem past an urn of plastic flowers set neatly on the front lawn, and up some brick stairs. At the door, she reminded her visitors to take their shoes off. Then she reviewed the rules of the house: the living room, with its spotless new off-white sofa and chairs, was strictly off-limits, as was the dining room, with its freshly polished table. The guests complimented the new house, and Shanell's mother, Donna Ward, a gentle, round-faced woman in her forties, was pleased. "God bless you," she said. The doorbell rang, and the members of her Wednesday-night Bible-study group filed into the living room in stockinged feet, offering kisses and blessings all around. Shanell and her friends retreated upstairs.

Shanell's bedroom is a small, blue-carpeted room with a black lacquered dresser and a closet full of Iceberg shirts, Coogli knits, at least ten fitted baseball caps, and lots of gear from Phat Farm, the clothing label owned by the former Def Jam president, Russell Simmons. Shanell's stepfather, Kory, poked his head in the door, held out one shoeless foot, wiggled his toes, and nodded in the direction of the Bible-study group downstairs. "I wish I was back in the fucking projects," he said, with mock exasperation, before disappearing back down the hall.

"The green or the black?" Shanell held up two brand-new pairs of Nikes. All the sneakers in her closet are Nikes, thanks to a dinner she recently had with some Nike representatives, one of whom sent her a note: "After you left dinner I said she is special because she has such personality & I am glad to be around to watch you *win* in this game." The green pair got nods of approval. Next, she held up a canary-yellow shirt from Phat Farm. "This shirt looks hot with the blue wife-beater, but will it throw the outfit off?" she said.

Finally, she decided on an outfit from Phat Farm—black stretch jersey, black nylon cargo pants, dark sunglasses, and, for contrast, the green sneakers. "How do I look?" she asked.

"You look like a rapper," Shan said.

National Recording Studios, on West Forty-second Street, is a place where a great many rap records get made. That night, it was the site of the party for the new Method Man–Redman album. Inside was a smoky crush of Def Jam executives, producers, chain-store buyers, hip-hop writers, interns, assistants, and aspiring rappers, all of whom had come to schmooze, drink free Bacardi, exchange cell-phone numbers, and take advantage of the free buffet. While the new album boomed through trunk-size speakers, Lady Luck, followed by her entourage of Shan, Saleem, and a friend named Kana, moved through the crowd, making sure to greet every Def Jam employee she encountered with hugs or kisses.

When she spotted a tall white man with a close-shaved head who was seated across the room on a metal folding chair and bobbing to the beat, she put on her sunglasses and went over to pay her respects. He was Lyor Cohen, who, before becoming president of Island Def Jam, managed such pioneering eighties rap groups as Run-DMC and the Beastie Boys. He greeted Lady Luck with an inquisitive look, then got up and shouted, "Todd! Todd!" Waving back was the rapper L.L. Cool J (born James Todd Smith), a sleek, muscular multimillionaire who was discovered by Def Jam at the age of fifteen when he sent the label a homemade tape in the mail. L.L. Cool J, who is now in his early thirties and is still one of the most popular performers in the business, made his way through the crowd like a movie legend at the Oscars. Lady Luck ran over to him, and when he saw her he stopped, smiled, flexed his biceps, and got his picture taken with Def Jam's newest star.

As the party was beginning to break up, Lady Luck headed for the door with Saleem, Shan, and Kana. On her way out, she ran into Russell Simmons. He wore a serene expression, as though he had just stepped out of a long, warm bath after an hour and a half of yoga. "Luck, you getting shit done?" he said.

The question caught Lady Luck off guard. "Nah," she said. "I'm still trying to find some beats."

Simmons stepped back and looked her up and down. Finally, he delivered his verdict: "You gotta get working, yo." Lady Luck nodded mutely and, before she could think of anything to say, Simmons had moved on.

Out on the sidewalk, in front of a long line of limos, four or five would-be young rappers were engaged in a "cipher"—a rhyming battle in which the combatants duke it out with escalating boasts and put-downs. Joining a cipher at an industry event like this one is a way for unknown rappers to get noticed, especially if they can take on—and defeat—a signed artist like Lady Luck. A crowd had formed, making a circle around the rappers, and Lady Luck suddenly found herself in the center of things, standing there in her sunglasses and with a borrowed cigar, still in its wrapper, clamped in her mouth.

"Niggers act niggerish, talk gibberish," a sturdily built black kid in a gray sweatsuit taunted, hoping to draw Lady Luck into battle.

Floating from the doorway toward his town car, Kevin Liles took in the scene, then said in Lady Luck's ear, "You ain't got nothing to prove." But Shan did. Luck whispered to Shan, "Spit!" He nodded but didn't move. Finally—and only after the town car, with Liles inside, had pulled away—Shan accepted the challenge. His chin held high, he stepped into the circle and started to rhyme:

> *I'm not hot,*
> *Nigga, I'm blazing.*
> *Y'all now facing*
> *Shan the Amazing.*

He got off a second verse before a challenger stepped into the circle. Someone in the crowd held up a fifty-dollar bill. Shan's opponent spat first. "I shit on you, I shit on your crew," he muttered, stamping around inside the circle. His rhymes were weak, and his voice was barely audible.

"Nah, that ain't it, Money," someone shouted.

When the kid had finished, Shan stepped forward, his baseball shirt flapping in the breeze:

> *Little-time hustler*
> *Trying to come up on a rise to this game*
> *You a youngster*
> *I can see it in your eyes.*
> *Frontin' like that, you deserve to die.*

The opponent stalked around the circle with his chin tucked in, mumbling his verse into the collar of his sweatshirt. His delivery lacked aggression, the thrusting self-confidence that rhyming on a sidewalk in front of fifty or so spectators demands. The crowd pressed in, shouting "Louder! Louder!" By the time the rapper was finished, the mood on the sidewalk had turned to scorn.

"Nobody loves you where you're at, Money!" someone yelled.

"Don't get mad, Money! Don't get mad!"

Shan delivered one last rhyme:

> *I sit with your chick in my crib,*
> *Gittin' my tip licked while the Knicks is on!*

The crowd dissolved and the fifty dollars disappeared, but Shan was feeling triumphant. Lady Luck, however, was not pleased. Sitting in the front seat of the limo that was taking them all back to Teaneck, she rebuked Shan for his reluctance to enter the cipher. "When I tell you to spit, you spit!" she said, turning to glare at her cousin, in the back seat. "It happens once. That one time was Hot 97 for me. You never know when that time is." She felt that she had lost face when Shan didn't obey her immediately, and that he'd missed a great chance to rhyme for Kevin Liles. When Shan didn't respond, she said, as if weary of the whole subject, "Lady Luck don't care. But the question is, are you going to get that one time. Because I'm going to eat regardless."

She asked the driver to pull into a McDonald's at Broadway and 125th Street. After Shan, Saleem, and Kana had gone to get burgers and fries, she said, staring into the darkness below the elevated train tracks, "I'm trying to take everyone with me, but there's a lot of pressure, yo. Niggas don't do what I tell them." She took a breath, then continued, "That thing with Russell freaked me out. He was looking at me real suspect. I want to make Russell Simmons happy, and Kevin Liles happy, and I still don't have the tracks I need. But it's like this joke I have with Kevin, where he says that if I ever write a wack rhyme, or make a wack record, and he hears that shit, he'll drop me off by the side of the road and make me walk home." She set her jaw. "And what I tell Kevin is 'Kevin, I'm never walking home.'"

Without hot tracks, Lady Luck will never become a star. Behind every rap hit are producers who mine stacks of old soul, rhythm-and-blues, rock, gospel, and classical records for catchy loops that they can layer over a version of the basic drum-and-bass beat that is the backbone of every rap song. Producers like RZA, Prince Paul, Timbaland, Dr. Dre, and Swiss Beatz, who can synthesize fragments of found music into hypnotic mosaics of sound, are stars in their own right—alchemists who can transform ordinary rhymes into platinum hits. At the moment, the producer Lady Luck is pinning her hopes on is Mahogany, the shy young man with the pretty hair and the gold-framed tooth.

Mahogany produced his breakthrough track in an apartment in the South Bronx, where he lives with his mother and his sister. He did his sound mixing on an MPC-2000 sampler, a piece of equipment that cost three thousand dollars and that his mother bought for him with the last of the insurance benefit she received after Mahogany's father died. For the better part of a year, he took his tracks to the offices of Jay-Z's label, Roc-A-Fella Records, where he was greeted without great enthusiasm.

"And then one day Jay-Z walked by and he heard this track," Mahogany told me. "It was called 'Celebration.' I must have given him that track four times, and that one time he was, like, 'Yo, I like this track.' And he must have been in a good mood that day, because he cut me a check right there, from his personal account, for three thousand dollars. And I was on cloud nine." Soon afterward, he sold Jay-Z another track. "I bought some records, a black Maurice Malone bubble coat and a pair of boots to match, and I paid my mom back for the MPC-2000."

In the rear of Mahogany's apartment is a closet-size room filled with CDs, tapes, and thousands of vinyl LPs. Although Mahogany's only credit on Jay-Z's Grammy-winning album was as the producer of a single track—based on the Talking Heads' "Life During Wartime"—it was enough to make him a Grammy winner, too. From that song he stands to make well over a hundred and fifty thousand dollars in publishing royalties, fifty thousand of which he has already received in the form of a music-publishing contract that has allowed him to leave his job, as a salesman at the Gap, and work on his music full time.

"This is my Benz right here," he said, pointing to a fully automated digital mixing board, which he bought with his first royalty payments. "I said, 'Let me get this, and this will help me get the car.'" Next to the mixing board was at least forty thousand dollars' worth of advanced digital electronics, including a Trinity Pro keyboard, decks of TASCAM DATs, a TASCAM CD-burner, a Planet Phat dance-synth module, state-of-the-art samplers, and other equipment that Mahogany uses to chop, cut, loop, and play with bits and pieces of recordings—from Millie Jackson, Thelma Houston, and Fela to Mozart and Philip Glass—which he mines from the thousands of vinyl LPs stacked perilously around the apartment. "I'm looking for weird loops, for unusual sounds," he told me. "The crazier the cover, the older the record, the hotter and the richer the sounds."

On top of the Trinity Pro keyboard were three DATs, containing seventy-five instrumental tracks—the cream of the producer's output over the past six months. "This is a track for Lady Luck," he said, pointing to a fourth DAT, which he loaded into the mixing board. As he turned one of the hundreds of knobs on the board, the room filled with the bouncy opening loop of Donna Summer's "Bad Girls," which Mahogany proceeded to modify in at least a dozen different ways, fiddling with the knobs on the mixing board while loading new drum tracks, toning down the snare, thickening the bass, and reshaping time signatures to create the standard 16-8-16-8-16-8 bar structure of a four-minute rap song. Running up and down the bass line, at appropriate intervals, was Mahogany's signature sound—a fizzy, four-second-long crescendo that suggests a computer-generated version of champagne being poured into a glass.

Mahogany told me that he still had a lot to learn about Lady Luck. "I don't know how good her ear is yet," he said. "I don't know if she's loyal. She's got to want to keep working, and not be content with the first thing she lays down. But, really, she has to be able to listen. I've got to see if she listens to me instead of the people she hangs out with. If I say, 'I don't like it,' she's got to be 'You sure? O.K., let's do it again.'"

An important step in the grooming of Lady Luck was a guest slot on the remixing of "Get the Fuck Up," a wildly popular underground hit by a young rapper named Pharoahe Monch. The song was to be part of Monch's first album, which would also feature guest appearances by two big-name rappers, Redman and Busta Rhymes. By adding new verses and guest artists to Monch's single, the rapper's label, Rawkus Entertainment, a division of Def Jam, hopes to extend the life of the song until the album's release, in late October. The practice of putting new artists like Lady Luck on tracks with established stars (who enhance their street credibility by associating with an underground hit) is similar to the old Hollywood strategy of launching promising newcomers by casting them in films with a Gable or Cagney.

Fiddling with her platinum four-leaf clover, tugging at her New York Giants football jersey, and sucking on the cap of her pen, Lady Luck was in the Rawkus control room, busily revising the twelve-bar rhyme that she hoped to inject into the remix. Next to her was DJ Enuff, sipping soda from Wendy's and picking at a plate of ketchup-smeared fries.

Beyond the glass wall of the control room stood Pharoahe Monch, a shy-looking, slightly overweight young man in a white T-shirt and baggy jeans. He looked down at the floor as if gathering his strength, then raised his head and started to rhyme:

> *Rub on your titties!*
> *Yeah, fuck it, I said it,*
> *rub on your titties!*

In the control room, the engineer spoke to Monch through a microphone: "I can hear jewelry rattling. Does that bother you?" Monch smiled sweetly and shook his head. Then he put his head down, looked up, and energetically delivered another rhyme:

> *Some might even say that this song is sexist*
> *Because it's asking girls to rub on they breast-es . . .*

A few minutes later, he stepped out of the booth. "It's like Doctor Banner turning into the Incredible Hulk," he said when I asked him about his ability to contain two such apparently different personalities in one body—one a diffident, mumbling kid from Queens, the other a superhero party rapper whose style gets its explosive strength from letter-perfect enunciation. "Rapping is something I have to do because I'm so introverted," he said. "I was much too shy to rock at the jams. I just stayed in my room and played video games."

I asked Monch what he saw as Lady Luck's contribution to "Get the Fuck Up."

"I'm analytical about my songs," he said. "I analyze Luck being on the song like this: Where the chorus was kind of degrading to women, she adds the element that it's all in fun."

In the control room, Lady Luck was conferring with a producer named Bink Dog, a smooth-mannered young man, who played with the rim of his white fishing hat while he talked. His plan was to have Lady Luck join Monch on the opening chorus of "Rub on your titties." Luck frowned. "Yo, that shit will make me sound gay," she objected.

"Better if she say something toward rubbing on her *own* titties," Bink Dog suggested.

"Maybe it *is* a little gay," someone offered.

"Be honest with you, that connotation cuts both ways," Monch said. "But that takes the song to a whole other level."

The engineer said that he was just about ready to start recording Lady Luck. To get her energy up, she paced the room, whooped, did a series of high karate-style kicks, and sang bits of harmony from old Bee Gees songs. Finally, stepping outside to the microphone, she started to rhyme:

> *Bitches in the back like crack getting cut up*
> *I speak on behalf of them broads you call stuck-up*
> *Act like a man and get cock-smacked the fuck up.*

The point of the verse was that Lady Luck could rhyme as hard as any man. As she punched in the rest of her lyric, her voice expanded with a rush of brash, street-talking self-confidence that brought a smile to DJ Enuff's face:

> *Luck—*
> *You know the name*
> *Assed-out in the bleachers, stay shitting on the game.*

Lady Luck flipped to another page in her notebook and laid down a second lyric—this one notably devoid of curse words. Then, while Monch, DJ Enuff, and Bink Dog debated the merits of the two verses, she sat with her sneakers off, drinking Tropicana orange juice from the carton. Finally, the elevator door opened and Kevin Liles breezed into the control room, followed by his chauffeur. "That motherfucking record!" he exclaimed as he grabbed hold of Monch. "That shit is running now! That shit is crazy, dawg! Real hip-hop. I *fiend* for that shit!"

He hugged Lady Luck to his chest, then put his hands on her shoulders, took a comic-book step backward, and nodded at the chauffeur.

"I pay him not to give you a ride home if you wack," he said.

He listened to both tracks in silence, then held his ring finger up in the air. "The first one," he said. "She set it off the whole way."

"You want to hear the first one again?" the engineer asked.

"Yes, ma'am," Kevin Liles said.

"That's the one," he said, when the verse was over. Lady Luck looked momentarily upset. The curse words would disturb her mother, but the decision was out of her hands. On his way out, Liles raised his arm and proclaimed, "May your life be strong and healthy and blessed."

Lady Luck picked up her cell phone and called home. "Mommy, I love you," she said. There was a pause, and—judging by the look that crept over her face—whatever her mother was saying had pulled her out of the character of Lady Luck and back into Shanell Jones. In a small voice, she said, "Remember, this is my rap career. This is paying our bills. No, I'm not saying those words like that." Then, "I love you, Mommy. . . . Please."

The next morning, Shanell was back in DJ Enuff's office, fresh from her workout with Pop and still bothered by a dream she had had the night before. "There was this girl I was scared of," she said, hugging a pillow to her chest. "She was light-skinned, like me, about my height, and we were friends until the end. We got into an argument, and my heart started beating real fast." Lying in bed, her heart racing and her eyes open, Shanell imagined that she'd heard something move in the hall. She had got out of bed and gone to tell her parents about the dream, but they were both fast asleep. "I got real, real scared," she said. "I turned the TV on, and I slept with that all night."

I suggested that this didn't seem exactly like Lady Luck. "It sounds crazy—talking about me and Lady Luck like two different people," Shanell said. "But Lady Luck is like this really flashy character who just likes to . . . not show off, but she needs to be the center of attention." She nestled her head into the safety of the well-upholstered couch. "Inside Lady Luck's whole body it's ice," she continued. "She's on top. She's arrogant and cocky. Playful. She's wild. Whereas Shanell Jones is like a real loving person—real emotional, real sensitive. You know what I mean? And I try not to get the two confused."

Teaneck High School, a dark brick building, serves a multiracial suburban community—white kids, black kids, Hispanics, a few Muslim girls in chadors, and a few boys in yarmulkes from the town's sizable Orthodox Jewish population. Life here comes in subtle shadings, not the bright colors of the cartoon world of Shanell's rhymes. No one sells crack on the street corners of Teaneck.

After weeks of worrying about what to wear on the first day of school, Shanell arrived well before the beginning of classes, in a yellow Phat Farm shirt over baggy Guess jeans and her diamond-studded platinum clover leaf. She had a lot of friends she was looking forward to seeing, especially her "mad cool" best friend, Evan. She took up a perch by a side entrance that is known as the "black door"—a reminder of the de facto racial segregation that was in place until the nineteen-sixties. Shanell is confident of her reputation for being the sharpest mouth in the school, and she offered a stream of good-natured commentary on the teachers and students passing by. "Yo, that nigga has a crease in his sweatpants!" she exclaimed, sipping from a bottle of Evian. "Yo!" she called out. "You iron your sweatpants for the first day of school?" Her target looked sheepishly away.

She was already, she told me, facing a dilemma: whom she should go with to the senior prom, next spring. "See, Redman and Method Man have promised to take me," she said, referring to a promise that the two rap stars made to her after her guest appearance on their last album. Then she added, "But there's also Evan. We eat meals together. I hear he wants to take me, too."

Seated at a desk in her homeroom, Shanell seemed to be avoiding the eyes of the boy sitting next to her. He turned out to be Evan, a handsome, slightly chubby white kid in a navy-blue Nautica T-shirt and wire-rimmed glasses.

"I hear that someone wants to ask me to the prom," she ventured.

There was a moment of silence before the object of this remark came up with an acceptable answer. "If that was true, and a person did want to take you to the prom," Evan said, "how would you feel about that?"

Shanell looked down at her desk. Living up to the demands of Lady Luck and, at the same time, accommodating the feelings of Shanell Jones was not going to be easy. Arriving at the prom with two of Def Jam's biggest artists was the kind of sweepstakes prize that might be advertised on "Yo! MTV Raps." On the other hand, Evan was her best friend. "I would be cool with that," she finally said. "But listen. I promised Red and Meth that I would go with them."

Evan nodded.

"So what I'd like to do is this. You'll be my date to the prom, but I'll show up with Red and Meth. Is that cool with you?" Her diamond clover glinted under the fluorescent lights.

"That would be cool," he said.

"So this girl comes up to me after math," Shanell said, her face brightening. "You know what she said? She had a dream about me last night. Kids be having dreams about me now. Isn't that just the craziest shit?"

ARTHUR KEMPTON

The Lost Tycoons:
The Fall of the Black
Empires

1.

By the time the "equal opportunity" generation of black Americans started going to college in the Sixties, Booker T. Washington's reputation had washed up on the wrong side of history, beached and moldering like the carcass of a whale. For these newest "new Negroes" he was as old-fashioned as the country blues. He seemed compromised and unheroic at a time when compromise was disreputable. It isn't surprising that his influence on twentieth-century black America is commonly given short shrift. Ironically, two men of high influence with the generation that scorned Washington, Elijah Muhammad and Berry Gordy Jr., were in many respects his followers in the institutions they built, and that is the reason they are among the most important black Americans of the last half-century.

When Berry Gordy's father came of age in Georgia, and while Elijah Poole was growing up there, Booker T. Washington was the "Wizard of Tuskegee," an authentic international celebrity, famous for the industrial training school he had set up in Alabama. Among other things, he was the most powerful black political boss America has ever known, serving as a dispenser of government jobs to blacks under several Republican administrations, and a broker of white philanthropy to Negro causes and institutions for more than thirty years. He accomplished this by exchanging his acquiescence in white authority over black American life for relative freedom of action for himself within its appointed boundaries. He used this dispensation as a charter to build and administer, often with his hand disguised and by purposeful indirection, an informal national organization disciplined enough to be called "the Tuskegee machine."

Elijah Muhammad came to different conclusions about the white man's intentions and the mutability of his basic nature, but in most respects the Wizard's indirect methods were the Messenger's model. Elijah felt morally superior to his oppressors and expressed it openly and contemptuously, but, like Washington, he never challenged their authority. On the several occasions in the early Sixties when police forcibly entered, even shot up, Muslim places of worship, the Nation's response was uniformly restrained.

For all their jail- and street-hardened patina, the paramilitary huffing and puffing that always succeeded in making the Muslims seem a little dangerous, the tacit understanding they mostly had with local law enforcement was mutually reinforcing. Muslims were generally left alone because they were understood to be supportive of authority, perceived as a kind of auxiliary constabulary that helped to keep order in unruly neighborhoods. Though Elijah's accommodation to white authority was superficially less congenial than Washington's, he rendered unto Caesar every bit as much. He used the cover he was thereby afforded to tend his "nation of shopkeepers" with as much unfettered authority as Washington had to run his "machine."

Forty years before Berry Gordy Jr. started to amass his fortune as a budding impresario of pop music, his father stole away from Georgia with the $2,600 he got from selling tree stumps. It seemed like a fortune to him. He was a practical man who understood that the white people he lived among were authorized to take whatever he had whenever they wanted it. The father's son inherited his assumption of a theoretical limit on how high white people would allow him to rise and the tenuousness of his hold on wherever he perched once he got there. But he reckoned the distance between ground and ceiling altogether differently. Berry Gordy Jr. dared to imagine he could have what the rich and powerful white boys had. That dream was no less audacious in its time, nor was its achievement any less a breakthrough, for having found its most meaningful fulfillment in a standing invitation to Hugh Hefner's parties and a credit line in Las Vegas as big as Sinatra's.

Not disposed toward humility, Gordy made himself into discretion's servant. Once he began beating his industry's establishment at its own game, he comported himself while in its sightlines as delicately as if he were integrating the University of Alabama. He gave his white trading partners in the music business white faces to deal with, and receded into the shadow and safety of his company's meeting rooms and shop floors to apply his monomaniacal focus and incalculable shrewdness to conquering by stealth. In this he was as much a Washingtonian as the real estate and insurance tycoons A. G. Gaston in Birmingham and Alonso F. Herndon in Atlanta, who both made and kept their money under the noses and out of the hands of hostile and capricious white overlords by working longer, being smarter, and knowing how to maneuver in the briar patch. And so, after his dream came true, on late Friday afternoons Gordy still prowled the offices of what had become the most successful organization in the history of the music business, admonishing any within it whose pace had slackened to keep working. "Haven't you heard?" he would growl. "Money's not on strike."

Late in 1960 Berry Gordy Jr.'s first label, Tamla, released its first million seller, "Shop Around," by the Miracles—a "gold record," in the industry's term of art. This gave him all the foothold he needed to begin imposing his will on a business that earlier had tried so hard to break it. The record was largely the work of Motown's cornerstone asset, the singer, songwriter, and producer William "Smokey" Robinson, although the polishing Gordy gave it in the studio was critical to its success.

The two had found each other when Robinson was seventeen and Gordy was still bobbing along in the singer Jackie Wilson's wake, writing songs and scouting talent. Smokey came to audition his group for Gordy and brought along a schoolboy's spiral-bound notebook filled with the lyrics of songs he'd written.

Gordy, ever self-serious—Robinson at first thought him "pompous"— and, comparatively, the seasoned professional, offered criticism that became advice that turned into ongoing instruction. Thus began a relationship that was unique among all the others in Gordy's life. Robinson was the only person not named Gordy to whom Berry Gordy Jr. was unwaveringly loyal, the only Motown employee spared the sting of the back of its chairman's hand. Early on he made Robinson a vice president, and they were bonded in their shared enterprise for thirty years. Smokey named his first child, the son his wife delivered after enduring eight miscarriages, Berry, and the daughter that followed, Tamla.

Gordy already had convictions about songwriting before he was entitled to have anything more than ideas. His ideas weren't notions but seemed to spring from his head fully and finally formed. His teachers were the radio and the record player, and the musicians he had befriended years before at the Flame Show Bar in Detroit. What Gordy knew about music was as circumscribed as his gift was particular: the two-minute-forty-five-second popular song. The pattern was "a verse, another verse, a bridge, a chorus, back to the verse, one more chorus and out. . . . " Perhaps because he was a musical subliterate, he attached less value to melodic inventiveness than he did to song structure—"layout"—and lyrical content—"concept."

"The key," he told Raynoma Gordy, his second wife, "is in creating tension with the hook. You introduce it in the chorus, bring everything back to the verse, distract on the bridge—that's the tension—and then send the tune out with the hook." The hook is an element of pop music trade craft borrowed from the advertising copywriter's tool kit, a line or phrase ingratiating enough to catch the ear and clinch the sale. Smokey Robinson, whose manic cleverness and gift for ironic wordplay—"sort of like holding words to a mirror and checking out reverse images"[1]—made writing hooks the strongest part of his package, while Gordy worked on other things.

---

[1]These attributes, refined, by then, into a definitive style, are evident in this quintessential Robinson lyric from 1967's "The Hunter Gets Captured by the Game":

> . . . *Secretly I've been trailing you*
> *Like a fox that preys on a rabbit*
> *I had to get you and so I knew*
> *I had to learn your ways and habits,*
> *You were the catch that I was after*
> *But I looked up and you were in my arms*
> *And I knew I had been captured,*
> *What's this old world coming to*
> *Things just ain't the same*
> *Any time the hunter gets captured by the game.*

"He'd take a tune of Smokey's," Raynoma observed, and literally turn it around. "No, man, you should come from this point of view. Start here in the first person, get rid of that third-person voice." Then, when a strong theme was evident, Berry would guide Smokey further. "Yeah, that's good, very visual. . . . This line here, make it more of a picture. . . . " Smokey would incorporate the input, and the line would be, "I will build you a castle with a tower so high it reaches the moon. . . . "

Here is Gordy in 1960, an editor before he'd ever finished reading a book, way before it was clear to his contemporaries that cinema would supplant music as the cultural touchstone of the young audience he was after, shaping the text of a song as if it were a screenplay, making sure it was both literary and visual.

Every week Gordy convened the company's producers and salespeople to decide what to bring to market of what they had lately made. These meetings were Gordy's means of quality control, an idea he had met on the Ford assembly line. In Motown's early days, he sometimes brought kids in off the street to participate—the modern focus group before its time. Robinson tells us:

> [Gordy] built the meeting around the artists; anyone with a song for the Supremes, for example, would play it. Then came the critiques. Sometimes we'd all agree on what seemed an obvious hit. But mostly revisions would be suggested, and mostly they'd be heeded. When we got to [Robinson's group] the Miracles that morning, I proudly played my tape of "The Tracks of My Tears."
> "You crazy?" Berry asked when I was through.
> "No. Why?"
> "You got a hit, but you buried your hook. Bring it up at the end, man. Repeat that shit—that 'it's easy to trace the tracks of my tears' refrain—until you wear it out."[2]

Smokey, already by then as popular a songwriter as any, applied the finishing touches Gordy prescribed. He repeated his hook—

---

[2]Smokey Robinson, *Inside My Life* (Jove Books, 1990), p. 125.

> *So take a good look at my face*
> *You'll see my smile looks out of place,*
> *If you look closer it's easy to trace*
> *The tracks of my tears*

—four times in two minutes and fifty-three seconds—"wore it out"—
planting it so deep in the consciousness of one generation of American
youth that it is rooted there still in our middle age. When the film director Oliver Stone needed an aural artifact of the middle Sixties to
evoke a hands-across-the-racial-divide-in-doomed-brotherhood feeling for the foxhole bacchanal scene in his movie *Platoon*, he used
"Tracks of My Tears" to produce the effect.

Robinson was the embodiment of Gordy's highest aspirations as a
songwriter, an alter ego who was the artist Gordy would have been if
he could have been more than a technician and a teacher. Gordy himself prospered by his prophetic sense of where his audience was
headed, even before he could know it would one day consist of "young
America" itself. He began engineering his records to sound good in
cars and on transistor radios. His methods turned making commercially successful records from something his peers thought of as
alchemy into an industrial science; in 1964, for example, forty-two of
the sixty records Motown released were hits.

Gordy never understood the business he was in the same way his
competitors did. They were in the music business; he was building a
brand. Even when its output was issued simultaneously on five different
labels, they all were "Motown records," identifiable by its production
elements and defined by its characteristic "sound," yet distinguishable
as the work of particular producers working with particular singers.
Distinctive and identifiable as the "Motown Sound" was, its precise de-
scription eluded even those most intimately involved in its creation:
"The sound is the bottom, you can hear the bass real good . . . ,"
Smokey Robinson suggested. "A lot of treble," countered Brian
Holland of the Motown writing and production team of Holland-
Dozier-Holland. Gordy, who liked to spin his story as folklore of urban
uplift, called it "a combination of rats, roaches, love, and guts."

Much as Motown would be known by its star performers, its producers were the company's real stars. Gordy paired artists with producers

on the basis of proven affinities; a hit record guaranteed a producer the next opportunity to work with the artist with whom he had been successful. These project assignments had the rhythms of a dice game; players stayed in as long as their hands stayed hot. As soon as they missed, another producer stepped up. The continuities that this system assured, in combination with the individual properties of the major Motown acts, established for each of them a particular identity, along with a common corporate identification that suggested a standard of quality and likeness of qualities—thus creating, in effect, a product line.

The model in Gordy's head of the record company he wanted to run didn't look like anything he'd seen in a car factory, as is commonly supposed, but rather more like an old-fashioned movie studio. He kept a stable of writers and producers on hand, churning out product. As early as 1965, Gordy was announcing, "We're signing people with talent to do songs we've already got on hand."[3] He controlled every aspect of his artists' working lives, from recording to performing to managing their careers and handling their money, and paid them all a straight salary. He created an Artist Development department to groom his young, unschooled performers for the stage, and hired Maxine Powell, doyenne of black Detroit's bourgeois social club set, to teach them how to carry themselves, eat in public, and give innocuous interviews. Along with running her in-house "charm school," Powell was sent along to chaperone girl groups on the road. Ten years before other record companies copied the idea and called it "tour support," Gordy had packaged his acts as the Motortown Revue and made them a roadshow, sending them all over the country on grueling bus tours to build a following and sell their records.

The producer's role in making records is like the director's role in making movies. Gordy made making records a producer's medium. As Carl Davis, a competitor from Chicago, described the process, "Motown used to put a picture frame together, paint in all the background, and . . . take the artist and put him in the picture. They would make a complete record, record it in a certain key. . . . Then the singer had to

---

[3]Quoted in Peter Benjamin, *The Story of Motown* (Grove, 1979), p. 90.

come in and sing the song in the key they had already determined, whether or not it was appropriate for the artist."[4]

Useful people kept turning up. One was Norman Whitfield, a pool-hustling sixteen-year-old who had hitchhiked from New York in 1961, impelled to set out for Detroit by the idea of a record company run by black people making black music that white people were buying. Whitfield was hired to work around the office and help babysit a kid Gordy had just signed and rechristened Little Stevie Wonder. Within ten years, Whitfield had become the most commercially successful black producer in the music business, and he was on hand to step in when, later, the departure of the company's most reliable breadwinners, the writing and production team of Eddie Holland, Lamont Dozier, and Brian Holland, could have damaged Gordy beyond repair.

Gordy himself wrote and published more than four hundred songs, some well known but none as good as Holland, Dozier, and Holland's or perhaps a hundred others made by the toilers on his factory floor. The talent there was stacked so deep that Nick Ashford and Valerie Simpson, popular songwriters of the highest rank, left Motown because they couldn't get enough work. But for six of Motown's sunniest years, 1963 to 1968, HDH were the company's mainstays; they made the Supremes a lucrative franchise and the Four Tops a going concern. As songwriters, they were not conspicuously gifted at either words or music, but they were master builders of danceable rhythms, another pillar of Gordy's faith. Dance music was Motown's leading export.

Once HDH got rolling, they became production engineers of what came closest to the assembly line Motown was often said to be. They were able to keep pace with the company's relentless release schedule by writing as many as two or three songs a day. Before they knew anything, they relied on the resourcefulness of the company's gifted studio musicians. They learned to work fast—a complicated production like 1966's "Reach Out I'll Be There," the Four Tops' greatest hit, might take two hours to record—by assembling songs from warehoused parts: one of these from their inventory of verses, one of those from their stockpile of hooks, bringing to bear classical influences they

---

[4]Quoted in Robert Pruter, *Chicago Soul* (University of Illinois Press, 1991), p. 77.

picked up, like the pipes they smoked as part of the college-boy poses they adopted when they got successful, and the gimcrackeries of the earliest generation of electronic musical devices.

HDH were stewards of a shop that was innovative in ways that only the aggressively self-taught can be when they are working under the pressures of time, budget, equipment constraints, and fierce internal competition, and buoyed by serial successes:

> After [the Supremes' "Baby Love"] became a hit, somebody wrote about the genius of handclapping on the backbeat. Said it was a new sound, revolutionized pop music. Hell, it wasn't even hand-clapping. Ain't no way we gonna pay twelve people session fees to clap hands. It was two by fours, man, two by fours hooked together with springs and some guy stompin' on them to make a backbeat. We knocked that song off in two takes.[5]

Continually present among the comings and goings of artists and producers were the musicians Gordy assembled in his house band, known around the company as the Funk Brothers, although they were never identified that way because Gordy didn't regard "funk" as a word fit for polite company. He plucked many of them out of Detroit's underemployed jazz players and suckered them into signing on for low wages with the unmet promise of being able to record the music they really loved on Motown's jazz label. These musicians were instrumental in defining the sound that sold 250 million records, and Gordy kept them fully employed for fifteen years, transforming them in the process from the unknown and idle into the uncredited and underpaid. Some were shrewd enough negotiators to end up making more than many of the singers anyway, yet a pair who didn't—bassist James Jamerson and drummer Benny Benjamin, who were among the most influential musicians of their time—were still the company's most exploited employees. On tour, they took to calling their designated sec-

[5]Earl Van Dyke, quoted by Gerri Hirshey in her book *Nowhere to Run* (Times Books, 1984), p. 189.

tion at the back of the bus "Harlem," and referred to the front, where the singing artists rode, as "Broadway." Feeling left out of the strenuous social climbing going on around them, their disposition toward what they could see of Gordy's ambitions turned gently ironic. For him, no place was warmer than the shadow of Ed Sullivan's smile. And like others of their tribe's unassimilable many, they would have known that when he got there they wouldn't be anywhere around.

2.

For more than forty years, those who joined the Nation of Islam, from the many thousands who were converted in prisons to the college-trained who briefly alighted during the height of its fashion in the late Sixties and early Seventies, were in some degree exposed to the extraordinary tale told by W. D. Fard—a detailed historical narrative appended to a creation myth. Billed as "Knowledge of Self and Others," it was church doctrine and, however seriously it was taken, it proved resistant to the occasional incursions of the truly orthodox and the scathing attacks by the fallen-away. It was the stuff of children's catechism and the entrance exam to the Nation that was the novitiate's highest hurdle.

The underlying premise of Fardian theology that separates it from traditional Islam is its repudiation of divinity that is not flesh and blood—the so-called "spook God." There were precedents on the disreputable fringes of African-American religious life; in repressive post-Reconstruction times self-declared prophets and messiahs started popping up all over the South and followed the migrations north into the bleak Depression years. Sooner or later, most began calling themselves God incarnate, from Father Jehovia to Father Divine to Father Hurley. Many preached a religio-political heterodoxy, and had their own strain of the black Christian nationalism that inhabited the cult-crowded urban landscape of the Twenties and Thirties. But none, even those who drew upon many of the same contemporaneous sources to tailor their own versions of holy writ, ever spun a story as elaborate as the one Fard set before his consignment of Detroit's weary, worn, and sad.

It goes something like this: The original man created himself 76 trillion years ago from a single atom. He was black, and called himself Al-

lah. Then he created others like him to assuage his loneliness. Allah
and the other godmen created the universe, then concentrated on developing their homeland, Earth. They populated it with "Asiatic black-
men" who were united by skin, religion (Islam), and natural disposition
(righteousness). Organized into thirteen tribes, they ruled the world
from their base in Asia.

Allah was the head deity, and his knowledge and vision determined
what was written. Every 25,000 years, another deity was selected from
among the god-scientists to write the history of the future. In the current cycle it was foretold that a race of devils would have hegemony
over the world for six thousand years.

The Tribe of Shabazz—"blackskinned," "straight-haired," with "delicate, fine" features—ruled magnanimously over the planet's "golden
age." They established centers of civilization in Egypt and Mecca. An
eccentric among them proposed that the tribe explore the rest of
Africa. Rebuffed by the leadership, he led a renegade group into the
bush. For the next several thousand years, these black men led a "jungle life"; they lost their cultural refinement and were altered genetically. Though they became more rugged physically, their hair kinked
up and their features grew flatter and thicker.

Eighty-four hundred years into the current 25,000-year cycle of history, a new god was born whose destiny it would be to destroy his own
people. His name was Yacub, and he is the Luciferian figure of the tale.
He was born in a suburb of Mecca, fiercely intelligent, hungry for
knowledge, with a precocious aptitude for scientific inquiry. When he
was six, it occurred to him that if he could create a race completely different from the Original People, they could attract and dominate the
Black Nation through "tricknology"—tricks, lies, and deception.

Yacub preached a distorted, materialistic brand of what was called Islam that appealed to the growing numbers of the disaffected. Yacub fo-
mented so much trouble that the Meccan elite was forced to negotiate
his resettlement, along with 59,999 of his followers, to the Aegean island of Pelan, where they set about creating their own civilization.
There, by means of a vicious process of unnatural selection, the "big
head scientist" began to eugenically engineer his "devil race." He
wouldn't live to see his work completed—it took six hundred years—
but artificial, blue-eyed people emerged who, while inferior to their

prototype in intelligence and physical strength, were genetically pro-
grammed to oppose freedom, justice, and equality; in short, made to be
natural enemies of the righteous Tribe of Shabazz. After an aborted assault on Mecca in 4000 BC, they were deported to the wilderness of
West Asia (Europe), where they became so degraded over the next two
thousand years that many regressed into apelike creatures with tails,
and those who retained human characteristics lived like animals.

Allah was finally touched by their suffering, and sent the mulatto
prophet Musa (Moses) to raise these wretched savages to a level of civilization that would enable them to rule as prophecy had ordained.
Only one group among them, the Jews, were consistently faithful to
Musa and his teachings, forsaking idolatry; they would be closer to the
Original People in their manner of worship than any of the others,
though still incapable of goodness. Under Musa's heroic stewardship
the light of civilization slowly filtered into Europe, until 400 BC, when
Nimrod, "the evil demon of the white race," rose up against him and
plunged West Asia back into darkness and savagery.

Allah next sent a black prophet, Jesus, who preached to the Jews and
was killed for his trouble. He was deified by conspirators who wanted
to obscure God's true nature. They also promulgated a book, the Bible,
that cleverly mixed truth and lies; this whole unholy conspiracy, called
Christianity, was orchestrated by the pope of Rome, who is the dragon,
or devil, disclosed in the Book of Revelation.

A third prophet, Muhammad Ibn Abdullah, was sent to the white
people in 600 AD, to reintroduce them to Islam and counter the rampant scourge of Christianity. He died in 632 at sixty-two of a broken
heart, and cursed the unregenerate Christians with his last breath, forever denying them access to Arabic language and culture, a denial that
set white civilization back a thousand years.

A period of protracted war between the two faiths followed. The
Crusades, represented in this account as a triumph of Islam, forced the
Europeans to look westward for new territories to defile. They sailed
into the Western Hemisphere intent upon profiting by the toil of others, and once they had exhausted the local supply of conscript labor,
they turned to East Asia to replenish it. Beginning in 1555, by "tricknology" and coercion, Europeans brought members of the Tribe of
Shabazz to America as slaves, stripping away as much original culture

as they could from subsequent generations and replacing it with Christianity to promote servility, renamed their chattel "Negroes," which meant "something dead, lifeless, neutral (not that nor this)," and made them pray to a mystery God, a "spook," who was too remote to be of any use at all. Four hundred years of this reduced the "so-called Negroes" in America to white people wearing darker skins. Uncivilized and lost in a western precinct of hell, the misplaced descendants of the Tribe of Shabazz needed a savior. Thus, the stage was ready for W. D. Fard Muhammad's entrance on the eve of the Great War.

Elijah Muhammad is represented here not as a prophet in the biblical sense, but rather as a courier, the last in the line of men dispatched by Allah to bring Truth to the benighted. His commission is both particular and urgent, since it is to prepare the so-called Negro in America to survive the imminent destruction of the world around him. He is the appointed intermediary between God and the Black Nation; no man's prayer can even reach Allah unless Elijah is mentioned in it by name.

Before the final destruction of the white world, Allah would send a warning in the usual ways—pestilence, natural disasters, climatological disturbances—to afford unsaved Negroes a last opportunity to clean up their lives and embrace Islam. In the time of the Judgment, it is said, anyone answering to a European name will be shunned by Allah. The instrument of divine retribution will be a wheel-shaped spaceship a half-mile in diameter called the Mother Plane, piloted by black scientists with psychic abilities, carrying fifteen hundred smaller ships, each equipped with three dynamite-tipped drill bombs. At the hour of reckoning, the Mother Plane will hover twenty miles above the earth, release its fleet of airships over England and America, and incinerate everything below. Two black scientists on every other street corner will direct the righteous to a safe haven, wherein they can survive the conflagration.

America will burn in a great lake of fire for 390 years. The saved of the Black Nation will emerge from the ashes of dead white civilization into a new Eden, where sickness, fear, and vice will not exist, where all memory of the oppressor will have been obliterated, where people will live for a thousand years and never look older than sixteen.

The narrative unfolds with the deliberateness and particularity of a textbook history and the sweep of epic fancy of a campfire tale. It was meant to be taken as literally as good Catholics take the Virgin Birth. While many thousands pledged their allegiance to it, this clearly required, at least for some, a suspension of no little disbelief. Yet allegiances could prove at times durable, as when Louis Farrakhan, present-day Templar of the diehard upholders of these articles of faith, invoked the Mother Plane in his speech at the Million Man March.

The doctrine's ingenuity lies in the way it is packaged to alternately jar and then gentle its small audience of country-bred Christians into an acceptance of a religion they were raised to think of as heathen. This is accomplished by its judicious consonance with much that is in the Bible. For example, Fard relied on conditioned Afro-Christians' ingrained association of four hundred years of slavery in America with the Jewish captivity to allow them to permit him, with a little elaboration, to appropriate for the so-called Negro the Old Testament "chosenness" of the Jews. Then, by demystifying Jesus altogether—as entirely human, black, illegitimately born, basely murdered, and unresurrected—he makes it easier for people for whom Jesus wasn't working too well to put others in His place as their intermediary between God and men.

But cleverest of all, Clegg suggests, is Fard's making the whole of creation and all subsequent history the responsibility of men, and then placing the ultimate disposition of mankind within a predetermined cycle of history, beyond the reach of men, and deliverance in the hands of "God, who would act in his own good time." Thus it encourages active self-help in personal life, but holds the political in abeyance.

The Nation had an entente with municipal governments, but it never "pressured" them about much beyond its own landholding and business interests. As a rule Muslims didn't vote and their leadership didn't take positions on candidates, for discouraging political activism well suited the purposes and disposition of the Messenger of Allah as he got older, sicker, and richer in the Sixties. By 1962, he was removing himself to Arizona's more congenial climate for months at a time. Elijah was now an established member of the propertied class and, with more to lose than ever, chary of antagonizing the government that held his tax exemption hostage. He was also trying to steer his organization clear of a threatened investigation by the House Un-American Activities Committee. He was learning to live under what was becoming the relentless oversight of the FBI. As times grew darker and meaner in the middle of the decade, Elijah Muhammad accrued stature from being a government-certified subversive without having to do more to earn it than sit in the shade on his staked-out place in that era's racial politics, chiding his people from time to time for trying to integrate into a sinking ship.

During the last twelve years of his life, when Elijah had to deflect internal challenges to his leadership, perhaps the clearest evidence of the power the Fardian gospel held for many within the organization was their willingness on those occasions to kill or die to uphold the absolute authority of Elijah Muhammad. Even after he was gone, the schemers around Elijah who had jockeyed so hard to succeed him could never bring themselves to subvert the Messenger's implicit will.

3.

Of the 535 singles issued by Motown between 1960 and 1970, 357—two thirds of them—were hits, while the industrial average of hits to misses was less than 20 percent. By 1967, whites were buying about 70 percent of all the records Motown was selling. Gordy wasn't losing his core black audience; one of his groups, the Temptations, was in the middle then of a three-year unbroken sequence of fifteen records that were all among the five most popular in the country among blacks when they were released, according to *Billboard* magazine's index of black audience appeal. What Gordy was doing was providing the industry's first measure of the relationship between the two markets when a black product line had equivalent appeal and equal access to them both. The prospect of selling more than twice as many of the same record to whites as they could to blacks is why "crossing over" has always been the Holy Grail for makers and sellers of black popular music. By the late Seventies, when sales of black music would account for about two thirds of the industry's $3.5 billion annual take, nearly all the profits were back in the hands of six conglomerates.[6]

But in the middle Sixties Motown still had plenty of what the pop culture business these days calls "street credibility." It suggested the possibility of blacks being acceptable to whites without compromising anything essential of themselves, which was what the street felt it ought to aspire to. The Temptations were as definitively the establish-

---

[6]In 1978 these were: EMI, Warner Communications, CBS, RCA, Polygram, and MCA.

ers of young urban black male style as rap stars are today. When they began wearing single silver bangles on their wrists in 1965, they started a fashion trend among African-American males that lasted twenty years. A year later, a dance called the "Temptation Walk," adapted from the group's stage choreography, had its season among black teenagers coast to coast. It wasn't until Gordy grew obsessed with re-making Diana Ross from Brewster Homes as "the black Barbra Streisand" that he let his finger slip off his people's pulse.

The Christmas 1968 edition of *Billboard*'s pop charts listed five Motown releases among its Top Ten singles. Gordy assembled his staff and announced, as if he were the CEO of some regular business routinely setting a target for next quarter's earnings, that henceforth the company would release nothing it could not confidently predict would become a Top Ten record, and none would issue under color of its flagship, the Supremes, that wasn't a prospective Number One. Of course, nothing like that would ever be possible in any business that depends upon anticipating the fashion cycles of the mercurial young, but then no other man who was ever in such a business would be more entitled to so arrogant a presumption. Anyone who felt indicted for most of thirty years by the implications of his family's "if you're so smart why ain't you rich" brand of bootstrap Calvinism might have been as susceptible as Gordy was to the warping effect a rapid transformation from factory hand into a ten-million-dollar-a-year tycoon had on his self-esteem. Later, "I earned $387 million in sixteen years" would become his one-size-fits-all rejoinder to almost any challenge.

Gordy's older sister made him a present that year of an oil-painted portrait which superimposed his face on Napoleon's torso against the backdrop of an enlarged section of a Detroit street map. It was intended to warm the splendid house that had cost a million dollars to build and appoint fifty years before Gordy bought it, and it hung over the cavernous fireplace beneath the frescoed ceilings in the gold-leafed living room. For Esther Gordy Edwards, a local politician's wife, the portrait would also have represented what her brother and his company had come to mean to black Detroit. The automobile industry's steady growth had produced a sizable, homeowning, black, and blue-collared middle class. Motown, the term of convenience for all of Gordy's Motown enterprises, now served as the quasi-official trademark for the city, and nothing could have better expressed the sense of

Detroit's emergent black establishment that it was settling into influence, even permanence.

What a week of riotous burning and bloodletting in the summer of 1967 undid psychologically in Detroit, the contraction of the American car industry over the next decade and a half made irreparable. White people bailed out, leaving behind a monument to their abdication, the Renaissance Center, a colonial fortress pied-à-terre for people who lived somewhere else and occasionally needed to use the city at night. African-Americans inherited Detroit when it was already assured of becoming what it is now—the poorest, blackest big city in the country.

The fancy house on Boston Boulevard would be Gordy's last home-town investment. After the riots, he moved the company's headquarters away from the scarred west side into a sold-off municipal office building downtown. He never intended it to be more than a way station. By late 1967, he was spending most of his time in Los Angeles, where the highest forms of low white culture were easier to engage. He was already moving his acts out of black show business onto television and into Las Vegas. Although it would take four years, he was planning to move Motown out of Detroit.

"Pops" Gordy's son had to have known that it was unwise for any black man to be too noticeably rich, too visibly powerful, or too openly associated with white women. So, for most of his public life, Gordy kept himself from public view. He refused awards and magazine covers, managed the press by staying out of its way, and, as Marvin Gaye put it, "married blacks and fooled around with whites." He held his company closely and privately. He refused to allow industry regulators to audit his sales figures. He spurned any of the tax-abating strategies that were standard in the music business, because these would have come between him and direct control of his money. Besides, he would rather give the government too much than endure its scrutiny.

While he invented much of what is modern in the record business, and many of his methods resembled those that Americans thought they had learned from the Japanese twenty years later, Gordy never outgrew certain of his received cultural assumptions. "Negroes just don't understand the kind of general market business I'm trying to run," he groused. Gordy figured he needed Italians to promote his records and collect his money and Jews to keep his books, manage his finances, and do his lawyering. Although white people never made up more than 10 percent of all Motown employees, by 1967 four of eight vice presidents were white, and in 1977 four fifths of all the senior positions in the organization were held by white executives. This inevitably changed the sense of being family that had been so much a part of the company's self-consciousness in its early days, and the basis of its morale.

There was still plenty of family around—Gordys comprised a third of the company's phone directory—but as layers of strangers and corporate policy were interposed between Gordy and the creative talent, Motown's artists and producers began to defend themselves against the sudden chill in the air by stiffening their attitudes about business. Once that happened, many got outside lawyers, asked to see the books, took another look at the substandard deals they'd signed, and left as soon as they could. Holland-Dozier-Holland, convinced that Gordy had reneged on a promise to give them stock or its cash equivalent, stopped working in 1968 and sued Gordy for millions.

With the future of the Supremes thus threatened, Gordy responded by pulling together a new team of writers and personally supervising the production of a couple of hit records that restored their luster long enough for him to launch Diana Ross. When Norman Whitfield took over, he integrated into the company's output the wilder strains that had entered black music from Memphis and California, and with Marvin Gaye and Stevie Wonder the company rode easily into the middle Seventies. Both Gaye and Wonder had to hardball Gordy into giving them the creative freedom they exercised ingeniously enough to make him so much richer that he had enough left over to make movies.

Nowadays Motown ceaselessly repackages the same old songs and spins off theme restaurants and Super Bowl half-time shows. A dozen or so memoirs have appeared in the past several years from Gordy's ex-stars and ex-wives, even former valets and publicists.[7] In each of these accounts a moment comes when Gordy is asked to rise to some

---

[7]These include books by Diana Ross, Mary Wilson (of the Supremes), Otis Wilson (of the Temptations), Tony Tucker (ex-valet of the Temptations and the Supremes), Michael Jackson, William "Smokey" Robinson, Raynoma Gordy, Martha Reeves, Claudette Robinson, Mable John, Kim Weston, and Marvin Gaye (the best of all these books, a posthumous "as told to" by the estimable David Ritz, called *Divided Soul: The Life of Marvin Gaye* (Da Capo, 1991)).

occasion of crisis in the narrator's life. "Don't worry," he says to them all. "I will always take care of you." These words haunt many stories and they are akin to the Godfather's kiss, because the many who heard them ended up more or less like former Temptations David Ruffin and Eddie Kendricks before they died, grinding away in failing voice in some forlorn oldies roadshow, sitting in a hotel room at dawn in a place like Tulsa, and drunkenly excoriating Gordy for having ruined their lives.

To Gordy, sentiment had its uses but the money mattered most, and the only kind of bargains he made were hard on somebody else. He divorced Raynoma Gordy almost as soon as she helped him start the company, and not long after that she was banished to New York to open an office and look after his publishing interests there. As soon as she was set up, he cut off the money and, in desperation, she sold five thousand copies of a Motown hit to a local distributor. Gordy had her arrested for bootlegging and hauled back to Detroit, where she had to sign away her interest in the business and any future claims upon it.

When Mary Wells turned twenty-one in 1964, the contract she had signed with Motown when she was seventeen became invalid and needed to be renewed. On the strength of a record called "My Guy," that year she was the biggest-selling pop female vocalist in the world. Wells was the first to make the company open its books to her, and whatever she saw she liked so little she immediately signed with another label. Although it could never be proven, it was widely reported that thereafter Gordy paid disc jockeys all over the country not to play her records. Her career was permanently blighted. A variation of the same story happened to Florence Ballard of the Supremes and Martha Reeves and the Vandellas, as well as David Ruffin of the Temptations. But as rancorous as many of these partings were, none of the aggrieved who are still around can bring themselves to speak of Gordy without awe and grudging affection. He gave them all when they were young the identities that became their lifelong addictions.

One of the hoariest truisms in the black music business is that a white girl who sounds black, in the right hands, can make millions. Gordy never found one of those, so he took a black girl and made her into a white girl who sounded black, and made more millions. If Smokey Robinson was his greatest achievement, Diana Ross was his crowning triumph. Once his Galatea was up and running, Gordy lost interest in making records or running a record company. She was his excuse to start making movies. For one thing, he was a premature synergist who recognized the cross-marketing potential of a movie and its soundtrack. For another, movies were the major leagues of white show business, as well as the stuff of Gordy's daydreams. He was a sucker for the detritus of white popular culture: he had, after all, once been entranced by Doris Day and Debbie Reynolds. He put up the money for *Lady Sings the Blues*, doctored the script, whispered in Ross's ear before she played every scene, and commandeered the editing room. The movie was hugely successful financially, if not critically; it cost $3.5 million to make in 1973 and grossed nearly five times as much. Diana Ross was nominated for an Academy Award.

This so emboldened him that two years later, during the making of her next movie, Gordy harried the distinguished British director Tony Richardson off the set and took over the picture himself. *Mahogany* made money but was an artistic disaster. Gordy filled half his entry in the 1977 *Who's Who* with his movie-making accomplishments, and never directed again. Ross's next movie with Gordy, *The Wiz*, a black *Wizard of Oz*, lost all the money the first two made, and she hasn't worked in films since.

Motown's assault on movie, television, and theatrical production petered out, and Gordy retreated to life as a Bel Air squire in a house Red Skelton had built. By 1979, the company's chief operating officer was someone named Michael Roshkind, and Motown was just another middle-sized record company in a marketplace becoming the property of giants.

4.

It could be said that Elijah Muhammad's troubles began again when the evidence of his serial dalliances with young secretaries couldn't any longer be obscured. But their root causes had more to do with the young people Malcolm X had drawn into the Nation. The young are activists by disposition, and these were living in agitated times; Elijah was increasingly isolated and so, it followed, was the curia in Chicago. These antagonisms within the organization produced two pockets of turbulence ten years apart. The first involved the falling away of Malcolm, the surrogate son.

Elijah's women and their children were a serious inconvenience to the archbishops of a church wherein adultery was a banishing offense. But they were disinclined even to snarl at the feeding hand. Instead, they went scurrying to find suitable scripture to support and explain the Messenger's behavior. They found it in a Koranic reference to honoring the concubines of a prophet, advised that in any case messengers of God were not to be judged but obeyed, and stashed the young mothers out of sight. Malcolm came upon this badly kept secret after a number of old-line members of Temple #2 had already left in disapproval. Malcolm, a moralist, feeling betrayed and left out besides, was noisy in his disillusionment. This gave his enemies in Elijah's court leverage to wedge themselves between Malcolm and the Messenger.

As the Nation's representative frequently called upon in those days to speak for it before thickets of cameras and microphones, Malcolm was almost always asked for comment on the news of the day. When he was interviewed after the Kennedy assassination, he tried to make the point, not unreasonably, that the violence endemic in American society had produced another violent result. But he stumbled over a metaphor about chickens coming home to roost that plainly suggested an indecent relish in the occasion, and landed in outraged headlines. Elijah, who well remembered when the newspapers in Detroit hounded Fard out of town, recoiled in instant alarm. This was the opportunity to distance the organization from Malcolm by issuing an immediate, stinging repudiation of its minister's impolitic remarks, then by suspending and silencing him for an indefinite time. Thus were established the positions from which they played their relationship's mortal endgame.

Once Elijah became convinced Malcolm was both disloyal to him and threatening to the Nation, he moved remorselessly to cut him away. He replaced his star on the New York stage with the understudy Malcolm himself had chosen and lovingly groomed, Louis X of Boston, who soon enough would seize as well the vacated national platform. Elijah brought his in-again-out-again apostate son Wallace, Malcolm's only ally in the royal family, snivelingly to heel. When it became clear that the break with Malcolm was unmendable, Elijah invoked his organization's command-and-control discipline against him, first to isolate, then to demonize him. As the campaign quickened and grew harsher, he allowed others to say in public what he expressed privately, that Malcolm was guilty of capital crimes. Eventually, some aroused vigilantes from the thuggish Newark mosque ended Malcolm's life. Elijah said he was surprised and deeply saddened to hear the news.

Ironically, Malcolm had invented the most effective weapon used against him, the newspaper *Muhammad Speaks*, which was as well a source of instruction in the Muslim way of commerce. For years, clean-cut men hawking newspapers in suits and bow ties were a regular feature of urban American life. Every male Muslim in the ranks was required to sell a consignment of papers, which they paid for in advance. This burden eventually weighed as heavily on each member as $88 a month. Obviously, this flimsily veiled form of taxation yielded substantial revenue in steady, predictable increments.

Although its publishers claimed a biweekly circulation of 600,000 copies, no one could say how many of these ended up in closets or the trunks of cars. Still, the paper was read in black America, and it was skillfully used to make the Nation's enterprises seem grander than they were and its voice in tribal affairs respectable and courageous. As the civil rights movement ripened into Black Power in the late Sixties, the African traditionalists and militant renouncers of white American society who were so much the seasonal fashion began to think of Elijah Muhammad and his program as a tribal totem. But Elijah was no cultural nationalist. He amplified the muted anti-African strand in Fardian doctrine by dismissing non-Islamic Africa as insufficiently "civilized." He never wavered much in the assumptions about Africa he had inherited from the missionary church culture of his youth. He disparaged Afros, beards, and traditional African clothing as a reversion to "jungle styles." While no one maintains that the Nation of Islam ever enforced a color caste, it remains true that none of its succession of public faces was ever dark-skinned. Muhammad Ali came closest, but Elijah never chose him and, much as he recognized the value of having the world's most famous athlete near the top of his marquee, never thoroughly approved of him either.

Elijah was as conservative temperamentally as any deep-country grandfather. He denounced the Black Panthers as "dangerous" and ill conceived; they drew government attention too near his places of business. Elijah had lived too long with the inconvenience of being considered by white people a dangerous man to tolerate his tribe's unruly young, who were disturbing his quiet empire-building by trying to be thought of as dangerous. His instincts formed in a place and time when a black man who had anything had to pretend he didn't if he wanted to hold on to it. So he kept a purposeful distance from this newest generation of black subversives. Nevertheless, the era's nationalist rhetoricians carried Elijah through the streets of black America like a plaster saint on a pole. As Jesse Jackson put it, "During our colored and Negro days, he was black." And by then, in Professor Clegg's estimation, he was presiding over "the richest black organization in American history." Elijah seemed well on his way to building the permanent black institutions others were just starting to talk about.

By the early Seventies, the Nation of Islam held enough legitimate property to share the class interests of the American establishment. In 1973, the Illinois state legislature, which in scratchier times had nearly decertified the Muslim schools, recognized "the Honorable Elijah Muhammad and his organization" for a "distinct, positive community program." A year later, Mayor Richard Daley declared an "Honorable Elijah Muhammad Day" in Chicago. When, in 1974, after all the years of surveillance, infiltration, and dirty tricks, the FBI sent a couple of its agents to talk to him directly, they came away impressed and reassured, reporting that Elijah said "he believed in law and order . . . and loved America very much."

Well into his seventies, infirm but not feeble, Elijah stuck close to Chicago, where he occasionally pruned his inner circle and made sure that the business of his Nation stayed business, and in those days business was better than ever. He was addicted to real estate, probably because of a landless youth spent absorbing his elders' abiding country faith in land as the only unassailable currency. This was a manic period of acquiring progressively richer properties in Chicago and conceiving grandiose construction projects. He put up an office building. He made plans for a hospital and a huge, Mormonesque tower to house an Islamic Center. High-living Chicago supporters bought Elijah a private jet. They festooned his head with a jewel-encrusted fez said to have cost $150,000. A two-million-dollar royal family compound of five houses was built in Chicago during the early Seventies.

Elijah seemed incapable of staying anywhere without buying a house; he bought his last in a Mexican resort town just weeks before he died. He was quiet about living well but unapologetic; he advised his rank and file to hold on to his unchanging hand and "wait until I pull them up." But all that seemed to trickle down was the taste for conspicuous consumption. Some of the local ministry had taken to dressing like pimps.

An attempt by an outlaw faction to assassinate Elijah's son-in-law, Supreme Captain Raymond Sharrieff, in 1971 provoked two years of a tit-for-tat internecine shooting war that left bodies stacked up on both sides. It was a lawless time, when some of the unreconstructed within a few renegade mosques robbed banks, dealt drugs, and murdered in Elijah's name. But it subsided as quickly as it took the Nation's permanent government to reassert its control. Through all of this, there was never enough damage to the organization's reputation as a solid enterprise to prevent it from being able to attract managers. But the recruits were too few and arrived too late to keep the greedy and the incompetent from mismanaging the best business the Nation ever had.

The Muslim farms never did well, but their existence required the directors of the enterprise to buy a fleet of trucks and create a national distribution network. It was in place in the inflationary time late in the first Nixon administration, when Elijah Muhammad saw an opportunity to bring a basic commodity to market in black neighborhoods more cheaply than the established food industry could. To do it, he had to maneuver into international commerce. Elijah's agents arranged to buy boatloads of frozen whiting from Peru. When the banks he dealt with refused to provide the letters of credit he needed, Elijah bought control of a small bank on Chicago's South Side.

The Muslims chartered ships and brought their fish into ports all over the United States. They did their own stevedoring and dared unions and port authorities to intercede. They succeeded in profitably selling fish in African-American communities for between a quarter and fifty cents a pound at a time when meat cost three times as much. Clegg asserts profits of the fish business exceeded a million dollars in 1975. Yet, within months of Elijah's death early that year, the Nation of Islam was nearly five million dollars in debt.

Elijah Muhammad died without leaving a will or publicly designating a successor. He did leave 3.2 million unspent dollars in the Honorable Elijah Muhammad Poor Fund. Before his silver-lined coffin had been lowered into its bronze and copper electronically sealed vault, a peaceable transfer of absolute power had already happened. The choice of Elijah's seventh son, Wallace Muhammad, was as improbable in one way as it was inevitable in another. After all, according to church lore, Master Fard had both named and ordained Wallace in utero, by inscribing the letter "W" on the back of a door in his father's house. But Wallace had been a prodigal ever since his conversion to orthodox Islam in the early Sixties. Only his inability to make an independent living made bearable his father's harsh and painfully public chastisements whenever Wallace openly expressed his disdain for the sectarian cult of manworship. Wallace's history suggested that he was a man accustomed to compromising an inconvenient principle. But it may have been that the presence of his father made him weak, because in the aftermath of Elijah's death he displayed boldness and courage in measures much larger than anyone but himself could have predicted.

Even before his father died, Wallace had beaten back the pretenders to his presumptive throne, including the wily Farrakhan. Upon ascending, he immediately purged the venal church bureaucrats in Chicago and many of their local franchise holders, dismantled the paramilitary Fruit of Islam, disclosed the Nation's indebtedness, and began selling off all the businesses except for the farms, the fish, and the newspaper. He officially renounced the doctrine of Fard's divinity, discounted the rest of his father's theologizing, summarily converted the organization to orthodoxy of the Sunni variety, opened it to people of all races, and renamed it the World Community of Islam in the West.

A man of priestly inclinations, Wallace lacked the wherewithal to keep the enterprise together. Farrakhan bided his time for three years, then departed with as many of the unreformed—probably numbering in the hundreds—as shared his desire to repossess the original Nation of Islam. The Nation he left behind had fed so long on itself that its business organization was thin enough to collapse as suddenly as a tissue-paper tent in a stiff wind. In the end, it is impossible to know how much money was lost or stolen, since for most of his stewardship

Elijah, constitutionally unwilling to think of himself as a taxpayer, avoided leaving any audit trails. But what he built over three decades was, within three years of his passing, an empire of empty shells.

Elijah's decision to die intestate snarled a probate court for more than a decade. Besides his eight children with Clara, thirteen others stepped forward to claim a share. Maybe he left no will to confound the IRS, which he knew to be circling overhead in a slow, descending spiral. The taxman landed, but by the time he could feed there were only bones left to pick. Elijah's reticence had the effect of assuring that his estate would eventually be handed over to Wallace and the family to settle once the appetite for public scandal had passed.

To the very end, Elijah loudly denied having any interest in who would succeed him. "There is no need for a successor when a man has got the divine truth and has brought you face-to-face with God," he had growled to reporters of his last public conversation. He had to have known what Wallace would do. For thirty years the Nation was a totalitarian state because its governor would let no other objective supercede holding it firmly together. Then he turned it over to a man he was sure meant to pull it all apart. We are left to conclude that Elijah Muhammad intended that the world he had created would end with him.

5.

There are still reminders of the permanent effects of Berry Gordy on at least one generation of Americans in a period that barely lasted twenty years and ended twenty years ago. Last November, on successive nights, NBC broadcast a two-part made-for-television movie about the Temptations. About forty-nine million of us watched each segment. The Motown Gordy knew is no less a historical artifact for seeming to be still alive in a culture that preserves everything it can sell for as long as it can be sold. Several years ago Motown's corporate foster parent, MCA, hoped to re-create Gordy in André Harrell, the young rap music mogul it hired to bring the company back to life. That he couldn't, and went without leaving a trace, assures that what Gordy built will never again have a modern form.

Gordy came early into knowing what our spent century has lately disclosed: Black America's most valuable natural resource is its popular culture. There has been a struggle going on for a hundred years over who would own the exploitation rights. Gordy was an industrial pioneer in turning black culture into a commodity—both its first, and arguably its best, mass producer and mass marketer. That he happened to be black made him, in a limited sense, revolutionary, even though he never served directly any cause but his own. His imprint is unmistakably upon the youngish men who currently comprise the music business's largest and richest black proprietary class ever. Nearly all these rap music tycoons—who, like Gordy, sell 70 percent of their goods to white people—have, at one time or another, said they aspired to be "the next Berry Gordy."

It is easier these days to make as much money in the music business as Gordy did thirty years ago, but it will be harder for this newest breed of his emulators to hold on to as much of it as Gordy has. The rap music sector of the industry, with its relatively low capitalization requirements and its huge windfalls, has more than a little in common with the drug trade. Because they are legitimate, rap music's captains are even more susceptible to contemporary America's drugs of choice—celebrity and easy money. What once assured the transmission of the essentially conservative social traditions of African-American life, and produced a man as implacably disciplined as Gordy, broke under the surge of a culture that teaches its young that the value of a human being is estimated by what he or she can consume. This idea has always been the beat that gives street commerce its regulating pulse, "cop and blow," which is at the core of black street culture, whose values have never been more consonant with those of the mainstream.

Given the music these quick-risen rap millionaires sell—all self-advertisement, sexual swagger, and emblematic rage, with brand names like "hardcore" and "gangster"—it seems unlikely that any of them will ever own an evergreen song catalog like Gordy's, which for two decades made him about $20 million a year. The summer before last he sold a half-interest in his publishing companies to EMI, a British conglomerate, for $132 million; he has the right to sell the other half in 2002 for another $250 million. Gordy is a rare phenomenon in American life; he was labor who became capital and ripened into idle rich in half a lifetime.

Elijah Muhammad's legacy belongs less to Louis Farrakhan—the man who publicly claims it now—than to the more than a million

African-Americans who converted to Islam in the last thirty years, most ushered into their faith by teachers who had first heard Fard's narrow catechism and then moved into a broader orthodoxy. The popularity of Islam among African-Americans bespeaks one response to the requirement that any who would feel intact in this society must learn to live constructively with the ineffaceable brand of Otherness it imposes on them all. The stories of black Americans converge around the points in each of their lives when they all face their own decisions about what kind of citizens they will choose to become of a country most can't help but love and can't help but know will break their hearts.

JOHN MORTHLAND

Songwriter

Every morning at five, she pours herself a cup of black coffee and heads upstairs to the little studio in her Mexia home. Though she is one of the leading country and pop songwriters of this century, she has not had a new song recorded by a major artist in many years. Still, she continues to write every day. For Cindy Walker, songwriting is its own reward.

Slowly, other rewards have been coming her way: induction into the Country Music Hall of Fame in Nashville in 1997, for instance, and into the National Cowgirl Museum and Hall of Fame in Fort Worth the following year. But unless you're the type that reads the fine print on record labels, you've probably never heard of her. If you are that type, you know that during half a century or so when songwriting was even more of a man's game than it is now, Walker wrote, first and foremost, "You Don't Know Me," a number ten country hit for Eddy Arnold in 1956 and a number two pop hit for Ray Charles in 1962. She wrote more than fifty songs for Bob Wills, including "Cherokee Maiden," "Dusty Skies," and "Bubbles in My Beer"; nearly two dozen for Ernest Tubb, including "Two Glasses Joe" and "Warm Red Wine"; and had nearly as many recorded by Jim Reeves, Tex Ritter, Hank Snow, and George Beverly Shea. She also wrote "Blue Canadian Rockies" for Gene Autry, "Dream Baby" for Roy Orbison, "China Doll" for the Ames Brothers, and "Barstool Cowboy from Old Barstow" for Spike Jones. Her unabashedly romantic, sentimental, Westernflavored songs have been done by Bette Midler and Grandpa Jones, Elvis and the Byrds, Cher and Willie Nelson (who is rumored to be planning an entire album of Walker tunes). Until this past decade, it was easier to count the number of country stars who hadn't recorded Walker songs than the number who had.

Yet she has always shunned the limelight, doling out interviews sparingly. It took me about five years of off-and-on requests to get one. She agreed to talk to me with one condition: "You cannot tell my age," she said, "because if people think you're older, they think you can't write contemporary anymore."

On the morning we were supposed to meet, the red ribbon was tied as promised around the mailbox in front of her house, which is hidden by trees and sits a couple blocks off U.S. 84 in Mexia. Her housekeeper, Willie Mae Adkinson, answered the door and led me back to the combination sitting room–dining room, where Walker and her cousin Bill Hearne, who is her driver and escort on her rare public appearances, were waiting. While Willie Mae fixed breakfast, Walker— an effervescent graying strawberry blonde in a yellow pantsuit—pulled a notebook full of materials for me from the neat filing cabinet in the corner. She read a poem she had written for Willie Mae, another for Chet Atkins, and finally, the one that she'd recited as her acceptance speech when she was inducted into the Country Music Hall of Fame, about the dress she wore, a gift from her mother. She showed videos of that ceremony along with her "soundies," short film clips shown on jukebox-like machines in bars and restaurants in the 1940s, and she played tapes of new songs. And once breakfast was over, she sat in her favorite easy chair and told her life story, punctuated with a lot of belly laughs and a little crying.

She was born at her grandparents' farm near Mart, not far from where she lives now, and grew up largely in that area, though the family moved around often because her father, Aubrey Walker, worked as a cotton broker. Her mother, Oree, was the daughter of F. L. Eiland, who wrote such hymns as "Hold to God's Unchanging Hand." "I was her playpretty," Walker recalls. "She taught me to dance and sing, but she didn't need to teach me much because it was just sorta natural with me." She wrote her first song, "Dusty Skies," after reading newspaper clippings about the Dust Bowl in her grandmother's scrapbook.

In late 1940, when her father took the family to Los Angeles on business, Walker persuaded Bing Crosby to cut "Lone Star Trail," her first sale. Later that year, she penned five songs that were recorded by Bob Wills, who then hired her to write for the five movies he was in town to shoot. A few months later, she'd finished 39 songs without a single rejection; after that, every singing cowboy in Hollywood wanted a Cindy Walker tune tailored to him. Walker always gave them what they wanted, from idealized Western landscapes to starry-eyed songs of chaste love to knee-slapping novelties. She also became a performer herself, appearing in two Gene Autry movies. To aid Walker's career, her father decided to keep the family in Hollywood, even if he was always shuttling in and out of town; she says he taught her to "learn the business end of music and make good deals and read every word of the contract." Her mother, who'd initially been wary of the move, came to like Hollywood. She threw big parties every year at Christmas for the performers and played the piano on all of her daughter's demos. "I didn't have a worry in the world about rent or food," Walker said. "I was free to write my songs, and that's what I loved to do."

She liked it so much that she never married. "I'm old-fashioned," she explained. "I believe that if you're married you have to stay with your husband and children, and they take all your time. I give all my time to my songwriting, and that's the way it is. It's simple, very simple." She liked it so much that she essentially ignored her own performing career; she didn't even write her sole hit, 1944's "When My Blue Moon Turns to Gold Again," and her record company was constantly complaining (justifiably) that she gave all her best material to other singers. When she and her mother decided to move back to Texas in 1954—her father had died of a heart attack six years earlier—she quit performing to concentrate on writing.

They moved into the same house she lives in today. Every October, right before the annual deejay convention and Country Music Awards, they'd take a train to Nashville, rent an apartment at the Continental and a piano, and conduct a writers' salon until April. Stars and unknowns would drop by and tell Walker what kind of song they wanted. If she didn't already have something along those lines, she would custom-write it to fit their image. "I wrote until the song was pleased with itself and I was too," she said. "If a song didn't like its words, I'd work until I got it perfect. You have to give every song a face, like a melody or a hookline, so you remember it—just like I'll remember you by your face." But Cindy had to be alone when she got down to work. "I can't write with anyone around me," she continued. "If someone's around, it takes part of the idea away. I wouldn't even tell Mama about a song until it was finished."

They made quite a pair—elegant, dignified Oree and giddy, giggly woman-child Cindy—and the artists, who always called Oree "Mama," just as her daughter did, relished the rare opportunities to stick around and enjoy some of her chicken and dumplings for dinner. If anyone considered it unusual that hit after hit was being written by a woman—practically the only woman, in fact, who wasn't co-writing with a male partner—nobody said anything. "People ask me this a lot, like it's some feminist thing, and all I can say is I don't know. I have no idea why there weren't other women songwriters," she said with just a hint of weariness at being asked again. "I never did have trouble with the artists because they wanted the same thing I did; they wanted a hit, that's how they made their living, and they didn't care who wrote the songs, whether it was a man, woman, or monkey. Plus I was lucky they loved Mama's playing—and they loved eating her cooking."

At the end of one Nashville trip, Eddy Arnold suggested a song title and theme to her. The idea didn't make a lot of sense to her, but she promised him she'd "let it cook." One night in her studio several months later, she said, "something started singing to me," and she wrote the opening stanza of a song that laid hearts on the line: "You give your hand to me / And then you say hello / And I can hardly speak / My heart is beating so / And anyone can tell / You think you know me well / But you don't know me." By the time she'd finished this uncharacteristically introspective tale of a man too shy to tell his true feelings to a female friend, Arnold had forgotten all about his initial idea. But he made the song a hit anyhow, and then Ray Charles made it a standard. The list of people who've cut "You Don't Know Me" since goes on and on. So does the list of country stars, from Merle Haggard to Ricky Skaggs, who continued cutting her songs through the seventies and eighties. In all, Walker says, her songs have made the country or pop Top Forty more than four hundred times.

But the Nashville trips stopped after her mother's death, in 1991. (Walker says she never knew how old Mama was.) Today, she tapes her new songs accompanied by her own piano and then sends them to Cousin Bill, who records demos at his Fort Worth studio with former Texas Playboy Leon Rausch singing lead. Last year, Rausch cut a CD of Walker tunes, including five new ones, for an independent record label; it did well in Europe but hardly sold at all in the U.S.

Walker still mails her demos to Nashville artists, but these days she rarely even gets a reply. She understands that—"I write lyric songs, and they play too loud today for you to hear the lyrics" and she keeps writing anyway. After all, songwriting is all she knows, and all she's ever done.

Punk: Undead

"Fuckin' A," moans a battered, middle-aged punk rocker who's splayed out on the sidewalk outside Prentis Hall at Detroit's Wayne State University, "Why do I have to keep playing Itchy?" While a three-chord hardcore band thrashes away inside, the spiky-haired fan wipes his bloody nose on the sleeve of a tattered oxford shirt with "Cash For Chaos" spraypainted on the back, glares at the bouncer who's just tossed him from the venue, and mutters to no one in particular, "He's always too fucked up to see straight by the time Negative Approach comes on."

Greg McCormick isn't your ordinary loser ejected from a punk club, however. In fact, he's not drunk, he's not actually "Itchy," and the show he's been kicked out of isn't even a real concert. No, McCormick, along with the bouncer, the band, and everyone else inside the auditorium, are attempting to restage, as meticulously and accurately as possible, a hardcore punk gig that originally took place in early 1982.

Called, appropriately enough, "hardcore reenactments," these events represent a strange new phenomena that's sweeping across the country. Part costume ball, part *Beatlemania!*, part punk passion-play, these elaborate rituals are taking counterculture nostalgia to its logical conclusion. By recreating concerts, notable incidents, and even entire tours from the hardcore era, hardcore reenactors—much like their spiritual compatriots in the Civil War reenactment movement—try to make themselves feel as if they're actually living in the past. "You know," says Keller Ayteal, a devoted participant in the Detroit-area scene, "they just don't make unintelligible high-velocity thrash like they used to."

In a quest for authenticity, reenactors seek out period instruments and clothing, study old fanzines, flyers, and set lists, and interview surviving scenesters. Indeed, for many of the participants, reenacting has become a lifestyle unto itself. The most hardcore of the hardcore reenactors even try to remain in character at all times, copying the bizarre haircuts, mannerisms, and odors of the scenesters they're portraying— some to the point of losing their jobs and moving back home to live with their parents.

In their zealous pursuit of the intense sensation that devotees call "period rush," hardcore hardcore-reenactors take a dim view of less-dedicated participants, whom they label "aips" (for "anachronistically inaccurate poseurs"). "I spent three weeks getting ready for the 10/22/82 Misfits/Necros/Void/GI show," attests a young man calling himself "Springa." "I listened to the *Process of Elimination* 7" nonstop, read nothing but *Smegma Journal* and *The Partyin' Press*, and soaked my clothes in cat urine. Then when I show up the aip playing Jerry Only is wearing a beeper and a Samhain t-shirt!"

Such transgressions are not taken lightly by the faithful. Unlike Civil War reenactors, who stop short of the atrocity of actual killing, hardcore reenactors fully recreate their fabled events slam for slam. Goatees, piercings, and modern slang are forbidden, and each event is policed by scene historians, who ensure that all attendees wear the proper band t-shirts and other era-appropriate accessories.

At a recent Detroit "gig," for example, items confiscated from the crowd included compact discs, a pair of Nike Air Jordans, a Green Day sticker, and snack foods like Sun Chips and Fruitopia; meanwhile, the reenactor impersonating Meatmen frontman Tesco Vee was deemed "too short," the fellow portraying Necros' guitarist Andy Wendler was "too punk," and the guy playing L-Seven singer Larissa Stolarchuk was "too feminine." Penalties for such infractions can be severe, ranging from simple ejection to a "role demotion" requiring the guilty party to portray a poseur wearing a dog collar and Izod shirt. Repeat offenders risk complete expulsion from the scene, a practice known as being "banned in D.C." even when the city involved is actually Milwaukee or Toledo.

Despite such harsh restrictions, the number of reenactors is growing rapidly; in fact, the reenactment scene is already larger than the original hardcore subculture that inspired it. Detroit's legendary Freezer Theater, for example, only held 200 attendees; in contrast, a recent reenactment of the Misfits/Necros/Negative Approach/Meatmen 4/8/82 show drew over 5000 people. Not surprisingly, the popularity of the reenactment scene has begun to alienate some of the pioneers who first strapped on guitars and began imitating their idols note-for-note. "I've been into this shit since Day One," sneers Detroit scene stalwart Pat Pend. "Where were all these bandwagon jumpers three years ago when we were doing Flipper live at the Second Chance 3/15/81 in Doug Abuse's basement?"

Indeed, dozens of different cities now have their own distinct scenes, connected by newsletters, conferences, and the Internet. According to Maura Bund, publisher of a reenactment zine called *Salad Days*, more than a dozen groups vie to best portray Black Flag, but none of them have nailed it quite right. "Ken Moore's Henry Rollins sings too well, while Steven Edie's Rollins is really just a copy of Phil Anselmo's Rollins."

Perhaps the most ambitious event in the reenactment repertoire is Fear's 10/31/81 appearance on *Saturday Night Live*, including the chaotic slam-dancing and subsequent "riot." "It's the Gettysburg of the reenactment world," explains Skip Schuul, who choreographed a recent staging. "Besides the people playing the band and all the stage divers, you need to have cameramen, stage crew, and a studio audience, to say nothing of stand-ins for the *SNL* cast. You wouldn't believe some of the people who try to pass themselves off as John Belushi."

Although tonight's Prentis Hall production is a far less extravagant affair, the participants are no less passionate. From teenage wannabes to aging weekend warriors like the aforementioned McCormick, the reenactors have left behind the present for a purer, "punker" past. "My old man says I'm behind the times, but I don't care," asserts McCormick. "I guess I'm just out of step with the world."

REBECCA MEAD

Sex, Drugs, and Fiddling

Although wrecking a hotel room is standard rock-star behavior, it is unusual for the instrument of destruction to be a bucketful of freshly cooked lobsters. Such unlikely use of crustaceans is among the many ways in which Ashley MacIsaac, a punk fiddle player from Nova Scotia, sets himself apart from other popular musicians, as I discovered one afternoon last spring, in Room 2018 of the Westin Hotel in Ottawa. The bathroom looked like the site of a lobster massacre: the walls and the floor and the mirror were spattered with bits of shell and stray gobbets of flesh. The tub was swimming with crushed ice cubes and the pink, poking antennae and tails of a dozen or so submerged sea creatures. In the toilet bowl, straw-thin legs floated listlessly. MacIsaac—who is on the short side, and built like a laborer, with sinewy arms and powerful legs—was standing by the sink in dirty black pants and an orange camouflage T-shirt, stamping vigorously with the heel of his battered leather boot on a fluffy white bath towel, before unfurling it to reveal smashed lobster body parts. He then called room service, and within a few minutes a waiter bearing mayonnaise and bread and salt and pepper was stepping gingerly over discarded T-shirts and scraps of paper, and sniffing the air, which reeked of brine and marijuana. MacIsaac mixed the mayo with lobster meat in an ice bucket, then smeared the

281

results on a roll and offered it to me. He is unfailingly generous—he'll give a seven-dollar tip on a three-dollar cab fare—and since I had already declined several invitations to join him in smoking pot, it seemed churlish to turn down a lobster roll on the ground that its preparation was insufficiently sanitary, so I ate. It was pretty good.

MacIsaac, who is twenty-four years old, comes from the island of Cape Breton, off the northern coast of Nova Scotia. Cape Breton is one of those places around which it is impossible to drive without imagining that you are in an automobile commercial. It is rich with pine-covered peaks and rugged cliffs and miles of deserted beaches; the barely trafficked roads are edged with hardy fishing villages, each comprising little more than a few score clapboard houses and a church. The island was settled two hundred years ago by Scottish emigrants, to whom the hills and the heaths of the place were a vivid reminder of the land they had left behind. Those Scots settlers also brought their music with them—their jigs and reels and strathspeys—and it evolved in Cape Breton into a distinct musical strain, more energetic and less polite than the traditional music that is usually heard in Scotland. These days, fiddle players perform every weekend at square dances in the village halls dotting the green, still countryside of the island.

MacIsaac is a prodigal talent in Cape Breton's musical tradition. Before his voice broke, he was a local celebrity, step-dancing and fiddling at square dances. By the time he was in his mid-teens, he had developed a vigorous style of playing, and his clarity and fluency rivalled the old-time masters of the genre. MacIsaac's first album, *Close to the Floor*, which he recorded in 1992, when he was only sixteen, demonstrated that proficiency. Within a couple of years, he had splashily extended his range, and a subsequent album, *Hi How Are You Today?*, released in 1995, married the old tunes with techniques from MTV— thrashing punk guitars and mesmerizing dance beats and nervy, witty samples, along with MacIsaac's rollicking fiddle. He even sang on a couple of tracks, in an off-key, ragged voice. The album, which generated a hit single, "Sleepy Maggie," a reworking of a traditional tune in which MacIsaac's fiddle playing slides under and around the ethereal Gaelic vocals of Mary Jane Lamond, was a phenomenal success in Canada, selling three hundred thousand copies. Because MacIsaac wore his hair in a Mohawk and liked to go onstage in a kilt and combat boots, he appealed to young people whose tastes ran to alternative music or hip-hop. But he also sold records to the grandmothers of those fans, and he has champions among the musical élite. Philip Glass, who has a home in Cape Breton and has become a friend and a supporter of MacIsaac's, compares his powers of innovation to those of Ornette Coleman. "Ashley grew up in a very complete kind of musical world and began learning at a very early age, but it is his own particular talent that has set him apart," Glass told me recently. "These are gifts that come from somewhere else. There are a lot of good players in Cape Breton, but even in a musical culture that is extraordinary he stands out."

The phenomenon of the prodigy can be seen in all the arts, but the phenomenon of the prodigy who struggles to deliver on his early promise is especially widespread in popular music, which relies upon putting onstage young people whose talent exceeds their maturity, and whose very rawness and inexperience constitutes much of their appeal. In the years since Ashley MacIsaac's début, his career has quieted down noticeably, and his appearance last spring in Ottawa, at an AIDS benefit, was something of a rarity. The day before the show, MacIsaac and I took a walk, and out on the street, which was clean and orderly in the best Canadian tradition, he seemed like a scruffy lord of misrule, somewhere between the Pied Piper and Pig Pen. Just down the road from the Parliament Buildings, a homeless man asked for some change. MacIsaac handed over a twenty-dollar bill and, flipping open a silver cigarette case, a gram of pot. ("I love you, man," the bum groaned, embracing him.) MacIsaac enjoys being recognized, and if he's not being recognized he wants at least to be noticed. When he saw a group protesting the United States' bombing of Yugoslavia later that day, he started bellowing "Death to Serbia!" at the top of his voice, to the consternation of protesters and passersby alike. Still later, as we walked by the canal that runs through the center of Ottawa, he charmed a pair of wary young student types into lending us their canoe by offering them twenty dollars and, for security, his passport. "Are you Ashley MacIsaac?" one of them asked tentatively as we paddled away from the bank. "Check my passport!" he yelled.

His appearance onstage the next night likewise seemed to be the product of a barely controlled chaos. MacIsaac was scheduled to appear at around ten-thirty, and when he got to his dressing room, at six, he rummaged in his pockets and drew out a folded piece of silver paper. "Fuck, I thought I lost my acid," he said, then put a tab ostentatiously on the tip of his tongue before swallowing. He smoked a couple of joints, got out his fiddle, and started to play traditional Cape Breton tunes. He played for fifteen or twenty minutes without stopping, and the rich, dense music echoed off the mirrors and swirled in the air as he segued from one intricate reel into another, his fingers never missing a note. Then the rest of his band showed up—a spoons player, a guitarist, and MacIsaac's younger sister, Lisa, who also plays the fiddle—and MacIsaac smoked some more pot, and did high kicks in the middle of the dressing room to warm himself up, then took another hit of acid and smoked some more pot, and then went onstage.

He had on the same black pants that he'd worn the night before, stained with lobster juice, and a blue T-shirt I'd seen lying on the floor of his room, and a pair of pink-tinted glasses. As he began, he held his fiddle down at a forty-five-degree angle, as if he were trying to drive it into the ground. He stamped his foot furiously, and scraped so hard with his bow that "Sleepy Maggie" sounded like a wild beast. He pirouetted while he played, and kicked his feet into the air before him, and after the second tune the horsehair on his bow started to fly off in wisps. At the end of the short set, he shook his head so wildly that his glasses fell off, and he crushed them underfoot; then he hurled his burned-through bow into the cheering crowd.

MacIsaac's transformation from a folk-music prodigy into a rock star began one summer evening in 1992, in the hamlet of South West Margaree, in Cape Breton. MacIsaac, who had just entered his senior year of high school, was playing at a square dance, and in the audience was JoAnne Akalaitis, the New York theatre director, who has a home on the island.

"I felt I was seeing something I had never seen before," Akalaitis told me. "I had been living in Cape Breton a long time, and I appreciate all the talent that is on the island, but he kicked it up. Nobody plays in such a physical, demonic way; nobody engages his body the way Ashley does. There is a kind of harshness, a volcanic ambience to his performance of the music. I was in a state of meltdown. I thought, This is a *great* performance."

Akalaitis was about to stage a production of Büchner's "Woyzeck" at the Public Theater, in New York, for which Philip Glass was composing the music; she invited MacIsaac to participate. His mother at first disapproved of the idea. "I said, 'No way,'" Carmelita MacIsaac told me when I visited her and Angus MacIsaac, Ashley's father, in Cape Breton. Carmelita and Angus, who is a retired electrician, live in a village called Creignish, just over the causeway from the mainland, in the same bungalow in which MacIsaac grew up. On the living-room wall hang his gold records; a cabinet is filled with trophies and recording-industry awards; displayed with equal pride is a fresh-faced high-school graduation portrait. "Some people were saying, 'Let him go, you're holding him back,'" Carmelita recalled. "Other people were saying, 'You're crazy, don't let him go down there; he's only seventeen, and he is going to lose his music.' And I said, 'Ashley will never lose his music.'"

In the end, MacIsaac went, and was transported. All he knew of New York was what he had learned from reading occasional copies of the *Village Voice*, which he could buy in Halifax, three hours' drive from his home. He got his first taste of celebrity at Newark Airport, where a limousine picked him up and ferried him into town, and soon he was in the heart of Manhattan's haute avant-garde, teaching members of Akalaitis's cast to step-dance, and witnessing the artist's life at close quarters. Akalaitis had arranged for him to stay at Philip Glass's apartment, and MacIsaac listened to the composer practice, though he had no idea of Glass's significance in contemporary music. "This apartment had seventeen hundred manuscripts in it, and there was one with, like, twelve hundred pages," MacIsaac told me. "I looked at what it was called—'Einstein on the Beach'—and I decided I would take page five hundred because that would be a cool souvenir. I realized afterward that I had better put it back."

"I don't think he'd ever seen a play before," Akalaitis said. "He didn't have a clue who we were. And he didn't know who David Byrne was, when we took David to see him once. But he learned quickly, and he was curious, and greedy, and interested." MacIsaac developed a following among his patrons' friends: One day, Paul Simon came around to see Glass, and MacIsaac played for him; Simon's wife, Edie Brickel, included him on her next album.

Although MacIsaac had been dropping in on the small gay community in Halifax since getting his driver's license, at sixteen, he was still half in the closet in Cape Breton. In New York, he suddenly found himself in a very gay crowd. "The first time he arrived at the theatre, all the company was sitting there, and he said to the manager, 'Are there any homosexual people here?'" Akalaitis recalls. "The company manager said, 'Yeah, about fifty per cent of them.' I think that was stimulating to him. That year, I remember looking out the window at the Halloween parade, and there was Ashley, at the head of the parade. He embraced a certain franticness of New York." He did so around the clock, vanishing off to night clubs after the curtain fell at the Public Theatre. "I was a club kid," MacIsaac says. "I went to the Limelight every night. I got laid a lot. I was considered a cute little boy."

Before MacIsaac left Cape Breton, he had been a quiet student who practiced the fiddle eight hours a day. When he returned home, after four months in New York, he had undergone a transformation. To the neighbors who heard of his New York exploits, he might as well have been visiting Sodom and Gomorrah. "I didn't have any real vision of my being a cool kid," MacIsaac said. "All of a sudden, I became this guy who was onstage, the entertainer." He was eager to advance his career, so he found himself a manager, Sheri Jones, who was based in Halifax.

His goals weren't specific, but his ambition was enormous. "He would say, 'I want to be rich and famous. I want to make money, and own a house on Cape Breton,'" Jones told me. "I realized that we could put a rock band behind him and it would appeal to kids. Ashley has that star quality that very few people have." Jones showcased MacIsaac at an industry event in Newfoundland in February of 1994. "Everybody had been saying, 'What are you going to do with a traditional fiddler?'" Jones says. "Then, the minute he hit the stage, people I had known for twenty years were all over me."

MacIsaac signed with A&M Records, and went on the road, touring with such mainstream artists as the Chieftains and Sarah McLachlan and Melissa Etheridge. He got excellent reviews for his quicksilver fiddling, and soon forged an outrageous public persona: step-dancing on

Conan O'Brien's show wearing nothing under his kilt; loudly telling interviewers that he was a "fiddle slut" who liked hearing Courtney Love sing about heroin. During breaks from touring, MacIsaac was also recording, and in 1995 he released *Hi How Are You Today?*, with its bizarre mixing of traditional and modern sounds.

Cape Breton purists criticized MacIsaac for messing with the music, and he defended himself aggressively. "Celts were the original punks," he told one interviewer. Unlike, say, the recordings made in the early nineties by American hip-hop producers who sampled jazz riffs, MacIsaac's music was a true fusion of new and old, and he knew the old as well as anyone. (In response to critics who accused him of corrupting his heritage with *Hi How Are You Today?*, he released a traditional album, *Fine Thank You Very Much*, on which he played old tunes in the differing styles of well-known Cape Breton fiddlers.) Even with a hit CD, MacIsaac was something of a naïf when it came to popular music; it was his producers who engineered many of the innovations on *Hi How Are You Today?* But the spirit of the album was pure MacIsaac, and its reception among the mainstream audience was ecstatic. In 1995, he pulled off an unusual feat by winning two Juno awards, which are Canada's equivalent of the Grammys, in the categories of best new solo artist *and* best roots and traditional album. That's a little like the winner of the Oscar for best short documentary walking off with the best-picture prize as well.

Stardom requires not just virtuosity but presence, and MacIsaac is extravagantly endowed with both. He has the swagger of a star, too. The first time we met, he picked me up at my hotel in a rented white stretch limo. He sat in the back seat like a prince, smoking a joint and holding forth on his plans for further fame.

In front of a rock audience, MacIsaac exhibits an air of edgy danger, and he is vividly, violently physical, disturbingly sexy. Like Kurt Cobain, or Shane MacGowan, formerly of the Pogues, MacIsaac is transfixing because you are never sure when he is going to spin out of control.

Even in the tiny church halls in which he plays in Cape Breton, he seems klieg-lit. I saw him at a square dance in the hamlet of Glencoe

Mills one day last summer: the place felt no bigger than a tennis court, and there were slices of home-baked cakes and bottles of soda for sale, and a loud ventilator fan cranking in the corner, and hundreds of people cramming in to watch and dance. On the handkerchief-size stage was Maybelle Chisholm, a legendary Cape Breton pianist, whose upper arms quivered as she pounded the keys, and MacIsaac sat next to her, all in black, with a studded belt and dark glasses, fiddling. He looked as if his coccyx had been fastened to his chair and the rest of him set in perpetual motion: His legs pumped and his arms sawed and his body swooped and his mouth hung agape and sweat dripped off him; it was clear that he was made for bigger places than this.

These traits insured that as soon as MacIsaac became famous he also became infamous. In 1996, *Maclean's* selected him to be on its annual honor roll of worthy Canadians, and he managed to get himself struck from the list by telling one of the magazine's writers about his underage boyfriend and his fondness for a particular sexual practice involving micturation. (The magazine ended up running a disapproving article that reprimanded MacIsaac for his "stunning recklessness about his image.") His exorbitant nature became even more apparent after he began to make money. (He says he earned three million Canadian dollars for *Hi How Are You Today?*) He bought a house in Cape Breton and started to renovate it in classic rock-star style—a sunken Jacuzzi, a bed on a circular platform. On the road, he would rack up huge hotel bills. One night on tour, MacIsaac's dinner companions insisted on picking up the tab, refusing his proffered fifty-dollar bill: MacIsaac stuffed the money into his mouth and ate it. Then, there was all the money that he was increasingly spending on drugs, including acid and mushrooms.

MacIsaac believes that drugs are an important element of his success. He doesn't have to be high to perform, he says, but he prefers to be. "The people who are paying to see me like it better when I'm high," he once told me. "It is a sad fact. I am not addicted, and I don't need to do it, but sometimes I have to, because I want to go out onstage and do what people expect to see from me. And that is not Ashley MacIsaac not on drugs, that is Ashley MacIsaac on drugs." Those around him saw what was going on, but no one did anything about it.

Sheri Jones, who was his manager at that point, recalls that every time she got a phone call late at night she feared the worst about MacIsaac.

Hi How Are You Today? had coincided with a revival of interest in things Celtic, from Frank McCourt to "Riverdance." It seemed possible that MacIsaac's successful record might be a one-off oddity, and he wasn't sure how to follow it up. He loved being a pop star, but he kept going into the studio, failing to produce anything A&M liked, and dropping out of sight. He was bored with touring, and in the spring of 1997 he disappointed his record company by backing out of a series of engagements in the United States. A year later, he returned to Cape Breton for a show, and, instead of playing his familiar songs, he stood onstage in a hooded sweatshirt, fiddle in hand, and rapped, badly, at the audience. When he trashed his trailer at a festival, Sheri Jones stopped representing him. After that, according to MacIsaac, he did nothing much except shuttle between Cape Breton and Toronto and take drugs, including crack cocaine. "I had enough money to enjoy myself, and I just went with it," he said. "I got pretty whacked out." Soon he was at the end of the money he had earned from *Hi How Are You Today?* About a year ago, he hit bottom. "I found myself walking down the streets after two days of being up at four in the morning," he told me. "I was walking with crackheads, smoking off some dirty old crack pipe, and when I got back to my hotel room and took off my shoes I was covered in blisters. I couldn't stand up. I said, This is fucking disgusting, and I got very emotionally distraught and called my parents. They said, Everything is O.K., come home, so I went home for Christmas, and everything has semi-cleared since then. Semi-cleared. Because if it was completely clear, it would be boring." But his reformation did not make relations with the record company any smoother. At the beginning of 1999, A&M was bought by Universal, and although MacIsaac went back into the studio this spring, he still failed to come up with anything that was sufficiently commercial. He started agitating to be released from his contract.

When I visited MacIsaac's parents in Cape Breton in June, they seemed to be enormously proud of him—his mother scurried to find an Ashley MacIsaac T-shirt and cap for me—and to be exceedingly defensive on his behalf. Angus MacIsaac said, "The last year, he more or less laid back, and now what he needs to do is get a recording out there and make some money. I think it will build his confidence, too." I warily broached the issue of MacIsaac's drug use—a Canadian magazine called *Frank* had published an interview with him a week or two earlier in which he had talked about smoking crack—and Carmelita MacIsaac became indignant. "I find some of the media will only put the garbage in," she said. "I went in the store one time and saw all these magazines with all this *garbage* in them, and I bought three or four of them and ripped them up right in the girl's face."

Even as MacIsaac brags to the press about his erratic behavior, it's never entirely clear whether his spinning out of control is actually part of the performance. When he was just nineteen years old, he told the Ottawa *Citizen*, "I don't think my gift is music at all. I think my gift is the power of marketing." For all his skill and his innovation, it often seems as if MacIsaac had concluded that notoriety will sustain him further than talent. He happily volunteers details about his sexual history: He has, on more than one occasion, boasted about the four years he spent with a sixteen-year-old boyfriend, a triumph over the laws of mathematics as well as over the pitfalls of romance, and the first time I visited him he told me how he met his first real boyfriend—a porn star, he said—at a "Big Dick" contest at the Limelight, in Manhattan. He has called himself the Antichrist. He has used aggressive pronouncements about his sexuality to offend not only the blue-rinsed portion of his musical admirers but also members of the gay community, who have been upset by his assertions that although he has had boyfriends, he might end up going straight and getting married. MacIsaac's list of transgressions is exhaustive, and exhausting.

His high public profile hasn't always bolstered his success. After his statements in *Maclean's*, his bookings for corporate gigs—the ones in which artists actually make money—and opportunities for commercial endorsements dropped off dramatically. This kind of routine self-sabotage betrayed MacIsaac's deep ambivalence toward his pop-star role. If you ask him about the music he plays, and what it means to him, he tends to deflect the question and bluster about his desire to make money. You get the sense that he'd much rather discuss his sex life—

real or imagined—than his musical one, as if his true private life were the one he conducts with his fiddle.

One Friday afternoon last July, MacIsaac and I drove from Halifax to Cape Breton. At the airport, he stood out among the tourists and business travellers. He was dressed all in black, was wearing dark glasses, and was carrying a large purple fiddle case, and he wore a peculiar safari hat that sat oddly high on his head. In the car, he took off the hat, and inside was a thick wad of Canadian dollar bills.

The previous day, he told me, he had signed a record deal with Andrew McCain, the chairman of a large Canadian food company who also owns a small independent label called Loggerhead Records. For weeks, MacIsaac had been trying to get out of his contract with Universal, and he had finally slipped free. (To accomplish this, he had walked into the company's offices and demanded a million dollars; when Universal refused, MacIsaac trashed the place.) He had approached McCain, who suggested that he go into rehab, but MacIsaac said that wasn't necessary. Loggerhead, whose recordings are distributed by Universal, had agreed to pay him a hundred thousand dollars, half of which he would get when the record came out and half of which the company gave him in cash. He said he had forty thousand dollars in his hat and in his pockets. I asked what had happened to the other ten.

"Well, five of it is on my finger," he said, and flashed a gigantic, hideous gold signet ring bearing a Mercedes-Benz symbol. He had stashed some of it under his bed. Several hundred had gone on taxi fares and big tips. Some of it had gone on what he said was a gambling game he'd been playing the previous night, in which he would ask someone to cut a deck of cards and then give that person the face value of the card, multiplied by ten, in dollars. Because it's impossible to listen to MacIsaac for long without wanting to impart financial advice, I said something responsible about how he had forty thousand dollars to last him until Christmas. "I don't know whether it's going to last me until Monday," he said.

When I saw MacIsaac a couple of months later, the ring was gone— someone had stolen it from his apartment, he said—and instead he was wearing a smaller version bearing the imprint of a dollar sign. I didn't ask about the forty thousand dollars. We were at a recording studio in Toronto, where he was laying down the final vocal and fiddle tracks on what was to be his new album for Loggerhead, *Helter's Celtic.* (It came out last month in Canada to good reviews, but so far no company has signed on to release it in this country.) MacIsaac had just flown to Toronto from Ireland, where he had been recording with the Chieftains; this evening, he was working on a remake of Hank Snow's country ballad "I'm Movin' On," which his new producer, Justin Gray, had turned into a hardrock squall. "You've done this much without me; I'm sure you can finish without me," MacIsaac said good-naturedly to Gray as he entered the recording booth with a lyric sheet in his hand. He stripped off his shirt, so that he looked like a satyr slightly run to seed, and started singing into the mike, wildly off key.

"How completely, bizarrely out of tune am I?" he asked Gray.

"It doesn't bother me," Gray answered. "The track is so far from the original already."

MacIsaac took repeated passes through the song, then he took his fiddle into the recording booth and played it over the Kiss-like backing track, an escalation through a scale here, a shimmering eddy of notes there. Then, for the next couple of hours, Gray sorted through the digital recordings of the vocals, trying to find enough good phrases among the repeated bum notes to build a single decent rendition of the song. MacIsaac seemed embarrassed that so much effort was being expended on his behalf, but he sat quietly and let the sound engineer do his work.

"No matter how many people you piss off, there are always more people who don't know that you pissed the other people off," MacIsaac told me at around four-thirty that morning, as we drove into downtown Toronto. We were in a 1971 Cougar that MacIsaac had recently acquired: It had no heat, and rattled alarmingly, and we were dangerously low on gas. I asked him whether he liked what the new producer had done. He was unenthusiastic but sanguine. "It has been doctored from what I initially set out for it to be, and the approach on the whole thing is a lot less edgy," he said. "The record company decided to try and make it radio-friendly, and I don't know if it was the right choice, but I gave them the O.K. to do it."

He seemed to be dealing with the pressure of being expected to deliver a smash-hit followup by insisting that he wasn't even attempting to match his earlier success. "If this record comes out and sells fifty thousand copies, which it will, it won't be a failure," he said. "It will be a fucking gold record. It will accomplish something, which is to hold me over for another six months, and give me some public persona in this country, so that I can look like I haven't been too much of a crackheaded fool. It will give me the space to go on and do more stuff, and give me the time, and that is pretty much all I was looking for." The *next* record, he was suggesting, would be the one he really wanted to make. What it might contain he wasn't sure: Mostly, he said, he wanted to shut himself in a studio and work privately, "so that I can be as fucked up and freaky and as prima donna as I want." And he still hoped to make some kind of recording with Philip Glass, who had invited him to perform with him the following week in Ann Arbor.

Then MacIsaac veered off into one of his outrage riffs. He told me how he'd fantasized about pretending to die, then having a sex change and coming back to Cape Breton as a prodigal girl fiddle player who played just like Ashley MacIsaac. He said he'd like to find a new place to live, other than Cape Breton. "I am happy to be there," he said. "But it's hard to be as maniacal as I would like to be at home when everybody knows me. There are definitely some things that aren't in Cape Breton that are in my life at this point, like harems of naked boys in India, say.

"So I haven't decided where I will go," he said, as the car shook perilously, and the gas gauge slipped beyond empty. "And actually, at the moment, I can't do it. But soon, I think, I am going to become weirder than Michael Jackson."

JEFF STARK

The Politics of Plagiarism

Tom Zé's eyes are large and dark, a pair of polished acorns. He is sixty-two years old, which you wouldn't know but you can actually kind of tell when you stare at the creases. He smiles a lot, like he's always laughing at his own absurdist in-joke. Sometimes, when he looks at you, his pupils are so bright that you can see a ghost of yourself. Other times he drops his head to consider a question. His features—the patchy beard, big nose, diminutive frame—are strikingly human. His eyes never wander.

His attention is remarkable. There are a million things happening at once in this shabby Victorian parlor, downstairs in the Irving Plaza concert hall. Later tonight, Zé is performing a rare U.S. show with the Chicago post-rock band Tortoise. Right now, the room is loud and complicated with the kinds of things that have to happen before concerts. A small television crew is interviewing David Byrne about Zé (pronounced Zay), whom the former Talking Head tracked down more than 10 years ago in Brazil. A photographer from a Brazilian newspaper is pacing impatiently, waiting for a chance to take Zé outside in the rain. And a stressed-out record company guy keeps coming into the room and looking over the translator's shoulder. There are things to do. Sound checks. Photographs. Brazilians who need nonexistent tickets. Dinner. Strangers to hug. And Zé's eyes never wander.

Tom Zé, who has made some of the most beautiful music in the world, is not a purist. Purists are boring, especially world music purists. The best contemporary musicians know this. That is why artists like Beck, Stereolab, Tortoise, the High Llamas and Sean Lennon are all fascinated by Tom Zé and Tropicalia, the 1960s Brazilian pop movement that he helped create. Beck *et al.* have looked beyond American-Anglo pop for inspiration and incorporated elements into their own work. They, like Zé, are not purists either.

If world beat is a genre of music loosely based on the idea of marrying native sounds with foreign influences or musics from other cultures, Zé made world beat music long before it went Deep Forest. In some ways, the Tropicálistas—including principally Zé, the young Gilberto Gil, songwriter Caetano Veloso and a strange, obscure and wonderful band called Os Mutantes—can be understood as corollaries to the dirty hippies jamming psychedelic music in the States. The Tropicálistas' movement was both political and social, set against injustice, restrictive sexuality and a military dictatorship. (Imagine Nixon's tenure, under martial law.)

"We speak about the government, the people that conspire with the government, the big corporations," says Zé, half in English, half with the help of a Portuguese translator. "If you live in a country like that, you have politics everywhere. You can't imagine."

Working with Brazil's rich rhythmic heritage—dense with the music of Portugal, the Caribbean, Africa and indigenous America—the Tropicálistas layered their pop songs with Brit psych, modernist poetry, found sounds and phrases ripped off wholesale from The Beatles and the Stones. Like most musicians, they were combining influences and reinventing in their own language. At the same time, there was never a question of where the components originated. Listen to the old Tropicalia records and you hear parts connected to parts connected to parts. It's some of the most angular, confusing and ecstatic pop music ever recorded.

Oddly enough, it's the riff from "Smoke on the Water" coming through the P.A. onstage at Irving Plaza. Zé turns to the guitarist and stops the set. There is something that he wants to say to the audience.

"I want to make a partnership with you," he says, "to take plagiarism into your home."

It is difficult to understand Zé because his English is so poor. He's trying to convince the crowd that the melody of "Hey Jude" is almost the same as the Brazilian national anthem. He has split the audience into halves and has them humming each song separately at the same time. It's hard to know what he's talking about.

For Zé, plagiarism is political. A liner-note essay from his 1998 record *Fabrication Defect* explains how the third world can cannibalize the first, settle a score and put an end to the notion of the traditional composer. "The esthetic of the fabrication defect will reutilize the sonorous civilized trash . . . It will recycle an alphabet of emotions contained in songs and musical symbols of the first world, that sealed each marked step of our affective and emotional life. They will be put to use in small cells of plagiarized material. This deliberate practice unleashes an esthetic of plagiarism . . . that ambushes the universe of well-known and traditional music."

Back onstage, the guitarist rips into "Smoke on the Water" again. Conga drums come in. He switches to the Stones' "(I Can't Get No) Satisfaction." Zé smiles. The music wanders everywhere, but he is unswerving.

As a performer, Zé was the weirdest in a weird movement. The military came down on the Tropicálistas with extreme censorship in late 1968. Some of the musicians were arrested, others banished. Zé went underground. He began recording with homemade instruments, experimenting with atonal riffs and continuing to write political songs. Zé, unlike his Tropicálista comrades who abandoned much of the strangeness of Tropicalia and became stars, lost his audience.

He languished for years until David Byrne found his records during a stay in Saõ Paulo. Byrne tracked down Zé and arranged to release the Brazilian's older songs on his Luaka Bop record label. The first collection, *The Best of Tom Zé*, is a pleasant mix of acoustic guitar melodies, strange sounds and Zé's soft, almost soothing voice. At the same time, it's very, very odd: One minute back-up singers coo lullabies, the next there's the sound of metal milling against a grinding wheel. Odd, and very, very pretty.

Zé in the Irving Plaza lobby: "Politics are in my songs in the same way that to be lovers—to have a relationship—is politics, the same way that staring at the moon is politics. For us Brazilians, politics is a very important matter, because politics is destroying us. It's fucking up the country. Politics are in my music because it is part of our food. It is very important."

Tom Zé is jumping up and down onstage at Irving Plaza. There are 1,100 people in the audience and the show is sold out. He is playing percussion by thumping his chest. Behind him, the members of Tortoise plink on vibes and shake rattles and play fuzzed-out guitar.

People in the audience are not really dancing: They are listening. When Zé asks them to, they sing entire choruses. Some speak Portuguese, many know the lyrics and sing along.

Zé is very pleased with a just-finished version of "Defect 2." He smiles at the mike, gleams at the lights and addresses the crowd. "You know that I no speak English," he says. This does not stop him.

"In Africa, I am the slave. In Brazil, I am the slave. In Brazil, the republic is the slave. But here, here I am the boss."

Fabrication Defect (1998), Zé's third record for Luaka Bop, is a concept album of sorts, based around some of the esthetic theories Zé has been toying with since he began studying music at a university in Bahia in the early '60s. An essay in the liner notes explains that Zé believes that people in the third world have been converted to "a kind of android," which allows them to serve "first world bosses." The androids, however, are not perfect yet, they have defects, which include the ability to think, dance and dream. Zé's album then is a celebration of those defects, broken down into 14 different songs, each celebrating a separate defect.

It's smart music, obviously, but the ideas never seem forced. The three-minute songs effortlessly segue from one to another. "Defect 1: Gene" is a sprightly tune based around ringing guitar patterns and chiming tambourines. "Defect 2: Curiosidade" is a quieter ballad, its acoustic guitar riffing off "Defect 1," with Zé baby-talking in the background.

It's almost suspiciously tight, musically at least. Did Zé ever abandon the album's concept for musical concessions? Is there a difference between the fabrication defect idea and *Fabrication Defect*? "My attempt was to make the record very simple: Defect one, to think, that is the most dangerous defect; defect two can be to love, to study, to dance, to think. These are all defects," he says. "But the songs I get to compose—like the winds in navigation—change the direction of the target. My own inspiration changes direction too. It fucked me up."

Not too much. There are moments when you can hear Zé's past, like the "vasolina-gasolina" rhyme he rips off from Caetano Veloso on "Defect 3: Politicar." And there are other moments when Zé sounds like the future, or at least hyper-contemporary. The record's figurative centerpiece is the loping, accordion-driven finale, "Defect 14: Xiquexique," which flips from found-sound to rhythm sticks, methodically builds new patterns upon each section and crescendos at five and a half minutes with all the different sounds ramming into one another. It's as dramatic and complicated and weird and exciting as the best songs by Beck, Stereolab or Tortoise.

Brazilian music, once again, is reaching critical mass in the States. Consider:

- Luaka is reissuing long out of print records by Os Mutantes this summer. (Talk about beach music!)
- Beck named a groovy Brazilian-influenced tune "Tropicalia," and named his last record *Mutations*, which sounds a lot like a mad shout-out to the Mutantes.
- A huge Tropicalia box set appeared last year with four CDs' worth of songs.
- *Fabrication Defect* popped up all over 1998 critics lists for best record of the year; Zé's tour earned stacks of press clippings; and you can still hear his songs in rotation on college radio.
- Zé's tour-only EP *Postmodern Platos* includes remixes by popsters like Sean Lennon and the High Llamas and sonic pioneers like Amon Tobin, Ui's Sasha Frere-Jones and Tortoise's John McEntire.
- That damn Banana Republic commercial and its little Brazilian anthem.

And so what does it all mean? What were the Tropicálistas onto that still resonates today? For starters, it probably has something to do with the essence of pop: miscegenation and the constant progress that comes with reinventing form by destruction. Then there's the lure of appropriation, the desire to turn a world of sounds into a private playground, and the absurd drama of dada, which allows for laughter in the face of tyranny. And there might be a little political residue, or at least a nostalgia for a time or place where to sing about politics seemed important, when it gave their music force and a reason to exist.

Ask Zé what the fuss is about and he'll answer with a bizarre riddle, one that says everything and nothing at once—the perfect Tom Zé quote.

"To respond, I will make a metaphor," he says, speaking quietly, his eyes narrowing in. "The ears of the dollar are more sensitive than the honors of the dollar."

TOM PIAZZA

Trust the Song

We have entered an era of mass confusion between people's ability to perform public tasks for which they are, presumably, trained, and their personal lives, which in healthier times are considered nobody's business. Former Vice President Quayle has even announced that marital fidelity will be "the issue" in the next presidential race. Sure—the heck with foreign policy, education, the economy, public works. . . .

"Trust the song, not the singer" is age-old wisdom. I'm glad that the singers and musicians, male and female, whose work I have loved over the years did not have to display certificates of marital fidelity in order to qualify as performers. Likewise the fiction writers. Nobody asked them to be moral exemplars in their personal lives. It was their work that was important.

Lately, though, the agenda of aesthetic discussion, along with politics, seems to have been lifted from an afternoon talk show. One example from recent memory: Philip Roth's Pulitzer Prize–winning *American Pastoral*, easily one of the best novels of the past ten years. At least three quarters of the people to whom I mentioned the book didn't really care what was between the covers of *American Pastoral*, but wanted to know if I had read Claire Bloom's memoir of her apparently troubled marriage to Roth.

To some people, an artist's work is only an avenue by which to get to the real point, which is the artist herself or himself. A kind of sacrificial element comes into play, a desire to consume the body and drink the blood. "Who are you, really?" is the question. But most creative people are trying to escape from the cage of who they are. It is a mistake to think that most artists and creative people are trying to express the self; they are more likely trying to complete the self, or even find its opposite.

These thoughts are occasioned by the career of the singer and songwriter Gillian Welch, since her brilliant 1996 debut CD *Revival*, and especially since her second recording, *Hell Among the Yearlings*, was released last year. Both discs consist of original material, strongly inflected by different kinds of traditional music as well as some rockabilly, folk, etc. One of the most talented and distinctive singers or songwriters to come down the pike in a long, long while, she and her partner and co-writer, the excellent guitarist and harmony singer David Rawlings, have gained a wide and appreciative following.

Behind that following, though, like hyenas following a wagon train, has come a chorus of scattered, carping voices, questioning Welch's right to use Southern themes and elements from traditional music in her songs. The problem, for them, is that Welch grew up in Los Angeles with music-business parents. Maybe the writers looked at her picture, thought she was a mountain girl and then were embarrassed when they realized they were wrong. Who knows?

I think that the voices questioning Welch's right to do what she does are putting the emphasis in exactly the wrong place. They belong to the same type of people who felt betrayed thirty-five years ago when it turned out that Bob Dylan was a Jewish kid from Minnesota instead of Billy the Kid's younger brother.

Here's the thing: First of all, Gillian Welch is not playing, or claiming to play, "traditional music," strictly speaking, any more than Bob Dylan was. She knows the repertoire and some of the techniques, but there are all kinds of elements in her music that are hardly orthodox old-time elements and that are clearly there as part of an international effect.

As for the often rural, and even rural-Gothic, subject matter of her songs—murder, moonshine, failed crops, etc.—well, what about it? "Caleb Meyer," the song all the reviewers mentioned from *Hell Among the Yearlings*, is about a foiled rape attempt somewhere in the vicinity of "them hollering pines." It's a good song, and I don't believe one needs to have been the victim of a rape attempt, or live near the hollering pines, to have written it or to appreciate it. If there's a better devotional song than "By the Mark," from *Revival*, I don't know what it is. It makes no difference to me whether Gillian Welch believes in Jesus or not; the song carries its own weight. Besides, it is about a kind of truth in life that we can recognize as truth whether or not we believe in Jesus in the first place. But both discs are full of terrific songs (and singing)—"Good Til Now" (with its faint echoes of Blind Boy Fuller's "Weeping Willow"), "Acony Bell," "My Morphine," "Winter's Come and Gone," "Barroom Girls," "Only One and Only." To make an issue of who is behind the lyrics and the voice moves the discussion into a completely different arena.

It seems to me that it takes an extreme poverty of imagination to propose, implicitly or explicitly, that people can write only about their personal experience (or worse, about the experiences peculiar to their ethnic/gender/regional/national group). It takes not only poverty of imagination, but hostility to the idea of the free human spirit. Any hope one might have left for a society like ours depends on the constant assertion of the possibility of that kind of empathy in the first place.

Of course, the farther from your personal experience you try to reach as an artist, the more effort, intuition, honesty, humility, and/or luck it takes. The farther you reach, the easier it is to do something that just doesn't work, doesn't ring true. But the question is *whether it works*, whether it rings true, *not* whether you have an inherited visa to enter that territory.

A few years ago, while I was attending the Iowa Writers' Workshop, Saul Bellow came to talk to us for a few days. In addition to a reading, he conducted a workshop and a question-and-answer session. During the Q&A, one student asked him about "stealing" from other writers—borrowing techniques, structural ideas, entering other cultural milieus. Bellow smiled wanly and said, "You are entitled to take anything you are strong enough to carry out."

Amen.

DAVID HAJDU

Duke Ellington and
Billy Strayhorn

Secretly dying of the cancer that would claim him within months,
Duke Ellington, sallow and thin, stood before the assembled in West-
minster Abbey on October 24, 1973, for the premier of his third and
final *Sacred Concert*, and a chorus sang the 74-year-old composer's
words: "Every man prays in his own language." Publicly, Ellington
spent much of his last decade communing with the divine in grand, if
unorthodox, devotional performances. Privately, retiring in the hotel
rooms that were his home for more than half a century, he used a
prayer book. His son, Mercer, later donated one of Ellington's vol-
umes, a 1966 edition of *The Catholic Hymnal*, to the Smithsonian Institution. When an archivist unpacked it recently, she called me. She had
found some photographs tucked between the pages, and she thought I
should see one of them before it was filed away, erasing any record of
its origin. It's a snapshot of a sweet-faced, bespectacled African-American man, Billy Strayhorn, half dressed, reading a book in bed.

What was Duke Ellington saying, in his own language? Why would
one man, reading in solitude, care to look at a picture of another man
doing the same? And what might that have to do with the music that is
Ellington's legacy?

This April 29 marks the 100th anniversary of the birth of Edward
Kennedy Ellington, one of the true pioneers of jazz. Duke reigns om-

nipotently over the cultural landscape, or at least its high ground: Concerts and conferences devoted to Ellington are scheduled at dozens of arts centers and institutions, from New York's Lincoln Center to Ohio's Cuyahoga Community College. A torrent of new Ellington CD collections and reissues will land atop the more than 150 titles in circulation. There will be a nationally syndicated radio series, musical celebrations in three dozen cities, even new ballets in Duke's honor.

Fleetingly, the face in that photograph from Ellington's prayer book shifts in and out of view. In panel discussions, as experts ponder Ellington the Legend, Billy Strayhorn is mentioned with reverence. In out-of-the-way cabarets in Manhattan and Istanbul, vocalist Allan Harris has been performing all-Strayhorn tributes. Filmmaker Irwin Winkler is now casting a screen version of Strayhorn's life. And the credits on virtually every new Ellington CD list William Thomas Strayhorn as composer or co-creator of some of the best-known pieces associated with Duke, including "Take the 'A' Train," "Satin Doll," "Chelsea Bridge," and suites such as "Such Sweet Thunder."

Yet Strayhorn, Ellington's chief collaborator and perhaps the most influential figure in his creative life, is still, somehow, but an ethereal presence. Though their careers are elementally inseparable, the true nature of their collaboration remains virtually unknown—or unspoken. As Strayhorn's biographer, I have explored their three-decade partnership extensively; indeed, some of the interviews quoted herein were gathered for my 1996 book, *Lush Life*. And the question remains: How to explain a relationship between men of such contrasts? Ellington, tall and commanding, a master jazz innovator who managed his orchestra and his expansive songbook like a small industry, a brilliant scholar of the streets whose regal air and grandiloquence, vaguely ironic, had the charm of an irresistible con game; Strayhorn, tiny, attentive, demure, a consummate composer and arranger, content to remain in Duke's massive shadow, a culture buff who relished New York (as well as Paris, eventually) and developed a taste—and oversize appetite—for high style in food, fashion, and nightlife.

In the section on Strayhorn in his 1973 memoir, *Music Is My Mistress*, Ellington was, as always, poetically obtuse on the subject: "He was not, as he was often referred to by many, my alter ego. Billy Strayhorn was my right arm, my left arm, all the eyes in the back of my head, my brainwaves in his head, and his in mine."

Many fellow musicians have called theirs a unique case of artistic intimacy. "Ellington's relationship with Strayhorn was one the likes of which I will never see and maybe the world will never see again," says Luther Henderson, the composer and arranger with whom Ellington and Strayhorn crafted many of their most ambitious projects, including several long-form works for symphony orchestra. "It was obviously a special relationship. Duke had an enormous love for Billy apart from his work," explains George Avakian, Ellington's longtime producer at Columbia records. "It was a love affair between the two, as artists," remarked the late trombonist and arranger Billy Byers.

That's the essence of the story, I am convinced: They loved each other. But what *kind* of love? As Ellington frequently noted, he and Strayhorn abhorred all categories, whether aesthetic, social, racial, or emotional. Moreover, it seems that Duke Ellington, a notorious Lothario, loved Billy Strayhorn more fully and deeply than he loved any woman in his life—excepting his mother and his sister, Ruth. No matter how many scholarly panels we convene, the complexity of their love remains elusive, even in our ostensibly enlightened age.

With a conjurer's regard for the allure of the unknown, Ellington always kept the details of his collaboration with Strayhorn a mystery. "Edward always used to say, 'Don't peek your hole card,'" explained the late Marian Logan, wife of Ellington's friend and doctor, Arthur Logan.

"[Edward] would never answer the question 'Who wrote this? Who did this?'" recalls Teo Macero, the arranger and producer who made several Ellington albums for Columbia. "He'd say, 'Sweetie . . . you know, I don't know. Maybe Billy, you know, me. . .' And it would go round and round and round."

Ironically enough, when he first met Strayhorn, in 1938, Ellington was hardly in need of a muse. Not even 40 and a bandleader for nearly 20 years, Ellington had proved to be not merely a skillful writer of distinctive popular songs ("Mood Indigo," "Solitude," "Sophisticated Lady") but also a serious composer of more intricate works ("Creole Rhapsody," "Reminiscing in Tempo") which had begun to redefine jazz as a music for the ears as well as the feet, earning due praise from highbrow critics and composers such as Aaron Copland. Ellington, however, recognized Strayhorn's talents as a pianist, composer, lyricist, and arranger when the prodigy, then 23, attended one of Duke's concerts in Pittsburgh. (The pair were introduced backstage by William Augustus "Gus" Greenlee, the charismatic sports impresario, nightclub owner, and presumed racketeer.) Ellington was so taken with Strayhorn's skills that he immediately implored him to write songs for the band, swiftly jotting down directions to his Harlem apartment, subway line and all— scrawls which Strayhorn ingeniously fashioned, within a week or two, into the swing classic "Take the 'A' Train."

Strayhorn had gone as far as Pittsburgh could take him. Conservatory-trained, he had already composed several sophisticated pieces merging jazz and the classical tradition; played bar piano all around town; led his own jazz trio; arranged for half a dozen local bands (black, white, and mixed); and written songs that would later become jazz standards, including "Something to Live For," "Your Love Has Faded," and his signature piece, "Lush Life." Highly regarded by the few who knew him, Strayhorn lost ground, nonetheless, as a result of two provincial pressures: his trio and his main big-band affiliation, both mixed-race groups, had been forced to dissolve after incidents of prejudice against Strayhorn, because he was African-American; and he was dropped from the best black band in town, because he was gay.

In a drumbeat after they met, Ellington had him move into his apartment on Edgecombe Avenue in Harlem's tony Sugar Hill district, where Strayhorn lived like one of the family with Ellington's girlfriend Mildred Dixon, Duke's only sibling, Ruth, and his son, Mercer. (Ellington was estranged, though never legally separated, from his wife, Edna.) The benefits of their collaboration proved exquisitely mutual: Ellington gained a second set of gifts to help expand his musical palette and take him beyond the big-band idiom into the worlds of the concert stage and the theater; Strayhorn, in turn, now had a world-class vehicle for his music and the freedom to compose without bearing public scrutiny and the risk of rejection for his homosexuality. That Strayhorn would toil largely behind the scenes, often contributing anonymously to the ever broadening Ellington canon, worked to the advantage of both.

And that Ellington might not have really required the young man's assistance would quickly become moot; they grew reliant upon each other. "His approval was like going out with your armor on, instead of going out naked," Ellington said of Strayhorn in a 1968 interview. "We had a relationship that nobody else in the world would understand." The composers worked together from 1938 to 1967—often closely, occasionally as a sort of musical tag team, trading portions of pieces in mid-creation. Wherever in the world his performances took him, Ellington called Strayhorn religiously, writing songs by phone, virtually every night. Their collaborative output includes dozens of jazz masterworks, from songs such as "Day Dream" and "The Star-Crossed Lovers" to extended jazz-orchestra pieces, from the Broadway musical *Beggar's Holiday* to film scores.

"Our rapport was the closest," wrote Ellington. Indeed, according to photographer Gordon Parks, who spent several days observing Ellington and Strayhorn in 1960, on assignment for *Life* magazine, "they were like one mind." Preparing for a Los Angeles recording session, the pair shared a small suite at the Chateau Marmont in Hollywood, Parks remembers. Ellington would start writing late in the evening while Strayhorn slept; around two A.M., Strayhorn would awaken and resume composing where Ellington had left off, while Ellington would take Strayhorn's place in bed. "One person would work until he got sleepy," recalls Parks. "They never seemed to be in the room at the same time. They were like Clark Kent and Superman. You wondered if they were really the same person, changing disguises in the bedroom." What's more, Parks says, "they didn't talk about the music. One would just leave it for the other one, and he would pick up as if he had been writing the whole thing himself."

Ruth Ellington described the communication between her brother and Strayhorn as virtually psychic. "I've seen [Strayhorn] walk into Duke's dressing room," she recalled, "and Duke would say, 'Oh, Billy, I want you to finish this thing for me.' Just like that. And Billy would sit and stare into his eyes . . . and Duke would stare back, and then Billy would say, 'O.K.' They wouldn't even exchange a word. They'd just look into each other's eyes, and Billy would go out and write what Duke wanted. That's why he and Duke got along so well—because he could look at people and see through them. If he looked at you, he could tell exactly what you were."

Ellington couldn't abide such an intrusion—from anyone other than Strayhorn. "He didn't like anybody who could read his mind," his son,

Mercer, remarked. "That's what gave him his strength over people. Pop knew everybody's weakness, but he would never, never, oh, man, *never* he'd never let anybody know his. Strayhorn was the only one. He let Strayhorn in the door. That door was *locked* for everybody else, and I do mean everybody—family, his women . . . me, too, before the old man was dying, and I was the only one sitting there."

If Ellington granted his collaborator unique emotional access, the key to it was their music. "Let me tell you the one thing that will explain everything there is to know about Duke Ellington, including that magic between Duke Ellington and Billy Strayhorn," said a friend of both composers. "Music. That's it. Duke Ellington lived, breathed, ate, and drank music. That's all that really mattered to him—nothing else. That's what he loved. And he loved Billy Strayhorn because they made music together."

Marian Logan, perhaps because she was the wife of a physician, had a more diagnostic view. "Everybody knows Edward had eight million women," she said. "You have that many—and you're never home for any longer than a day every year—and you don't have to get overly close to none of them, and you don't have to worry none about them getting too close to you. The only real partner that man ever had was Billums [Strayhorn]. He called him his 'musical companion,' you know. Strayhorn adored that. [Edward] kept everybody else very far away, built a wall around himself—a big, gold, shiny wall. The only person inside with him in there was Billy Strayhorn. He wouldn't let his own doctor in, believe me.

"Edward had a kind of intimateness with Strayhorn that he never gave his girlfriends, none of them," Logan continued. "He trusted him [because] of the one thing that cut way down deep into him, and that means the music. It's hard to explain what it was. He had a very, very, very deep love for Strayhorn, and Strayhorn obviously loved Duke, too, to work with him like that for all those years. You can call it whatever you want. It had all to do with his music, and I think it was the only kind of love Ellington was truly capable of."

Though artistically plausible, Logan's assessment overlooks paternal love. From the onset of their association, Ellington included Strayhorn in his familial circle—and inserted himself in Strayhorn's; Duke would wire Billy's mother, Lillian, back home in Pittsburgh, on her birthday and Mother's Day. A generation older and far more prominent than his junior partner, Ellington would seem an obvious father figure. Then again, he avoided the obvious in most matters of business, art, and family. "That's the way it probably looks, a father-and-son thing, but it wasn't that simple at all," recalls Lena Horne, Strayhorn's dearest friend and confidante. Horne, who still keeps Strayhorn's portrait on her nightstand, also worked with Ellington and had something of a fling with him once. "Duke didn't want to be anybody's father—hell, no! Not even his own son's, and certainly not Billy's. He wasn't old enough to be a father!" she says with a big laugh. "Duke was young forever—he thought he was, anyway—young and sexual. Listen to his music. He never aged a day, till Billy died."

When Billy Strayhorn, then 51, succumbed to esophageal cancer on May 31, 1967, Ellington, then 68, fought to come to terms with it, while those around him struggled to understand Ellington's reaction. Mercer, who served as road manager for the orchestra at the time, recalled his father as angry and distraught. "He said, 'Why me? Why did this have to happen to me?' Only time I remember him ever saying, 'Fuck it,' he didn't want to play." Shortly after Strayhorn's death, pianist Donald Shirley, a friend of both Ellington's and Strayhorn's, went backstage to see Duke at the end of a performance and found him alone at the piano, head bowed, playing Strayhorn's "Lotus Blossom" over and over.

Ellington's grief was so deep that his publicist, Joe Morgen, circulated what has been considered a fabricated interview with the deceased, reportedly to deflect rumors about the musicians' close relationship. In it, an uncharacteristically tough-talking Strayhorn justifies his bachelorhood by claiming, loopily, that his apartment was too sloppy for any gal to stomach.

The degree to which the mercurial love between the pair may or may not have seeped past the chalk lines of heterosexual friendship is unknowable, though it proved to be anything but imponderable. As Strayhorn's biographer, and the president of the Duke Ellington Society, I've been asked literally scores of times if their relationship had a homosexual component. In the muted Ellingtonian tradition, I've tried to dodge the question gracefully.

Yes, Strayhorn was gay, and he undoubtedly had a love for Ellington; however, Strayhorn was known as monogamous and appeared wholly devoted to each of his four main companions in turn. Might he have longed for a more amorous involvement with Ellington? Perhaps, some have said. "I think that if Strayhorn could have constructed a relationship with Ellington, then he would have," Mercer told me. (Mercer died at 76 in 1996.) "He loved him that much."

As for Duke, Mercer said—with no hint of spin—he had always simply assumed that his father's bond with Strayhorn, his legendary sexual appetite, and his seemingly boundless sense of adventure likely led to some experimentation with Strayhorn. "I don't know for a fact—I didn't watch them," he said. "I just presumed as much. So did the cats [in the band]. One told me he walked in on them one time. I never pressed the issue. It seemed like a given."

A few of those close to Duke Ellington discussed homosexuality with him directly. According to Sam Shaw, producer of the 1961 film *Paris Blues*, scored by Ellington and Strayhorn, "Duke talked to me about Billy and the whole subject of homosexuality. In certain [African] tribes, the priests wore blue robes, which were the symbol of their status. They were considered holy, and they were bisexual—part of the African culture. Duke accepted that as part of nature."

Some of Ellington's personal beliefs, feelings, and preferences—including, for instance, his habit of wearing blue clothing—are more than just subjects of gossip because they had a significant effect on what he brought to the public. This year, as innumerable celebrations acknowledge his contributions to twentieth-century culture, one accomplishment may go little noted: Duke Ellington accepted, nurtured, supported, and empowered a small, shy gay man whom he loved as a soul mate, and he gave voice to that man's music through his own. There's a sound within the sound we think of as Ellingtonia, and much of it is a world apart from the assertive drive of big-band swing. "Passion Flower," "Lotus Blossom," "A Flower Is a Lovesome Thing," "Minuet in Blues." In dozens of Billy Strayhorn compositions that Ellington performed and recorded with his orchestra, the listener encounters expressions of humanity's subtler shades—a gentleness, a sensitivity, sometimes a sadness, arguably a gay sensibility, there on the jukebox from the same band that played "It Don't Mean a Thing if It Ain't Got That Swing." Though Billy Strayhorn could swing when he wanted (having written Ellington's theme song, "Take the 'A' Train," the leitmotif of the whole swing era), other things meant a thing to him too. Billy Strayhorn composed eight songs about flowers.

"The music of Duke Ellington is regarded as so great and so important now," notes Kevin McGruder, executive director of the organization Gay Men of African Descent. "To think that some of it is the voice of a gay man making distinctive statements of his own is quite something. It's a real testament to Duke that he embraced Billy Strayhorn the way he did and gave him that outlet. I can't imagine any other bandleader of his time doing that."

During the seven years between Strayhorn's death and Ellington's, of cancer on May 24, 1974, the aging composer turned his attention to God. He created three major works of sacred music and performed them in churches and temples, accompanied by singers, dancers, and a full orchestra. "He started channeling his music and his deep capacity for love toward God," explains the Reverend Janna Steed, a United Methodist theologian now writing a book about Ellington's religious music. "His theology was quite simple. All Duke was saying, basically, is 'God is love, and love is the answer to everything.'"

For reference, he always had his prayer book.

ROBERT LLOYD

Gone North

"I usually have a hard time talking about things directly, you know?"

—Tom Waits, not just whistling "Dixie"

I.

Morning. A truck-stop diner along Highway 101 near Santa Rosa, California, north of San Francisco. A horseshoe counter, tables, booths. Plain but clean. The focal point of the room is a large painting of an eighteen-wheeler on a country road, a painting that somehow speaks not of modern power but of classical repose: the Peterbilt as stag. The customers are mostly in their 40s, 50s and 60s, dressed for hard work or unfashionable comfort, the men almost invariably bearded.

In a booth by a window sit two patrons: One of them, Most Obviously Not From Around Here, is me. The other is Tom Waits, a musician and occasional actor. (His next film, *Mystery Men*, a superhero comedy, is due out this summer.) Formerly of Los Angeles, he has lived in the area several years with his wife (and co-writer and -producer), Kathleen Brennan, and their three children, and has taken on something of the local coloration. He wears unprefaded denims and big boots, and the only remaining emblem of his erstwhile cloth-cap-and-pointed-shoes flophouse-jazzbo neoboho fingersnappin' self is the Dizzy G. soul patch parked subtly beneath his lower lip. The towering monolith, or towering inferno, that was famously his hair has collapsed into something more like a brushfire.

Born on the eighth anniversary of the bombing of Pearl Harbor, Waits will celebrate 50 years on Earth three weeks before the end of the century. But like some other people who do not punch clocks, unless it's to stop them from ringing, he seems to exist outside of conventional time, and—judging at least by the person on his records, which range from his folkish 1973 debut, *Closing Time*, to the bop prosody of *Small Change* and *Foreign Affairs*, to the taxonomically confounding vaudeville of *Swordfishtrombones* and *Rain Dogs* and the stone-age blues of *Bone Machine*—even to have lived backward, from premature middle age into middle-aged youth, from (apparent) sophistication to (deceptive) simplicity. His first new album in six years, *Mule Variations*, which incorporates, refines and extends these previous researches into something at once fresh and familiar, is set for release April 27. And it was in this very diner that he sealed his new surprising-yet-not-really-when-you-think-about-it deal with Epitaph Records, the Los Angeles-based independent best known for the punk pop of Pennywise and Rancid, and founded by Brett Gurewitz, formerly of Bad Religion. Though he can claim Jackson Browne as a onetime labelmate and has been covered by the Eagles and Rod Stewart, Waits is by persuasion an outsider. "I think they're all great," he'll say later of Epitaph's young, enthusiastic and musically inclined staff. "I came from the whole period where *record guys*, it's like meeting guys from *DuPont*—they start looking at you like they want to lift up a part of you and look underneath, you feel like they're smelling meat."

On the table are a tape recorder, its red recording light on, two cups of coffee, a hat and a pair of reading glasses. Waits rummages in his pockets, producing various sheets and scraps of scribbled-upon paper that he spreads before him. He picks up his glasses to study the documents, then lays them down again. His voice when he speaks has the friendly rustle of dry leaves.

Tom [*leaning forward confidentially*]: The Washington Monument sinks six inches each year. *Six inches.*

Me: You brought notes?

Tom: You don't think I'd come unprepared, do you? I'll tell you what's good here: specials. If you're hungry go for the specials. It's like your grandma. They got borscht here. They got turkey loaf. This place hasn't really been discovered yet. [*Indicates the truck painting.*] That's the table I usually try to get. Just to be near the painting. It's kind of like the *Mona Lisa*. The *Mona Lisa* has no eyebrows—you ever notice that?

Me: Maybe that's the secret of that painting, more than the smile.

Tom: The shaved eyebrows. That's what I go for . . . When I was a kid, I had a friend whose dad was a truck driver. His name was Gale Storm. We had moved to National City, and his dad was coming through town, and he picked me up and he took me back up to L.A., to Whittier, to stay for a weekend. And I rode in the truck all the way up there. I was just like, "I'm gonna—I don't know what I'm gonna do, but I'm changed."

Me: How did you end up in this neighborhood?

Tom: It just seemed a good place to go—*north*. You live in L.A., you go south, there's *more* L.A.

We bought a house here several years ago right along the railroad tracks. And it was one of those things, they show you the house and you sit on the porch, and as you sit down on the porch there's a train going by, right? And the engineer *waves* to you. And then a cardinal comes and sits down right near your shoulder, and you hear the train whistle blowing, and the sun is going down, you have a nice glass of red wine. You think, "This is it." You buy the place, and the next day they say, "That was the *last time* that train ran. No cardinals have *ever* been seen around here. It must have been some freak thing." Then you quit drinking, and you're stuck with a house on a busy road, and the traffic noise is deafening. That was my introduction to the area. Now I live out. Way out.

Me: You must be well-established here by now.

Tom: I'm not well-established at all—but I'm here.

Me: You ever go down to San Francisco?

Tom: I go down sometimes—in for a weekend of excitement. Watch women's wrestling, or mud wrestling. Midget female mud wrestling. It's big there—it's huge. It's bigger than the *opera*—in fact, they call it "The Little Opera."

Me: And have you been playing music in the time between records?

Tom: The standard answer? I've been in traffic school.

Me: You know, you can get through that in a day.

Tom: They wanted to make an example out of me. I didn't have a good lawyer, and I just said, "Look, I'll do the time."

Me: Traffic school is hard.

Tom: It *is* hard. People don't really give it the weight it deserves.

Me: To get something out of it.

Tom: Exactly. More than just a diploma. I feel better *as a person*. I graduated vaya cum laude . . . Actually, I've been breaking in other people's shoes. Just on the side. Just to stay busy. You get 'em new, you're unhappy with them—I wear 'em four or five weeks and mail 'em back to you. No obligation necessary.

But just 'cause you're not fishin' doesn't mean there aren't fish out there. You can go out there when you want, when you're ready to do it . . . We've got a piano called a Fisher. And that's what we use to catch the big ones.

Me: Could you stop playing music and still be happy?

Tom: I thought about that. I don't know. I'd probably end up gluing bottlecaps onto a piece of plywood. I don't know how long I'm going to last. Until I get sick of it. Sick of myself.

I get a lot of weird mail. I get letters from guys that say, "My wife and I ran a hotel for many years, and we've sold it. The folks that took it over are a nice couple, and if you're ever in town, you should go visit them. Tell them that you spoke to us." And I don't know those people. They've already told me some people that they know that I should go and talk to and tell 'em that I know these people that I don't know. And then they tell me about the fact that he had bypass surgery and he has two blood clots, and his wife had a 14-pound hairball removed from her and then they mounted it, you know, on a . . . *globe*.

You know there's a device that they invented during World War II that could print 4,000 words on a surface the size of a piece of rice?

Me: I did not.

Tom: That's what I'm here for. Here's something else: Now, I hope you never have to use this, but if you're ever pursued by a crocodile, run in a zigzag fashion. They have little or no ability to make sudden changes in direction. But they're fast, they're very fast. In fact, there are probably more people that are killed by crocodiles than there are by . . . anything. More than heart disease. And I hear they're headed west.

Waitress [*returning*]: You're not going to eat? Not yet?

Tom: Still nothing.

Waitress: Nothing from nothing is nothing. You want more coffee? [*He nods. She refills the cups and moves on.*]

Tom: You can sit here as long as you want. [*A pause, as he consults his notes.*] A mole can dig a tunnel 300 feet long in one night. A grasshopper can jump over obstacles 500 times its height. You know what creature has the largest brain in relation to the size of its body? The ant. An ostrich's eyeball is larger than its brain. You put those two things together and . . . I don't know what that means. I'm not going anywhere with that.

Me: Where do you pick this stuff up?

Tom: Just livin' . . . The Ringling Brothers at one point were exhibiting Einstein's eyes, Napoleon's penis and Galileo's finger bones, all on the same bill. Different tents. 'Course I missed that. You ever hear of Johnny Eck? He was a Ringling act. The Man Born Without a Body. Johnny Eck had his own orchestra and was an excellent pianist and he'd stand on his hands and wear a tuxedo.

I used to take the bus to the Troubadour and stand out front at 9 o'clock in the morning on a Monday and wait *all day* to get up and do 15 minutes onstage . . . 'Cause you know, you never had confidence, you have absolutely no self-esteem, but you have this mad wish to do something public at the same time. You're sitting all day next to a guy with a silver trumpet who's on acid, you're sharing cigarettes and drinking Tabs. And then like a whole Mexican family with nine kids comes in in matching vests and pants and studs and hats, from ages 19 down to 4, and they get up and do "Guadalajara," "Eres Tu?"— remember that? Break your heart, just break your heart . . . I saw Miles Davis there. Professor Irwin Corey. They swing a spotlight around right by the cigarette machine to pick you up:

And nowwww, ladies and gentlemen, the Troubadour is proud to present . . .

And they'd say your name, and they'd walk you up to the stage in the spotlight. I used to watch other acts do that, and I'd be in the audience with my coffee, and I said, "That's it. That's it for me."

You know this group called That Mean Old Man Next Door?
They've got a record called *Tijuana Moon*.
Me: I like the name.
Tom: I just made it up.
Me: Did you?
Tom: Could be the other way. Could be a group called Tijuana
Moon.
Me: Could be. It's confusing sometimes.
Tom: You ever try to get a sandwich made for you in England? It'll
just make you crazy. "Put a little more sauce on that." And it's your
sandwich, you're gonna pay for it *and* you're gonna eat it. But they
look at you like [*snooty voice*], "I won't do it." "Put a little more lettuce
on that for me." "I can't do it." "And don't cut the crust." "I *have* to
cut it off." I used to get in arguments. I used to end up going over the
counter. I'd say, "Gimme that bread, god*damn* it. Let me have that
thing. *I'll* show you how to make a goddamn sandwich." I was young. I
was rude. But there was something real and sincere about my reaction.
[*The waitress approaches with a coffee pot.*]
You got a decaf? I got to calm down.

II.

Driving me back to my hotel in the big black Silverado he calls (today, at
least) Old Reliable, Waits detours to a flower-bedecked makeshift roadside shrine dedicated to the memory of 12-year-old Georgia Lee Moses,
the subject of "Georgia Lee," a lilting Irishy lullaby on *Mule Variations*.
   "It's a good spot," he says as we pull over to a grassy plot of trees and
brush by a freeway onramp. "She'd run away from home, been missing
for like a week. I guess this is where they found the body." He takes a
plastic point-and-click camera from his pocket and shoots a picture.
"Not to make it a racial matter, but it was one of those things where,
you know, she's a black kid, and when it comes to missing children and
unsolved crimes, a lot of it has to do with timing, or publicity . . . and
there was this whole Polly Klaas Foundation up here, while Georgia
Lee did not get any real attention. And I wanted to write a song about
it. At one point I wasn't going to put it on the record, there were too
many songs. But my daughter said, 'Gee, that would *really* be sad—she

gets killed and not remembered and somebody writes a song about it and doesn't put it on the record.' I didn't want to be a part of that."

Waits recorded 25 tracks for the 16-song *Mule Variations*, which takes its title from the fact that "Get Behind the Mule," a low-slung gospel blues more or less about persistence, had been attempted in several styles; but the mule is an apt enough totem for the record, stubbornly itself and not as pretty as a horse. Like Bob Dylan's *Time Out of Mind*, it's a mature work that trades away a young man's flash effects for an older one's plain speaking—a step forward that can sound like a step back—and like that record, it alternates between mutant blues and bravely sentimental ballads. ("It's got a lot of ballads," he says, "which I was nervous about at first," but which makes the album more immediately accessible than the elemental *Bone Machine* or the troll-cabaret *The Black Rider*.) While he has not abandoned his familiar lyrical complement of drifters, town-edge dwellers and sideshow freaks (like the "not conventionally handsome" "Eyeball Kid," whom the singer gives his own birth date), his subject here overwhelmingly is Home. (He will say no more about it than "You write about what you go through.") Waits—who moved several times as a child, and conceived a fondness as an adult (in what might be termed his Bukowski phase) for flophouses and fleabag hostelries, living notoriously for a spell in West Hollywood's Tropicana Motel—was formerly a poet of transients, and of transience; *Mule Variations*, a family man's album, is by contrast founded primarily upon household images: "Evelyn's kitchen," "Beulah's porch." "Never let the weeds get higher / than the garden," he advises in "Get Behind the Mule," while at the "House Where Nobody Lives," "the weeds had grown up / just as high as the drawers," and the unsavory neighbor of "What's He Building?" "has no dog and he has no friends and his lawn is dying." "I hope my pony knows the way home," sings the weary traveler of "Pony." "Picture in a Frame" provides a swell little metaphor for commitment and the civilizing influence of small gestures. "Filipino Box Spring Hog" concerns a barbecue. And in the breathtakingly intimate "Take It with Me," perhaps the most beautiful and most beautifully sung song in his canon, domestic pleasure inspires a vision of transcendent permanence:

> *Children are playing*
> *at the end of the day*

Strangers are singing
on our lawn
It's got to be more
than flesh and bone
All that you've loved
is all you own
. . . I'm gonna take it
with me when I go

"Come On Up to the House," the raucous hymn that follows, appropriately caps the album with a general offer of refuge.

What makes Tom Waits most valuable, and continually attractive to succeeding generations of listeners looking for something . . . nonstandard, is—apart from his heart and his humor—his restlessness, his perfect willingness to destroy the lab for the sake of the experiment. (He's the kid you knew who made models just to blow them up.) Except for *Closing Time*, a singer-songwriter album in an age of singer-songwriters, he's gone his own way, often too far from the pack even to be called *out of step*, but he's been influential around the significant fringes. (Beck, Sparklehorse, Nick Cave, Giant Sand and Los Lobos all owe him something.) Most important, he has never—as pop stars so often do in their middle years—equated quality with either technique or technology; if anything, he's a bit of a Luddite, standing for the "junkyard choir," the real room sound, the unplannable accident. He'd far sooner hit something with a stick than plug something in. There is an element of cultural bravery in all this, even if unintended, and Waits has become a kind of hero to the pop discontent. His appearance last month at the South By Southwest music conference in Austin was the weekend's hot ticket.

Because it gets relatively little airplay—being too strange for the stations that play his chronological contemporaries and altogether unrelated to the business of modern rock radio—Waits' music is spread most often, like a seditionary pamphlet, from friend to friend, lover to lover, parent to child, teacher to student—a conspiracy of Tom. On the Internet one finds testaments from fans who first heard him . . .

. . . in the fifth or sixth grade [when] my science teacher listened to Bone Machine *every day before we students arrived . . . from my ex-*

*boyfriend, and I am certain that it was the best thing he gave me at all
. . . from a Swedish girl driving thru Omaha with my cousin . . . in my
AP History class . . . in Trondheim, Norway, as an exchange student . . .
in my dad's record collection . . . via a girl I fell in love with during my
early years as a poor starving acting student in a small Miami art college—she was a dancer who ultimately stepped on my heart and squashed
it into the cheap beige carpet that covered the floor in my dorm room.
Thank god for her, anyway . . .*

They are every last one of them hoping he will come to their town,
now that he has a record to promote. But Waits, who has scant patience for touring ("I like to come home before I get angry"), will likely
make only a few appearances in a handful of "major markets."

"You don't feel the need to get up in front of a crowd and play, obviously?" I ask as we drive along a frontage road.

Tom: Not unless I can wear a leotard and a bathing cap and some
fishing boots. That's what I'm looking for, some new channel, so you
don't feel like you're doing a medley of your hits—not that I've had
hits. I'm just saying that after a while you sit down at the piano and
start *feeling* like a lounge act. Everybody wants to hear this song or
that song . . . This used to be all fruit stands, eucalyptus trees, used-car
lots. There's an old Buick right there. Is that a Buick or an Olds? See
the one I'm talking about? The four-door?

Me: It's the only one you *could* be talking about.

Tom: It's an Olds . . . fifteen hundred dollars—Jee-*sus*. My first car
cost me $50. It was a '55 Buick Special.

Me: Did it run?

Tom: Oh God yes. Swing low, sweet chariot. It was just a . . . boat.

Me: Do you have other cars than this?

Tom: I got an old Caddy. I got a '72 white Suburban that no one in
the family will ride in. My vehicles have always been humiliating for
the kids. This one, it's like a motel, and they even complain about this.
I say, "You're nuts. You could *live* in this car."

Me: A family of five.

Tom: Comfort. Roadability. Reliability—hence the name "Old Reliable." Smoked windows. For anonymity. 'Cause there's times when you just want to sneak in, do your business and sneak out.

III.

Later that same day. An old roadhouse Italian restaurant 40 minutes out into the countryside, amid the green hills and spotted cows. "It's got the largest Elvis Presley decanter collection in the West," Waits had said. "That's something you gotta see. And they also have this tilted floor, and glasses fly out of your hand. I was gonna suggest perhaps later this afternoon meeting me there to see if we could get a glass to fly out of our hands. It's very chic. Big line around the block. Guy wears a uniform at the door. Little band. Very chichi. I don't even know if you can get in the way you're dressed. . . . I never go anywhere without a tuxedo. At least the upper half of a tuxedo. Might be able to get away with your own pants, if you stay seated. In fact, you might want to bring a chair that you're already in, and just sort of scoot towards the door."

No one is at the door, in a uniform or in line. The interior is strictly red checks and paneled walls. There's no band, but there is an old upright piano, an enormous rack of antlers, a collection of dusty paintings, including one of John Wayne, "the patron saint," says Waits, "of all Italian restaurants." And in wall-mounted glass cases, dozens of decanters of varying shapes and sizes—nary an Elvis, however.

Me: Do you feel isolated out here?

Tom: I guess I used to, but I don't really anymore. I think what happens is that when people move to the sticks, they still want all their products and services, and they get out here and then gradually the place they thought was bucolic and serene starts looking like all the places that they left, because they brought with them all the things that made the place they used to live in look so . . . crappy. And they have to keep moving further away, but they're really bringing it all with them.

When I went back to Los Angeles after having not been there for a while, I was surprised at how many *words* you see when you're driving. It's *shocking*. Every square inch of space that you can see from your windshield there are words. *Hundreds* and *hundreds* of words. In places you never would imagine. And I found myself unable to drive safely. Even after seven years of traffic school, I was having problems with focus and attention. I was going to lose my diploma.

There was an earthquake in 1812 in the Midwest that changed the direction of the Mississippi River. Did you know that? Church bells rang as far away as Philadelphia.

Me: From the earthquake?

Tom: I don't mean it was Sunday.

Me: Is this how you spend your time?

Tom: I can't finish a book, you know, but I snack on information. The origin of pumpernickel bread, for example. Napoleon's horse ate the best bread. All the soldiers were livid. What they really wanted was to eat as well as Napoleon's horse ate. And he ate pumpernickel. His horse's name was Nikolai. Nikolai . . . pumper*nickel*.

Me: I think of that as a German word, and yet it's apparently from the French.

Tom: And yet. And yet. It's just one of those things that . . . gives you a reason to live.

Me: Keeps you mystified.

Tom: Like this place. [*Portentously:*] Notice the plastic pitcher. The plastic tumbler. It was at one time glass. You know how the nicer restaurants have a piece of glass? They finally just said . . .

Me: Flew off the table too many times.

Tom: The overhead was just amazing.

[*A waiter approaches.*]

Waiter [*noticing the tape recorder*]: You're not going to tape me, are you?

Tom: No. We're going to listen to music. But only we can hear it. We're dogs.

Waiter: Well, crank it up.

Tom: It is cranked up. What do you mean, crank it up?

[*A puzzled pause. After which Waits orders lasagna.*]

Waiter: And some soup?

Tom: I'll have some soup. In preparation for my lasagna.

[*The waiter withdraws.*]

Me: You're really putting on the feedbag this evening.

Tom: It's a matter of being polite. If you don't eat, they'll get you later. "Well, why'd you come in here? To laugh at us? To laugh at our decanters? Our crooked floor?"

Me: When you were living in Hollywood 20 years ago, did you ever imagine you'd wind up a country squire?

Tom: Then, no. Now, neither. You do get addicted to noise living in the city. There's a great deal you have to recover from if you leave. When I first came out to a small town, there's a guy with a dustpan and a whiskbroom, a policeman, in the middle of the street, sweeping up glass. And then I ordered a coffee in a little café—the waitress says [*sweetly*], "Hi, how are you?" "I don't think that's any of your business, how I am. I'm just drinking my coffee." Took me a while.

Me: You had the shell on. The protective coating.

Tom: It's a little drop of Retsin. That outer candy shell that seals in the freshness.

Me: Do you feel countrified yet?

Tom: I don't know. I hope I'm becoming more eccentric. More room, you know. More room in the brain.

Me: Did you feel limited by Hollywood or New York?

Tom: Well, gee, after a while, it just gets . . . change is good. I can go there if I want. They didn't get rid of it.

Me: No, they did. It's gone.

Tom: I was afraid that might happen if I left. But I have film; I have a lot of it on film . . . Western Avenue, you know, is the longest street in the world. I hear it runs down to Ensenada.

Me: Tierra del Fuego.

Tom: La Paz. You get on Western and you just keep driving and it's pretty unbelievable. A lot of hair-care places. I think there's probably more hair-care places on Western than there are in Hollywood. You think of Hollywood as obsessed with its hair, but folks who live way out on Western are just as interested in hair care and hair-care products.

[*The waiter brings soup.*]

Tom: What was that big high-speed chase that came through here in the '30s—remember that?

Waiter: Gosh, I forgot about that.

Tom: There was a bank robbery in the city, and it was like a . . .

Waiter: You're talking about the '30s or the '70s?

Tom: The '30s. There was a shootout at the creamery—you know the creamery? Big shootout. Three guys dead. The car was on fire, the whole place.

Waiter: I missed out on that one.

Tom: I thought maybe you'd heard something recently about it. It's all in the Library of Congress.

Waiter: That's the first time I heard it.

[*The waiter withdraws.*]

Tom: They don't like to talk about it here—afraid they're gonna lose business. I think they stole like half a million dollars. On back roads from Petaluma. Like a Bogart movie. There was a dairy right behind here, and that's where they had this big shootout. . . . And afterwards they all came here. And they all made up.

Me: They sat down together.

Tom: You gotta eat. You have to stop a minute and just . . . eat. My stepfather's mom dated Al Capone.

Me: Really?

Tom: Went out on a few dates.

Me: Nothing serious.

Tom: I don't know.

Me: Could have turned into something.

Tom: Could have developed. Who knows? How much of what really happened do you tell? The reason that history is so distorted is 'cause most people aren't talking. Most people really don't want you to know the truth.

[*The waiter returns with lasagna.*]

Waiter: Tom, you ready for that lasagna?

Tom: Um, yeah . . . I was going to ask you about the Elvis decanters. Was there an abundance of Elvis decanters here for a while? Or did I just create that, out of a desire to see more of them?

Waiter: Well, that may have been. The bartender at one time, who was married to Dolores, who's bartending now, he was an impersonator of Elvis. Maybe you saw him.

Tom: No, I could have sworn I saw . . .

Waiter: I think there's a couple in the bar.

Tom: There's *got* to be.

Waiter: He may have taken them when he left.

Tom: There it is, you see.

Waiter: The '30s, though.

Tom: The '30s. A high-speed chase. Big bank job. A shootout. All
along the Shoreline Highway. Ended up at the creamery. Three guys
dead. And afterwards they came over here. It's in the library.

Now I've got to ask a question. Those stories about the glassware.
I'm surprised you brought a glass. You set a glass down on a table
here. There are certain places here where a glass will fly off the table
and hit the wall?

Waiter: I've heard that. [*Pointing*] Over there.

Tom: Is that why there's no glassware on that particular table? First
thing I noticed—that you'd gone with the plastic cups. A safety feature. What else has happened over there?

Waiter: Pictures.

Tom: Pictures have fallen?

Waiter: Fallen off the wall. That one . . .

Tom: I just saw it move.

Waiter [*concerned*]: Do you want your check now?

Tom: No. I came *for* that.

[*The waiter withdraws.*]

Tom: You notice on trash day how somebody's going through the
trash, you stick your head out the window and say, "What the hell you
doing in there?" And then they leave and you start going through your
own trash? You start re-evaluating the quality of your own trash, wondering if you made some terrible mistake, if you've thrown out something that is now going to be essential to your life.

Kathleen and I came up with this idea of doing music that's
surrural—it's surreal and it's rural, it's surrural. [*sings*] *Everybody's doin'*
it doin' it doin' it. Surrural. She'll start kind of talking in tongues, and I
take it all down. She goes places . . . I can't get to those places. Too, I
don't know . . . pragmatic. She's the egret of the family. I'm the mule. I
write mostly from the world, the news, and what I really see from the
counter, or hear. She's more impressionistic. She dreams like Hierony-
mus Bosch. She's been a lot of things. She drove a truck for a while.
Had her own pilot's license. Worked as a soda jerk. Ran a big hotel in
Miami. She was going to be a nun. When I met her, she was at the
corner of nun or ruin. So together it's *You wash, I'll dry.* It works.

She's exposing me to all kinds of things I'd never listen to. It's kind
of like trying on hats. "Is that me?" You have to kind of let it all down

and not worry about what's hip and what's cool. I guess I'd been trying to find some music that's my own music—it's like home cooking, you know? Of course if I'm making something just for *me*, I'm not very picky, I might just pour some sugar in my ear, suck on a piece of dirt in my mouth, light my hair on fire. I'm fine with that.

What I did for a long time was put my head on other people's bodies. You look for your own niche. How have all these things synthesized in you? You take your Elmer Bernstein and you take your 7 inches of throbbing pink Jesus and you put it together and you try to make some sense out of it. Melt it, crush it, saw it, solder it. I've always had diverse influences, and I never know how to reconcile them. There was a point where I wasn't sure whether I was a lounge act or . . .

Me: A main-room act.

Tom: Yeah. "Am I too hip for the room?" I don't know. "I'm not hip *enough* for the room." Or am I just, like, you know, a garage sale? It's an ongoing dilemma. Where are you, what are you? In popular music, the key word is "popular," and popular usually connects something very temporary—*once* popular, then they call you *once*-popular.

Me: Ninety-five percent of everything is temporary.

Tom: I'm okay with that. . . . But it's nice to think that when you're making your music and you bring it out, someone's going to pick it up. And who knows when or where? I listen to stuff that's 50 years old or older than that and bring it into myself. And so you are in a way having communion and fellowship with folks you have yet to meet, who will someday hopefully bring your record home and—you know, they're running a little lingerie shop down on Magnolia—and put it on, and bring it together with the sounds that they hear in their own head. It's nice to be part of the dismemberment of linear time.

The meal is finished, the check paid. On the way out, half a dozen decanters representing Elvis Presley in the several stages of his fine, fine, superfine career are discovered in the bar. Outside, a red Corvette is parked. Waits hands me his camera, and I take his picture posing proprietarily by the car. For a second, he looks about 17. Then he climbs into his hulking black Silverado and drives away, into the cow-covered hills, back to the family, as night falls on the countryside.

Money Boss Player

Lost in the legend of Sean "Puffy" Combs' cultural-moment-defining birthday bash last November 4 is the curious story of the first notable to "arrive." That is, the first player, one who had arrived—in terms of "blowing up"—years before 29-year-old Puff, but with much the same mind-set and in much the same style.

There he was—"like the first boy at a high school dance," says hip hop writer Nelson George—at a minute past 10, strolling solo into Cipriani Wall Street. He looked around, shifted caterpillar eyebrows side to side, and spotted a place to alight: *Ah, a throne.*

The ticket clutchers, all giddy with big-night expectation, were just starting to drift into the cavernous marble hall. (Cipriani's, a grand ballroom of a lunch joint, is Manhattan's latest testament to the fact that the '80s, *his* decade, never ended—conspicuous consumption only got more acceptable.) Waiters already tipsy on free Cristal sailed around in tight tuxes, hoisting lacquered trays. This might have been a coming-out party of sorts for hip hop—the scions of Manhattan society had been angling for tickets for weeks—but the man whose rock-star name is The Donald seemed used to it all.

Casually, he mounted the stairs ascending to the comfy VIP section and settled into a centrally located armchair. He leaned back, looking studious and pleased, a corporate king in his trademark blue suit and shiny Ferragamo shoes. If Canibus, say, had sat in that chair, somebody would probably have popped a cap in his drink faster than you can say

"L.L."—that was *Sean's* chair. But that was The Donald up there. And he had just anointed himself First Guest of the Birthday Party.

The word NOTORIOUS flashed on the wall above him in blue neon graffiti.

Trump Daddy smiled.

West Coast, East Coast: Meet the Gold Coast, and the player most. Donald J. Trump, 52, is such a player he doesn't even *listen* to hip hop music. "The problem is," he explains, "my life is so *wild* I just don't have time."

And yet Trump has blessed the mike on numerous rap records. Last year his voice could be heard on Method Man's megasmash *Tical 2000: Judgement Day* (Def Jam) and Pras' somewhat-less-than-megasmash *Ghetto Supastar* (Ruffhouse/Columbia). "I hear I'm all over the place," Trump says offhandedly, although, he admits, he's never actually listened to any of the tracks.

"I'd never heard of Method Man," he confesses, "until Russell [Simmons, co-founder of Def Jam] asked me to call and leave him a message."

"Hey, Method Man," he freestyled onto the Wu-Tang rapper's answering machine. "This is Donald Trump, and I'm in Palm Beach, and we're all waiting for your album. Let's get going, man—everybody's waiting for this album!"

Sure. You can picture it: Trump, Puffy, and Martha Stewart, all playing Nintendo on the 50-inch screen down at Mar-a-Lago—the opulent seaside estate Trump bought from the old-money Post family and turned into a controversial party-hardy, celebrity-studded playhouse. (It's also where Puffy was reportedly caught getting busy in the sand with an unidentified woman last spring.)

"I know who Method Man is *now*," Trump adds.

But "Pras?" he asks, voice drifting off. Still not quite sure.

"Now, after knowing you," Trump says on Pras' album, "I know that you're gonna be right up there, and I hope very soon you're gonna be in the leagues with me. So good luck, man. And do good!"

But no matter if Trump Daddy can't keep it all straight in his slightly oversize head. The feelings of kinship are strong—on both sides. Method Man breaks it down this way: "I like Trump's style. It's like,

'I'm rich, fuck y'all, I build my buildings and put my name on them. Fuck y'all.'"

"How weird was it walking into my dad's booth at the U.S. Open and seeing Puff Daddy there?" asks Trump's daugher Ivanka, 17, a hip hop fan. "Or going to the Grammys, the phone rings, and my dad's like, 'Yo, Puff, what's up?' And I'm like, 'You are *not* talking to Puff Daddy!'"

Trump was hip hop before he himself knew. For one thing, he was rich—a billionaire who reveled in his money. And he didn't care who cared. He was a real estate mogul, and he built big, and he built flashy, and yes, he put his name on everything from Trump Tower to Trump Plaza to Trump Parc to the Trump International Hotel and Tower. When people dissed him—whether it was city government, banks, or the media—his response was indeed, *Fuck off.*

"Every time I see Tina Brown [media queen and former editor of *Vanity Fair* and *The New Yorker*]," The Donald says, "I give her the finger." (Brown printed some player-hating pieces about him. "She treated me like total shit!") The Top Ten Comeback Tips from Trump's 1998 best-seller, *Trump: The Art of the Comeback* (Times Books), read almost like a rap song. (The Lox's '98 Bad Boy Entertainment hit, "Money, Power & Respect," comes to mind.) "Be paranoid . . . Be passionate . . . Be lucky . . . Get even." Puffy is currently writing his own book on the art of blowing up, possibly inspired by Trump's many best-sellers.

"Trump is respected by people in hip hop because he's not a corporate guy," says George, author of *Hip Hop America* (Viking Penguin, 1998). "He's a self-made entrepreneur, and that's key to the hip hop mentality. They respect him for being a 'fuck you' hero."

By midnight that night of The Party, Cipriani's was packed and pounding with the music of the hip hop superstars now constellating in the room: There was Mase and Jay-Z and Missy Elliott and Heavy D and crazy Busta Rhymes clowning, his mouth opening in a ghoulish laugh. Puff Daddy still hadn't arrived yet. His big entrance would come right after Muhammad Ali's.

And there was The Donald, amid all the flashing neon, still up in the elevated VIP section, still sitting in The Seat.

Meanwhile, Fergie, Duchess of York, and Kevin Costner didn't seem to be able to find chairs.

Stripper girls in Plexiglas booths were rubbing at their leather thongs, making men in baggy zoot suits go crazy.

"I think Puff Daddy is a great guy," said Trump.

A security guard ventured over and asked him to find another seating arrangement. "Sean said he wanted me to sit with him," Trump said blandly. And he never moved.

"I've been around the world / And Ay-Ay-Ay / I've been player hated." Puff Daddy, on his 1997 hit "Been Around the World."

Trump can relate. A whole battery of power players from the upper echelons of New York society—including Victoria Newhouse, wife of media mogul S. I. Newhouse Jr., and billionaire David Koch—are reportedly gearing up to try to block Trump's most recent development: Trump World Tower, the world's tallest residential building (some 90 stories), set to rise on a plot of land smack-dab across the street from the United Nations. Newscasting legend and elder statesman of classiness Walter Cronkite has called designs for Trump's pet project "gross."

"Those people are going to end up moving into my building," Trump told *The New York Observer.* "'Cause it's much better than where they live."

The naysayers never did understand him. Not his love of excess or publicity or gold-plating. They never got that Trump . . . is *Trump.*

"He's shunned socially by old money," says Jessica Rosenblum, president of Stress Entertainment and a longtime hip hop maven. "But now hip hop is saying 'Hey, you're our kind,' and he's saying, 'Hey, cool.'"

"Donald doesn't *have* flavor," offers one recording-industry executive, who asked not be named, "but he knows where the flavor *is.*"

Cut to Puffy and Donald shaking hands at the Polo grounds in Long Island's exclusive Hamptons residential area—in effect thumbing their noses at all those stuffy longtime residents who, not so many decades ago, would have found some convenient way to keep either one of them from attending their lawn parties. Now, those very same people routinely pull out all the stops to try to get into one of Puffy's Hamptons parties—where Trump can always be found, possibly sitting in Puffy's chair.

Hip hop has seen itself in Donald Trump, and vice versa. "He has been taken by the energy and the chutzpah of the rap world," says George, "especially the entrepreneurs."

"The Hamptons has a certain rigid society," Trump says. "And people like Puffy and Russell and Andrew Harrell [president of Bad Boy Entertainment] have done really well within it. The reason is because they're fun. The Hamptons people are boring."

By the same token, some people in the hip hop world seem to think Donald Trump is fun too. "There's a lot of people out there who have money but they're not all accepted. Donald is," says DJ Funkmaster Flex, with whom The Donald spent time at Interscope Records honcho Ted Field's Fourth of July party last summer in the Hamptons.

If Bill Clinton is, as Nobel Prize–winning author Toni Morrison insists, "the first black president," then, using the same weird logic, Trump may be the first African-American billionaire. He doesn't see color if it gets in the way of having a good time, and he seems to have the best time when he's kicking it with his homies. "I think that these hip hop guys are smart, and they're fun, and I don't give a shit, because if I didn't like them I wouldn't bother," he says. "Because I don't *need* anybody, and I don't *need* anything."

"Hey, Russell," The Donald says. "Will you send me a lot of money, please?"

On a fine winter morning, Trump is poised on his own throne high in Trump Tower talking on the telephone to the godfather of hip hop.

"We told Donald he was the illest man alive, and he called a doctor," says Russell Simmons through the white noise of the speakerphone.

"I love ya," says The Donald with a smile.

"We told him he was the *shit*—and he said, 'Fuck you, too!'" says Simmons.

"I love ya, Russell, I love ya, baby," Trump says. "I was really mad about that one—Russell calling me 'the shit,'" he continues, hanging up the phone. "I thought Russell liked me! Kara Young had to explain it to me."

It was Simmons who introduced Trump to model Young—now a former flame of *both* men—after he and Marla Maples split. It's Simmons and Harrell whom Trump hangs out with several times a week into the wee hours at Moomba, N.Y.C.'s watering hole for the ultra chic. It was Simmons and Harrell Trump picked as judges for last year's Miss Universe pageant in Hawaii. "You know I own that, right?" Trump asks.

The skyline of Manhattan stretches out behind him like a personal kingdom.

"I own the Empire State Building, too," he says. "Did you know that?"

What could be more hip hop than self-promotion? The Slick Ricks, the L.L. Cool Js, the Jay-Zs—The Donald's right up there with them in representing for self. He tosses a copy of *Crain's New York Business* across his mahogany desk. It rates his Trump Organization the third most successful privately held corporation in New York City. (*Forbes* sets Trump's net worth at $1.5 billion.) "We're bigger than we ever were!" Trump crows.

It wasn't so long ago, though, that he was assed-out. After his celebrated rise in the '80s, he plunged to more than $900 million in debt in 1990. The Donald admits he stopped working as hard. "I was having too much fun!"

But now he's back. And "a *lot* of people in the music business can relate to that," says Funkmaster Flex. "He made it happen, and he came back to make it happen again."

"Trump," says Rosenblum, "has a ghetto pass."

And he couldn't feel more at home with the pantheon of hip hop entrepreneurs with whom he's recently become so chummy. "They're all moguls, and they're all great businessmen," Trump says. "They have a real sense of where the market's going, they have a sense of the future—and that's the ultimate businessperson."

Stumbling onto a concept, he adds, "I think hip hop has done more for race relations, and more for respect among everyone, than anything. Because these guys really are respected. I can tell you—hey, the most important white people have *total* respect for these guys."

HEATHER HEILMAN

Lawsuit Blues

"Do you know how good you are?" Tom Hoskins once asked elderly, belatedly famous Mississippi John Hurt.

"Yeah, I know it," Hurt said. "And I been knowin' it."

Occasional bragging notwithstanding, Mississippi John Hurt was a gentle, sweet-natured man. Those who knew him say so, and you can see it in the photographs and hear it in his voice. He was small, barely over 5 feet. His eyes were kind. There was usually a brown fedora tilted toward the back of his head and a cigarette in the corner of his mouth.

Mississippi John Hurt was not a Delta bluesman, though he is often thought of as such. Scholars consider him more of a folk artist than a bluesman. His voice is calm, bemused, free of any emotional anguish. His music seems simple to the casual listener, but he is a virtuoso guitarist whose intricate, layered style continues to influence other musicians. He died a modestly famous but disappointed man, upset by the battles that had broken out over efforts to control him and his career.

Last May in Grenada, Mississippi, a judge decided that 109-year-old Gertrude Conley Hurt, the musician's first wife, and 17 of her descendants are the rightful heirs to the estate of Mississippi John Hurt. They won the right to share in Hurt's royalties, which these days amounts to less than $20,000 a year.

The decision was the result of a suit filed by Gertrude's family against Hurt's manager Tom Hoskins and Rounder Records. The suit also claimed that Hoskins, who rediscovered John Hurt in the early 1960s, manipulated Hurt and essentially robbed the musician of the proceeds of his career. Plaintiffs asked the court to set aside a 1963 royalty contract they claimed was unfair, but the court dismissed the charge. Gertrude's family says that's because their lawyers bungled the case, and are considering refiling the suit.

According to the May ruling, Gertrude's family will share royalties with Hoskins and John William "Man" Hurt, John Hurt's son by Jessie Lee Hurt, the woman he spent 40 years with and who was or was not his second wife, depending on whom you ask. So far, though, the family hasn't collected a cent, unless you count the change tourists leave on John Hurt's grave.

"We're just trying to right a wrong. I want my grandmother to get justice," says Lonnie Conley Hurt, the grandson of Gertrude and John Hurt. "Money would be good, but it's not about the money. It's about this family."

Hoskins says he loved John Hurt like a father.

"I promised him I would take care of Jessie and her two grandkids, and that was my intention," he says.

This is not a simple story.

It all began with a fiddling contest in Winona, Mississippi, where a white fiddler named Willie Narmour came to the attention of a talent scout for Okeh Phonograph Corporation. Narmour told the man about another talented musician in the area, a guitarist named John Hurt. And so the first white stranger came to knock on Hurt's door, asking him to come to the big city and make records.

In 1928, at the age of 35, John Hurt traveled from his home in Avalon, Mississippi, to Memphis, where he made his first record, a single for the Okeh label.

"I sat on a chair and they pushed the microphone right up close to my mouth, and told me not to move after they found the right position," Hurt later said. "Oh, I was nervous, and my neck was sore for days after." The song was "Nobody's Dirty Business" with "Frankie" on the back side. He was paid $20 a song.

Then he went back to Avalon, where he finished the farming season as a sharecropper. That winter, the record company invited him to New York City to do more recording. He spent about a week in the city and cut an album's worth of material, as well as a Maxwell House Coffee jingle. One of the songs he recorded was "Avalon Blues," about his tiny hometown in Carroll County where the hill country rolls out into the Delta. He wrote the song one homesick night in New York and recorded it the next day.

It could have been the beginning of a successful and storied career. But it didn't work out that way. The Depression came. Hurt's records made little impact. Back in Avalon, Hurt farmed cotton and corn on 13 acres and turned over half his crop to the white landowner. On Saturday nights he played dances in Avalon and surrounding towns.

Thirty-five years passed.

In the early 1950s, Folkways Records rereleased a couple of the songs Hurt had recorded for Okeh as part of its American Folk Music series. One of the songs was "Avalon Blues." Hurt didn't know about it—the people at Folkways assumed he was dead—but the record gained him a small group of new fans.

In Washington, D.C., 20-year-old Tom Hoskins was learning to play the guitar when his friend Dick Spottswood turned him on to Mississippi John Hurt.

"I thought, I wanna play like that," Hoskins says. "How the hell is he doing that?"

When he heard "Avalon Blues," a bell went off in Hoskins' head.

"Everybody thought he was dead. Nobody knew. But I thought 'Avalon Blues'? 'Mississippi' John Hurt? I started looking for Avalon, Mississippi, on the map," Hoskins says. He couldn't find it in a current road atlas, but he finally located the town in an atlas from 1898. With a tape deck and $100 in his pocket, he hit the road.

In March of 1963 he arrived in downtown Avalon, which consisted of Stinson's general store, post office, and gas pump. Locals in the store told him he could find Hurt about a mile up the hill, at the third mailbox on the right. Hoskins knocked on the door of the little shack situated in the middle of a cotton field.

"Yeah, who that?" came a voice inside.

"I'm looking for Mississippi John Hurt," Hoskins said.

"Heh, heh, heh," came the sly laugh.

Hurt opened the door with a wide grin, which fell when he saw an unknown white man standing at the door. Jessie, his second wife, ran out the back door to the house of landowner Mr. A. R. Perkins for help in this unexpected crisis.

"What do you want?" Mr. Perkins asked when he arrived.

"I want to listen to him play the guitar," Hoskins answered.

"He ain't got a guitar," Mr. Perkins said.

"He can play mine," Hoskins said.

Hurt hadn't played for two years, but his skills were still there.

"I couldn't believe I was hearing what I was hearing and seeing what I was seeing," Hoskins says.

Hurt had been with Jessie for more than 35 years and was raising their son Man Hurt's two kids when Hoskins met him.

"She was the love of his life," Hoskins says. "He married Gertrude when he was young 'cause he wanted some, but Jessie was the one."

Gertrude remembers it differently. Withered by advanced age, she lives in a humble four-room frame house in Greenwood and is looked after by her grandchildren. She spends her days in a recliner in the corner of the living room, watching television and the comings and goings of her extended family. Despite her physical frailty, she is mentally alert and can be quite vehement on the subject of Jessie. She says the rift in her decade-old marriage was caused by conflict between John's music and her increasing involvement in the church.

"But he never stopped supporting me," Gertrude says. After she and John split up in the mid-1920s, she entered into a common-law marriage with Willie Conley. She remembers Jessie as a "loose woman" who traveled from southern Mississippi to a logging camp near Avalon in the hopes of finding a man. She claims Jessie was already pregnant with Man Hurt when she met John.

Gertrude says John never married Jessie. However, a search in the Leflore County Courthouse turned up the 1927 marriage record of John Hurt and Jessie Nelson. But John never legally divorced Gertrude, with whom he had two children. John once told Tom Hoskins that when he and Gertrude decided to split up he talked to his white boss about it, and his boss told him he would take care of it. In those days legal niceties weren't thought to apply to poor black sharecroppers. No one expected that John Hurt would one day have a legacy to fight over. When Hoskins met Hurt, he was making $28 a month taking care of Mr. Perkins' cows, while Jessie did the Perkins' laundry.

Avalon was a community of a few hundred people then. In such a small place, Gertrude's children and grandchildren couldn't have avoided knowing John and Jessie, and there's no reason why their relationship wouldn't be friendly. But Gertrude's grandchildren say they were more than just friendly with John and Jessie. They were family.

"We knew Miss Jessie wasn't our real grandmother, but we treated her like a grandmother," granddaughter Irene Smith says. Gertrude sometimes looked after Man Hurt, while Gertrude's descendants stayed close to Jessie even after John's death.

But Man Hurt remembers it differently. In a letter to the Greenwood paper last year, he said the only father and mother he ever knew were John Smith Hurt and Jessie Lee Hurt. "The only reason they are trying to claim my father is trying to get his royalty," he wrote of Gertrude and her grandchildren. "They only want his money."

"That hurt," says Lonnie Conley Hurt.

"He was here two months ago, sat down, and had dinner at our table," he comments about Man Hurt.

Lonnie Conley Hurt navigates his battered Mercury along a rutted dirt road in the hills of Carroll County. As the windows rattle, he comments, "This car gets good gas mileage. Sixteen miles a gallon."

Lonnie, now 51, has returned to Mississippi after many years in Indianapolis. He had to leave Mississippi to make a living, but he always knew he'd be back. His family is here, and he loves the countryside. "The fishing is good, and you can hunt anything you want," he says.

"Mississippi hasn't changed much," he says, a polite way to say racism is still alive and well. But he's older and has learned how to get along. "If some people don't want to be with other people, well, that's their right," he comments.

At the top of the hill are two modest ranch houses. One belongs to Lonnie's mother and the other to his sister Mary Hurt Wright, who teaches in Chicago but spends her summers here. Behind Mary's house is a decrepit three-room, tin-roofed shotgun shack with holes in the floor, hay in the middle room, and no doors in the door frames. This is the house where John Hurt lived with Jessie all those years, the house where Tom Hoskins found him one afternoon in 1963. The family has moved it up the hill to their property to prevent it from being torn down. Lonnie wants to clean it out, fix the roof and floor, and keep it as a remembrance. Mississippi John Hurt fans would be welcome to visit.

Lonnie says that as a young man, his grandfather was the most influential person in his life. As he looks at the house where his grandfather lived and thinks about the conflict that now divides his family, he begins to weep.

"If you could have known my grandfather you'd understand," he says. "My grandfather was a very, very special person. I'm not talking just because of his music or the money he made, I'm talking as a person. When I was a kid he would talk to me. He encouraged me to make something of myself, without ever yelling at me. He taught me not to be bitter about the way things are. He's a part of me."

Everything changed when Tom Hoskins showed up and talked John Hurt into traveling to Washington, D.C. Hurt would later say he first agreed to go because he thought Hoskins was "the F.B.I."

"My grandfather left his whole way of life," Mary Hurt Wright says. "Everything was altered."

Hoskins, Dick Spottswood, and Spottswood's wife drove down to Mississippi to bring Hurt back to Washington. As they were loading up the car, Mr. Perkins suddenly "remembered" that Hurt owed him $100 for feed and seed. He couldn't leave until he paid up, Perkins said. It was common for landowners to keep sharecroppers tied-down with imaginary debts, and Hoskins knew it.

"Are you sure it's exactly $100," he asked Perkins, "not $97.50?"

But Spottswood's wife, with a cooler head, took $100 out of her purse and handed it to Perkins, while Hoskins commented that he should have held out for $1,000.

Hoskins tells this story as a commentary about the ways of the good ole boys, but another listener might hear something else in it. Some might think, here is a white man buying from another white man the right to a black man's labors. Or, if that is too harsh a judgment of Hoskins, Lonnie would say it's also too harsh a portrait of Perkins, a man Lonnie remembers as far kinder and more generous than most white landowners, who protected his workers from the Klan and whom John Hurt always called on when he visited Avalon after the move.

In Washington, Hurt signed a contract with Music Research, Inc., a company formed by Hoskins and Spottswood with Hoskins as president.

Gertrude's family still believes the contract was unfair. According to Irene Smith, her grandfather was only barely literate and probably didn't understand the three-page document.

"He took advantage of him because he knew he couldn't read and write," Mary Hurt Wright says. "My grandfather wouldn't have signed it if he understood it. But he was a sharecropper all his life. If Hoskins gave him a few hundred dollars, that seemed like good money."

It might be, though, that she and her family have an inflated idea of how much Hurt's music earned for anyone.

According to the contract, Music Research and Hurt agreed to a 50/50 split of all Hurt's earnings, whether from recordings or performances. For recordings made by Music Research, Hurt was to receive 15 cents per record sold, in addition to 2 cents for every song that was his own composition. In other words, for an album of 12 songs, each written by Hurt, he would receive 39 cents for each record sold. This was at a time when an album retailed for between $1.50 and $3. It also gave Music Research power of attorney over Hurt's affairs and exclusive rights to make or arrange recordings. The contract was originally for five years and promised Hurt that he would earn at least $500 in that time.

In his defense in the lawsuit, Hoskins produced a slew of affidavits of record-industry experts, who said the contract Hurt signed was in line with industry standards and comparable to those of Lightning Hopkins, Mississippi Fred McDowell, and Big Joe Williams. If anything, Hurt's contract was more generous than most. But just because a contract was typical doesn't necessarily mean it was fair.

Charles Kingman Mitchell, a lawyer for the National Association of Independent Record Distributors and Manufacturers, discussed underhanded record company practices in his affidavit.

"Unfair record company accounting practices often wiped out all royalties, no matter what the artist's contract provided," he said. "In general, if an artist of Mr. Hurt's stature was paid at all it was because of the personal integrity of some individual at the record company rather than because of enforceable contract provisions. The system was entirely corrupt."

"There is, in my opinion, nothing at all wrong with the agreement, given its time and circumstances," he wrote.

According to Hoskins, the contract was never enforced during Hurt's lifetime. Instead, all the proceeds of his music went directly to Hurt. And Hoskins says his work for Hurt went far beyond the normal duties of a musician's manager. He drove John and Jessie around since neither could drive a car. He enrolled grandchildren Andrew Lee and Ella Mae in school and sent them to summer camp. He took them to the doctor, paid for their clothes, and bought them groceries.

In Washington, Hurt recorded 39 songs for the Library of Congress, the last a love song dedicated to Jessie. In July 1963, at the age of 70, he made an appearance at the Newport Folk Festival.

"He was an absolute hit," Hoskins says. "He played guitar like nobody else did."

Then he went home to pick cotton, but in a month he was back up north to play the Philadelphia Folk Festival. He was lauded in *Time* magazine and the *New York Times*, and appeared on the *Tonight Show*. That fall, Hurt, along with Jessie and their two grandchildren, moved to an apartment in Washington, D.C., where Hurt made recordings and played in coffeehouses and on college campuses.

Even at the height of his popularity, according to Hoskins, Hurt's income was modest at best.

"While the fees for his appearances were very respectable, he was not able to work as often as a younger performer might be able. Additionally, someone had to travel with him, which added expenses for food, tickets, etc.," Hoskins wrote in an affidavit. Others have contended Hurt could have made more money if his career had been managed better.

Mississippi John Hurt was suddenly famous, but he could never get used to that fact. He was a 70-year-old product of the segregated South who was always a little uneasy around his white fans.

"He had a certain amount of disbelief that all these young people just adored him," Hoskins says. And although Hurt liked the attention and the travel, he was not entirely happy.

Dick Spottswood had moved Hurt into an apartment in northeast Washington, D.C., a crime-ridden inner-city neighborhood. Hoskins thought he should have been living in Takoma Park, Maryland, an integrated, Bohemian suburban area.

"He was miserable being stuck there," Hoskins says. "He was more comfortable in Mississippi." Hoskins and Spottswood had a falling out over this and other questions about Hurt's career, and Music Research fell apart. Hurt was caught in the middle and unhappy about the way he was being treated financially. Some of his Northern relatives intervened and fired, or attempted to fire, Hoskins.

After two years in Washington, Hurt packed up and went back to Mississippi. While some of his biographers have written that he bought a house there, Mary Hurt Wright says that isn't true.

"My grandfather never owned a house in his life." Instead, she says he lived in poverty in a rented apartment in Grenada and "could barely eat."

Hoskins says he helped Hurt out as much as he could.

"All the money went directly to John," he says. "But it wasn't much more than nickels and dimes. I couldn't live on it."

Nobody disputes the fact that John Hurt died in his sleep in Grenada on November 2, 1966. He had no will and an estate worth $2,542.18. Hoskins helped Jessie file the petition that allowed her and Man Hurt to be named John Hurt's only heirs. Gertrude's family said in their lawsuit that they were given no notice of this and that the filings made by Jessie were "based upon fraud and fabrication."

Mary Hurt Wright thinks Jessie was ill-used by Hoskins.

"After my grandfather died, Miss Jessie lived in a housing project," Wright says. "She had nothing. Tom Hoskins even took my grandfather's hat and his guitar."

But Hoskins says that from 1964 until Jessie's death in 1981, he gave all royalties to Jessie.

"I didn't take a penny," Hoskins says. "It was my intent to take care of Jessie and the grandchildren. I promised John I would do that. I wouldn't take money away from them."

In 1990, Hoskins entered into an agreement with Rounder Records allowing the company to license the recordings of Mississippi John Hurt. The company currently has three of his albums in their catalog. Hoskins was paid a $2,500 advance and receives 15 percent of the list price for every record sold. Another Rounder artist, Bill Morrissey, has recently released an album of Mississippi John Hurt covers. Rounder will pay around 75 cents for every one of those sold to Wynwood Music, which administers the copyrights to Hurt's songs. Wynwood will in turn pay half of that to Hoskins.

The records made for Okeh in 1928 are now owned by Sony, which pays Man Hurt modest royalties.

Rounder Records was named in the suit brought by Gertrude's family, but co-owner William Nowlin said he would be happy to pay royalties to whomever the court decided was entitled to them. So far, according to Nowlin, the company has not been informed they should pay royalties to anyone but Hoskins.

Hoskins, who has no children of his own and who makes his living buying and selling old phonographs, has named Hurt's granddaughter Ella Mae his heir. She currently lives in Tacoma, Washington, and has five children. Her brother, Andrew Lee Hurt, died two years ago. Her father, John William "Man" Hurt, now lives in Minneapolis and has a sporadic career as a blues musician.

Hoskins said he bears no ill will toward Gertrude's descendants. But he's concerned that if the royalties are divided among a large number of people, they will be of little value to anyone.

"I have no animosity toward those people," he says, "But my loyalty is to John Hurt."

"Without Tom Hoskins, there wouldn't have been a Mississippi John Hurt," Lonnie Conley Hurt admits. "But he should have known better than to think a man my grandfather's age down here would've had just one wife and one son. If he and Man Hurt had done what was right, there wouldn't have to be all this hiring lawyers."

If Tom Hoskins had never gone looking for him, Mississippi John Hurt most likely would have died in obscurity in Avalon, and his music with him. There would be no royalties to fight over. But would Hurt have been better off if no strange white man had ever knocked on his door?

Hoskins comments that although Hurt had been poor in Mississippi almost his whole life, it had been a "good poverty."

"He was respected by everyone in the community, both black and white," Hoskins says. Still, he doesn't believe Hurt was content.

"No black man in Mississippi in the 1960s could have been happy," he says.

But neither was Hurt happy in Washington. He returned to Mississippi as soon as he could—just like his grandchildren, who left to make money and to make something of themselves, but came back, drawn by the pull of family ties, by the land, and by the blues.

John Hurt is buried on a hill in Carroll County, in a secluded family cemetery, a clearing in the woods lined with simple grave markers and colorful wreaths. His headstone is a plain stone block with his name and the dates of his birth and death. Still, it's the most substantial monument here. On it, blues pilgrims—the spiritual descendants of Tom Hoskins—have left behind a drawing of the musician and a handful of coins.

NEIL STRAUSS

Unearthing the New Nashville's Wax Castoffs

Where do wax figures go when they die?

For more than a quarter of a century the Country Music Wax Museum was one of Nashville's most colorful tourist magnets. One in every nine visitors to Nashville walked through its doors, gawking at life-size replicas of Hank Williams, George Jones and Dolly Parton.

This was no ordinary wax museum. Performers like Minnie Pearl and Johnny Cash donated clothes and instruments and even tended to their characters. Once, after Jim Reeves had died and his ex-wife dropped by to brush the hair on his exhibit, employees saw she had put a picture of herself on the mantel.

But the Country Music Wax Museum quietly shut its doors two years ago, a casualty of Nashville's self-conscious rush toward modernization. In 1971, when the museum opened, Nashville was a small city with a handful of studios; today the population of the metropolitan area has boomed past one million, and there are 400 music studios. Professional hockey and football teams have moved into town, and health care has replaced country music as the city's number-one moneymaker.

The wax museum was once part of a thriving tourist mall, along with the Hank Williams Jr. Museum, Barbara Mandrell Country and the Car Collectors Hall of Fame. Now they, too, are closed, and there are plans to supplant them with a traffic circle, offices and a Ritz-Carlton hotel.

But what happened to the cherished wax figures of country music greats with their vintage finery and original instruments?

Not even officials of the Country Music Hall of Fame across the street knew the answer. This reporter crisscrossed Nashville on the trail of the missing wax figures, encountering tales of a vanished promoter, a Kennedy campaign consultant and a Taiwanese herb vendor. But nothing could prepare him for what he found.

None of the three shopkeepers who remain in the area—once called the gateway to Music Row but now nicknamed "death row"—knew the figures' whereabouts. Rumor had it that they had been sold to the Music Valley Wax Museum, a newer attraction on the city's outskirts, where the Opryland U.S.A. theme park, since demolished, had lured the tourists who once kept the mall's shops in business.

"They did offer their collection to us," said Doris Harvey, the assistant manager of the Music Valley Wax Museum. "But they didn't want to break the set, and we already had many of the same figures."

Inquiries at the Country Music Hall of Fame revealed little. Administrators said they were never offered the figures. But one employee brought out a charmingly crude wax museum coloring book she had recently bought for 99 cents at the local grocery.

Virginia Brazzell, the proprietor, found the books in the back of the store when she bought the place some two years ago. Phone calls to former employees of the museum produced the vague conjecture that the figures had been melted down.

More than 60 figures were missing. And it wasn't so surprising in a city that likes to reinvent itself every few years, complaining about the loss of tradition while paving over its past.

"The city decided that they want the convention business," said Jim Cook, the owner of Hat Country, a wax museum neighbor that is going out of business. "But they can't create that new image of Nashville without killing the old one."

Years ago the Country Music Wax Museum was tied to the most powerful people in the city. Aurora Publishing, a failed book and entertainment venture that had managed to pull most of Nashville into its orbit, founded the museum. One of its first chiefs was Paul Corbin, a political operative who worked on campaigns for John F. Kennedy and Robert F. Kennedy. After their assassinations, Mr. Corbin found respite from politics in wax figures, often borrowing their boots to wear around town.

But the museum's most notorious operator was Dominic De-Lorenzo, an Aurora founder described by former employees as a good-looking, slick-talking charmer who persuaded Nashville luminaries like Chet Atkins, Minnie Pearl and the newspaper mogul John Seigen-thaler to invest in the publishing company and museum. It was while dining at the Peking Restaurant, a country star hangout, that Mr. De-Lorenzo discovered the museum's future: Daniel Hsu, the son of a leading herbal medicine authority from Taiwan, who had given up his microbiology studies at Vanderbilt University to open the restaurant.

Mr. Hsu soon became majority shareholder in Aurora, and Mr. De-Lorenzo left Nashville for New York and disappeared, leaving behind a pile of creditors, some of whom believe that he faked his death. Mr. DeLorenzo's son, Dominick, who used to spend his summers working at the museum, said his father died of cancer in 1980.

Under Mr. Hsu, the wax museum thrived and the area around it blossomed into a tourist mecca of offbeat novelty stores and shrines to country stars. In a bold move in a world of Hank Williams Jr. fans, Mr. Hsu opened a Chinese art museum above the wax museum. And when Mr. Hsu learned that a relative of Mr. Seigenthaler's was an artist, he commissioned her to make new wax figures.

The last one she made was of George Strait. A faded wood sign above the old museum still advertises the addition to the collection.

With Opryland closing, tourism slumping, the Hall of Fame moving downtown and tour buses rerouting to the more package tour–friendly Branson, Missouri, the death knell for the neighborhood rang in 1997 when a city-sponsored study determined that a business district would be more useful.

By then, Mr. Hsu had left to work for his family's herbal medicine business in California, selling the buildings to a developer named Jim Caden, who converted them into office space and a shoe store.

"They all wanted us out of there," said Phyllis Shoemake, a former wax museum employee who now distributes herbal medicines, including Mr. Hsu's. "They thought we were an eyesore. Now it's a ghost town."

One of Mr. Caden's office buildings became home to a magazine called *Country Weekly*. And it was there that the trail of the wax figures got warm again. Visitors reported seeing the Hank Williams dummy in the reception area, leaning against the wall in his original suit designed by Nudie the Rodeo Tailor.

And, sure enough, a reporter for *Country Weekly*, Bob Cannon, knew exactly where the figures were: they had never left the building and were locked up, deteriorating, in the basement. "The weird thing is, if you go down there at night, it's real spooky," he said. "You have 40 wax figures looking at you. And they all look like Buddy Ebsen, whether they're male or female."

After ignoring phone calls for a week, Mr. Caden eventually agreed to open the storage room, which was once home to the car collector's museum. "But," he warned as he unlocked the door, "I don't want you to write anything making fun of the South, or some of the positions these figures are in."

Inside, the pieces looked more as if they belonged to a country music chamber of horrors than a wax museum.

"That," said Michael Horton, the building's maintenance man, "was Ronnie Milsap's head."

He gestured to a wax face that had been smashed by vandals. Barbara Mandrell's head, with a hairpiece she had designed, was impaled on a stick, yards away from her torso. Johnny Cash, all in black, stood against the wall, one arm hanging below his knee. Pop Stoneman's autoharp rested on a bench, covered with detached fingers. Uncle Dave Macon's gold teeth had been stolen. And Hank Williams Jr. lay on his back with two disembodied hands across his chest and a giant crack running along his neck.

Just who owns these figures—62 of them not counting various busts and body parts—is in some doubt. Mr. Caden said they either belonged to him, to Mr. Hsu or to Aurora. "But," he added, "I don't even know where Daniel Hsu is, to be quite honest." Mr. Hsu, who works in the Irvine, California, office of Brion, his family's herb company, did not return phone calls.

Fortunately, Nashville's delinquents didn't recognize the value of what they were vandalizing, and left the costumes intact. When Mark Medley, the archivist for the Country Music Hall of Fame, walked into the storeroom to determine the collection's worth, his jaw dropped. There were clothes from the entire Carter Family, Jimmie Rodgers' singing brakeman outfit, a rare Gretsch guitar that once belonged to Jim Reeves, handwritten lyrics from the Stoneman Family and more than a dozen stage suits by Nudie, the rhinestone-loving designer who created country high-fashion in the late 1940s.

"This collection of suits is really the most complete I've ever seen," he said. "Their historical and monetary worth is considerable."

"It's so strange," he continued. "These things belonged to people who are so exalted, and now their costumes end up on the floor."

Just how long they will stay on the floor is anybody's guess. "I don't have a clue what I'm going to do with them," Mr. Caden said. "I thought some bolt of lightning would strike us, and we would figure it out. But we really have no plans."

And so the figures remain in limbo, a waxy analogy for country music itself as they decay untended while Nashville races after its cosmopolitan dream.

J. R. JONES

Prove It All Night

Larry Ribs' guitar is a work of art. The Fender Jazzmaster was new when he bought it in 1965, but after three years of abuse in south-side juke joints and Rush Street bars it was already beat to hell. A girlfriend took him to a theatrical-supply store on State Street, where he bought a bag of white rhinestones and using seashell glue he pasted them all over the front of his guitar. Toward the bottom, where he'd run out of rhinestones, he later glued a chrome naked-chick silhouette that had fallen off a truck's mud flap into the street outside his home. The last piece, added years later, was a hat pin of the word "Chicago" in art deco lettering, which he fastened to the headstock.

Since he was a teenager Larry has never wanted to do much more than play guitar in a rock 'n' roll band. For the last five years he's been working at the Lakeview Lounge, a dank honky-tonk on Broadway just north of Argyle, playing three nights a week, six or seven hours a night, 30 minutes on and 30 minutes off. The Lakeview is the sort of drinking establishment even the most charitable person would have to call a dive. A sign on the inside door warns THIS IS NOT A PAWNSHOP but more than once I've been approached there by someone trying to sell me a tuxedo or an overcoat. One Friday night an old man keeled over backward off his bar stool. The band quit playing and a few patrons gathered around, but after a few moments he pulled himself off the floor and dusted himself off. Larry ended the uncomfortable episode by launching into "Blue Moon," and after a while the fellow staggered home.

Larry, bassist Raul Chabarria, and drummer Gilbert Canchola call themselves Nightwatch, but on the sign outside they're just "live entertainment," and to the regulars they're simply "the band." They play directly behind the bar, serving up songs like cans of Miller Genuine Draft. Because the drums and amplifiers stay set up all week, the stage looks well lived-in, like some kid's messy bedroom. The fake wood paneling behind the drum kit is decorated year-round with silver tinsel and Christmas lights; a string of red cardboard letters declares HAPPY VALENTINE'S DAY. A stuffed Benny the Bull perches on Gilbert's bass drum like a gargoyle, and just behind Raul a purple sombrero adorns an unused cymbal stand. A small disco ball hangs from the ceiling between the bandstand and the bar, and a wall switch within arm's reach of Larry turns on a colored light, sending pink champagne spiraling around the room.

"The Lakeview is a laid-back type of place from yesteryear," says Larry. "We try to keep a comfortable atmosphere, not too much excitement. We're not gonna go 90 miles an hour. Take a sip of whatever you're drinking in between songs and just take your time."

Six hours is a lot of time to kill, and when they're playing to a near empty room—which is often—Larry, Raul, and Gilbert can sound as bored as they are, walking through tunes they've played literally hundreds of times. But they can play just about anything—blues, R & B, country and western, classic rock, big-band and jazz standards, Latin ballads, Italian crooners, on and on—and when they get an audience, the energy comes rushing back. Larry, a Polish man in his mid–50s who wears a Greek fisherman's cap to cover his bald pate, is the main attraction: When he steps out for one of his delicate, jazzy solos, you might think you're a couple blocks south, at the Green Mill. Raul, a squat Mexican with long graying hair, is the mike man, the band's singer, comedian, philosopher, and all-around bullshit artist. Gilbert, whose lined face is topped by a startling Mohawk, is the wild card. At the beginning of the night his drumming can sound pretty rusty, but after a while he'll fall into the groove—and when that happens Nightwatch is the best bar band on the planet.

The line between band and audience dissolves as soon as the three men step off the bandstand, but even when they're up there it's pretty faint. You play drums? Come on up—Gilbert would rather knock one back and hang out with his friends anyway. Want to take a turn at the microphone? Go ahead—if you can remember the lyrics, Larry and Raul probably know the song. If not, they can almost certainly fake it.

The clientele at the lounge is as strange and varied as the band's repertoire. "One thing unique about the Lakeview is you have practically every nationality," Larry says. "Guatemalans, Bosnians, Germans, Pakistanians, Koreans, Puerto Ricans, Polish, Irish, a little bit of everything comes in here. You have Afro-Americans from Chicago and Africa, you've got Jamaicans, you've got Ethiopians, American Indians. And it's a place where the most trouble you'll run into is maybe some old-timers getting into an argument at the bar or something. No violence. Kathy [Battaglia, the proprietor] is well-known by everybody. And we get people come back in there who haven't been there in four, five, six years."

When Kathy took over the business in 1979, the neighborhood was thick with country people, folks from the southeast who'd moved to the city in search of work, and on weekends the lounge was so packed she had to turn people away. Raul played there with a different lineup in the late 80s, cranking out straight country and western four nights a week. But the urban hillbillies were displaced by Koreans and Vietnamese, and after a while Kathy cut the live music back to three nights a week. The winter months are especially tough, and if not for the bar's late license, which permits it to serve until 5 AM on Saturdays, the lounge might have locked its doors long ago.

"This place is dying," says Michael, a slight man with a mustache and glasses who's lived in Uptown all his 40-some years. "People don't want to come out and drink anymore. They'd rather sit at home and get drunk, or surf the Internet. Or they go to someplace like Goose Island."

"If you leave it up to your wonderful mayor he's gonna turn us into a desert," says Larry. "This is one of the greatest cities in the world, but now, since the year 2000 is coming, he's trying to wipe the slate clean. He don't want none of this Al Capone shit, and all that."

"What happened to history?" Raul asks. "That's part of history—Capone and Dillinger."

"He don't care, he don't like it. I truly believe he hates the history of Chicago."

"But his old man wasn't like that."

"He was like that too. They're all jealous of Al Capone because he was bigger than they are, he had more power. They don't want to admit it."

I started going to the Lakeview Lounge about four years ago. An old friend of mine had discovered the place during his drinking days, and every few months we'd drop in for a few beers. When I started working for the *Reader* my friend said, "Whatever you do, don't write about the lounge. Every asshole hipster in town will be in there making the scene." But the word's already out: The last time we went there together, an entourage of handsome young people in black leather coats filed in until, about a dozen strong, they had taken the place over, soaking up the ambience and requesting their favorite oldies. "This place is over," my friend declared. "I mean, I'm glad for these guys. They deserve it. But I'm never coming back here again."

My friend may be heartbroken, but Larry, Raul, and Gilbert don't give a damn about protecting "authentic" Chicago from marauding hipsters. They're trying to earn a living, and while Kathy pays them a flat rate for an evening's work, they rely on the tip jar as well. Customers who drop in every four, five, six years can't keep a business open, and it's no fun playing all night to half a dozen barflies.

Raul grew up in Bridgeport—the Irish enclave where Richie Daley was raised. Raul's father emigrated from Mexico to Texas, then moved to California and finally Chicago, where he did grunt work in restaurants before landing a job at the Silver Cup Bread Bakery, on Federal near Garfield. Later he worked as a floor manager for Wonder Bread, and all told, Raul spent about 15 years as part of Bridgeport's Mexican-American community. "I could count them on one and a half hands," he recalls. "I had some trouble, but no big deal. I can't really say it was a traumatic experience. Back then they didn't have words like 'spic' and 'wetback' and all that. If they called you a bad name, they'd be calling you 'Mexican.' Which is what I am!"

His father loved music and played classical guitar, performing at parties, weddings, and funerals with his own band—three guitars and an accordion playing traditional songs from Spain and Mexico. "My dad had a lot of guitars. He played mandolin, too, and electric bass. And he had a lot of friends who were musicians. Basses and trumpet players—I can't even count the people he knew. Then my brother, he played, and one of my sisters, she sang, so we had our own little family gathering." Raul listened to all kinds of music: His family owned a phonograph, and an uncle gave him a stack of big-band albums. At 15 he took up the guitar, learned a few chords and scales from his father, then dropped it. Two years later he came back to it in earnest. An Italian friend of his father's taught him some music theory, struggling with English and scrawling out notes and chords on paper, but Raul learned more from his records, playing one over and over until he'd worked out an entire song.

One day he was hanging around a neighborhood restaurant when a friend dropped a coin in the jukebox and punched in a Little Richard single. "I didn't know who this guy was, but when I heard it, it got to me. I didn't know if the guy was black or white, or what the hell. About a week later I went to the record store, and I remembered the song— 'Long Tall Sally.' Back then they used to have the picture on the sleeve, and there he was. But still I couldn't figure it out, 'cause you know, Little Richard, he wore so much makeup!"

He bought a Silvertone electric guitar from the Sears catalog and formed a band with his brother, playing house parties and backyard barbecues. Then an uncle offered him a set of Ludwig drums that someone had abandoned at his house—a bass drum, snare drum, and tom. Raul got one of his cousins, a sheet-metal worker, to cut him a crude cymbal, and he draped a chain over it to kill the ringing. When he was 16, he was invited to join a rock 'n' roll band that sometimes played at the Mary McDowell Settlement House, a community center near 47th and Ashland built half a century earlier by reformers from the University of Chicago. The Polish-Catholic parishes had been suspicious of McDowell's progressive and Protestant leanings, and during the '30s and '40s the settlement house had become a haven for the growing population of Mexicans in Back of the Yards, providing sports, after-school activities, and naturalization classes. Yet the band Raul joined was led by a Polish kid, Larry Rybakowski—Larry Ribs.

It's 9:30 on a Thursday night, and though the band doesn't go on until 10, Raul is already at the bar, having a bottle of Rolling Rock and a smoke with Caroline, a blond woman in torn blue jeans, a brown rain-coat, and a backward baseball cap. Caroline used to tend bar at the Lakeview, but lately she's been working at the Wooden Nickel, near Wilson and Racine. She has a toy, a tiny microphone that plays back whatever you say into it, and as she points it at me Raul's voice hisses from the scratchy speaker: "I don't see nothing. I don't hear nothing. I don't say nothing!" Caroline unleashes a raucous laugh and plays it again. "I don't see nothing. I don't hear nothing. I don't say nothing!" A pair of handcuffs dangles from one of her belt loops.

On work nights Raul usually takes public transportation up to the north side. He lives in the same building as Larry, a cheap two-flat a block from where the settlement house once stood. Raul lives upstairs in the back. Larry lives downstairs with Sherry, his girlfriend of a dozen years. During the day Larry looks after their seven foster chil-dren, actually Sherry's grandkids, but on the nights he has to work, Sherry takes over so he can nap for an hour or so before driving in. Tonight when he arrives he heads straight for the bandstand. He runs up, plugs in, fusses with his amp, and finally comes out from behind the bar, sliding into a booth with a glass of Coke.

By the time Gilbert shows up it's well after ten. He's a soft-spoken man in his 60s, and with his Mohawk and flak jacket he's a dead ringer for Travis Bickle, the psychotic Vietnam vet in *Taxi Driver*. Raul grins and says, "We call him Robert No Dinero."

The place is nearly empty. "Time to rehearse," says Larry. "Nights like this, we brush up on stuff that we haven't played." They open with a snaky walking blues, Larry peeling off a few clean, well-shaped licks before the tune crumbles to a halt. They run through an instrumental version of "Mercy, Mercy, Mercy," a 1967 hit for north-siders the Buckinghams. "All right, Larry!" Caroline cheers. "The rest of you guys are fired." She holds her toy microphone in the air: "I don't see nothing, I don't hear nothing, I don't say nothing!"

"Hey, we have Caroline," Raul says over the PA. "Hey, Larry, she brought her cuffs, but she forgot her whip. You're gonna cuff us up and beat the hell out of all of us, and we're gonna love it. We're gonna scream in ecstasy." They play B.B. King's "The Thrill Is Gone" and "Patricia" by Cuban mambo king Perez Prado. On the Doobie Brothers' "Long Train Runnin'" Larry abandons his usual clean sound for a screaming fuzz-toned solo. They sail into the first verse of "Me and Bobby McGee," and Raul coaxes Caroline up to the bandstand; she delivers a passable Janis Joplin impersonation, a cigarette and a bottle of Bud dangling from one hand.

"Thursdays are always a little bit more bizarre than Friday or Saturday," Larry says between sets. "You get all these crazy people coming in." He and Raul talk shop, kicking around forgotten names from the 50s and 60s: Philly organist Bill Doggett, Elvis's bassist Bill Black, assorted Chicago tenor men. Gilbert wanders over and Larry tries to get him to talk to me. "Come on, he's doing a write-up on us, man. We don't know nothing about you. We know you're Puerto Rican." Gilbert glares at him and stalks off. Larry cackles. "He's Mexican. They hate that!"

"That's like calling a Polish person Lithuanian," Raul says.

"The most aggravating Mexican in the world," says Larry, eyeing Raul. "Everybody hates the son of a bitch. They've hated him for 40 years. I've known people that still hate him. They like him and hate him at the same time."

Larry and I get to talking about the current music scene. "I think rock 'n' roll is dying," he says. "Where's the stars now? There's no stars. There's just a flash of light, and they go down. Guns 'n' Roses, any of them. Look at your TV commercials—buy a tape of the 50s, tape of the 60s, tape of the 70s. How about the tape of the 90s? Look at your videos—what do they start at, $250,000? So the first money you make on that record you gotta pay for that damn video before you get anything. You got everybody working against you, man."

This brings him back to the mayor's war on taverns, which is closing the bars and lounges where he learned his trade. "Where's the tribute to the great musicians of Chicago? Where are they supposed to play? He's *killing an art.* And Chicago has made a lot of great musicians, from the early 1900s to the 20s, the 30s, the 40s, they all got their start here. I seriously think this guy, with the year 2000, he wants space cadets. He's throwing this city's history away." Larry gets up and heads back to the bandstand. "That's it, man. These are the last days of rock 'n' roll."

Larry grew up in Pilsen and Back of the Yards. Both his parents were children of Polish immigrants, and his father worked as a machinist all his life. His childhood memories are dominated by the stockyards and packing plants. "Big factories—Swift, Armour, all of them," he recalls. "As a kid I'd go in there, hang around with a couple of my friends. You'd see a lot of cowboys riding around on horses, and cattle as far as the eye could see. The cowboys would run the cattle to the slaughterhouse, the sheep and pigs and all that."

Most of his neighbors were Polish, Irish, and German. Mexicans generally lived north of 47th Street, north of Mary McDowell. But Larry fell in with the Mexican students at Saint Augustine, the German parochial school at 50th and Laflin, and they introduced him to the settlement house. Their parents might have glared at each other across 47th, but Larry and his friends shared one interest more powerful than ethnicity. "The Mexican music, these American-born Mexicans liked that stuff for the family," he explains. "But outside the family they were into American rock 'n' roll. Little Richard—one of my friends was a Little Richard nut. And this other Mexican guy, this older guy in the settlement house, was a big jazz freak. He knew every jazz record and star there was. Remarkable."

Like Raul, Larry can pinpoint the day he discovered rock 'n' roll. In 1959, when he was 14, his family took a vaction to Oubwa, Wisconsin. His uncle had opened a bar in the small town, and Larry was glued to the bandstand every night. "It was the first time I'd ever seen a three-piece rock 'n' roll band," he says. "And it really lit a match. They had a fabulous lead guitar player, who was—ooh, he was just whaling the hell out of the guitar all night. It just blew my mind. So I'd hang around the stage all the time. Something just fascinated me, watching these guys play." He'd been admiring a guitar that hung in the window of the Mort Herold School of Music at 51st and Ashland, and when he got back to Chicago he marched into the school and rented it for six dollars a month.

Herold, a world-class accordionist, gave Larry an after-school job cleaning up, and he used his earnings to pay for guitar lessons. Herold didn't really play guitar himself, but he knew enough to get Larry started, and before long Larry began studying with Joe Richardson, a jazz guitarist in his 50s who taught at the school. "Very quiet—you had to strain your ears to hear him talk," Larry recalls. "Very smooth guitar player. Till today my technique isn't as smooth as his. His pick control was just beautiful." He worked with Richardson all during high school, going through every guitar book in the shop. "At the end of four years he told me to move on and find another teacher. But I'd learned pretty much what I wanted to know for what I wanted to do. I just wanted to play in a rock 'n' roll band."

With his friend Bobby Villalobos, Larry formed the Dy Counts—a play on the name of the popular combo the Vy Counts. When their first drummer quit, Larry invited Raul to join. They played Little Richard, Elvis, the Ventures. Raul liked to throw in some jazz standards, and Larry's all-time favorite was "Honky Tonk," a 1956 boogie-woogie hit by Bill Doggett. A group leader at Mary McDowell booked the trio at Back of the Yards festivals, sock hops at the settlement house, dances at the YWCA. One time he sent them to UIC's mental hospital to serenade the patients. "That was cool," Larry recalls. "We didn't get paid nothing. It was just for exposure."

Playing at the settlement house, Larry caught the eye of Johnny Thunder, a 22-year-old singer whose band gigged every weekend at the Sky Blue Lounge at 47th and Laflin. Thunder's real name was Jerry Costello, pronounced, "Castillo"; part Bohemian and part Mexican, he'd grown up in Back of the Yards and spent his own not-so-distant teenage years hanging around the settlement house.

"He was a huge guy with a real low voice, rough voice," says Larry. "He was like a comedian—his singing wasn't very good but his stage presence made up for it. He was the best mike man I ever seen." Thunder needed a lead guitarist. Larry was only 17, but Thunder promised to set him up with fake ID. "So I got some IDs. Used to carry two wallets. I always looked old—I had a high forehead and everything. And I acted old. I didn't act silly like some kids. So I passed. And I learned

how to behave in a lounge, and your mannerisms and things like that."
The Sky Blue was "just a little corner bar—fights galore every week-
end, a real smoky dive type of a bar," but compared to playing with the
Dy Counts it was a big-time gig. Larry was a professional.

"All right, now we're gonna get Skip up here," says Raul. "The drummer's got to go to the washroom. He can't hold it no more. He's blowing up." Skip, a young guy who does lenses at the Pearle Vision Center
in Lakeview, settles down behind the kit for Chicago's "Colour My
World," the Wilson Pickett hit "Mustang Sally," and the Surfaris'
"Wipe Out." Gilbert returns, and the band closes the set with "My
Way" and "Viva Las Vegas."

Caroline, the woman with the handcuffs, is gone: Kathy Battaglia arrived shortly after 11 and asked her to leave. When she refused, Eddie,
another patron, was dispatched to throw her out. Larry launched into a
swinging 12-bar blues to drown out the ensuing argument. Eddie
grabbed Caroline by the shoulders and they struggled. Kathy got on
the telephone, and eventually Caroline stormed out. The band
watched from the stage but kept playing.

For the midnight set, Raul croons a loving "Blue Moon," Larry's
languid solo decorated with deft arpeggios and hammered notes. Then
it's on to a Johnny Cash medley, with Raul blowing over the top of his
beer bottle to mimic a train whistle on "Folsom Prison Blues." Larry
cradles the whammy bar of his guitar, laying some gorgeous vibrato on
Santo & Johnny's 1959 instrumental "Sleep Walk." He hits the disco
ball switch, and Raul glides through a couple Italian ballads: "It's Now
or Never," Dean Martin's "Return to Me."

"We try to cover the ethnic part of it," says Larry. "Polkas, Italian
music, Spanish music. We had a hard time with the Pakistanian stuff."

After the set he and Raul get to talking about the racial strife of the
60s. Larry remembers driving right into the infamous 1966 southwest-
side march where someone hurled a brick at Martin Luther King. "I
seen a big crowd, thousands of them," he says. "So I pulled over and it
was a big black march. The American Nazi party was there, their headquarters was there, and they had a big sign on the door: NIGGERS GO
HOME!"

Raul claims he once visited the Nazi headquarters in Marquette Park. "I was working there at Chez a Go-Go on Pulaski," he says. "I said, 'What's this?' So I walked in. The guy says, 'What do you want?' I says, 'Hey, can I join the Nazi party?' 'What nationality?' 'Mexican.' 'Get out of here! *Now!* Is this a joke? Get out!' 'I just wanted to know!' Then he says, 'Here's some of our literature—pass it around.'"

"Look at the Bible," says Larry. "The Tower of Babel. Now if I remember the story correctly, everybody was getting along great. They're all working together. And then God came along and screwed it all up. Zap! He made everybody a different nationality. So they couldn't work with each other, couldn't understand one another. Then they all took off to their own countries. He's the one that started it all! Everybody was getting along great!"

The night winds on into morning. Sometime during the one o'clock set the crowd swells to eight—yet the band is hot, shifting easily from Glenn Miller's "In the Mood" to Frankie Lymon & the Teenagers' "Why Do Fools Fall in Love?" to Conway Twitty's "It's Only Make Believe" to the Shadows' "Apache" to Santana's "Europa." Two Hispanic guys wander in between sets, and the musicians are so grateful for the extra ears that they empty out their Latin song bag: "Black Magic Woman," "Oye Como Va," "La Bamba," "Guantanamera." A few of the regulars stagger around the bar dancing, and the band jumps into "El Rancho Grande." Raul sings, "My name is Pancho Villa I got the gonorrhea I caught it from Maria Beneath the apple tree-ah And now I cannot pee-ah . . . "

By 3 AM almost everyone except the band is three sheets to the wind. Raul and Gilbert have downed a couple beers, and Larry drank a glass of red wine around 11, but they're still pretty straight. According to Kathy, Larry once packed up his gear and walked out on a busy Saturday night because Gilbert and Raul were too plastered to keep it together. "When he did that I told those other two guys, 'Without him, you're out of here. You're fired.' But they wouldn't leave," she says. Larry was lured back, and now they all pace themselves. "You gotta keep your smarts about you, you gotta stay under control," Larry says. "You don't get bombed while you're doing a gig."

They circle back around to the beginning of the night, giving "Mercy, Mercy, Mercy" another workout. They take a request for the Stones'

"Honky Tonk Women," then play one of my favorites, "Theme from 'A Summer Place.'" Percy Faith's 1960 single is an exercise in schmaltz, but shorn of its syrupy strings it cuts clean to the heart. Finally they relax into a medley of Ventures hits as if it were an old jacket: "Ram-Bunk-Shush," "Walk, Don't Run," "Perfida." Kathy shakes a tambourine. Larry and Raul switch instruments, and as Raul tears into "Long Tall Sally," he could almost pass for a teenager again. "We're gonna have some fun tonight Have some fun tonight Everything's all right Have some fun tonight Have some fun, some fun tonight . . . "

Larry played with Johnny Thunder for three years, on Fridays and Saturdays and sometimes weeknights as well. He earned $15 or $20 a night plus free drinks, though a good gig might earn him as much as $25. The Sky Blue Lounge catered to Poles, Irish, and some Mexicans; Thunder and his band—Larry, a rhythm guitarist, and a drummer—performed on a stage in the back corner. "But a lot of the places we played at didn't have a stage," he says. "We'd either stand on the floor or play on a pool table—they would put a sheet of plywood on the pool table. One time they made a stage out of beer cases." They played the Tropic Lounge at 63rd and Winchester, a late-license place with an oval bar; they played J.W. Hummel's Lounge on 63rd near Maplewood; they played Casa Madrid near 25th and Lake and just about every other bar in Melrose Park.

Casa Madrid was known for its Sunday-morning jam sessions. "We would play till five o'clock, close down till like seven, and lock the doors—no one else could come in. The jam session would start at seven o'clock in the morning. Bands from all over Chicago were coming into the place all night long, waiting for the jam session, and it would go on till maybe two o'clock in the afternoon. Nat Adderly came in one time. The Everly Brothers came in; they were playing at the Manor Lounge. One of them played my guitar—it was brand-new at the time, candy apple red. He was wearing a vest with metal buttons on it. He looked at the expression on my face and said, 'Don't worry. I'll take my vest off.' I thought that was really nice of him."

Johnny Thunder was an unreliable bandleader, often showing up late and insulting patrons from the stage, so Larry ditched him for

Buddy DeVito & the Fabulous Storms. For about six years he bounced back and forth between the two bands, but the set list was always the same: rock 'n' roll, R & B, country and western, 12-bar blues. As a guitarist, he could write his own ticket. "If you had a badass guitar player, you had a good band," he says. "Phil Orsi always had a decent band. He had a real good guitar player named Clark Dufay. He was well-known while I was just starting out. I had a lot to do to catch up to him. There was other bands like Stop, Robby and the Troubadours, the Gems—they played the Cherry Lounge at 25th and Pulaski. Another band called Poobah, they were very good. The Mob—they would dress in pinstripe suits, like the mob, with the white ties and all. They were excellent musicians."

By this time Raul had gone pro as well, playing guitar with a group called the Fabulous Three. He and Larry saw each other at Casa Madrid jam sessions, or if one had an early gig he might get off work and go watch the other's last set.

But the 50s were over. Buddy Holly was dead. Little Richard had become a man of the cloth. Presley had returned from Germany to make dopey movies. In February 1964 the Beatles appeared on *The Ed Sullivan Show*, and almost overnight acts like Johnny Thunder became yesterday's news.

"I was playing for Joe Hummel's when The Beatles hit," says Larry. "I didn't even know who The Beatles were. I wasn't paying attention to the radio. I was playing more of the black style—'Willie and the Hand Jive,' 'My Girl,' and all that stuff. And I didn't like The Beatles. To me they sounded like a garage band, like I used to sound when I was 14. They did good songs, but I knew a lot of musicians that quit the business because they didn't want to play this stuff. The owners of the bars wanted them to play Beatle music, and they refused, so they lost their jobs. 'Hey, I spent all my life trying to polish my playing, and here I gotta sound like I'm 15 years old again in order to sell? This is bullshit.' So a lot of them just quit."

"The Beatles!" someone calls out. "Nineteen-sixty-four: The Beatles!" Larry leads the band into Freddy King's "Hideaway," a rolling blues instrumental Eric Clapton recorded with John Mayall in 1966. It's just after ten on Friday night, and again the lounge is nearly deserted. A young couple settles down into a booth with bottles of Budweiser, looking a little uncomfortable among the half dozen regulars seated at the bar.

"It's Michael's birthday, a very good friend of ours," Raul announces after the song. "So we're all gonna get together and, uh, beat the hell out of him." The band plays "Happy Birthday to You," segues into a chorus of "The Old Gray Mare," then returns to "Happy Birthday," Raul turning the last line into a coda: "Get plastered you—"

"Bastard!" the patrons shout.

"—good guy, happy birthday to yoooou . . . "

Cheers and applause.

"All right, here's a Beatles song for Mikey. He wasn't born when the Beatles were playing but—"

"Yeah I was," protests Michael. "But I was still in diapers."

"He's in diapers again," cracks George, an aging country boy in a green windbreaker. They're perched on a pair of bar stools, Michael savoring a shot of Jägermeister while George drains a can of MGD. Raul sings "And I Love Her," and Gilbert plays his toms with his hands to simulate the bongos on The Beatles' recording. The song is way out of Raul's range, but they have better luck with "Ticket to Ride." I ask Michael how old he is.

"Forty-four," he says. "Forty-four, born in '55."

"That's right, that adds up."

"It's the wonder of mathematics."

"It's the wonder of time. If you live long enough, you die."

"That adds up too, doesn't it? But you can't think about that on your birthday."

The musicians set down their instruments, and before long Larry and Raul are deep into a discussion of the merits of classical guitar. "If you want to be a serious concert classical guitarist—like Segovia Gova—you gotta sleep, eat, and shit that stuff," says Raul. "All your life. Don't watch TV, read the paper—no no no no! And then *maybe* you might make it."

"That's a different world," says Larry.

"But look at the money they make! If they start when they're 12 years old, by the time they're 40, that's it, man. They can retire."

"The trouble with that is, the better you get at it, and the deeper you get, the more boring you get. Your audience gets less and less and less. Look at Segovia—you ever listen to Segovia?"

"Yeah, his stuff is boring."

"Come on! You're lucky if you can sit through one song. You know what I think it is, though? You got two kinds of people: intelligent people and personality people. You get a guy who's really intelligent, he'll tell you the reason for everything all night long, and he could be the most boring person in the world. That, to me, is a well-learned classical guitar player. But then you get some asshole with personality up there and there's people coming out of the woodwork! Do you want to be intelligent, or do you want to turn people on?"

At 11 sharp Larry's back on the bandstand, checking his tuning, and his solo on Duke Ellington's "Take the 'A' Train" positively smokes.

Raul and Larry met as teenagers at a community center near 47th and Ashland. Their first band played sock hops at the settlement house, Back of the Yards festivals, dances at the YWCA.

By the summer of 1965 Larry had a wife to support, and he wanted to move up in the business. He was backing Johnny Thunder at the Crystal Pistol in Old Town, and Thunder was on a rampage. Larry and the drummer, C. J. Young, started hanging out with Joel Santiago, a black organist whose band was playing at the bar next door. Santiago told them he had a contract with one of the city's biggest agents for a cross-country tour and maybe even a trip to Japan. The three of them started rehearsing on the side. Larry and Young quit Johnny Thunder, and their band, the Versatiles, set out for Fort Dodge, Iowa, with Larry's wife, Joan, and a female vocalist in tow.

"But things didn't work out at all," says Larry. "We got as far as the first gig, and around that time the riots started and all of that. We got a bad rap from the first place we played because the owner didn't like the idea of a white girl singing with a black organ player. So then the agent dropped our contract, and of course the girl went back to Chicago."

They decided to keep moving west anyway. Santiago knew the midwestern bar circuit and assured the other two that he could land them gigs as they traveled. From Fort Dodge they drove to Sioux Falls,

South Dakota. "We would pull into town and he would take us to the place. We'd sit in and cut the band out of a gig," says Larry. "In the black world, if the people like you, you're onstage and you're tearing the place up, [the owner] will fire the band he's got and hire you. That's how it was, so that's how we got our gigs." But then Young decided to head back to Chicago. "He took off in the middle of the night and left me, and he had the trailer that pulled the damn organ and everything." Larry and Santiago picked up Buddy Miles, a 19-year-old drummer from Omaha who'd later back Wilson Pickett, Jimi Hendrix and Carlos Santana. They moved on to Denver, where they played regularly for a few months, but then Miles left too. The tour was over.

Larry wanted to see Hollywood and decided to push on, convinced he could find a gig as soon as he rolled into L.A. But no one on the Sunset Strip was interested in Little Richard or the Ventures. "They were playing a different kind of rock 'n' roll music. Bob Dylan, the Byrds. See, I never joined the hippie thing, with the long hair, the mod clothes, and all that. I was kind of an oddball. I still had the greaser look. So it was hard." He hung around music stores, jamming away in hopes that someone might notice him, and while he did manage to scare up a few gigs, the pay was terrible. Finally he landed a job as a session guitarist for a studio owned by Johnny Otis—the guy who'd written "Willie and the Hand Jive."

"I'd sit there all day with earphones on," Larry says. "He would send scouts at night to hear local bands and ask them if they had any original material. If they did, come on down and record for nothing, and then he would push the song through people he knew in New York and different states. I was paid $20 a day just for hanging around the studio. Bands would come in every hour and I would overdub, or play solos, or whatever they wanted."

That September Joan got pregnant, and Larry took her back to Chicago. They had two sons together, Larry Jr. and Mike (who shows up at the Lakeview every few weeks to watch his old man), and Larry returned to Johnny Thunder and Buddy DeVito. But after two and a half years his marriage ended, and with bills piling up, Larry quit the music business. In May 1959, when he'd first walked into the Mort Herold School of Music, the number one single was Wilbert Harrison's "Kansas City." That winter, in January 1968, it was The Beatles' "Hello Goodbye." Larry got a job as a toll collector.

"Larry!" Raul calls out. "I want to be a star on Broadway, man."

"You are on Broadway."

It's an old gag but everyone laughs. "I promised Larry I'd make a star out of the man," Raul tells me. "He was in rust! We had to get Rust-Oleum and beef him up again. Broadway! And from here we're gonna go to Hollywood—Hollywood and Sheridan Road, right down the street."

"You know who's getting into baseball?" asks Larry. "Garth Brooks!"

"Puke!" says Raul. "He won't do it. Come on!"

"Can he afford it?" asks Michael.

"He can buy the team, man!" says Raul. "Larry, what's his famous saying? 'I've made more money than my kids' kids' kids' kids' kids' kids will ever make'?"

"Yeah, but those guys are owned. They can't take a shit without it being on paper."

"Can you imagine him coming in here and sitting in with us, if his agent found out? 'No! Don't get up—you can't do that. You can't get up and sing for nothing.' 'But I wanna go up!'"

"Give him five bucks," Michael suggests.

"Yeah, there we go! Unless we pay him five dollars."

"Then you'd get sued," says Larry. "It's all on contracts."

Kathy arrives a little later and throws her arms around Michael, wishing him a happy birthday. "I'm 44, born in '55," he tells her, though as the evening drags on he's beginning to look more like 55, born in '44. The band swings into "Honky Tonk," Larry's old favorite, and on one verse the guitarist and singer do a call and response, Raul urging the audience to help him out: "Nah-nah-nuh-nah—nah-nah-nuh-nah!" When the song is over a patron in tan tights, white go-go boots, and a knee-length vinyl coat climbs onstage and commandeers the microphone for a high-camp rendition of Elvis's Vegas showstopper "An American Trilogy." Then, swinging his hips, he's Tom Jones, singing "It's Not Unusual."

The next set opens with "Mercy, Mercy, Mercy," which is coming together nicely. The band plays it as an instrumental, but Larry jazzes it up with more colorful chording, and it sounds rich. "It's harder to do a song as a trio," he admits. "You gotta fill in all the holes. It could be done better if we did some background singing. But I'm not a singer, I don't have no range, and neither does Gilbert, although Gilbert could carry a tune if he had to. So we do it instrumentally. Where normally a background singer would be doing it, I'll do it with the guitar. That's the name of the game: fill in all the holes." After years of covering pop songs he knows how to put one across. "What helps people remember songs is certain licks, dominant licks that stick out. So you make sure you get dominant licks down. Like the solo on 'Hotel California'— make sure you get that solo down, 'cause that's the kicker of the whole song. Or the opening chord of 'Hard Day's Night'—make sure you got that chord. Those are your p's and q's; if you watch those, the song should go over pretty good."

More people trickle in after 2 AM, and eventually every seat at the bar is filled. There's a mix of regulars, working-class Latino guys, and goateed yuppies; a pair of black women sit front and center. The band plays the Miracles' "Ooh Baby Baby," and Larry's solo is a study in dynamics, lightly strummed chords flowering into an ardent lead. The crowd whoops and applauds. Then it's the Drifters' "Some Kind of Wonderful," Al Martino's "Spanish Eyes," and just as the crowd is beginning to mellow, the rhythm of "Viva Las Vegas" snaps everyone awake—everyone but Michael and George, who are both passed out on the bar, sleeping on their arms.

Raul has worked his share of day jobs: during the late 60s he made bridges at a south-side dental lab, and in the 70s he spent a couple years in the shipping and receiving department of a steel distributor. But the only career he's ever had is music. After high school he played guitar with the Fabulous Three and gigged steadily on the weekends, playing Club Laurel at Broadway and Bryn Mawr. He enrolled in the college of music at Roosevelt University but spent so much time on the road that he never finished his degree. By the time Larry was making his ill-fated trip to the west coast, the Fabulous Three were playing at

Sgt. Pepper's and Barnaby's, both near State and Chestnut. They still wore suits and greased their hair, but when they landed a job as the house band at the Webster Hotel in Lincoln Park their agent convinced them to get hip. "So we started wearing jeans," says Raul. "The drummer grew a beard, the bass player grew a beard. I grew a mustache and had my hair long." They worked there Tuesday through Saturday, still filling in at Sgt. Pepper's on Sunday and Monday. "On Sundays you had to play Beach Boys music, 'cause they had these 'beach-bum specials.' 'Giddy-up, giddy-up, giddy-up, 409.' And we had to dress like the Beach Boys, with the stupid colors and white pants, all this shit."

The Fabulous Three split up around 1968, and Raul joined a band called the Bossmen—not to be confused with Toronto's Bossmen, whose vocalist David Clayton-Thomas would join Blood, Sweat & Tears, or Detroit's Bossmen, whose guitarist Dick Wagner would write songs with Alice Cooper. Chicago's Bossmen were south-side Mexican rockers, two of them Texans who'd moved north like Raul's father. According to Larry they were a popular and well-respected combo, but after about three years that fell apart. Then Raul spent most of his time with Four Deep, a slick outfit with its own lights and PA that toured the midwest hotel-lounge circuit.

"When you're on the road you gotta play six days a week," he explains. "Sunday was your only day off. Course it was early license: you're talking about from 8:30 to 12, and then Saturday was the long one, from 9 o'-clock till about 1:30, 2 o'clock. We would contract for a month, and then while we were playing there the guy would book us somewhere else. We were always booked maybe two months in advance."

During the 70s Raul also pulled down good money sitting in with wedding bands in the north and northwest suburbs. "Play here Friday and here Saturday, and sometimes they'd have what they called double-headers—one wedding during the day and then in the evening you'd play with another band. But you didn't know nobody. 'So-and-so agency sent me, you need a guitar player?' Because when you book a wedding for a four-piece, they expect four pieces." The wedding circuit enlarged his already formidable repertoire. "I knew it all, man. There wasn't too much that I didn't know. I was like a sponge. And the stuff that I couldn't grasp, I didn't worry about. 'Yeah, we'll try that some other time.' Some of them had their own notebooks. They would say, here's a book, just flip the page, and they had the chord changes written out and everything. I'd just sit there and strum away, and at the end of the night: 'Here's your money, you did real good, and we'll see you some other time.'"

After the Fabulous Three and the Bossmen, the wedding circuit seemed like hack work, but it was better than punching a clock. "I would just roll around with my amp and guitar in my car, and I'd get these jobs. Then I started getting hooked in, because I did that for almost a year, this guy had me working. And good money. I said, This is better than getting with a group and traveling on the road—all the aggravation, cars breaking down, equipment being stolen—and it's a little easier. But these groups I went with, you gotta do what they're doing."

The bandleaders could be rigid; one even made the band play with a click track to regulate the tempo. Raul wanted to sing but seldom got the opportunity, and he began to tire of playing from fakebooks or bumbling along while the other players called out chord changes. "Oh yeah. I've heard this song but I've never played it: 'Well, you know it now.'" It's a line he's carried with him ever since: whenever the band at the lounge has brazened its way through an obscure request, he'll laugh and tell Gilbert, "Well, you know it now."

Around 1986 Raul landed a steady gig at the Lakeview, playing bass for guitarist Pat Kelly's band. Kelly was an "all-around guy," but the band played country and western to keep the patrons happy. Finally Raul had a chance to do some vocalizing. Kelly "didn't like singing sometimes because he didn't have that accent," Raul remembers. "City guys trying to do country. But we'd pull it off. A lot of people were from the south, and once in a while Indians. But it changed. We started noticing, 'Well, they don't want to hear country, now they want to hear old rock 'n' roll and what's happening now.' So I said, 'Come on, man. We gotta change with the people. Drop the Johnny Cash and drop the Hank Williams.'"

In the 70s the Lakeview Lounge had been a piano bar. The pianist who performed there owned 40 percent of the business, which he sold to Kathy Battaglia in 1977. Two years later the other partner decided he wanted to unload his share. "I wanted to sell out," Kathy recalls, "but I got talked into buying the rest of it. That's how I got stuck here." She had lived nearby all her life; she grew up over her father's grocery store, the Quality Market on Broadway, when Edgewater was still mostly Irish and Sheridan Road was lined with mansions. By all accounts she's a tough customer, holding her own in a mean part of town and trying to maintain a good reputation in a business that often brings out the worst in people. There's never the slightest doubt whose bar it is. One patron keeps nagging her to buy a CD jukebox, but she'd rather hear the country-and-western 45s that have been here forever, and often she stocks the old jukebox from her own collection.

In the last 20 years she's seen numerous musicians come and go. She went through a string of piano players, and then her southern clientele prompted her to audition country bands. She landed drummer Al Miracle and pianist Phil Fields, who were followed by guitarist Jimmy Johnson and later Pat Kelly.

Gilbert joined Kelly and Raul on New Year's Eve in 1988, shortly after his 50th birthday. His father, a railroad worker, died when he was four, leaving behind seven kids. Gilbert grew up in Little Italy, near Morgan and Harrison. He fell in love with the big bands—Glenn Miller, Harry James—but in 1955 he saw *Blackboard Jungle* and got turned on to Bill Haley and Little Richard. At 20 he took up the drums, and by 1963 he was gigging around town in various country and soul bands, playing Club Laurel (where Raul gigged with the Fabulous Three) and the F&Z Lounge, a hillbilly bar at Sacramento and Milwaukee. In 1975 he moved to San Diego and gigged full-time, playing six nights a week. After returning to Chicago in 1980 he got a job delivering paint for Sherwin-Williams, then spent more than a decade working at Cook County Hospital. Since 1996, playing drums at the lounge has been his only job, but he also takes care of his ten-year-old daughter, and few are the nights when he doesn't arrive late. Larry claims that Gilbert's wristwatch is actually an Aztec sundial.

In 1993 or so, Pat Kelly decided to move to the west coast, and Raul went through an endless succession of guitarists before Larry joined. The years hadn't been kind to Larry. In the mid–70s he remarried and got a job driving a forklift for a publishing company, then bought a trailer and a few acres in Quincy, Michigan, where many of his relatives had relocated. His new wife, also named Joan, had a child of her own, and she and Larry had another son, Jeffrey, but the marriage ended in 1984. Larry moved back to Chicago and lived with his mother for a while, collecting welfare, then built himself a hot-dog cart and started selling red hots around Back of the Yards.

Raul was scratching around for work and used to kill time with Larry; a few years after Raul got his gig at the Lakeview, he asked Larry to sit in with him and Gilbert. Larry's band at the time, a country outfit called Guitars and Cadillacs, was falling apart, so he hauled his gear up to the north side, and before he knew it, he and Raul and Gilbert were putting together a set. He gave up the hot-dog cart. After 25 years he was a professional musician again, playing in a neighborhood juke joint not too different from the Sky Blue Lounge.

On Saturday the lounge stays open until five and the band plays seven sets. Before they start, Raul introduces me to a regular, a towering Bosnian man with miserable eyes. He sits down across from me in a booth and begins an interminable monologue in what might graciously be thought of as broken English. He's wearing a battered tweed hat, a plaid shirt buttoned to the neck, and a striped V-neck sweater. Raul sits with Larry at the bar, laughing.

The band begins its first set, and the guy talks loudly over the music. "Hey Bosnia, can you yodel?" Raul calls from the stage. Eventually I hear the words "Bill Clinton," and the guy grunts and thrusts his pelvis forward. I try to shush him and point to Raul, who's singing "Girl From Ipanema."

"I'm sick of *singing!*" Raul screams. The band is pacing itself, starting off with a string of languid jazz standards: Cole Porter's "Night and Day" and "Begin the Beguine," "Moonlight in Vermont."

Francine, a Native American regular, comes up to say hello, and the Bosnian puts an arm around her shoulders, muttering something in her ear. She doesn't know what he's saying any better than I do, but she understands him perfectly. "Not me," she says, smiling. "I have a boyfriend." He grabs her rear and she grimly removes his hand. "OK," she says. "Just because I'm Indian doesn't mean I'm a pushover." She heads into the ladies' room, and he turns his attention back to me.

Michael is here again, sipping a glass of tequila and chatting with Gilbert and Louarine, the bartender. "Hey," he offers helpfully, "I let him do me last week. I was just trying to be a nice guy." Shortly after the Bosnian leaves, two couples walk in, clad in black from head to toe. The band puts out mightily for them, darting from one song to the next: Duane Eddy's "Ramrod," the Ventures medley, Herb Alpert's "The Lonely Bull," The Beatles' "Day Tripper," Perry Como's "It's Impossible." Michael and Francine head out onto the floor for the Ventures' "Walk, Don't Run." "Hey, Michael, don't hurt her," Raul calls out.

This is the sharpest set of the weekend, hands down. The band always lights up when the younger crowd comes in. They mix with the regulars like oil with water, but they're always there to listen, and they tip well. "There's about three different groups of them," Larry says. "All of a sudden they'll walk in the door and there'll be 15 of them. Seems like some of their friends are from out of town, and when they come to town they take 'em over by us. So we're starting to get to know them. We call them yuppies, but they're all fine people. They just got good careers and everything."

There's no point in catering to them, either—they don't come to hear Beck. "A lot of times that doesn't make it," says Raul. "You can play the number one top song, and they're looking at you like you're crazy. Then you pull out something a little older: 'Oh now, there we go, there we go.' And they're clapping and they're dancing. It seems like they hear a certain song, they drink more, and everyone wants to dance and sing. Human beings are very unpredictable. 'Oh, what's the name of that song? That was *beautiful*.' That song's older than anybody in the place, man. You never know."

Once, many years ago, while Raul was playing Freddy Fender's "Before the Next Teardrop Falls," a woman rushed up to him crying, stuffed some money into his palm, and begged him to play something else. "I'll never forget one thing my dad used to tell me when I was younger," he says. "One song to a certain person—I don't care if they're younger than you or your age or older than you—one song might mean something to that person. And you'll see the response

'Oh, thank you very much.' So you discipline yourself. Every chance I got, I would learn a song that I could sing in the job, thinking, 'Hey, one of these days that might come in handy.'"

Some songs he's played until they're worn-out, devoid of any charm or meaning for him, but when you're angling for tips, you sing what people want to hear. "They won't let go of certain songs," he marvels. "I hate 'Black Magic Woman.' I used to like it. And 'Proud Mary' and 'Wipe Out.' And 'Guitars, Cadillacs,' by Dwight Yoakam? I used to love that song. Now I'll play it if I have to. After a while, anything gets to you. I don't care if you're making top money, or you're not making top money, or somewhere in between. Even Larry: walk out, pack up, the hell with this shit. You ask yourself, 'What am I doing it for?' But then it comes to you. 'Oh yeah—'cause I like it.'"

The band cranks on into the dawn, swaggering and funky on a clean, loose-limbed workout of Ray Charles's "What'd I Say," dark and menacing on their millionth rendition of "Black Magic Woman," quiet and melancholy on Eddy Arnold's "Make the World Go Away."

Michael sits down with me. He tells me he used to own a house in the neighborhood, but then he got divorced and moved into an apartment a little farther north. He also used to drink at a pizzeria up the street, but it shut down for a while and he started coming to the Lakeview. He remembers the days before Larry and Gilbert arrived, when Raul and Pat Kelly played country-and-western tunes all night. "I've been coming here for years and I've never seen a fight," he says. "These are good people." I ask him if he had a happy birthday. "Oh sure," he says ironically. "In a way, I'm still celebrating my 21st birthday."

"Make the world go away," croons Raul. "Get it off of my shoulders . . . "

Just after 4 AM the band takes the stage for its seventh and final set. The young folks are long gone, and no one is going to help them out by sitting in at this hour. The musicians trudge through "Oye Como Va," "Lady," "La Bamba," "How 'bout 'Night Train'?" Larry's shoulders are sore, he told me before the set, but the band rolls out the James Brown instrumental before relaxing into a leisurely doo-wop progression. "I'd like to thank everybody for coming out here to the Lakeview Lounge," says Raul. "Like to hear it for Louarine the bartender, she's been here all night. We got Mr. Larry Ribs on guitar,

Gilbert on drums, and myself, Raul. And let's hear it for the boss, Kathy, for putting up with all this petty shit."

The tune trails off, and the workweek is over. "Sweet Home Alabama" comes on the jukebox. Louarine hasn't even announced last call yet, but as soon as the band quits the place clears out. Gilbert climbs up on his drum stool to kill the light over his head, and Raul chats with some patrons at the far end of the bar. He and Larry might go out for breakfast, passing houses where other people are getting up to go to church, or they might just drive home. Larry lays his gaudy Jazzmaster gently in its case and snaps the lid shut.

Old Songs in New Skins

The pop moment I've found most affecting in the last few months comes at the end of *Little Voice*, when Michael Caine's wiped-out sleazeball promoter gets up drunk on a nightclub stage and sings a horrible, self-flagellating version of Roy Orbison's "It's Over." The classic song has been rubbed smooth by decades of overplay, but now it's ripped into someone else's story so violently you may never again be able to hear it as an innocent object, as a kind of toy. Now it has been brought into a play about real life—or the play of life itself.

I couldn't get Caine's scene out of my head. I began to think about how songs survive—and one of the ways songs survive is that they mutate. Once you start thinking this way, it's like listening to a new radio station: a vampiric, surrealist station where nobody knows what time it is and everything happens at once.

Sometimes this happens subtly, around the margins, in soundtracks or commercials. The song is moved just slightly off the map we normally use to orient ourselves—but in a way that, in a year or ten, may completely change how we hear it, what associations we bring to it. Pop songs are always talked about as "the soundtrack to our lives," when all that means is that pop songs are no more than containers for nostalgia. But lives change, and so do soundtracks, even if they're made up of the same songs.

Etta James's "At Last" was a Top Ten R&B hit in 1961, and a small pop hit. After that it lived a quiet life in a small, neat house on a poor street—until last year, when the musical director from *Pleasantville* came knocking. In James's hands the record is a soft exhalation after years of silent suffering, a sweep of passion so full of doubt it all but turns in on itself, and it came to orchestrate the most romantic scene in the film: a boy and a girl, connecting for the first time, driving into the sylvan glade of Lover's Lane as the novelty of their emotions brings new color streaming into their black-and-white '50s sitcom world. The bucolic setup was too good to leave to the movie, though—and now, just months after the film's release, you can see the scene replayed, tree for tree and leaf for leaf, in a Jaguar commercial. But while in the movie the song is a forgotten voice brought back to speak as if for the first time, blessing the young lives it's dramatizing, in the commercial the song completely escapes. It's too unrushed, too patient, to be used as the commercial wants to use it: to make you want something right now. So it turns and walks away—not back to the history books, but back to Pleasantville.

Where Bob Dylan's "The Lonesome Death of Hattie Carroll" has gone is a much trickier question. Dylan supposedly wrote it after attending the 1963 March on Washington, where he and others sang for equal justice. There was a story in the paper about a rich man's son in Baltimore, one William Zantzinger, who, drunk at a society party, had beaten a black hotel worker to death. The song Dylan wrote was solemn, elegant, and almost unbearably painful. In the last verse his tone turned bitter and ugly, and he sprang the fact on which, for him, the story turned: "For penalty and repentance . . . A six-month sentence." When you listen, it's as if Dylan can barely expel the last word. It breaks and stumbles, as if the singer will never not be shocked.

Thirty-four years later, in 1997, *Homicide* ran three episodes about the murder of a Haitian maid employed by a rich Baltimore family; the father, played by James Earl Jones, had shielded his guilty son. Why? Because of William Zantzinger, the Jones character says, and he tells the old story in Bob Dylan's words, as if they are now part of a bible, as if a white man's crime should pay for a black man's, an eye for an eye, a tooth for a tooth—even if in both cases the eyes that close are those of a poor black woman. "'In the courtroom of honor, the judge pounded his gavel, to show that all's equal and that the courts are on the level,'" Jones explained, so long after the fact, or before the new fact, that it was impossible to read his tone: "'The ladder of law has no top and no bottom.'" But the law had a top and a bottom for Zantzinger, Jones was saying: Doesn't my boy deserve the same? A song that was once so clear, that sounded as if its words might be chiseled over some courthouse door, now seemed to make no sense at all.

Then last December 8, testifying before the House Judiciary Committee, Princeton history professor Sean Wilentz stirred the broth one more time. Among a group of scholars arguing against Bill Clinton's impeachment on various constitutional grounds, Wilentz seemed to come out of nowhere, pugnacious, angry, granting Republican representatives no more respect than he would a well-dressed lynch mob. He denounced the argument "that if we impeach the president, the rule of law will be vindicated if only in a symbolic way, proving forcefully that no American is above the law and that the ladder of law has no top and no bottom." Nonsense, he said: The offenses of which Clinton is accused put no constitutional principle in jeopardy—and if you vote for impeachment for any reason found outside the constitution, out of vengeance or for gain, "History will track you down."

With those last words, Wilentz recovered the voice of the song that, through blind quotation, he had made part of the official historical record of the nation—a voice of suppressed and bitter fury. ("I got tired of Henry Hyde describing Clinton as if he were William Zantzinger," Wilentz says.) In his way, Wilentz was singing a Bob Dylan song as badly as Michael Caine sings "It's Over" in *Little Voice*—and as fully. I can't listen to Roy Orbison's original anymore: compared to Caine's version it sounds bloated and strained, where Caine's is all sweat and self-loathing. The song itself may be over—or, rather, definitively appropriated, never to be given back. As for Dylan's song, like Etta James's, you can think it has just begun to travel, a mutant now, limbs fallen off, strange sores appearing, the sores growing into whole new bodies.

ALEC WILKINSON

Who Put the Honky Tonk in "Honky Tonk Women"?

There goes Ry Cooder to Cuba in 1996 to make a record with some African guitarists, but as it happens the Africans can't leave Africa—they've lost their passports or they can't obtain visas; exactly what occurred even Cooder's not sure, it was all very sudden. He rides from the airport in a taxi past buildings in pale colors, past motorcycles with eight people onboard, past the loopy trucks from Russia that haul semitrailers resembling moving vans, except that the trailers have windows and seats and carry passengers because the country doesn't have conventional buses, and right away he's happy to find himself among such tranquil festivity, and then he's in Havana—a picturesque and singular American at large, a man whom Walter Hill, one of the directors for whom Cooder has scored movies, says is "the most talented person I've ever known," who is not simply "a singer or a guitarist or a folklorist or a collector of indigenous musics or a rock 'n' roller or a bluesman but a very great artist who uses all these things to make the material of his own music," a traveler now at a loss in the landscape of fascinating rhythms and tricky chord changes. His eyes take in palm trees, old Studebakers and Lincolns, decrepit buildings, streets in deep shadow, the ocean and the wide-open tropical sky. The clear blue air smells vaguely of diesel fuel. He smokes cigars as big as hammers that last all day and make the inside of his head feel like a fabulous nightclub.

Cooder is fifty-two. He is tall and big-boned and a little bit portly. He doesn't fit easily into chairs. He has black hair, a wide and pleasingly proportioned face, and dark eyes. Lenny Waronker, the record executive who signed Cooder to his first contract, in 1969, describes Cooder as a young man by saying, "Of course he looked tremendous," and he pretty much still looks tremendous, does yoga and is the picture of rude health. Cooder, though, seems indifferent to what he looks like. From having walked behind him to tables in several restaurants, I know that he is the sort of person whose arrival in a room people notice. Partly this is because he has a head-bobbing walk that makes the movement appear to be a collection of gestures he is still practicing, but it is also because he is strikingly handsome. He has never, though, put an especially flattering picture of himself on the cover of any of his records. On most of them his features are obscured, or the lighting is unsympathetic, or he is making a goofy face, or there is no picture of him at all. Cooder is averse to self-promotion. He has never changed the color of his hair. He has no tattoos. He has never appeared in a beer commercial or made an arrangement to wear the clothes of a specific designer or connived with a press agent to be photographed in the company of a famous actress or released photographs of how he looks sitting around his house or ones that reveal his body or that portray him engaged in lewd activities, and it is unlikely that he will—it is difficult to persuade him to have his photograph taken at all. The photographs of him that best reveal the warmth and complexity and depth of his nature have been taken by his wife, Susan, to whom he has been married for almost thirty years.

By temperament Cooder is diffident and retiring. He is more apt to find fault with himself than with someone else. He worries a lot and is subject to unbidden apprehensions and is pleased to observe that his son, Joachim, who is twenty and plays drums, seems to worry about nothing at all. He has a versatile and agile intelligence, and he reads a great deal, and his talk is expansive and idiosyncratic. Walter Hill describes Cooder's conversation as a kind of "verbal jazz. It's very poetic," he says. "There's a kind of circularity to it." If you ask Cooder how he happened to record a certain song, "Hey Porter," for example, by Johnny Cash, he might say that what makes modern American music different from the music of other cultures is the jukebox, and that before World War II, during the jazz-band era, that is, musicians made records to promote their performances, so that people would come to see them—records were novelties, almost—radio hadn't yet embraced regional music, and there weren't that many radio stations anyway. After the war, people developed the habit of going to bars and cafés and feeding the jukebox, and if you were a musician and wanted your record to be chosen from among the fifty others offered, you had to come up with something conspicuous and memorable, and so the music of the period—Johnny Cash, say, with "Big River" or "Hey Porter" or "Ring of Fire"—was very poignant and microcosmic in its compression of experience, the best songs were honed to something that resembled miniature masterpieces—proof of this was that nothing else was going to come into your mind while you're listening to them—and meanwhile everyone was working to get a hit, even Howlin' Wolf, even Muddy Waters, and these great records were made in very informal settings, hotel rooms sometimes, and the offices of record companies where the employees pushed the furniture to the walls at the end of the day and set up microphones, and so the records had a warmth and informality that has surely been lost, because at a certain point technology overtook sentiment—bound to happen, there was so much money involved—and so you began to hear more of the equipment used in making the record and less of the music, more of the science and less of the feeling, and you can't go back now, no, you can't, you sure can't, and the only time you can perhaps is to a place like Cuba, where they still have beautiful music, and not so much of a technological society.

Cooder went to Cuba with the producer Nick Gold. Making a record in Cuba was Gold's idea. Cuban music having its origins in strains of African music, Gold thought something worthwhile would undoubtedly come of having Cooder and the Africans play with Cuban musicians. Without the Africans, there's nothing to do but start auditioning Cubans and asking the whereabouts of musicians Cooder knows from records. Twenty years earlier, as part of a cultural exchange, he was briefly in Cuba with some American jazz musicians. He brought home a wagonload of records and a tape someone gave him of a performance by a musician playing a type of guitar called the *tres*. Cooder found the music in Cuba deeply alluring—he loved the seductive and intricate rhythms, the concise and lyrical melodies, and the music's capacity to succinctly express emotion—but he says, "I was too young and uncertain to know what to do about it; I couldn't just go up to someone and say, 'Let's record,' so I went home and thought about it for twenty years." Occasionally when he met someone familiar with Cuban music, he played him the tape of the *tres* player and asked if he knew who it was, but no one did.

Cooder doesn't like to perform. He would rather play music in a recording studio than in public, with the result that he has probably been seen onstage less often and by fewer people than any other popular musician of his stature. More than ten years have passed since he appeared on tour to promote one of his rock 'n' roll records. Seven years ago, he played a series of concerts with Little Village, whose other members were John Hiatt, Jim Keltner, and Nick Lowe. Last year, with a collection of Cuban musicians and Joachim, he performed at two concerts in Amsterdam and one in New York at Carnegie Hall, all of which were sold out. Rather than occupy a position at the front of the stage, he sat toward the back, on a folding chair, beside Joachim.

Cooder withdrew from performing partly because he doesn't like leaving home, partly because there are areas of the world, especially northern Europe, where he feels an unease that is close to dread, but mainly because onstage he feels exquisitely self-conscious. "I don't like being watched," he says, "and I don't like being an entertainer. You get up there, and it's all so loud, and the stage is so big, and how you do is all so critical, and I thought, I can't stand there one more time and say, 'Ladies and gentlemen, and especially you ladies . . .'" Furthermore, once a show was over, he tended to become despondent. "I felt like a withered balloon under a chair on the day after a birthday party," he says. "People who love the applause should have it, but I don't care for it."

Very few people hear Cooder play guitar anymore. He lives in Santa Monica, California, and mainly he plays by himself or with only a few people present, in a recording studio usually somewhere in Los Angeles or the practice room he has at home in what used to be the garage. Joachim has a friend named Sunny Levine, who mixes records in the bedroom he occupies in his parents' house in Pacific Palisades, the next town north from Santa Monica. Recently Joachim asked his father if he would play guitar on a song that Levine was working on, and Cooder said that he would, so one afternoon I went with Cooder to Levine's room, which had a view out a sliding glass door of the roofs of the Pacific Palisades and beyond them the ocean, and Joachim and a friend of his sat on the bed, and Cooder sat on a chair in the center of the room, with his back to the view, and untangled guitar cords and plugged himself into a small amplifier and put on some headphones and tinkered with his guitar until he got it to produce the swampy, raspy, low-down, growly tone that he wanted. Sunny set up a microphone by the amplifier, and for Cooder's benefit we listened to the song, which was a trancy, ethereal dance tune with a guy sort of half singing, half whispering a refrain that went more or less, "I used to love you," something, something, "but that was enough for me," and Cooder said, "Uh-huh . . . that's nice . . . well, all right, I can do something on that." He recorded three takes, each lasting several minutes. On the first, he played a restrained and sinuous figure involving two dense chords. On the second, he played a rhythmic and piercing tenor line that had a slightly Indian feel to it. On the third, he added a series of steplike bass figures. He started beating time with his foot on the floor, and then he closed his eyes and his head began moving from side to side and back and forth like a bird's, and his knee rose higher and higher until his foot was pounding on the floor, and he was frowning and flinching and wincing, and he looked like a holiness preacher at a tent revival, and I felt like I was sitting in the amen corner.

Cuba: Cooder and Gold have no simple time organizing the musicians. Nearly all of them are elderly—the oldest is eighty-nine—and one of them Cooder hoped to find is dead. Few of them have phones, and most people in Cuba, he learned, don't answer the phone anyway.

"Down there when the phone rings," Cooder says, "it's like a dog bark-ing—no one pays any attention." After a few days, Cooder and Gold have chased down and invited and talked from retirement a collection of suave and spry and elegantly accomplished men and one woman, nearly twenty altogether, and they set up shop in Old Havana in a stu-dio called Egrem, which is on the second floor of a sprawling, rickety, wooden, and termite-ridden apartment house. Egrem belongs to the government. It is hardly used anymore and has been allowed to dilapi-date. Water leaking from apartments above has soaked the tiles on the ceiling. When the tiles dried out, they shrank, and some of them fell off and others hang loose, but something about the age of the walls and the shape of the room is sympathetic, and anything recorded here sounds warm and natural and true and has the breath of life, and later, in California, when Cooder plays back tapes of music recorded at Egrem, he sometimes says, "You can hear the room, can't you?" The tape machines at Egrem are old and over the years have been repaired with whatever materials were at hand—"It's real dime-store engineer-ing," Cooder says—and he and Gold send to Mexico City for parts, and they're almost ready to make a record. What they need is a singer. Someone suggests Ibrahim Ferrer, who is seventy and two years earlier, having no work, completely gave up the idea that he was ever going to sing again, but he's graceful and thin as a reed and moves like a cat, and his voice is fit.

To conduct the musicians, Cooder hires Juan de Marcos González, who is considered the best *tres* player on the island. Cooder plays González the tape, and González's eyes open wide as umbrellas, and he says, "How did you get that?" Cooder says, "Twenty years ago" and "present from someone" and "kept it all this time," and González says, "It is me, when I was a young man."

After a Havana hangout that no one remembers the exact location of anymore, Cooder and Gold call the record *Buena Vista Social Club,* and the rest of the story is perhaps sufficiently familiar that I needn't add that the record sells more than a million copies and wins a Grammy, and as a result every agent and promoter and performer in America sees dollar bills when he looks at the map of Cuba, and in February 1999 the *New York Times* prints an article (MORE AMERICANS GOING TO CUBA AS PERFORMERS) that fails to mention Cooder and instead says that seventy country-and-western and rock 'n' roll acts and Burt Bacharach and Jimmy Buffett and MTV are all going to Cuba, most of them together, and you might think that a life on an island, even a hard life on a semi-impoverished island, with palm trees and sugarcane and the smell of diesel fuel and raw sewage in the air and the ocean and the wide-open tropical sky, such a life, bereft of seventy American pop acts and Burt Bacharach and Jimmy Buffett and MTV, is not an existence a person would necessarily rush to describe as one of deprivation, but even if Cooder thinks so, he is far too gracious a person ever to say such a thing.

Under his own name, Cooder made eleven records from 1970 to 1987, and then he quit making them. The records consist of songs he found beautiful for one reason or another. Some of the songs are so primitive in their structure that they are hardly songs, and some are so complicated that they would tax the capacities of most popular musicians. The records include songs he wrote; songs from the catalogs of blues, soul, rhythm and blues, rock 'n' roll, rockabilly, and jazz; Hawaiian songs; cowboy songs; drifter, tramp, and hobo songs; Mexican songs; American songs from bygone times, especially the Depression and the Dust Bowl era; pop songs, gospel songs, folk songs, and songs from the Caribbean. They represent a variety unexampled in the repertoire of any other popular musician. "The biggest inspiration I had," he says, "was to take *norteño* soul music and fuse it with Mexican music. It was my great big idea to do that. I was listening to *norteño* stuff—accordion and rhythm and boleros. This is the seventies. You got a culture that is centered around northern Mexico and the border and southern Texas, people who got across the border but didn't go far. They play this music with an accordion, which was brought to them by Germans that worked on the railroads, and so they play these polkas, but in a Mexican style." Cooder learned to play the accordion well enough that he could go to San Antonio and teach songs to the accordion player and bandleader Flaco Jimenez and then come back to Los Angeles and teach them to the singers he worked with, and finally he got Jimenez and his band and the singers together in Los Angeles to make a record he called *Chicken Skin Music*.

The rhythms of Cooder's arrangements are distinctive and highly eccentric. He describes them sometimes, especially the earlier music he recorded, as having the feel of "some kind of steam device gone out of control" or as having "a weird teapot effect, like the lid's about to blow off." Such a keen sense of the divisions and stresses of rhythm were inspired partly, he says, by listening as a young man to a record of brass music made by a group of black men who had found in a field the instruments belonging to a regiment of Civil War soldiers who had dropped them when they fled an engagement. No one had taught the men how to play the instruments, and they had arranged the music to suit their own ears. If you happen to be unfamiliar with the sound of a typical Cooder arrangement, one way I can think of to describe it is to say that when Cooder was a young man, he was brought into the studio to assist the Rolling Stones in recording their album *Let It Bleed,* and one day he was playing guitar, goofing around, clicking this and popping that, and Mick Jagger came dancing over and said, "Oh that's very interesting, what you're playing; how do you do that? You tune the E strings down to a D, and you put your fingers there, oh, I see, and you pull them off quickly like that, yes, that's very good," and Cooder showed him the whole thing—he was young, he didn't know that sometimes you got to keep your stuff indoors—and the next thing he knew, the Rolling Stones were picking up royalties for "Honky Tonk Women," which sounds precisely like a song arranged by Ry Cooder and absolutely nothing like any other song ever arranged in thirty years by the Rolling Stones.

The first of Cooder's ancestors to arrive in America, around the time of the Revolution, came from the Low Countries—that is, the area including Holland, Belgium, and Luxembourg. He spelled his name Kuder, and one of his descendants married into a family in Ohio named Ryland.

Cooder grew up in Santa Monica. His father went to World War II, then, with a GI loan, bought a house on a hill above the Santa Monica airport. Cooder was an only child. As a boy, he often had trouble sleeping. In the middle of the night, from the window of his bedroom, he aimed binoculars at the planes landing and taking off and at the people

on the night shift coming and going from a factory where aircraft were
built. The activity suggested a world at one remove from his own—
men and women who worked while the rest of the world slept—and he
tried to imagine what they did. When he was about four, his parents
gave him a radio. "The guy on the air would tell the time and give the
ads brought to you by whoever," he says, "and it was reassuring." Part
of Cooder's apprehension derived from an accident he had when he
was three. He was fixing a toy car with a knife, and the knife slipped
and entered his left eye. For a year after that, he says, "all I remember
is sitting in dark rooms and going to hospitals and seeing doctors. A kid
can't foresee anything like that, and once it happened it seemed as if
the sky could fall in, as if at any time something can go wrong in a big
hurry, and forever." He was eventually fitted with a prosthetic eye. His
left eyelid occasionally droops, which makes him look sleepy.

One night in the year after the accident, when Cooder was four, he
was lying in bed in the dark on his back. The door to his room opened.
A friend of his father's, a violinist, came in and laid something on his
stomach. Cooder asked, "What's this?" and the man said, "It's a guitar."

Throughout his growing up, Cooder kept mainly to himself. He
rode his bike to the ocean. He liked to visit the airport because "it was
quiet and peaceful, and the little planes looked like toys." Sometimes
he took the bus to the beach or down to Venice, where the oil wells
were. "To me that was heaven," he says. "It was messy, and it looked
like the desert." When he got a driver's license, he liked to drive downtown and look at the old buildings, whose appeal for him was strong
but obscure. "It's empty enough to where you could like something in
there," he says. "I just don't know what it is, I'm sure I don't."

He didn't care for school. "It was like something I thought I'd never
survive," he says. "Like it was Devil's Island, and I was each night making
one more mark on the wall, crossing off the days." By the time he was
sixteen, he played guitar well enough that he was working as a sideman
on various records. When he was eighteen, a producer engaged him to
help the legendary figure Don Van Vliet, who performed as Captain
Beefheart, make his first record, *Safe as Milk*. Van Vliet's outfit was called
Captain Beefheart and His Magic Band. Cooder was taking the place of
his guitarist, who had suffered a nervous breakdown. Van Vliet lived in
the desert. Cooder would drive out to rehearse with the band. Occasion-

ally the guitarist would appear at a rehearsal, and Van Vliet, whose manner with the members of his band was imperious, would order him to return to his room. One day the guitarist showed up carrying a loaded crossbow. "The first thing I thought," Cooder says, "is that he's going to point it at me, since I'm taking his place, and the next thing he's going to hiccup and shoot me." Van Vliet ordered the guitarist to put down the crossbow and go back to his room. Cooder finished the record and then decided to enroll at Reed College in Portland, Oregon, where he lasted only a year. "I liked the trees, I liked nature, I liked being up in Portland," he says, "but once you've recorded with Captain Beefheart and looked down the barrel of a crossbow, you might get a little bored in college." While he was in Oregon, he kept getting calls to return to Los Angeles to contribute to various records. Finally, he had missed enough school that he was summoned by his adviser, who asked him to explain the absences. Cooder described what was involved in playing on sessions. The adviser asked, "Do you get paid?" Cooder said, "Last time I played about a week and made $5,000." The adviser recovered himself and said, "What are you doing here?" and Cooder said, "Well, it was kind of my parents' idea."

Many rock guitar players consider their guitar to be an accessory to their appearance. They match its color to their outfits. They have guitars made in peculiar shapes. They have flags painted on them, or maybe the insignia of a liquor company. They have the necks and bodies inlaid with mother-of-pearl dragons or death's-heads or devils or snaky patterns of geometric figures. Cooder's guitars are homely. He plays guitars that a lot of other musicians would be embarrassed to be seen with. He cares about how a guitar sounds, not how it looks. He plays guitars that look as if he bought them at a yard sale on a trailer lawn in Arkansas where the lawn wasn't grass but pavement and the only other things for sale on the floppy little card table set up for the affair were some not thoroughly washed jam jars and glasses, a few pieces of cheap pewter flatware, a drink box without a lid, some filthy children's clothes, and a fan whose blades don't turn anymore and whose motor (you would discover when you got it home) makes a bad smell when you plug it in.

Most of Cooder's guitars are built for him from parts obtained from other guitars. He has an affection for the sound of guitars that no longer exist. A person can examine a photograph of, say, Robert Johnson or some other historical figure holding a guitar and try to determine what company made it, but the guitar in the picture might not be the one the musician played on his records. It might have belonged to the photographer, or it might have been rented as a prop for the occasion. Even if the guitar in the photograph is the one the musician played, it was undoubtedly a cheap guitar that likely ended up stolen or pawned or changing hands in a card game and by now the strings have pulled the neck out of line or someone left it in a basement that flooded or ran over it while backing out of the garage.

When Cooder finds a guitar with a sufficient number of companionable qualities, he sends it to a guitar builder and repairman on Staten Island named Flip Scipio. Describing Cooder's collection of guitars, Scipio says, "He has a *few* vintage instruments, but he also has things that seem to be out of the trash can. There's a certain kind of music he wants to play where you need cheap instruments. You can't use a $13,000 guitar to play a song that was recorded in a hotel room in Chicago in the fifties by a blues musician who bought his guitar at Sears." Cooder says, "Everything I got is irreplaceable, junk though it may be."

Cooder is not attempting merely to reproduce the sound of cheap, old guitars. He is obsessed with finding a sound that is resonant and authentic to his ear and that frees his mind from thinking about anything else when he's playing. Scipio says that Cooder is "always looking for the big note, the sound that makes all the inhibitions fall away." Not having the sound that he wants frustrates him the way not having a sufficient grasp of the grammar and vocabulary of a foreign language frustrates a traveler abroad who has something important to communicate about what he is feeling.

Cooder is receptive to intuitions and impulses and the texts of dreams. As a young man he dreamed one night that he was lost in the jungle. "You could see the sky through the tops of the trees," he says, "but that's about all you could see. Everywhere else you looked was just the trees. I knew that if I kept on walking, I would probably come to a place where I could see where I was, so I continued and eventually found a little clearing. By now it was night, and I thought I would lie down and get some sleep, and just as I did I heard this *crash, crash, crash* coming through the jungle, and out jumps Curtis Mayfield, from the Impressions, looking like a savage, with the war paint on his face and his chest and the bone in his nose and the necklace of teeth and a spear in one hand and a shield in the other and the black-rimmed glasses he wore. He had this guitar strung on his back, and the guitar was made out of bark and leaves and branches and snake skins, and it had barbed-wire strings. I said, 'Whoa, so that's it, that's the secret—the barbed-wire strings.' He said, 'If that's what you think is the reason for the sound, then I can't help you,' and he turned around and disappeared back into the jungle. I had that dream twenty years ago, and I never forgot it."

One night a few weeks ago Joachim's band, Speakeasy, was playing at a club in Hollywood, and I went with Cooder to see them. The band has eight members—two sisters who are singers and six guys, who among them play drums and percussion, guitar, lap guitar, violin, accordion, trumpet, and trombone. Joachim has known the younger of the sisters since they were classmates in the seventh grade—that year, she and Joachim performed together in the school's talent show; she sang and Joachim played drums. The girls are tall and slender and have dark hair and big, dark eyes and sharp cheekbones—not long ago, a movie star offered to keep one of them—and from time to time Cooder's laywer is occupied making phone calls to executives in the record business who would like to separate them from the band. The lawyer, Cooder says, instructs the executives "to stay the hell out of Dodge."

Speakeasy plays music like Cooder played during Joachim's child-hood, which is to say, some rhythm and blues, some ballads, some rockabilly, some car songs, and some country songs. Cooder some-times helps them with arrangements and teaches the guitar player parts.

Cooder and I arrived at the club early and drank two margaritas. There was a stage at one end of a dance floor and a bar to one side. Cooder said that the place was similar to plenty of clubs he had played during the early days of his career, when he traveled with a guitar and a mandolin and played by himself. "I used to love to come to these places early," he said. "Arrive and watch the waitresses set up and lay out the napkins. It was a nice, quiet time." Before long, he grew nervous, though. He began to pace. Then he sat down and tried to keep still. He went to talk to the sound man, because he said they usually only know how to set up microphones for heavy-metal bands and that his son's band was more complicated than that. Joachim arrived, and I heard Cooder tell him, "The song's too slow."

"Still?"

"Give it a bit of a groove tempo. It'll still feel down, but it won't be so down," he said, the way another kind of father might say, "Quit chasing the ball. Don't swing until you get the pitch you really want."

Several bands were on the bill for the evening, and Speakeasy had been engaged to play first. While the members were setting up their instruments, Cooder sat at a table toward the back of the room and said to no one in particular, "See how good I'm being—I'm just sitting here." He was especially anxious because Eliades Ochoa, who played guitar on the *Buena Vista Social Club* album, was in Los Angeles making his own record and had said he would come hear Joachim. Eliades arrived with his girlfriend, who had an oval-shaped face and long, shiny black hair and wore a T-shirt and a full, pleated skirt. Neither she nor Eliades speaks English. Around eight-thirty, the two beautiful sisters stood in the center of the stage, and the boys stood on either side of them, like parentheses, and the girls sang like angels, and the boys played wonderfully, while Cooder ran up and down the stairs to the sound booth, making suggestions.

Afterward we helped Joachim load his drums into his car. Then we drove Eliades and his girlfriend to their hotel in Hollywood. Eliades wanted a cigar, and Cooder tried to find a place where he could buy one. "What we need is one of those yuppie places with fancy cigars," he said, and he thought of one, but when we arrived it was closed. Eventually we pulled up in front of a convenience store next door to their hotel, and Cooder sat double-parked in the car, and I went in with Eliades and his girlfriend and stood with them in front of a glass cabinet filled with cigars that I felt sure could only disappoint someone from Cuba. After a lot of deliberation with his girlfriend, Eliades bought two cigars, and I followed them back outside. Cooder had parked the car and was walking toward us. The evening was a little cool, and he was wearing a blue duffle coat, like a boarding-school boy. Eliades was wearing jeans and a shirt and cowboy boots and a straw hat in the shape of a cowboy hat. He is short, and Cooder towered over him. The three of them stood talking. Cooder doesn't speak Spanish, so the talk was mostly gestures and a few words, with Cooder leaning toward Eliades as if he were addressing the brim of his hat. Cooder thanked him for coming to hear Joachim. They all nodded. Cooder seemed fatigued by having seen to all the details of the evening, among them their comfort. For a moment the three of them stood there—an exotic American, a notable Cuban, and a woman for whom "Señorita" seemed the only proper form of address, three figures on the Hollywood pavement, awash in the shimmering light that was a mixture of the light from the streetlamps, neon and car headlights, and the illumination from the windows of the big hotel. Cooder patted Eliades on the shoulder, and then he and his girlfriend started walking toward the hotel, Eliades rocking from side to side on the worn heels of his boots like a small boat in heavy weather. Not until the crowd on the street had absorbed them did Cooder turn toward his car.

BEN SANDMEL

Mr. K-Doe Goes
to Washington

On the Fourth of July in Washington, D.C., in the shadow of the
Washington Monument, a gospel band is eating lunch. The musicians
are fueling up for their impending performance at the National Park
Service's annual Independence Day Concert, held outdoors at the Sylvan Theater. Their at-table chit-chat stops suddenly when a striking
figure enters the back-stage hospitality tent.

The man sports a cobalt blue suit, some seriously big hair, and an intense yet abstracted stare. The musicians, who accompany gospel diva
Shirley Caesar, are dressed in mundane street clothes. They realize
that someone of importance has arrived, but are a little fuzzy when it
comes to his name.

"Aren't you a famous singer?" one of them asks.

The important personage pauses dramatically. "Yes . . . I am," he
replies. Several more seconds pass. He seems to be letting the full pro-
fundity of this fact sink in.

"Well, who are you?" his inquisitor continues.

"Let's just put it like this," the blue-bedecked man intones. "There
ain't but two songs that will stand the test of time, until the end of the

world. One of them is 'The Star Spangled Banner.' The other one is 'Mother-in-Law.'"

In the 38 years since "Mother-in-Law" reached Number One on both the national pop and rhythm & blues charts, the man born Ernest Kador Jr.—better known as Ernie K-Doe—has traversed a wide range of peaks and valleys. Besides hitting big with "Mother-in-Law," K-Doe says that one of his most triumphant summits came in 1962, when he "beat James Brown on stage" during a hometown concert at the Municipal Auditorium in New Orleans. K-Doe also recalls playing such R & B shrines as New York's Apollo Theater and the Regal Theater in Chicago. Many of his other '60s recordings—"A Certain Girl," "Te-Ta-Te-Ta-Ta," "Shirley," "Tain't It the Truth" and "Hello, My Lover"— were regional hits that became perennial favorites, but did not sell well outside of the South. Nevertheless, they are classic performances that enhanced the legacies of Ernie K-Doe and producer/arranger Allen Toussaint as masters of the New Orleans R & B genre.

During the 1980s, a more distinctive facet of K-Doe's talent emerged during weekly broadcasts on New Orleans' community radio station, WWOZ-FM. A typical show consisted of K-Doe spinning his own old records while screaming such pronouncements as "I'm a Charity Hospital baby!", "Yeah, I'm cocky—I'm supposed to be cocky!" and even the ultimately immodest "How great thou art!"

This ranting rhetoric spawned a cottage industry in bootleg tapes of his radio programs, but it didn't do much for K-Doe's career. He was taken off the air, to the dismay of his many fans, although he still returns as a special guest during fund drives. He fell on hard times, drinking heavily, and his lovably loose performances descended into sloppy embarrassments. K-Doe earned a reputation for being difficult and unreliable, and few venues would take a chance on booking him. It looked as if the valleys might mark the end of his line.

Happily, however, Ernie K-Doe was saved by love. In 1994, he married Antoinette Fox, who has turned his life around both personally and professionally. Antoinette helped him stop drinking. "It was like God removing a devil from his body," she says. She now makes sure that he is prompt and clear-headed on the bandstand, and spends hours designing and hand-sewing his elaborate stage outfits. "I'm a seamstress by trade," Antoinette explains. "I learned from my grandmother.

When I was a little girl, I never played outside with all the other children. I was sitting at that old Singer sewing machine with her."

Together, Antoinette and Ernie run the Mother-in-Law Lounge at the corner of Claiborne and Columbus. This friendly neighborhood bar and shrine to K-Doe has become a must-see for discerning tourists who flock to New Orleans as a musical Mecca. It also draws a diverse local crowd that ranges from green-haired grunge types to middle-aged couples. K-Doe sings there on the majority of weekends, and can be found holding court almost every evening. Special events include the annual renewal of Ernie and Antoinette's wedding vows, each January. The public is always invited.

Most significantly, K-Doe is performing nationally again, and playing select showcase gigs at that, instead of grinding out endless sets on the club circuit. In February 1998, he received a prestigious Pioneer Award from the Rhythm & Blues Foundation at the organization's annual banquet, which was held that year in New York. K-Doe accepted the award, which came with a five-figure stipend, by cutting up during the ceremony and cheerfully disrupting the proceedings with an unauthorized encore. The audience included Stevie Wonder, Gladys Knight and emcee Smokey Robinson, who was reduced into hysterics at the podium by K-Doe's antics.

That set and another great one at the 1998 New Orleans Jazz & Heritage Festival sent the message that Ernie K-Doe was back on his feet. Thankfully, being clean and sober hasn't turned him dull. His voice is strong, he's still good for some bursts of fancy footwork, and he knows how to work a crowd. He can hold his own on stage, and there's nowhere he'd rather be.

"I'm just like a rabbit," K-Doe says. As with many of his pronouncements, there is often a distinct tinge of surrealism, at least at the beginning—and frequently at the end, too. Beyond his solid musical talent, a major part of K-Doe's appeal lies in his anarchic, loose-cannon charisma. He is a charming New Orleans eccentric with a wild sense of humor and a flair for vivid verbal imagery. At the same time, K-Doe is extremely street-wise and savvy. There are moments when his outrageous persona seems to be a calculating ploy that serves him well in public; in one-on-one conversation, he is much more reflective and rational. Still, K-Doe's endearing spaciness is never far beneath the surface. "When you throw that rabbit in the briar patch," he continues, "that's exactly where he wants to be. And that's me, on stage. I'm happy then, and I'm making others happy, too."

This palpable, infectious happiness—combined with K-Doe's impressive credentials and cleaned-up act—prompted Nick Spitzer, the artistic director and co-host of the Independence Day Concert, to invite him to perform in Washington. "We always feature a New Orleans or South Louisiana artist, but we've never had any of the great, classic R & B heroes," explains Spitzer, who once served as Louisiana's state folklorist. He currently produces and hosts the New Orleans–based public radio program *American Routes*. "It seemed like the right time to bring in Ernie K-Doe," Spitzer goes on, "and pair him up with the great R&B pianist Eddie Bo. They're good friends, and they have often played together over the years." Beyond entertaining a large crowd in Washington—later estimated at 60,000 people—the concert will be carried by some 150 radio stations across America, with K-Doe's segment broadcast on WWOZ, the aural home of his former on-air glories.

Rewind to July 3rd, when both the Ernie K-Doe and Eddie Bo entourages are assembled at New Orleans International Airport for an early-morning flight to Washington. It's just been announced that the flight has been delayed for three and a half hours. Antoinette K-Doe and her cousin, Tee Eva Perry, are trying to catch up on their sleep. Perry owns and operates a praline shop and sno-ball stand on Magazine Street, just three doors down from Trent Reznor's recording studio. She also has appeared in several music videos and in the movie *JFK*, and has been singing and dancing with the K-Does for the last five years. Tee Eva and Antoinette refer to themselves collectively as "the Paradise Ladies." They always dress identically on the road, to Antoinette's specifications, and at the moment they are sporting lime-green tights while fidgeting in their tortuously rigid airport chairs.

But Ernie K-Doe is feeling good, despite arriving early for nothing, and he's in a very talkative mood. "I used to play in Washington back in the '60s," he recalls, "at the sweet old Howard Theater. I was on a big show there with Del Shannon, Chuck Jackson, Smokey Robinson and the Miracles, and a young lady called Baby Face Washington. I played at the White House several times when John F. Kennedy was president, but I never got to meet him. This time I'm going back under

President Bill Clinton. What would I say to President Clinton if I got to meet him? 'Come on up on this stage and blow your tenor saxophone!'

"Am I nervous about playing in front of such a big crowd? Let's just put it like this: I am ready for them, and I hope they are ready for me. I haven't missed yet. There is a first time for everything, but I don't believe that this will be it. And I'm glad that I had the pleasure of making a record that will stand the test of time, because people gonna have a mother-in-law until the end of the world. There is plenty of competition for me now, because the young generation has heard about Ernie K-Doe, and now they are going to get a chance to see Ernie K-Doe, and they will find out that their parents was telling them the truth.

"As far as the young generation with their rap music, you're putting me on the spot, now, but let's just put it like this. Rap, to me—and I could be wrong—but the way I feel about rap is it's a phase. With rap you really don't have to sing. Not like guys like me, B. B. King, Jackie Wilson, Bobby 'Blue' Bland, Joe Hinton, Joe Tex, Johnny Adams . . . I like to *sing*, and when I listen at rap I would say there's no real *singing*. But I would also say this: *They* know what they are doing, even if *I* don't.

"I have a new CD that's a gas, man," K-Doe proudly proclaims. "Warren Hildebrand put it out [*The Best of Ernie K-Doe*, Mardi Gras Records]. And I got a song on there called 'You Done Did It, Baby.' It goes 'You done did it, baby, you made my love come down.' It's the first blues song that I ever recorded; the others were all different styles, this is my first real blues, on record. And in this record, the lady that I'm singing to, I call her 'booty.' Every woman in the world carry a booty, and she thinks that her cargo is the best in the world. I'm relying on all the ladies in the world to let this be their national anthem. When I holler, 'Oh, booty! Good booty! Welfare booty! Every kind of booty!' then all the ladies gonna stand up and holler, 'I got one!' and then the lady across the hallway she gonna holler, 'I got one, too!' All the ladies is proud of what they're carrying around. It's a ladies' theme song. I want the ladies to feel proud about themselves. And I want them looking forward to me making my comeback."

A crowd has gathered during this soliloquy, but it's neither libidinous nor irate women, as might be expected. It's a group of boy scouts in full uniform, en route to a field trip in the nation's capital. They instinctively sense the presence of greatness, although they cannot identify the celebrity whom destiny has booked on their flight. No matter. Ernie K-Doe, resplendent in an orange suit and shoes, does not disappoint them. As the scouts wait patiently in line, he graciously signs autographs and poses with them for snapshots.

The plane lands in Washington, and the musicians plus their retinue are whisked straight to the stage for a rehearsal and sound-check. The afternoon heat is stultifying, and everyone retreats to an air-conditioned trailer, where a deli tray awaits the hungry travelers. The caterer, obviously, is not from New Orleans. "What the hell is this?" several people ask with revulsion. They rummage through the bottom layers of piled food, muttering imprecations about red beans, hot sausage, and French bread, but their search is in vain. The portobello mushroom and roasted pepper sandwiches remain uneaten. So do the bowls of cous-cous and tabouleh.

The rehearsal is a great success, however. K-Doe and Eddie Bo both know that this is a big gig, and because it's live, on national radio, there can be no lulls, wasted time, or "dead air." A short, tight set of eight songs is worked out and run through, and a few minor adjustments are made. They finally check into the Phoenix Park Hotel to rest up for tomorrow.

Besides K-Doe and Bo, the Independence Day Concert features a wide spectrum of other artists, including Shirley Caesar, Latin percussionist Tito Puente, and bluegrass icon Ralph Stanley. By mid-afternoon on July 4th, these stars, their band members and other concert performers are all milling about the hotel lobby. Later in the evening, at what K-Doe calls the "after-party," many of them will join in an impromptu, unlikely, multi-cultural jam session. Right now, it's fascinating just to watch them interact.

Each headliner is a leader of his or her respective genre, but there's no contest when it comes to picking the day's snazziest dressers. K-Doe wears his cobalt blue outfit for the ride to the concert site; soon after his arrival—and his cryptic conversation with Shirley Caesar's band—he heads to the trailer to change yet again. After lengthy preparations, K-Doe and the Paradise Ladies emerge wearing identical red-white-and-blue Uncle Sam outfits, replete with tall, floppy stovepipe hats.

Fully in character, Antoinette addresses Ernie as "Uncle Sam."

"Y'all behave," he replies, "or I'm gonna start signing them dollar bills on the left!" Like many K-Doe-isms this sounds good, but no one seems to know exactly what it means.

K-Doe and Eddie Bo are relaxed and nonchalant about the upcoming show, but the Paradise Ladies are extremely excited. "From a little girl," Tee Eva says, "this has always been my American dream, to be an entertainer, singer and dancer. Now here I am, and I'm very happy! I'm so proud that Antoinette and Ernie chose me to perform with them. It's the Fourth of July, and here I am in Washington, D.C.! The three of us have such a great time singing and traveling together. Ernie is such a wonderful person to be around. I get a real good education from him 'cause he knows his music so well, he instructs and teaches. And Antoinette is amazing, too."

"I thank God that Ernie is finally getting the recognition that he deserves," Antoinette reflects. "I thank God that he's living to see it. God has been a healing process for the two of us. I respect Ernie because he respects ladies, and he never tries to clip a lady's wings, in business. That says a lot about him, especially for a man from his generation. They don't like to see a lady fill a man's shoes. But he respects me as a bar owner, and he supports me and Tee Eva 100 percent. I love performing with him, and sewing our costumes gives me an outlet for different sides of my personality and my creativity.

"The main thing to understand," Antoinette points out, "is that I'm married to the man, not the legend. The legend belongs to the people. I know him as the legend but I love him as the man behind the legend. As long as you can separate those two things then you can handle it. I respect his career, and he respects mine. When I'm busy at my sewing machine, the legend leaves me alone."

Waiting to go on, the legend has a backstage guest—a DJ named Libby Gates, from WWMG, an oldies station in Charlotte, North Carolina. "I've known K-Doe's music all my life," Gates says, "and I've known him and Antoinette for five years. People in New Orleans may take Ernie K-Doe for granted, but our station has his music in heavy rotation. My co-workers don't believe that I'm friends with someone so famous."

By now it is show time. Eddie Bo opens up with hot versions of his two biggest tunes, "Check Your Bucket" and "Check Mr. Popeye," and then Nick Spitzer brings on Ernie K-Doe and the Paradise Ladies. Their patriotic outfits elicit roars of approval as K-Doe tears into his first song, "Honey, Hush." With a 28-minute set there is no time to warm up gradually, but K-Doe doesn't need to. He is already in a full frenzy, inspired by the sight of a sea of faces and the Washington Monument thrusting skyward. "Here's one that sold a million for Ernie K-Doe!" he screams, launching into "A Certain Girl." When K-Doe feels inspired, as he does now, a song's published lyrics are heavily interspersed with such phrases as "I'm cocky but I'm good!" "Burn, K-Doe, burn!" and "Get up on your feet for Ernie K-Doe!" Sometimes, this last command is followed by the order, "Now, bow down on your knees to Ernie K-Doe!" but not today. Many people obey his exhortation to stand, however. K-Doe clearly has the audience in his spell, with one notable exception—the poor, confused woman on the far right of the stage who's attempting to "sign" his remarks for the hearing impaired.

"A Certain Girl" is followed by an over-the-top rendition of "Mother-in-Law." K-Doe and the Paradise Ladies bow, blow kisses, and leave the stage. Eddie Bo plays "Hook and Drag" with his fine band, and then brings back K-Doe and company for an encore/finale of Jesse Hill's New Orleans R & B classic "Ooh Poo Pah Doo." All too quickly it's over, though the crowd is screaming for more.

Backstage, an exhausted but exultant Ernie K-Doe appraises his performance. "It went good, man, very nice! I enjoyed myself! You got over 60-some thousand people out there. That shows you I still have drawing power. That makes me feel good, a Charity Hospital baby from New Orleans, dressed up like Uncle Sam, on the Fourth of July, in Washington, D.C.!

"And it proves my point, too," he concludes. "Let's just put it like this. There ain't but two songs that will stand the test of time . . . "

●   ●   ●

Ernie's Oeuvre

K-Doe's best sides are bootlegs, and he doesn't see a penny.

At the present time there is no definitive collection of Ernie K-Doe's original '60s hits on CD. Bootleg anthologies hit the market on occasion, but K-

Doe does not get a penny of the proceeds. Except for an occasional song on a larger, multi-artist anthology, the following is the extent of his work that is currently and legitimately available on CD:

The Best Of Ernie K-Doe *(Mardi Gras Records). Despite the title, this collection does not include the original renditions of K-Doe's hits from the '60s. The versions here, recorded in the '90s, emphasize K-Doe's surreal side more than his musical ability. This is particularly apparent on his treatment of "Georgia on My Mind," which would have made Fellini go get a day job.*

Fever! *(DuBat Records). Another latter-day recording that's more notable for antics than musicianship, but is entertaining nonetheless.*

BILL FRISKICS-WARREN

Unbroken Circle

*Therefore, since we are surrounded by so great a cloud of wit-
nesses, let us also lay aside every weight . . . and let us run with
perseverance the race that is set before us.*

—Hebrews 12:1

Few have heeded this exhortation with such devotion as June Carter
Cash, and not just as a woman of faith. A member of the first family of
country music—as a daughter, wife, mother, and grandmother—she
has, for much of her 70 years, fixed her eyes on another, albeit related,
goal: preserving and expanding the Carter Family circle and its musical
legacy. This has often meant putting her career on hold to care for
children and ailing family members. Other times it has meant working
in the shadow of her husband, Johnny Cash, or of her mother Maybelle, aunt Sara, and uncle A.P., the trio that, in 1927, helped usher
country music into the modern era.

Recently, though, it was June's turn to take center stage. On a hon-
eysuckle-perfumed evening in mid-May, a host of 200 gathered at the
Cash estate north of Nashville to bear witness to the race June has run.
The occasion was the release of her new solo album, the aptly titled
Press On, a clutch of exquisitely unvarnished songs that functions much
as a musical autobiography.

The festivities took place under a tent up the hill from the Cashes'
sprawling, three-story house overlooking Old Hickory Lake. There

was plenty of Southern cooking (corn cakes, fried green tomatoes, fudge pie), no booze, and an odd mix of family, industry weasels and celebrities. Included among this last group were George Jones, Connie Smith, Naomi Judd and Jane Seymour.

Nothing, however, galvanized the proceedings quite like the moment the Man in Black, his wife at his side, stood before the assembly like a hillbilly Isaiah and announced: "Her time has come now." A full-minute standing ovation followed, after which June, sitting down with her autoharp, confessed, "I've been real happy paddling along after John, being Mrs. Johnny Cash all these years. But I'm sure thrilled to be up here singing for you tonight."

Throughout the evening, June invoked family members who have gone on: Aunt Sara and Uncle A.P., Ezra "Eck" Carter (her father), and Mother Maybelle, whose 1932 L5 Gibson round-hole guitar she played on her rendition of "Wildwood Flower." June also summoned long-gone friends from her "rock 'n' roll years": Hank Williams and Elvis Presley (she toured with both), as well as Tennessee Williams, James Dean and writer-director Elia Kazan, with whom she kept company as a drama student in New York in the mid-'50s.

By the time she closed her set, by turns hilarious and poignant, urging her guests to sing along to "Will the Circle Be Unbroken," the matriarch of the Carter-Cash clan had not only enlarged the cloud of witnesses who had surrounded her, she had testified to the power of that circle, the nurture of which has been her life's calling.

Along the way, Valerie June Carter, born June 23, 1929, in Maces Springs, Virginia, has enjoyed a kaleidoscopic career of her own. As a gangly tomboy with a sure-fire sense of timing, June's hayseed-improv provided comic relief for countless Carter Family shows during the '30s and '40s. On radio and on the road with her mother and sisters Helen and Anita, she was a mainstay of perhaps the most in-demand country act of the '40s and '50s, one that boasted a young picker named Chester Burton Atkins.

"We had probably the hottest show on WSM back then," says June, her azure eyes ablaze, sitting in the Cashes' downstairs den, a museum-like vault that holds dozens of photos and momentos from the couple's fabled career. "According to Artists Service, the outfit that booked dates for Opry acts back then, WSM made more money from the Carter Sisters, and from Mother Maybelle and the Carters, than they made from anyone else on the Opry. We went through a year of working shows with Hank Williams when he said, 'I will not close for the Carter broads.' And it's true. Hank never closed for us."

But it wasn't just as part of the family act that June achieved acclaim. Not quite 20, she had her first Top 10 hit, "Baby, It's Cold Outside" (with Homer & Jethro), in 1949. As a solo artist in the mid-'50s, she toured with the young Elvis Presley, with whom she also shared a manager, Colonel Tom Parker. After that, as a protégé of Elia Kazan, who directed Marlon Brando in *On the Waterfront* and *A Streetcar Named Desire*, June studied acting at New York's renowned Neighborhood Playhouse. She appeared on the Jackie Gleason and Jack Paar shows, and in 1958 made her first movie, *Country Music Holiday*. The picture co-starred country crooner Ferlin Husky ("Gone"), Zsa Zsa Gabor, boxer Rocky Graziano, and the Jordanaires.

During the late '50s and early '60s, when her mother and sisters were on the road without her, June worked on the Opry, anchoring the Prince Albert segment of the program with her gags and gregarious stage presence. "I could carry the first part of the show, just cutting up and playing banjo, guitar, and autoharp," she remembers. "Once I carried it for two hours when [the other regulars] were late getting there." During this time, June also played dates with some of country's biggest names, including Marty Robbins, George Jones, Buck Owens and Eddy Arnold. Her days in the spotlight, though, would be numbered after she met the Man in Black.

"I first heard of Johnny Cash through Elvis Presley," she explains. "Elvis would make me go into these little cafes and listen to John sing when we played in the South—in the Carolinas and all down through Florida and Georgia. Then, one night backstage at the Opry, this man walked up to me and said, 'I want to meet you. I'm Johnny Cash.' And I said, 'Well I oughta know who you are. Elvis can't even tune his guitar unless he goes, "Everybody knows where you go when the sun goes down,"'" adds June, alluding to a line from "Cry, Cry, Cry," Cash's first hit for Sun Records.

By 1961, June was singing and doing standup with Cash's road show and, before she knew it, falling for Cash and trying to save him from his self-destructive ways. She immortalized the mix of desire and trepidation she felt at the time in "Ring Of Fire," a chart-topping hit for her future husband in 1963.

"It was a terrible shock when I found out John was taking pills," June wrote in *Among My Klediments*, her 1979 autobiography. ("Klediment," she explains, is mountain parlance for anything that one holds dear.) "He dropped a few pills in front of me in Macon, Georgia, one afternoon, and I could hardly believe it. I knew he didn't sleep much at night. You could hear him roaming around his room if you were anywhere near. I could remember how it had been with Hank Williams a few years before when Hank took so much medicine for his bad back, and how my sisters and I worried about him.

"But the show always had to go on, and ours did. And I found myself fighting hard with Johnny Cash. It was only later that I began to realize I was fighting him for his life."

"June saved my life," admits Cash, 67, sitting at home with the woman who, for years, flushed his pills down the toilet. "And after that, June and her family kept me steadily on course at times when the rudder was shaky. Maybelle was a great friend, she and Pop Carter both. They were like parents to me. My parents were living in California at the time. They were happy, after they got to know a little about them, that I was spending a lot of time with the Carters because they were people who truly cared for me, as did June. They knew she did. So it was their love and care for me, and the musical influence, and the musical sharing, eventually, with all of them, that was very binding. And we're all still kind of bound up that way."

After she married Cash in 1968, June threw herself into being a good wife and mother. "John had four daughters the day I married him, and I had two," she explains. "That gave me six daughters right off the bat, so all of a sudden I'm a big mother now. And then I had our son, John Carter. And then—I don't remember what year it was, but this was another big surprise—I was named Youth for Christ mother of the year. I said to myself, 'How did I get this?' And I thought, 'Good Lord, I've got seven kids, that's how I did it.' I was still working on the road and carrying one of them with me. John Carter would be waiting in the wings until I'd done my part on the show and could run right off and nurse him."

Now that their kids are grown—John Carter Cash has a 3-year-old of his own—June has lately been nursing her husband, who suffers from Shy-Drager syndrome, a degenerative nerve disorder. She spent a good deal of time taking care of her sister Helen, who died last year after a long illness, and also has been seeing to her kid sister Anita, who has been in poor health. In fact, apart from touring at her husband's side and releasing a 1975 solo album, *Appalachian Spring* (the Cashes also won Grammys for two duets, "Jackson" and "If I Were a Carpenter"), June has for more than three decades abandoned her own career for family.

"June has been so devoted and attached to everything that I've been doing all these years," says her husband, "that she never really put any thought into doing anything of her own."

"It was just a choice I made," says June, sounding less like someone who subscribes to the submissive housewife cant of Phyllis Schlafly than like a woman who knows her own mind.

"I guess I could have tried to record," she adds, "but I didn't. I didn't even give it a thought. My ex-sons-in-law, Rodney Crowell, Marty Stuart, and Nick Lowe, all would say, 'What's wrong with you? Why don't you record again?' And I'd say, 'Well, I'm awful busy.' It's amazing that I've got an album out after all this time."

"I'd been wanting June to do this for years," says Cash. "She's had it in her to do it. Although she downplays them and diminishes their worth. I knew these songs of hers. I knew that they were very worthy of being on the record. And now what with the diversification of the market, there's a place for her work. There hadn't been before.

"There hadn't been a place for the work like I did with American," Cash continues, talking about *American Recordings* and *Unchained*, the raw-boned mid-'90s albums he made for Rick Rubin's American Recordings label. "There hadn't been. But when you can win a Grammy for some of that kind of work, you realize there's a market for it."

"When John recorded his last two albums, he did them the way he wanted to," says June. "And I said, 'Well, if I could do an album the way I wanted to, I might be interested in doing one one of these days.' Well, Rick Rubin heard me say that. We were playing a lot of places he wanted us to play—the House of Blues in L.A., a lot of rock 'n' roll places and colleges. We were playing for a lot of young people and it was a lot of fun. They accepted John so well. And they accepted me the same way. I could see no difference in any audience that I'd ever had."

Vicki Hamilton, a veteran of the hard-rock trenches who had worked with Guns N' Roses and Motley Crue, was among the converts in this latter-day audience. "Vicki had never been caught up in my music or anything like it," June explains. "But one night, while standing in the wings with Tom Petty and Rick Rubin, she asked Rick if I was ever gonna record again. And Rick said to her, 'I'd love to see her record. Why don't you do it?' So Rick asked me if I would talk to Vicki, who had been thinking about starting her own label. He gave me her number and I called her up and she said, 'I love that song about I used to be somebody. It made me cry.' And she said, 'If it can make me cry, as tough as I am, it can make a lot of people cry.'"

With backing from Hollywood-based Risk Records, Hamilton released *Press On* in April on her independent label Small Hairy Dog. Recorded at the Cashes' home studio—a converted log cabin set deep in the woods on the couple's estate—the album embraces the homespun aesthetic June learned from her mother, aunt and uncle. With plenty of relatives and friends pitching in, including master guitarist Norman Blake, the record harks back to the family picking parties June knew while growing up in southwestern Virginia.

The Cashes' son, John Carter, co-produced the album (with J. J. Blair); two of the couple's erstwhile sons-in-law, Marty Stuart and Rodney Crowell, played on the record; and June's daughter, Rosie, sang harmony on three tracks. June also duets, her pitch wavering on occasion, with her husband on "The Far Side Banks of Jordan," a moving witness to the couple's belief that they will be reunited after they've died and gone on. "I believe my steps are growing wearier each day / Got another journey on my mind," warbles Cash in his craggiest baritone. Penned 20 years ago by Nashville schoolteacher Terry Smith, the song is very much in the spirit of "Will the Circle Be Unbroken," the Carter Family perennial that closes *Press On* and, in many respects, serves as the record's statement of purpose.

Press On also includes two other Carter Family songs, "Diamonds in the Rough" and "Meeting in the Air." But unlike *Wildwood Flower*, the 1988 reunion album June made with her sisters and her daugher Carlene, *Press On* is more than a Carter Family tribute record. Most of its

13 songs, eight of them written or co-written by June, revisit events unique to her life.

"I Used to Be Somebody," the song that touched Hamilton so deeply, finds June looking back wistfully on the 1950s. "I used to be somebody / Dear Lord, where have I been / I ain't ever gonna see Elvis again," she mourns, alluding to the time when the circles she ran in included Hank Williams, Patsy Cline and Elvis Presley. These weren't just passing acquaintances: June is Hank Williams Jr.'s godmother; she and Cline were confidantes; and she was like a big sister to Elvis, among other things, teaching him to tune a guitar, spurring him to get his first motorcycle (June had hers first and has the pictures to prove it), and coaching him as he crammed for his first Hollywood screen test.

"I tried in two weeks' time to teach Elvis everything that I had learned during the whole time I had gone to school," June recalls. "When he first started, he was way over the top. And I thought, 'Please, Elvis, don't embarrass me. Please don't take a bad movie. You could do a part like Brando. Don't do this to me.' But he did. And do you know that I have never, to this day, seen one of his movies all the way through. I was disappointed because I knew an Elvis that was capable of doing so much more."

"I Used to Be Somebody" also reflects on June's days as a drama student in Manhattan in '56 and '57, a move brought about at the urging of director Elia Kazan, who had heard about June from a colleague, screenwriter Budd Schulberg. "Budd had come to a show that I had done in Sarasota, Florida, with Elvis," remembers June. "He and Kazan were fixing to do a movie called *A Face in the Crowd*. [The film, about a country bumpkin turned TV star, featured Andy Griffith in his big screen debut, and Knoxville native Patricia Neal as his co-star.]

"Kazan didn't know too much about country music and asked Budd if he should go see Elvis," June continues. "But Budd said, 'I'm not so concerned about Elvis Presley. June Carter is who you need to go see. She's the most unusual girl I've ever seen. I have never laughed so, I have never cried so, I have never had the time I had when she was onstage.'

"So Kazan came to see me one Saturday night at the Opry. I didn't know it was him at first. All I knew was there was this strange little man who kept following me around. He had a camera, and he kept taking my picture, all kinds of ways. Finally, he walked up to me and said, 'My name is Elia Kazan and I wonder if you'll come with me and go get a little something to drink.' So we went across to Linebaugh's, down there on Lower Broad, and got a coke and he said, 'I'm going to make a movie in New York. I need to go around and see what country music is like. Will you take me to some of the country places around here?'

"Kazan stayed in Nashville for two weeks and then said, 'I really wish you would come to New York City. I want you to go to school.' I said, 'Gosh, I have a little girl. What am I gonna do?' 'You'll take her with you,' he said. 'And if you don't have the money, I'll send you.' I said, 'Oh, I have the money. If I go, I don't wanna be beholden to you in any way. I'm also a good old girl, and I'll stay that way, thank you. And Mother Maybelle will skin you alive if you try to make it any other way.'"

In New York, Kazan took June everywhere with him, exposing her to culture and cultures she'd never imagined. "I was thrown into this group of people," she says. "I didn't know what they believed, or if they even believed in God at all. I'm not a Pentecostal. I was raised in the Methodist church, but one of my first memories was looking for Jesus' face in the clouds—looking there, just searching for it—and I never once ever thought there was any other way. And here I am praying, not just saying the blessing before every meal, but praying for every person I met."

As June's comments suggest, these were heady, often conflicted, times for a young, God-fearing woman from Appalachia. To compound matters, June had just split with her first husband, honky-tonker Carl Smith, the man with whom she had her first daughter, Carlene. This emotional roller-coaster notwithstanding, June held her own in the drama classes of Sandy Meisner, who groomed Gregory Peck, Robert Duvall and Mary Steenburgen for their Oscar-winning careers. "I think I could have been a good actor," June maintains, and as anyone who saw her with Robert Duvall in the opening scene of *The Apostle* can attest, she is indeed a gifted improviser.

"Bobby paid me a great compliment," says June, referring to Duvall, who often stays with the Cashes when he's in Nashville. "He said, 'This is my first movie to direct, and I really would be so happy if we could do our part first, so I'll be comfortable.' And so we did. We improvised it. I must've sung I don't know how many songs. He loved 'Far Side Banks of Jordan.' That's the one John and I did on this album. It's my favorite song to sing with John."

Over the years, June has appeared on TV dozens of times, including episodes of "Gunsmoke," "Little House on the Prairie" and "Dr. Quinn, Medicine Woman." She also has starred in several feature films, but nothing, she says, gave her as much satisfaction as an actor as when Meisner, her former teacher, asked her to be the one who presented him with his Kennedy Center award.

"It was the greatest compliment that Sandy could have paid me," beams June. "Robert Duvall, Mary Steenburgen, Gregory Peck—these wonderful people that he taught were all in Washington to watch him get this Presidential award, and he had to choose someone to give it to him. And of all these people who won Academy Awards, I was the person he chose. That let me know, according to Sandy Meisner, that I could have won an Academy Award, if I had chosen to go that way."

June's considerable acting résumé aside, in country circles, it is for her comedy, be it her famous "mud hole gag" or her unforgettable "Aunt Polly," that people revere her.

"I'll never forget June Carter in this chartreuse-green chiffon dress, doing her comedy bit," says Opry star Connie Smith. "She kept me in stitches. Her timing is so great." The queen of country comedy, the late Minnie Pearl, went one better, having once said that June, who started doing routines as a kid, had the best timing of any comic she had ever known.

"My uncle A.P. used to say, 'We don't have any comedy on the show and it would really be great if you would do something,'" June recalls. "So here I was, this little bitty kid, and I got this big board, a plank, and put it under my arm. I'd just walk across the stage. They'd be trying to sing some of their funnier songs and I'd just walk across the stage pulling that plank. And they'd turn around and look at me until my Uncle A.P. would finally say, 'What are you doing?' And I'd say, 'We'll, I'm looking for a room. I've got my board.' That was my first bit.

"So I did these improvisations. I could just talk about anything and it seemed to be funny. I had a great following. People would want to hug my neck and pinch me. They'd send me cakes in the mail. They'd crochet me bedspreads."

This humor is evident throughout *Press On*, notably on June's many between-song asides, but nowhere so much as on "Tiffany Anastasia Lowe." The song is a cautionary tale that June wrote for her granddaughter, Tiffany, an aspiring Hollywood actress besotted with the movies of director Quentin Tarantino (whose surname June pronounces "Tarantina").

"Quentin Tarantino's women sometimes get stuck with a hypodermic needle," June sings. But before she can add, "They dance a lot and lose a lot of blood," she breaks into a belly laugh, an unguarded and utterly beguiling moment that brings to mind the associative, and often hilarious, monologues of Woody Guthrie and the young Bob Dylan.

The former comparison couldn't be more fitting, given that Guthrie's "originals" appropriated many a Carter Family tune, and quite a few lines of verse. "If you want to sing a Woody Guthrie song, I can sing you the Carter family song where he got it," smiles June, noting, among other examples, how "This Land Is Your Land" draws heavily on the Carters' "Lulu Walls."

"Woody's widow even acknowledged as much at his induction to the Songwriters Hall of Fame," June adds. "Woody would always write to Uncle A.P. At one point, Uncle A.P. sent a him a telegram and Woody carried it 'til it was worn out in his billfold."

When pressed—and not without also citing Mother Maybelle's picking and the trio's harmony singing—June says the Carter Family's role as a repository of Anglo-Celtic ballads is her forebears' most significant contribution to the music of the twentieth century. "Uncle A.P. collected a lot of the ballads as they'd come across the mountain, or from different parts of the country," she says. "There would be people from Ireland, from Scotland, from some of those places, that might have a poem, or even just a piece of a poem. Somewhere, they had to survive."

As testimony to the ongoing power of this canon—one to which all country music, and much rock and pop, of the past 70 years refers—June framed her new album with a pair of Carter Family songs ("Diamonds in the Rough" and "Will the Circle Be Unbroken").

"I put bookends on it," she says. "My heart and soul is still a part of what my family was. I dedicate so much of what I've done to my mother, and to my Aunt Sara. They were both committed to doing the same kind of thing when they were together, to continuing on with it. I owe them so much, and still do.

"I think God put his hand on the Carter Family and said, 'Okay, you can be A.P. Carter, you can be Maybelle Carter, you can be Sara

Carter,'" June continues. "God also put his hand on people like Hank Williams, and said, 'You can be Hank Williams,' and to Johnny Cash, 'You can be Johnny Cash.' And God put his hand on Elvis Presley and said, 'You can be Elvis Presley.' But God has done that very few times. And God has been good enough to let me stand in the shadow of all these people—people that have either been very close to me, or that have been my blood. And somewhere God has said, 'Okay, June, you are a part of this some way.'"

DAVE MARSH AND
DANIEL WOLFF

No Hiding Place

America's most powerful singer and songwriter is over seventy years old and lives quietly in Birmingham, Alabama. Her daily life centers on her family, her church, and her Deep South community, which she, unlike almost all her contemporaries from the golden age of gospel—Mahalia Jackson, Sam Cooke, James Cleveland—never left.

Perhaps she's simply husbanding her energy for better purposes, in the manner of her nearest regional and demographic analogue, Eudora Welty. Maybe she long ago gave up on getting an honest count—from record companies or reporters or, for that matter, history. Maybe Dorothy Love Coates just lives in a place where none of this matters. Listening to her sing, in a voice that still has the tremendous dramatic force of her youth, you could believe it might actually be that simple. Or maybe it's even simpler than that. Maybe, as Coates tells us in the words of one of her most powerful songs: "I've got Jee-ee-sus, and that's enough!"

By Coates' definition, that's a lot. In her music, the African-American tradition of the social gospel comes to full, fierce life. Her pursuit of justice has remained consistent and scathing over the last half century. Appropriately enough, when she did surface recently—in the movie *Beloved*—she led a chorus of local women trying to exorcise the ghost of slavery through song. That is one way to summarize her life's work: a gospel warrior trying to win souls for Jesus and, at the same time, right some of history's wrongs.

As she says in another of her greatest records:

> *I went to the rock to hide my face*
> *But the rock cried out, "No hiding place*
> *down here!"*

Coates was twenty-three in 1951, when her group, the Gospel Harmonettes, signed with Art Rupe's Los Angeles–based Specialty Records. She was twenty-seven when Rosa Parks was arrested in Montgomery and the subsequent boycott of that city's bus system began a new, militant phase of the Civil Rights Movement. The next year, the NAACP was banned in her native state of Alabama. Meanwhile, Mahalia Jackson and Roberta Martin and great quartets like the Dixie Hummingbirds and the Soul Stirrers toured the country, separate and unequal. This was a kind of true underground music world, composed of church rallies—or "programs"—known only to the faithful, and "hit" records played on a select few radio stations, surfacing mostly after being plundered by pop, rock, and r&b acts.

The great majority of soul and R&B stars were church-trained, or at least church-experienced. Singers like Lou Rawls, Wilson Pickett, and Aretha Franklin were minor gospel stars; Sam Cooke was a major one. The list is so long that it would be easier to name the postwar black singers who didn't have a gospel background. "How much of r&b comes from gospel?" an interviewer once asked Bobby Womack, who has dwelt in both worlds. "All of it," he replied without hesitation—or much exaggeration.

This most dynamic of all forms of American music attracted a strong cult following among knowledgeable nonbelievers, including such important early recording impresarios as John Hammond and Jerry Wexler. Nevertheless, as Womack and dozens of others learned, if you wanted to make some dough in this life, gospel was not the place to do it. The hours and living conditions were ridiculously bad, the circle of acclaim narrow, and mammon beckoned at every turn. Even those with the tremendous level of commitment necessary to stay in the gospel world found their work crossing over . . . without them.

Coates' songs were the basis for a number of secular hits. The best context for listening to her gospel standard "(You Can't Hurry God) He's Right on Time" is alongside the Supreme Court's 1954 *Brown* v. *Board of Education* decision and the incredible upsurge in gospel-based R&B that began at the same time. Except you're liable to find that the song won't stay in that context. Dorothy begins, "You can't hurry God," and as the Harmonettes answer, "You just have to wait," we've jumped from 1954 to 1966, from the Supreme Court to the Supremes. The difference in the gospel song and its love child are striking. Holland, Dozier, and Holland wrote the number-one hit "You Can't Hurry Love" on the other side of the major, nonviolent Civil Rights demonstrations.

Motown's calculated sound was trying to bring us together—on the dance floor, anyway—with a strategy that might best be summed up by a line from the song: "It's a game of give and take." Diana Ross's slinky whisper is hanging on for the possibility of love. The broad-shouldered, stern-faced Coates is waiting on—and, with a shout, working toward—justice. With the Civil Rights Movement still before her, she's asking that old question: Do the Christian God and the African-American church pacify or inspire? The gospel song is about patience weighed against activism, acceptance as opposed to all-out defiance. And the greatness of "He's Right on Time" is that it doesn't resolve the contradictions but holds them on both shoulders, like wings, and announces that He *will* come, and in the meantime, justice is something we have to work toward.

It's no coincidence that the golden age of gospel corresponds to the golden age of the Civil Rights Movement. The power of the churches that produced the gospel singers and their ideas powered the Movement, too, uniting the black community and reaching out beyond that community to white people of all faiths. Coates' home church is Birmingham's Sixteenth Street Baptist, where, on a bloody Sunday thirty-six years ago this autumn, a bomb blew four little girls into bits and Civil Rights mythology. Sixteenth Street Baptist was chosen for the bombing because it was a kind of ground zero for the Birmingham movement, just as the Birmingham movement was a kind of ground zero for the Civil Rights struggle as a whole, an Omaha Beach where the forces of the enemy finally began their retreat. Of all the musicians and singers, pop and gospel, who got involved in the Movement (and there were a great many), Coates wrote the most and the best songs and may well have sung at more Civil Rights meetings than anyone else. The greatest recordings of Dorothy Love Coates and the Gospel Harmonettes evoke the passion, conviction, fear, and sorrow of that era—and of a timeless struggle for heavenly justice here on earth.

Listen to her best-known songs, and you get a picture of exactly what that struggle entails. In "I Won't Let Go," it's a shouted list: "Working, toiling, praying, hoping, trusting, believing, waiting, watching." The depth of the commitment is in the very title of "Ninety-Nine and a Half Won't Do" (which is the basis for Wilson Pickett's soul hit of the same name). A couplet from "He's Right on Time" provides an overview:

> *I don't know how or when He'll come*
> *But don't let Him catch you with your*
> *work undone!*

The social gospel is not only the great lost cord that knits together the New Deal and the Salvation Army, the Civil Rights and antiwar movements. It also helps illuminate the full impact of gospel music on the world of rock and R&B. That impact may *seem* purely stylistic, because its most obvious manifestations are. There's clearly a direct line, for instance, between gospel and the kinds of quartet harmony that drive group singing from doo-wop to The Beatles to Boyz II Men. At this year's Rock and Roll Hall of Fame ceremonies, Eric Clapton and others drew out the connections between their guitar playing and that of such gospel-derived players as new inductees Pops Staples and Curtis Mayfield. The indelible high "woo" that can be traced from Little Richard to Paul McCartney to heavy metal and beyond stems directly from the leaps made by the great Marion Williams of the Clara Ward Singers. Sam Cooke's raspy sweetness, which made its way to Rod Stewart and D'Angelo, maybe even to Lauryn Hill, had its origins in Cooke's gospel group, the Soul Stirrers, and its original lead singer, R. H. Harris. Then there are all those songs, from "Mystery Train" and "Stand by Me" to "I Believe I Can Fly," that have gospel origins.

Coates' extraordinarily concise and moving songwriting ability is inspired by the work of Memphis minister William Herbert Brewster. Author of "How I Got Over" and "Move On Up a Little Higher" and a community organizer in the days before Dr. King—when, in Brewster's words, "there were things that were almost dangerous to say, but you could sing it"—Brewster was pastor of East Trigg Baptist, one of the churches where young Elvis Presley studied the ecstatic moves of his gospel heroes.

It may be that this performance quality had the greatest effect on early rock 'n' roll: moments of ecstasy—running the aisles, knee drops, the rending of garments, leaps past all good judgment into true conviction—that eclipse any benchmarks of popular stagecraft, whether James Brown or Iggy Pop or P-Funk or, for that matter, Kirk Franklin.

Less often acknowledged are the other ways in which gospel has left its signature. The most crucial lies in its vision of community. In his new book *A Change Is Gonna Come*, Craig Werner traces that gospel impulse to Bruce Springsteen's "reason to believe" (in his case, most often called the power of rock 'n' roll) and the hope of a better tomorrow that runs through the work of artists like Public Enemy, Tupac, and Wyclef Jean.

This vision of social change may not be something you usually associate with gospel singers, since that style grew up in the black Pentecostal church. Its goal of putting people in direct and ecstatic contact with God would seem to jump past the importance of change in the material world. But any study of black churches will show that there's a strong social gospel current from Dr. Martin Luther King Sr. and the Reverend C. L. Franklin, Aretha's father, to the Reverend Jesse Jackson; from the Golden Gate Quartet to Kirk Franklin's avowedly "revolutionary" choir. For people ensnared first as slaves and then as sharecroppers, religion might only be able to promise salvation in the next life, but it had to offer the possibility of hope in this one, too. That's why the Civil Rights Movement had to center itself in black churches. That's why it could.

Most white nonbelievers cannot, or will not, see this connection between gospel and rock because of that two-syllable word (which in Coates' case sometimes extends to four syllables): Jesus. The irony is that many rockers and rock fans are happy to ascribe the visionary spirit of their music to Robert Johnson and his deal with the Devil. But a compact with Jesus, made not at some midnight crossroads but just up the road in a church in broad daylight, makes them cringe.

Why is it, then, that nonbelievers rarely have the same kind of trouble with the Christian convictions of, say, Flannery O'Connor, Walker Percy, or W. H. Auden? Their Catholicism and/or Anglicanism may strike many intellectuals as odd, but it's not alien. It is a mostly cool, somber, and meditative belief. On the other hand, the religious side of James Baldwin continues to alienate many of those same readers. Once a boy preacher in churches much like those where Coates has plied her trade, Baldwin espouses a faith that is hot, sweaty, flamboyant, and demonstrative. The whole point, with both Baldwin and Coates, is to transgress the mind/body dichotomy and bring the spirit out of the mind and into the house.

Because nonbelievers see this as simplistic (or simply too close for comfort), they often overlook the craft and intelligence involved. Both Coates and Baldwin use their belief in nuanced ways that go far beyond street-smart. The manner in which Coates reveals biblical tales of sin and redemption to be stories of oppression and liberation has its antecedents in the slave era. As James Cone demonstrates in his book-length analysis *The Spirituals and the Blues,* there is "a complex world of *thought* underlying the slave songs." Both Coates and Baldwin interweave threads of gospel with unmistakable commentary on the community and the world, and Coates' sense of narrative is arguably even sharper and more pointed than Baldwin's. She is a master storyteller, remaking familiar narratives such as "Hide in the Rock" and "Strange Man" with great precision and insight. And no one has used the vernacular voice with such deft shadings since Zora Neale Hurston. Not being able to hear and respond to that degree of talent simply because of subject matter is as intellectually stunted as not appreciating Mark Twain because he writes about sweaty, smelly urchins.

If you can get past the word *Jesus*—its existence at all, let alone its centrality and the atomic emphasis Coates places on what she calls "the great Emancipator and the heart regulator"—you get to hear Dorothy Love Coates sing. She is not just a finely nuanced writer; she is a once-in-a-lifetime vocal performer. Her voice has a hint of gravel in it at all times, which makes it definitively earthy, whether she is whispering or shouting. And she does both, often. Like all the great gospel singers, she has an emotional range of expression next to which all other contemporary singers pale. But even when Coates just bears down and almost recites—so slowly that you don't miss a hint or an implication—her voice is a transfixing vehicle, sweet and sharp at the same time.

Once you're ready to hear her testify about Jesus in that voice, you come face-to-face with seminal classics like "That's Enough." And once you hear that song's mood of stout defiance, its almost military cadence, and Coates' biting portrayal of her role in society ("There's always somebody talking 'bout me / Really, I don't mind"), you realize that singers and songwriters like Bob Dylan have been listening long and hard to this tradition. Years before he became a putative Christian himself, Dylan wrote "Blowin' in the Wind" (based on the Negro spiritual "Many Thousands Gone," also known, not insignificantly, as "No More Auction Block"), and the Old Testament–based "When the Ship Comes In." Dylan—who, like Springsteen, has used Coates' niece, Cleo Kennedy, as a backup singer—has never stopped reaching for biblical language or looking for an elusive spirituality in his music, and his persona as the prophetic outcast owes much more to the church than to the blues. He'd be the first to point out to you the absurdity of that hoariest of clichés, "the devil has all the good songs." Whatever it was Satan gave Robert Johnson, it couldn't have been the conviction that "He takes care of my enemies when they try to get tough." And that's not a quote from Marilyn Manson; it's one of about a dozen good lines Coates tosses off in the course of "That's Enough."

The blues/gospel division has never been as absolute as critics would make it. Thomas Dorsey, who has been called the father of modern gospel, went back and forth between the divine and the secular. Before him, during the Second Great Awakening of the 1840s and '50s, the stringing together of prayer, Bible stories, and the hymn tradition produced a new kind of religious song that one scholar has called "the distinctive badge of the camp meeting movement." Son House, Charlie Patton, Skip James—the great bluesmen who contributed so much to what we now call rock 'n' roll—all played God's music as well and, like Clara Ward or Aretha, passed back and forth across dividing lines misrepresented as inviolable. In that context, calling Coates' amazing vocal delivery "bluesy" is to retreat to the familiar; you could as accurately call Tom Waits a gospel singer.

The solitary confessionals of despair and longing that mark songs like Dylan's "Blind Willie McTell," Springsteen's bleak stories of desolation, and the most doleful ballads of Van Morrison are part of that need for each person to recount the tale of his or her individual woes. Call it the blues impulse—Ralph Ellison did. But the joyous spirit of rock 'n' roll, which encounters and transcends those woes not individually but as a group, is the gospel impulse. You have heard that conviction expressed a thousand or a hundred or a dozen times, depending on how old and picky you are, from John Lennon screaming out his definition of God ("A concept by which we measure our pain") to R. Kelly's conviction that not only can he fly, he's about to. You recognize it because the rock and R&B and hip-hop that form our musical lingua franca owe their very soul to gospel music. The stuff that drives you (as the MC5 put it) "crazy out of your mind into your body" comes as much from the churches as the juke joints.

Dorothy Love Coates recorded perhaps her most piercing, mesmerizing song, "Strange Man," in the spring of '68, about the time that Dylan was making *The Basement Tapes* and *John Wesley Harding*. Coates' gospel matches any dream of St. Augustine or wheels-on-fire vision. And in its attempt to exorcise the catastrophe of the end of Dr. King's dream and, at the same time, hold on to the possibility of grace and salvation, it ranks among the great acts of faith set to music.

In the first two verses, Coates tells biblical stories: the woman at the well and the adulterous woman about to be stoned. Both praise the person who has saved their lives, but neither knows his name or understands how he has recognized her. They don't know anything about the "strange man," except that

> *When he spoke, my soul caught on fire*
> *And I'll remember this day till the day I die.*

In the third verse, Coates tells the story of her own conversion, a testimonial deep and personal. The truth of it leaves her voice next door to a sob:

> *I felt that same power, Lord*
> *My soul caught on fire*
> *I'm just glad he stopped by in Alabama*
> *The Lord stopped by, one Tuesday evening*
> *Blessed my soul and gone.*

The shock of the story becoming contemporary is transfixing. The agony and heartbreak, the reference to Alabama, are not coincidental. Coates is singing not only about her own conversion but also about the miracles she has seen wrought by the Movement, and particularly by the work of her friend and compatriot Dr. King. She's seen her hometown—"Bombingham"—transformed; she's seen grace rolling out of her very own church like righteousness in a mighty stream; she's seen her people, denied the very smallest human dignity, rise up toward full citizenship. And that very spring, she saw it end with Dr. King's assassination. She had known all along that what was happening there, in the beloved community they had created, was temporary, because she knew all things on this earth must pass. But her voice bears testimony to that glimpse of what a just world might look like. They had done not only good work but God's work; and it was not only right but righteous.

All of this is contained in the way she sings the story of "one Tuesday evening in Alabama." She doesn't sound free; she sounds like her heart will break. And yet she sings it with all the tremendous power in her body. It's a testimonial of faith—whether or not you think faith comes from God. Frankly, at the moment when Dorothy Love Coates testifies, if you could believe in her God, you damned sure would.

It's this impulse that has shaped Coates' persona, in song after song, as a gospel beacon: a defiant, guiding light. That's why the congregation will urge her to take her time as she announces, "The mean things you say don't make me feel bad," and then roar their approval when she adds, "And I can't miss a friend I've never had." She works within a tradition of what W.E.B. DuBois, in *The Souls of Black Folk*, called Negro folk song. Without that tradition, the confessions of our greatest contemporary singer-songwriters become nothing but so much whiny self-pity. With it, they become stories we all can share. "It has been neglected, it has been, and is, half despised, and above all it has been per-

sistently mistaken and misunderstood," DuBois wrote, "but notwithstanding, it still remains as the singular spiritual heritage of the nation
and the greatest gift of the Negro people." Dorothy Love Coates
stands as living proof that those words, written nearly a hundred years
ago, are no less true today.

JIM WALSH

Baptism by Bruce

Why was I compelled, at the end of September, to trek to Philadelphia for two of Bruce Springsteen's six shows with the reunited E Street Band? And why does the thought of his appearance at Target Center this week quicken my pulse like no other rock show has this year?

For answers, we need to go back to a warm summer night in 1978. That was the first time I saw Springsteen in concert—at the old Metropolitan Sports Center in Bloomington, with 7,000 other loonies who, I am quite sure, could tell you exactly what they were wearing, who they were with and what various flights of fancy their lives have taken as a result of that night.

Me, I was 19 years old. That night, I remember Springsteen—scrawny, bad-ass, animated like no rocker I'd seen before or since—jumping into the crowd during "Spirit in the Night," and us ending up in front at the end, pogoing and pounding on his motorcycle boots during "Rosalita." I remember him singing a lyric that sent tremors through my nervous system, a lyric that I have come to regard as not only the quintessential Springsteen missive, but the lyrical embodiment of rock 'n' roll itself. More on that later.

After the show, at a house in South Minneapolis, a bunch of my fellow Catholic-school grads were partying after a high-school play. I found my friend/kindred music spirit Paul Kaiser, and dragged him out to the front steps.

"Man, I saw something tonight . . . ," I stammered. I quoted the lyric, then just shook my head and looked at my feet. I was embarrassed; it was too personal. He laughed, "Bruce Springsteen, huh? You can't explain it, can you?"

It was true: I had never witnessed anything so raw or so exuberant, and I couldn't articulate what it had done to me. So I split from the party, walked home to my folks' house, got in bed, and started writing—and, thanks a lot to Springsteen, haven't stopped since.

What I was trying to do that night was hold it in my hands, to capture bliss in a bottle. I was 19, I was nothing. My dreams were just that. I ached to see things, to be something, anything. I wanted to know if love was wild, I wanted to know if love was real.

A lot has happened since then. I grew up. Found love. And—and this is a big "and"—that stammering fool at that party went on to make his livelihood out of trying to explain the unexplainable. All of which has made me a lot tougher to impress than the 20-year-old kid who blew an entire hospital paycheck on a customized E Street Band jacket with "Jimmy the Saint" stitched above the heart.

So, frankly, on the flight out to Philadelphia last month, I was a little worried. Because, while I knew it wouldn't—couldn't—be *the same* as the four- and five-hour spiritual trips the E Street Band regularly provided me with in the '70s and '80s, I didn't want to come away from another sterile '90s arena show, or some lame nostalgia trip, feeling dead inside.

So this was something of a test, I decided, as the lights dimmed at the First Union Center in Philadelphia.

Unlike the start of most concerts, where shadowy figures dart on stage under the cloak of darkness, the E Street Band came out one by one, under a soft golden light, waving and grinning like old friends showing up to a pot-luck dinner. It was the first time I'd seen them together in 11 years: pianist Roy Bittan; drummer Max Weinberg; keyboardist Danny Federici; guitarist Nils Lofgren; guitarist Steve Van Zandt; Bruce's wife, singer/guitarist Patti Scialfa; saxophonist Clarence Clemons; and Springsteen.

That's when I fell into the dunk-tank of nostalgia, and decided to enjoy the water. Largely because, while most rock stars' music makes you think about their lives, Springsteen's music demands that you think about your own. So when Weinberg locomotive-thrashed his high-hat cymbal and Springsteen whispered the opening line to "Candy's Room," the hair on the back of my neck stood up.

The next song, "Adam Raised a Cain"—a cauldron of father-son tension—was followed by "The Ties That Bind," and I realized the last time I'd heard either one in concert, I was the son, and that now my job is to provide my kids with that heat, with something to butt up against.

By the third song, "Prove It All Night," I was a puddle. It took me back to something I hadn't thought of in years, when me and my band mates, armed with spray paint one night after practice, climbed some railroad box cars and a rusty tower to deface a billboard on Hiawatha Avenue with "Prove It All Night!" and "Bruce Springsteen and The 'E' Street Band Rule!"

And so on: During "Jungleland," after Springsteen howled, "Kids flash guitars just like switchblades, hustlin' for the record machine / The hungry and the hunted *explode* into rock 'n' roll bands," Van Zandt ripped off a thunderbolt lead. For that 10 seconds, he became Johnny Rey, Kevin Martinson, Bob Stinson, Dave Alvin, Terry Eason, Slim Dunlap, Robert Wilkinson, Ernie Batson, John Freeman and every other guitar player in every dive I've watched spill their guts over the past two decades.

When did I know that the test was over? That I had passed? That would have been during "Cadillac Ranch," when I found myself hopping from foot to foot like a drunken Muppet, and lolling my head like a bobble-head doll who'd just regained his innocence, and lost his critical faculties.

The next night, Springsteen encored with "Thunder Road." It was the last time he would sing it as a fortysomething (he turned 50 September 23). So when he sang, "You're scared, and you're thinking that maybe you ain't that young anymore," he backed away from the microphone and, sincerely taken aback by the moment, laughed.

The next lyric is the one that got me stammering some 20 years ago, but he didn't even sing it. He let the crowd do it, and the sound of all those voices raised to the Pennsylvania heavens got me thinking about how this whole country has been made to feel old of late, by an entertainment industry that pushes teenybopdom like bubblecrack, by the malling of neighborhoods, by a culture that worships technology and materialism over community and spirituality.

As a result, in the past year, I've had people aged 25, 30, 40 and 50 tell me that they feel old. One is my 48-year-old brother-in-law, Neal, who attended the first show with me. He had never been to a Springsteen concert, but afterward said, "All my favorite acid-rock bands came back this summer, but seeing them just made me feel old. This made me feel young."

And why not? In this, the Age of Irony, Springsteen is thoroughly unironic, and romantic. The musical landscape has shifted dramatically since the E Street Band was last on the road, and seemingly overnight, "rock 'n' roll" has taken on the same dirty-word obsolescence as "feminism."

Yet there is Springsteen, an unabashed, unapologetic rock 'n' roll disciple. The blond-wood Telecaster still smokes, his wrist is still wicked quick, he still mugs mightily and mighty goofily, he still talks between songs (though, sadly, not as much as before), and still jumps off the risers. Pretty spry for an old guy.

My dad, who turned 71 this year and still can't believe it, had a favorite saying when we were growing up: "I still feel like I'm 16." Now I know that he wasn't talking about arrested development. He was saying that the more life that happens, the less you know about the meaning of life. Instead, the mystery just deepens.

When I was 16, I thought I'd have more figured out by now. But the thing nobody tells you is that you never do figure it out, completely. Sure, you can attain a certain level of personal peace and happiness, but the hunger you were born with shifts, the dreams change, the search for wild love remains insatiable.

That's why it's impossible for me to call Springsteen's music a relic. Those songs are ageless, and those two shows in Philadelphia reminded me in no uncertain terms that when it comes to live performers, no one—*no one*—comes close. Nobody has ever knocked me out, picked me back up, given me a shot in the arm, broke my heart and resuscitated it, all in the span of the same three hours, the way he has, and did.

When I was younger, Springsteen's music provided me with a road map to manhood, and gave me permission to be both saint and sinner.

Now, songs such as "Badlands" still make me "want to go out tonight and find out what I got," but they elicit less of an ache, because I know that nothing compares to the art of real life, and that music can be found in the mundane.

To wit: The Sunday after I got back from Philadelphia, my son, Henry, and I went to House of Mercy Baptist Church in Lowertown St. Paul. Some local musicians were staging a tribute to the Louvin Brothers, a country-gospel group from the '50s and early '60s that has influenced Springsteen, and many others.

By the time 72-year-old Charlie Louvin himself came on, 4-year-old Henry was pretty restless. On our third trip to the drinking fountain, Henry stopped in his tracks at the back of the church. His mouth dropped open. He was staring outside.

"I just love the city lights," he said, genuinely wonderstruck. "C'-mon, Dad." We went outside and sat down on the cool hard steps. He snuggled up next to me to get warm, and started caressing the stubble on my chin, the way he does when he's especially affectionate.

We were quiet, and we sat that way until he put his arm around me and said, "Let's just sit here for a while and look at the city lights, and then we'll go back in and hear the music. OK?" Good idea, I said, before my throat lumped shut.

I was 40, I was nothing. Inside the church, a once-in-a-lifetime show was taking place, but Henry and I stayed on the steps. Because at that moment, we—or at least I—could hear the music just fine. It had drifted from the Philadelphia heavens, and was now echoing off the buildings of downtown St. Paul. It was a choir.

It was me at 19, feeling scared. It was my brother-in-law, feeling old. It was my dad at 71, feeling 16. It was my son at 4, feeling awed. It was everyone who has been made to feel out-of-touch, unhip, or hopeless. We were all there.

Maybe you were, too, singing along to a familiar lyric: "Show a little faith, there's magic in the night."

OTHER NOTABLE
ESSAYS OF 1999

Joan Anderman, "Eva Cassidy's Gift" (*Boston Globe*, January 31, 1999)

Noah Baumbach, "Keith Richards' Desert Island Disks" (*New Yorker*, November 29, 1999)

Louis Black, "The Memory of Music" (*Austin Chronicle*, December 20, 1999)

Franklin Bruno, "Thompson's Twins" (*New Times Los Angeles*, June 10, 1999)

David Cantwell, "The Voice" (*No Depression*, September/October 1999)

Carly Carioli, "Girl Talk: Waltham's Waltham" (*Boston Phoenix*, September 17, 1999)

Aaron Cometbus, "Martov" (*Cometbus* #45)

John Darnielle, "A Small Place" (*Last Plane To Jakarta* #4)

Bill Ellis, "Musician's Life, Music Echo Mystic Philosophy" (*Commercial Appeal*, May 8, 1999)

Josh Goldfein, "Touch & Go *v.* the Buttholes" (*Chicago Reader*, April 16, 1999)

Karen R. Good, "The Show, The After-Party, The Hotel" (*Vibe*, August 1999)

Abbey Goodman, "The Roots of Good & Evil" (*Stress* #17)

Fred Goodman, "Stepping Outside the Family, But Not Straying From It" (*New York Times*, June 13, 1999)

Robert Gordon, "Introduction to Another World" (*Oxford American*, Southern Music Issue #3)

Adam Heimlich, "Playa Hating With Love" (*New York Press*, March 31, 1999)

Christine Hill, "View Over Berlin" (*Music* #3)

Gerri Hirshey, "B.B. King" (*Rolling Stone*, December/January 99)

St. Huck, "The Beat Goes Online" (www.suck.com, March 29 and 30, 1999)

Mark Jacobson, "Steve Earle" (*Men's Journal*, June/July 1999)

Michael Jarrett, "Tales of Twang: Producing Country Music" (*Pulse!*, July 1999)

Frank Kogan, "Je T'aime... Moi Non Plus" (*Village Voice*, November 23, 1999)

Todd Lesser, untitled interview with Ian MacKaye (*Monozine* #6)

Miles Marshall Lewis, "A Dollar A Holler" (*L.A. Weekly*, April 30, 1999)

Ken Lieck, "The Genius of Love" (*Austin Chronicle*, March 22, 1999)

Glenn MacDonald, "Instructions for Dancing" (*The War Against Silence*, October 14, 1999)

J. Marlowe, untitled review of Simon Reynolds' Generation Ecstasy (*Ugly American* #13)

Eric McHenry, "Cordon Sanitaire" (*The Baffler* #13)

Margaret Moser, "The Singer Not The Song" (*Austin Chronicle*, June 14, 1999)

Mitch Myers, "Ghost Track" (*New City Chicago*, May 10, 1999)

Terry Pace and Robert Palmer, *Muscle Shoals Sounds: The Rhythm of the River* (*TimesDaily* [Florence, Alabama], series running seven consecutive Sundays, beginning June 13, 1999; reprinted as a whole, August 1, 1999)

Sarah Luck Pearson, "The Suit" (*L.A. Weekly*, March 26, 1999)

Mike Perry, "A Pilgrim's Progress" (*No Depression*, July/August 1999)

Keith Phipps, Nathan Rabin and Stephen Thompson, "The Least

LIST OF
CONTRIBUTORS

Vince Aletti, formerly a rock critic at *Rolling Stone* and a columnist for *Creem, Crawdaddy, Fusion,* and *Record World* (the last as a weekly chronicler of the rise of disco from 1974 to 1978), has been an editor and critic at the *Village Voice* since the mid '80s. His interview with Madonna appeared in the "Male/Female" issue of *Aperture,* which he coedited.

Jay Babcock can't be stopped.

Lester Bangs (1948–1982) was one of the earliest rock critics and writers. A collection of his work, *Psychotic Reactions and Carburetor Dung,* was edited by Greil Marcus and published in 1987.

Maureen Callahan has written for *Sassy* magazine, MTV, *New York* magazine, and *Spin,* where she is currently an associate editor. She lives in Brooklyn, New York.

Rosanne Cash is a Grammy Award–winning singer and songwriter whose books include *Bodies of Water* and *Penelope Jane: A Fairy's Tale.* Her essays and fiction have appeared in the *New York Times, Oxford American, New York Magazine,* and various other periodicals and collections. She is currently editing *Songs Without Rhyme,* a collection of short stories by songwriters. Ms. Cash lives in New York City with her husband, John Leventhal, and her children.

Eddie Dean is a contributing writer for *Talk* magazine and *Washington City Paper*. His work has appeared in the *Wall Street Journal*, the *Washington Post*, and the *Journal of Country Music*, among other publications.

Sasha Frere-Jones is a musician and writer living in New York with his wife and two sons.

Bill Friskics-Warren has written about music for the *Washington Post*, the *New York Times*, *Oxford American*, *Puncture*, the *Journal of Country Music*, and the *Nashville Scene*. He is also a contributor to the forthcoming third edition of *The Rolling Stone Encyclopedia of Rock & Roll*.

George W. Goodman is a former reporter for the *New York Times* and a former assistant editor of *Look* and *Ebony*. He is at work on a biography of Sonny Rollins.

David Hajdu is the author of *Lush Life: A Biography of Billy Strayhorn* and the forthcoming *Positively 4th Street: The Lives and Times of Joan Baez, Bob Dylan, Mimi Baez Fariña, and Richard Fariña*. He has written on music and the arts for the *New Yorker*, the *New York Review of Books*, and the *New York Times Magazine*, and his work has won the ASCAP–Deems Taylor Award and the New Visions Award. Hajdu lives in New York and teaches at The New School.

Heather Heilman was a staff writer at the *Memphis Flyer* from 1999–2000. She has a graduate degree in writing from Bennington College in Vermont.

Geoffrey Himes has contributed to such books as *The Blackwell Guide to Recorded Country Music* and *The Rolling Stone Jazz & Blues Album Guide*. He has written about music on a weekly basis for the *Washington Post* since 1977. He has also written about music for *Rolling Stone*, *No Depression*, National Public Radio, *Crawdaddy*, *Down Beat*, *Sing Out*, *Oxford American*, *Country Music Magazine*, and others.

Selwyn Seyfu Hinds is the former editor-in-chief of *The Source* and is currently the chief creative officer/EVP of 360hiphop.com.

Dave Hoekstra has been a *Chicago Sun-Times* staff writer since 1985. He is also a contributing writer for *Playboy Magazine* and has been a contributing editor for *Chicago Magazine*. He also writes for the *Journal of Country Music*, in which this piece appeared.

J. R. Jones studied writing and literature at Knox College and the University of Alabama. His work has appeared in *Kenyon Review, New York Press, San Diego Reader,* and the *Chicago Reader,* where he is a staff writer and editor.

Arthur Kempton was born in New Jersey in 1949 and now resides in Brooklyn, New York. He has written for the *New York Review of Books*, among other publications, and is currently writing a book about African-American popular music.

Robert Lloyd is a writer and musician living in Los Angeles, not necessarily in that (or any) order.

Greil Marcus is the author of *Double Trouble, Invisible Republic,* and *Lipstick Traces*.

Dave Marsh has been a music critic for more than thirty years, including stints at *Creem, Rolling Stone*, and, currently, *Playboy*.

Keven McAlester wrote the included soufflé during his stint as music editor of *New Times Los Angeles*, a weekly newspaper for which he penned the column "Bad Teeth." He has temporarily abandoned the trenches of fractured grammar to direct a documentary film about Roky Erickson, though he continues to freelance for *New Times* and other charitable publications.

Rebecca Mead was born in London in 1966 and educated at Oxford and at New York University. She has worked at the *Sunday Times* of

London and *New York* magazine, and has been a staff writer at the *New Yorker* since 1997.

David Moodie was formerly the features editor of *Spin* magazine and a founder of *Might* magazine. He is currently editor-at-large at *Spin*.

John Morthland has been writing about music since 1969 when he began working as an associate editor at *Rolling Stone* magazine. He has also been an editor at *Creem* and *Country Music* magazines and is the author of *The Best of Country Music*. He is currently a contributing editor to *Texas Monthly* magazine and lives in Austin, Texas.

Since 1987, in the interest of public safety and morale, the staff of *Motorbooty* magazine has endeavored to mock the people, places, and public relations campaigns which so sorely need mocking.

Susan Orlean has been a staff writer at *New Yorker* since 1992. She has also contributed to *Outside*, *Vogue*, *Esquire*, and *Rolling Stone*. Her book, *The Orchid Thief*, was a *New York Times* Notable Book of 1999. She lives in New York City.

Tom Piazza's books include *The Guide to Classic Recorded Jazz*, which won the ASCAP–Deems Taylor award, and the short-story collection *Blues and Trouble*, which won the James Michener award for fiction. His most recent book is *True Adventures with the King of Bluegrass*. Since 1997 he has been the Southern Music columnist for *Oxford American*. He lives in New Orleans, where he is finishing work on a novel.

John Rockwell is editor of the Arts & Leisure section of the *New York Times* and former director of the Lincoln Center Festival. Between 1972 and 1991 he was a music critic for the *Times* and from 1974 to 1980 its chief rock critic. He is the author of *All-American Music: Composition in the Late Twentieth Century* and *Sinatra: An American Classic*.

Nancy Jo Sales is a contributing editor at Vanity Fair.

David Samuels is a contributing editor of *Harper's Magazine* and a regular contributor to *New Yorker*. He lives in New York, and is writing a novel.

Ben Sandmel is the author of *Zydeco!* with photographer Rick Olivier. Sandmel has also written the liner notes for over 100 albums, and contributed to publications including *Esquire*, *Atlantic Monthly*, *Rolling Stone*, and *Oxford American*. Sandmel currently plays drums with the Hackberry Ramblers, a Cajun and western swing band, and produced the group's Grammy-nominated album *Deep Water*.

Tony Scherman is the author of *Backbeat: Earl Palmer's Story*. He has written about American music and culture for almost twenty years for the *New York Times*, *American Heritage*, *Atlantic Monthly*, *Entertainment Weekly*, and many other publications. He lives outside of New York City with his wife and daughter.

Karen Schoemer has written about pop music and pop culture for the *New York Times*, *Newsweek*, *Rolling Stone*, *Spin*, and many other publications. Her essay about Frank Sinatra appeared in the anthology *Rock She Wrote: Women Write about Rock, Pop and Rap*, and she contributed chapters about Linda Ronstadt and Dusty Springfield to *The Rolling Stone Book of Women in Rock*. She is currently writing a book about pop singers in the late '50s and early '60s.

Jeff Stark was tricked into writing about music in 1996. He has edited music sections for *San Francisco Weekly* and *Salon*. He lives in New York.

Neil Strauss is a pop music critic and reporter at the *New York Times*. He has also written for *Rolling Stone*, *Spin*, *The Source*, the *Village Voice*, and *Entertainment Weekly*. He co-wrote the *New York Times* bestseller *The Long Hard Road Out of Hell* with Marilyn Manson and edited a book of radio-related writings called *Radiotext(e)*.

Jim Walsh is the music columnist for the *St. Paul Pioneer Press*. He lives in Minneapolis with his wife, Jean, and their two children, Henry and Helen.

Author of the award-winning *Ramblin' Rose: The Life and Career of Rose Maddox* and *Cry: The Johnnie Ray Story*, **Jonny Whiteside** is a veteran music journalist whose work has appeared in *L.A. Weekly*, *Variety*, and the *Journal of Country Music*.

Alec Wilkinson is the author of five books, including *Big Sugar* and *A Violent Act*. Since 1980 he has been a writer at *The New Yorker*.

Daniel Wolff is the author of *You Send Me: The Life and Times of Sam Cooke* (Quill).

CREDITS